Operating Systems

Operating Systems

HAROLD LORIN
IBM Systems Research Institute

HARVEY M. DEITEL
Boston University

 ADDISON-WESLEY PUBLISHING COMPANY
Reading, Massachusetts · Menlo Park, California
London · Amsterdam · Don Mills, Ontario · Sydney

Library of Congress Cataloging in Publication Data

Lorin, Harold.
  Operating systems.

  (The Systems programming series)
  Bibliography: p.
  Includes index.
  1. Operating systems (Computers) I. Deitel,
Harvey M., 1945–   joint author. II. Title.
QA76.6.L639   001.64'25   80-10625
ISBN 0-201-14464-6

Reprinted with corrections, November 1981

ISBN 0-201-14464-6
DEFGHIJ-HA-89876543

To the students
of the IBM Systems Research Institute
who listened patiently while the material matured.

Harold Lorin

In loving memory of my father and my mother,
Morris and Lena Deitel,
and my uncle, Joseph Deitel.

Harvey M. Deitel

THE SYSTEMS PROGRAMMING SERIES

*The Program Development Process
Part I—The Individual Programmer — Joel D. Aron

The Program Development Process
Part II—The Programming Team — Joel D. Aron

*Mathematical Foundations of
Programming — Frank Beckman

*Structured Programming: Theory
and Practice — Richard C. Linger
Harlan D. Mills
Bernard I. Witt

*Coded Character Sets: History and
Development — Charles E. Mackenzie

*The Structure and Design of Program-
ming Languages — John E. Nicholls

*The Environment for Systems Programs — Frederic G. Withington

*Communications Architecture for
Distributed Systems — R. J. Cypser

An Introduction to Database Systems,
Third Edition — C. J. Date

Database Security and Integrity — Eduardo B. Fernandez
R. C. Summers
C. Wood

Interactive Computer Graphics — James Foley
Andries Van Dam

*Compiler Design Theory — Philip M. Lewis II
Daniel J. Rosenkrantz
Richard E. Stearns

*Sorting and Sort Systems — Harold Lorin

*Operating Systems — Harold Lorin
Harvey M. Deitel

*Recursive Programming Techniques — William Burge

*Modeling and Analysis: An Introduc-
tion to System Performance Evaluation Methodology — Hisashi Kobayashi

Conceptual Structures: Information
Processing in Mind and Machines — John F. Sowa

*Published

Foreword

The field of systems programming primarily grew out of the efforts of many programmers and managers whose creative energy went into producing practical, utilitarian systems programs needed by the rapidly growing computer industry. Programming was practiced as an art where each programmer invented his own solutions to problems with little guidance beyond that provided by his immediate associates. In 1968, the late Ascher Opler, then at IBM, recognized that it was necessary to bring programming knowledge together in a form that would be accessible to all systems programmers. Surveying the state of the art, he decided that enough useful material existed to justify a significant codification effort. On his recommendation, IBM decided to sponsor The Systems Programming Series as a long term project to collect, organize, and publish those principles and techniques that would have lasting value throughout the industry.

The Series consists of an open-ended collection of text-reference books. The contents of each book represent the individual author's view of the subject area and do not necessarily reflect the views of the IBM Corporation. Each is organized for course use but is detailed enough for reference. Further, the Series is organized in three levels: broad introductory material in the foundation volumes, more specialized material in the software volumes, and very specialized theory in the computer science volumes. As such, the Series meets the needs of the novice, the experienced programmer, and the computer scientist.

Taken together, the Series is a record of the state of the art in systems programming that can form the technological base for the systems programming discipline.

The Editorial Board

Preface

This book is written for students of operating systems who have learned enough of the introductory material to know that there are many questions, many problems, and many points of view. It is written particularly for students whose imagination and curiosity have been stimulated by basic material they have already seen. The word "students" does not imply only people who participate in a formal course; it is used to suggest those who wish to know more. In this sense, the authors and many other workers in the topic area are "students"— people who are continually fascinated by the area and motivated to discover some as yet undiscovered fundamental principles.

The book contains a broad spectrum of material. It is concerned with the relationships between operating systems and the hardware on which they run; with the relationships between operating systems and other components of that collection of programs that is understood to form a "systems software environment"; with interfaces to various kinds of users, casual and professional; with the intersection of operating systems design and software technology; with fundamental algorithms of resource management; and with new concepts in resource management in the face of evolving computer systems structures. The book lays the foundation for the emergence of opinion and unifying philosophy in the minds of its readers.

Some of the material is basic and might well be found in an introductory course. This material is included in order to remind the student who has seen it, and to fill the holes in the backgrounds of readers whose prior knowledge is partial or incomplete. It is also treated in a way that combines basic ideas with some more sophisticated reflection on the implications of these ideas.

Much of the material reflects trends and directions in current operating systems research and advanced technology. There has been a profound change in the topics at the center of investigation. Resource management algorithms, for example, are receiving less attention than are problems in structure and interprocess communication. For this reason, many of the traditional operating systems topics are presented late in this book.

We are truly in a time of great change in perspective, a time during which many basic questions are being revisited. Basic questions such as ''What should an operating system do?'' ''Who should see its interfaces?'' ''What new functions should be placed in operating systems?'' and ''What new functions should be placed in subsystems?'' are on the minds of designers in large corporations and researchers in universities. This book provides some insight into opinions surrounding these issues.

The approach is informal and nonmathematical as befits the goal of the work—to establish an intellectual framework within which one may understand the problems and directions that surround the concept of an operating system.

The authors wish to acknowledge the contributions of many people who gave unselfishly of their time from busy schedules to assist us in preparing this text. Our thanks to Cora Tangney of the IBM Systems Research Institute for her careful handling of the early versions of the manuscript; to Charles Gold of IBM Corporation for his encouragement throughout the project; to Alan Scherr, Roy Heistand, Walter Doherty, Gerry Gottlieb, Lance Vaughan, and Dr. William Henneman for a long and profitable interchange in the topic area. Barbara Deitel worked long hours correcting galleys and page proofs. Dr. John Porter and Joe Dempty of the Boston University Academic Computing Center made the resources of the Center available to us to ensure the timely production of the text. President John Silber of Boston University and Deans Geoffrey Bannister and Irwin Price provided an environment uniquely amenable to this academic endeavor. William B. Gruener, our editor, carefully directed the production of this text from conception to production. We are deeply grateful for his guidance and insights. Our production editor, William J. Yskamp, did an impeccable job bringing the book to publication.

New York City   H. L.
Framingham, Massachusetts   H. M. D.
January 1981

Contents

About the Authors   xix

CHAPTER 1
INTRODUCTION

1.1	Views of a System	1
1.2	Hardware Layers	5
1.3	The Hardware–Software Interface	20
1.4	Concept of Operating Systems	24

CHAPTER 2
FUNCTIONS OF OPERATING SYSTEMS

2.1	Concepts	33
2.2	Environment for Program Creation and Operation	39
2.3	Defining an Environment for Access	41
2.4	Creating an Interface for Operations	53
2.5	Managing a System to Meet Performance Goals	54

CHAPTER 3
TYPES OF OPERATING SYSTEMS

3.1	Taxonomy	61
3.2	Real-Time Environments	65
3.3	Real-Time Software	69
3.4	Batch Operating Systems	72
3.5	Single-Stream Systems	74
3.6	Multiprogramming Systems	81
3.7	Time-Sharing Systems	88

3.8   Multipurpose Systems   92
3.9   Networking and Distribution   .   94
3.10   Influences on Design   96
3.11   Understanding a Machine   96
3.12   Knowing the User   98
3.13   The State of the Art   99

CHAPTER 4
STRUCTURAL ISSUES IN OPERATING SYSTEMS

4.1   Systems Concepts   107
4.2   A Time-Division Approach to Operating Systems Structure   108
4.3   Systems Services and Worker Programs   108
4.4   Request Time   109
4.5   Select Time   109
4.6   Compile Time   109
4.7   Activation Time   109
4.8   Run Time   110
4.9   Postrun Time   110
4.10   Systems Services and Privilege   110
4.11   Single-Time Systems   111
4.12   Universal Computer-Oriented Language   112
4.13   Load Time   114
4.14   Link–Edit Time   114
4.15   Allocators   115
4.16   Subsystems   115

CHAPTER 5
THE RUN-TIME ENVIRONMENT

5.1   The Nature of the Run-Time Function   119
5.2   Structure in the Run-Time Environment   122
5.3   Process and Primitives   131
5.4   Vertical and Horizontal System Structures   139
5.5   Other Notions of Structure   146
5.6   Interface Definition   146

CHAPTER 6
THE KERNEL OF THE OPERATING SYSTEM

6.1   The Basic Kernel   161
6.2   Interrupt Handling   162
6.3   Dispatching   166
6.4   I/O Support   172
6.5   Memory Contents Manager   179
6.6   Other Elements in the Run-Time Environment   182

CHAPTER 7
SYSTEMS SERVICES

7.1	The Concept of Systems Services	187
7.2	The Control Stream Reader	188
7.3	Location Assignment and Loading	189
7.4	Program Combination and Linking	191
7.5	The High-Level Scheduler	193
7.6	System Generation	195
7.7	Systems Services and the Run-Time Environment	197

CHAPTER 8
SUBSYSTEMS

8.1	Concepts of Subsystems	201
8.2	Subsystems and the User Community	207
8.3	System–Subsystem Splice Levels	209
8.4	Database Management Systems	211
8.5	Interactive Programming Systems	214

CHAPTER 9
RESOURCE MANAGEMENT

9.1	The Notion of Resource Management	221
9.2	The Notion of a Resource	221
9.3	Policy	222
9.4	Programming Stylistics	224
9.5	Fundamental Economics of Resource Management	226
9.6	When Resource Decisions Are Made	229
9.7	The Limits of Resource Management	231

CHAPTER 10
PROCESSOR MANAGEMENT

10.1	Fundamental Notions of Multiprogramming and Time-Sharing	237
10.2	High-Level Scheduling	238
10.3	Low-Level Scheduling	241
10.4	Intermediate-Level Scheduling—Three-Level Systems	250

CHAPTER 11
FILE AND OBJECT MANAGEMENT

11.1	File Management	257
11.2	The Multics File System	258
11.3	Dynamic Linking in Multics	259
11.4	Protection and Integrity	260
11.5	Authorities and Capabilities in Multics	261
11.6	Generalized Notions of Object Management	262
11.7	Monitors	265

CHAPTER 12
ASYNCHRONOUS CONCURRENT PROCESSES

12.1	Program Synchronization	269
12.2	Lock Tactics	270
12.3	Parallel Processes	273
12.4	Operating System Structure	273
12.5	Producers and Consumers	274
12.6	Interprocess Communication	279

CHAPTER 13
REAL STORAGE

13.1	Introduction	285
13.2	Real Memory Systems with Absolute Compiling	285
13.3	Real Memory Systems with Relocatable Compiling	286
13.4	Fixed-Size Block Allocation	287
13.5	Variable-Size Block Allocation	287
13.6	First-Fit versus Best-Fit	288
13.7	Contiguous Storage Allocation	289
13.8	Memory Compaction	289
13.9	Fragmentation	289
13.10	CPU and I/O Load in the Programming Mix	290

CHAPTER 14
VIRTUAL STORAGE

14.1	Paging and Segmentation Systems	293
14.2	Paging	293
14.3	Locality and the Table Lookaside Buffer	297
14.4	Virtual Memory, Memory Management, and Paging	299
14.5	Management Strategies and Paging	301
14.6	Simple Demand Paging	302
14.7	Intermediate-Level Scheduling	306
14.8	Program Progress, Paging Rates, and Thrashing	307
14.9	Segmentation	308

CHAPTER 15
INTERMEDIATE-LEVEL SCHEDULING

15.1	Overview of the Systems Resources Manager	315
15.2	The Service Unit	316
15.3	Work-Load Levels, Objectives, and Performance Groups	317
15.4	Performance Periods	319
15.5	Interval Service Value	319
15.6	Response versus Utilization	320
15.7	SRM Goals and Techniques	321
15.8	The Earliest Version of SRM	322

15.9   Domains   322
15.10   Other Aspects of Balancing and Tuning Systems   323
15.11   Dispatching Mechanisms and Tactics   324
15.12   Conclusion   325

CHAPTER 16
VIRTUAL MACHINES

16.1   Several Operating Systems Sharing a Single Machine   329
16.2   Influence of Virtual Memory   331
16.3   Control State and Problem State   331
16.4   Input–Output   331
16.5   Minimizing Performance Burdens   331
16.6   Run-Time Environment   331
16.7   Conversational Monitor System   332
16.8   Distributed Processing and Networking   332
16.9   Conclusion   333

CHAPTER 17
AN ASSESSMENT

17.1   The Value   337
17.2   The Costs   339
17.3   Problems   341
17.4   The Universalist–Perfectionist View   342
17.5   The Toolmaker's View   343
17.6   Structural Concepts   344
17.7   The Compatibility–Innovation Issue   345
17.8   Distributed Systems   346
17.9   Conclusion   348

BIBLIOGRAPHY

                                                                 353

INDEX

                                                                 363

ABOUT THE AUTHORS

Harold Lorin

Harold Lorin has been on the faculty of the IBM Systems Research Institute since 1968. He currently teaches in the area of systems structure and management with particular attention to distributed processing, multiple-machine structures, and operating system design. In addition to teaching courses at the IBM Systems Research Institute, his activities include presentations and consultations with various IBM development and marketing organizations, using organizations and participation in professional development activities internally and outside of IBM.

Previously Mr. Lorin has been on the Senior Staff of the Service Bureau Corporation, with the UNIVAC Division of Sperry Rand, with the Systems Development Corporation and with Strategic Air Command Headquarters. He has held a variety of professional and management positions in systems design, software development, and systems marketing. His activities have involved him in the design, evaluation, and functional review of a large number of operating systems and subsystems for various classes of computing systems.

Mr. Lorin's books include *Parallelism in Hardware and Software*, Prentice-Hall, 1972; *Sorting and Sort Systems*, Addison-Wesley, 1975; and *Aspects of Distributed Computing Systems*, Wiley, 1980. He has published journal and encyclopedia articles and has made presentations to various symposia in the area of operating system and distributed systems design and management. His published articles in the area of operating systems include, "Operating Systems," *Encyclopedia of Computer Science and Technology*, Marcel Dekker, 1978; "Considerations in Operating Systems Design for Multiprocessor Structures," (with B. Goldstein), Proceedings of the International Workshop on High-level Language Computer Architecture, May 1980; "Operating System Design Considerations for Various Multiprocessor Versions of SWARD,'' IBM Systems Research Institute TR73–007, February, 1980; Operating Systems Structure for Polymorphic Hardware (with B. Goldstein), IBM Thomas J. Watson Research Center RC8172, April 1980.

Mr. Lorin is an adjunct faculty member at Hofstra University and has participated in professional development seminars for various universities and professional societies including ACM, New York University Graduate School of Business, Polytechnic Institute of New York. He is an occasional reviewer for *Computing Reviews*.

Harvey M. Deitel

Dr. Harvey M. Deitel has 17 years experience in the computer field including the research and development of several large-scale operating systems and the design and implementation of numerous commercial systems. He received the Bachelor of Science and Master of Science Degrees from the Massachusetts Institute of Technology where he did extensive development work on the Multics operating system. He received the Doctor of Philosophy Degree from Boston University where his dissertation research examined the problems of developing very large-scale, structured software systems.

Since 1965, Dr. Deitel has been concerned with the problems of developing operating systems. He worked on three of the largest operating systems ever undertaken, namely IBM's OS, IBM's TSS, and M.I.T.'s Multics. He has consulted for Advanced Computer Techniques Corporation, Computer Usage Corporation, Harbridge House, Inc., American Express, IBM Systems Development Division, IBM Advanced Systems Development Division, IBM Thomas J. Watson Research Center, M.I.T.'s Project MAC, and numerous energy and real-estate companies.

Dr. Deitel is currently on the Computer Science Faculty of Boston University where he teaches graduate courses in systems programming, operating systems, and software engineering. He has received numerous teaching commendations, and has been rated nationally among the top computing teachers in the country.

Dr. Deitel is a member of several professional honoraries including Tau Beta Pi, Eta Kappa Nu, and Sigma Xi. He holds the CDP Certification of the Institute for the Certification of Computer Professionals, and is a member of several professional societies including the Association for Computing Machinery, the Institute of Electrical and Electronics Engineers, the Society for Computer Simulation, the Data Processing Management Association, and the American Management Association.

Dr. Deitel's publications include *Absentee Computations in a Multiple-Access Computer System*, MAC–TR–52 1968 Advanced Research Projects Agency, Department of Defense; *Introduction to Computer Programming with the BASIC Language*, Prentice-Hall, 1977; *Structured Software Development*, Ph.D. dissertation published by University Microfilms, 1980; *Software Engineering*, to be published by Addison-Wesley; and *PASCAL Programming for Computer Scientists*, to be published by Prindle, Weber, and Schmidt.

1
Introduction

1.1 VIEWS OF A SYSTEM

A complete computing system can be thought of as a hierarchically structured composite of *hardware* and *software* elements. Figure 1.1 shows a structure of four layers. Each layer represents a set of functions and an interface. The interface is a set of visible conventions used to perform the functions in the layer. The characteristics of that interface we call a "view" of the system.

There is a *hardware layer* that represents the *visible architecture* of the machine. The hardware layer includes a *processor* consisting of an *instruction set,* a population of *program visible registers,* and an *addressing scheme* for memory referencing. The hardware also involves relationships between "box" components such as *channels, control units, processors,* and *memories.*

The hardware layer presents a view of the system meaningful to designers and developers of *operating systems.* These highly specialized persons undertake to develop an enhanced view of the computer system. The operating systems designers create a *megamachine,* an extended systems architecture to serve as an efficient target for *compilers* and *programmers* of applications. The operating system provides *interfaces* that make it easier to develop programs for the system by reducing the amount of code that must be written, and by simplifying the exercise of certain functions.

Operating systems interfaces do not entirely hide features of the hardware. A compiler writer, for example, planning the generation of code must have some knowledge of machine characteristics beyond those represented by the view defined in the operating system.

The *target* for compilation is the megamachine consisting of the software-defined operating systems interfaces and some portion of the native instruction

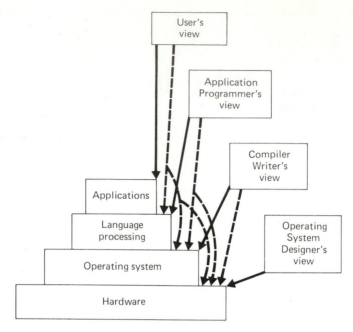

Fig. 1.1   Layers and views of a system.

set of the hardware architecture. Similarly, a programmer in assembly language will use a mixture of operating system and hardware-provided functions.

The notion that the encapsulation of a lower level by a higher level may not be complete is shown in Fig. 1.1 by broken arrows leading from the "views." These broken arrows suggest that each view of the structure is composed of a combination of the view defined by a layer and a partial view of a lower layer. Just how large a view of a lower layer it is advisable to permit or require at any level is an issue of current interest.

At the next level, the view of the system seen by the *applications program-mers* writing in a higher-level language is largely defined by *language specialists* and *language processor specialists*. The language specialists are concerned with the convenience of expressing problem solutions to a computer system. They worry about *program structure* and *expressive power, syntactic and semantic clarity*. Processor specialists are concerned with *lexical and syntactic analysis, code generation, optimization*, and *side effects*. They are also concerned with the *efficiency of translating* and with the *efficiency of translations* from languages such as COBOL to machine language.

Just as the operating system layer may not completely hide the hardware layer, the high-level language layer may not completely hide the operating system layer. Certain interfaces of the operating system may be passed upward through the compiler. For example, the idea of acquiring more storage for the execution of a section of a program is an operating systems concept frequently made available to an application programmer. Some designers argue that this concept should be hidden from a person interested in solving a problem. Others argue that it is a valid tool. In this disagreement, one begins to see the difficulties in determining the proper view to be offered at any level, and what is the proper distribution of concepts or capabilities among levels. How does one assure that a particular view defined by any level really enhances the productivity of those who are expected to interact with the system at that level?

Another consideration of the view of a programmer is that the programmer's view of the system may not be totally defined by PL/I, COBOL, or other programming languages. Apart from glimpses of the operating systems interfaces passed through by the compiler, a complete image of a system commonly contains views presented by *command languages, utility routines,* and *editors.* These software elements exist in the programmer's view in order to provide a complete set of applications development and operational tools. There is, therefore, a potential *multiplicity of views* at the same level, and care must be taken to assure the coherence of a systems image at any level at which independently conceived modules are exposed. Is it best to try to achieve a unity of view by imposing homogeneity of syntax and semantics at a given level? Is it best to allow a multiplicity of language forms and expressive conventions, each efficient for a particular set of functions done at a particular time?

One extends these considerations by asking if it is desirable to allow the view of the system to be altered at different stages of application program development. For example, it is not uncommon for a programmer to write a program in a *higher-level programming language* and then at various points in the *debugging process* to descend to lower levels, ultimately to machine-level dumps of memory. Is this a phenomenon to be encouraged? Should a system show only the higher-level view?

An additional dimension to be considered in thinking about systems views derives from the varieties of user specialties that may surround a system. How does the concept of programming relate to the concept of operating? Is the idea of separate roles for operators and programmers inherent in a computing system or are there circumstances in which the roles should be combined? How does this affect the design of languages and system structure?

The hierarchy in Fig. 1.1 shows the progression from hardware through *problem solver.* There are other hierarchies and they intertwine with the problem-solving hierarchy.

Consider Fig. 1.2. This figure describes an operational–management hierarchy that attempts to define the system views of a hierarchy of operational specialists. There is an engineer responsible for maintaining hardware. He or she

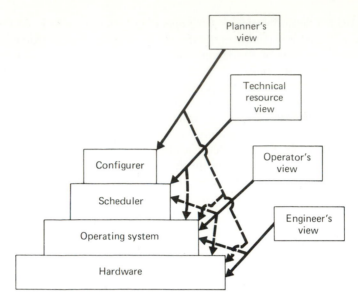

Fig. 1.2   System views of operational specialists.

may be supported by diagnostic routines that are part of the operating system and consequently the engineer's *total systems view is an operating system and hardware composite*.

Similarly, an *operator* must have some view of the hardware and of the operating system through which he or she provides and obtains information about system status. In addition, the operator may require a view of the system that includes notions of the relative importance of *keeping programs on schedule* as opposed to *intensive utilization of equipment*. These concerns cause the operator to interface with a higher-level software component called a *scheduler*.

The reader may infer from Fig. 1.2 that the set of operational–managerial interfaces may be considerably more complex than the problem solution hierarchy. In fact, there is a rich variety of role definitions involving systems specialists for *configuring, installing, tuning, evaluating,* etc. suggested in the hierarchy of Fig. 1.2.

In the hierarchy of Fig. 1.1, observe the last-mentioned member of the hierarchy, the *user*. The concept of a user is necessarily vague because it is so general. Airline reservation clerks, automobile designers, and corporate vice-presidents may all be users. The divergence in background and in need for services is as wide as the diversity of job assignments in the economic community. It is this divergence that makes the definition of a proper user view so difficult for systems designers.

Users are interested primarily in the information they can get from the system. As a group, they wish to have minimum awareness of the unique properties of information processing devices. Some users may program and thus perceive programmability as an added value. These users have problems that require algorithmic treatment of data that cannot be predefined. *The challenge of systems design is to create problem-solver interfaces of minimum contamination with computer concepts.* Some users do not wish to program. They are able to predefine (or have predefined for them) the processes they wish applied against data. The challenge to systems designers is to provide adequate structures for these processes to strike balances between generality and efficiency.

The *level-of-view* concept provides a context in which decisions can be made about proper views for various levels. To draw an analogy with a power utility is very tempting. The user interface for obtaining light in most parts of the world is remarkably easy to learn and perform. The flick of a switch produces what the user desires. In order to support this splendid interface, a lower-level structure of enormous complexity must be defined.

It is conceivable that the *user interface* could be made more complex and still be acceptable. This might even be economically desirable in the face of changing technology. It is conceivable that the user might be asked to know more about electric power in order to simplify the complexity of what goes on at a generating station, at a power control center, or even at a generator-manufacturing site. It is even conceivable that the price of electricity might be reduced in this way.

In the world of computing systems technology, economic parameters and user anticipations change rapidly. In each generation of a system, the issue of effective views must be revisited, the distribution of function between levels must be reconsidered, and the permissible complexity at each level must be reevaluated. How much complexity can be hidden? How much function can be moved from one layer to another and at what cost? How many levels should there be?

1.2   HARDWARE LAYERS

The hardware level of a computing system consists of a number of hardware components that have functional attributes and structural attributes. We will discuss in this section those aspects of hardware that might concern an operating systems designer.

1.2.1   Functional Aspects

The nature of a hardware system derives from the interconnection of packaged elements with varying degrees of autonomous operation and strongly distinctive attributes. Processors, memories, channels, printers, disks, drums, tapes, and teleprocessing lines are interconnected to form a functional system.

At one stage of design the systems programmer thinks about these various classes of devices as "black boxes" and considers only the nature of the relationships between them.

How concurrently a channel and a processor operate will determine the nature of support for I/O processing, and whether it is profitable to undertake software mechanisms for obtaining CPU–I/O concurrency. The relationship between memory and I/O affects memory allocation tactics.

The designer tries to determine how functions can be distributed in the system. Does the *channel* look intelligent enough to execute specialized *I/O programs* and manage local *buffers*? One recent phenomenon, due to technological change, is the enlarged distribution of intelligence into previously passive devices. The operating systems designer may face a complex of processing units distributed throughout the family of boxes. This has been true for some time, but it is of growing importance now.

Among the first operating systems designers to face issues of the distribution of functional elements of an operating system were those associated with the CDC 6600 in the mid-1960s. This system contained a powerful central processor that shared memory with ten smaller processors of different architecture. The operating system designers initially chose to place operational and I/O control functions in the small processors. This represented a radical departure from usual system design.

How deeply should an operating system respond to hardware detail? For example, if a memory is organized into independent memory banks such that memory locations 0 to 256K–1, 256K to 512K–1, etc. can be referenced concurrently, should the mechanisms of the operating system use this knowledge in granting memory to programs? Is it worthwhile to put data in one bank and programs in another so that instruction and data references may overlap, or does this hardware optimization require excessively complicated software?

At another stage of design, the designer considers the specific attributes of the boxes of a system. The box called the *CPU* (Central Processing Unit) is still first among peers. Although processing power in the form of instruction analysis and execution rate represents a decreasing percentage of total systems costs, it is still from the attributes of processing units that major concepts of systems design are derived.

The CPU characteristics that an operating system designer must consider are the *addressing structure*, the *interrupt structure*, the *instruction set*, and the *protection mechanisms*.

1.2.1.1   Addressing structure

The operating systems designer must understand and partially decide how programs are to be associated with memory locations, how real machine location

addresses will be formed, and how application programs will be structured for a
given machine. The designer must explore in detail the addressing mechanisms
of hardware. He or she searches for the existence of base registers that can be
used to offset program origins. The designer assesses to what extent code can be
shared by programs logically existing together in a *multiprogramming* environment (in which CPU service is quickly switched from one program to another).
The designer also assesses whether running programs can profitably be only
partially represented in memory, or whether all of the code of a program had best
be brought in as a precondition for CPU service.

There are machines that have simple addressing mechanisms involving only
the address field of an instruction and an index register. There are machines that
allow *double indexing* and machines that have *indirect addressing*. There are
machines with *segmented two-dimensional addressing* that support the concept
of associating logical *segments* of a program with each other on reference during
program execution. There are machines that organize blocks of single linear
addresses into fixed size *frames* so that a block of addresses can be associated
dynamically with different physical locations of memory without disturbing the
representation of addresses in the program. The specifics of these mechanisms
suggest memory management strategies in the operating system.

Systems like OS/MVS (IBM's System 370 Multiple Virtual Storage system), OS/MVT (IBM's System 360 and nonvirtual memory 370 system), Multics (a Honeywell operating system), and OS 1100 (UNIVAC's 1100 operating
system) reflect operating systems designers' responses to the memory management hardware in each system. The impact of memory addressing hardware on
operating systems design, and the close interconnection of hardware and software concepts will be discussed thoroughly in this text.

1.2.1.2   Interrupt structure

An *interrupt* is a mechanism used for achieving coordination between concurrently operable units of a computer system, and for responding to specific
conditions within a processor. There are varieties of interrupt structures that exist
in different hardware architectures, but all interrupt designs share the feature that
the occurrence of an event changes the sequence of operations in the processing
unit.

Figure 1.3 shows a hypothetical interrupt system. The box labeled S.V.
represents a simple *state vector*. The state vector represents the status of a
program running on a processor. It is a very general concept that represents what
has to be restored to processor registers or made accessible in memory in order to
resume a program if the program is suspended at any point. The full definition of
a state vector is a combined hardware/operating system structure. The simple
hardware S.V. of Fig. 1.3 contains the registers of the processor that contain the
results of arithmetic operations, (AC, MQ). The S.V. also contains the processor's single index register (IX) and a base register that points to the lowest

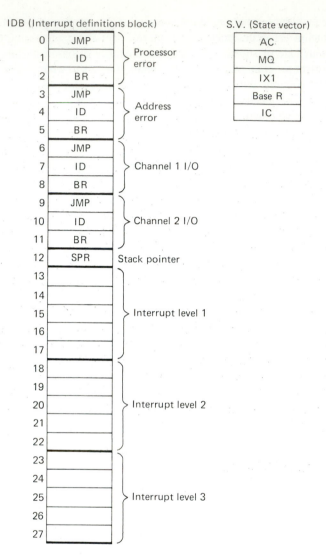

Fig. 1.3 Hypothetical interrupt system.

physical memory location to which the running program can refer. To address memory, an instruction (Load AC,1000,I) would form the address 1000 + the contents of the index register. If IX contains 23, the indexed address is 1023. However, the actual machine location is not developed until the contents of the base register are applied to the indexed address. If the base register contains the value 10,000, then the actual referenced location is 11,023.

The last entry in the S.V. is the instruction counter that points to the next instruction to be executed by this program. The status of this program is thus represented by AC, MQ, IX, and IC that together define the point in its computations that the program has achieved. Note that the program's ability to refer to particular devices or data sets is not defined by this S.V. Neither does this S.V. define the status of those devices or data sets. This implies that there is a software-defined extension to the S.V. somewhere in memory. We will discuss the nature of the software-extended S.V. at length in later chapters.

The box IDB contains the heart of the interrupt structure. It is designed with diverse elements of various real interrupt schemes.

The *IDB* (Interrupt Definitions Block) is a hardware-defined control structure that always occupies locations 0 through 27 in memory. The first twelve locations contain four entries of three words each. Each entry is associated with a particular type of interrupt. There are four interrupt types defined for this processor: processor error, address error, channel 1 I/O, and channel 2 I/O.

Processor error interrupts occur when a parity check has failed, when a division by zero is attempted, when an overflow occurs out of the AC, etc. *Address errors* occur when an invalid address is referenced in memory. This may be an address beyond the available locations in the configuration or an address computed below the base register limit. A channel 1 interrupt occurs whenever an I/O operation completes on channel 1; a channel 2 interrupt occurs whenever an I/O completion occurs on channel 2.

Each three-word entry contains a JMP word, an ID word, and a base register (BR) word. The base register word defines the lowest memory locations that the routine that will handle the interrupt may address. The ID (Interrupt Definition) word describes the specific reason for the interrupt. For example, on a *channel interrupt* it names the device, tells whether it is an *input* or *output completion*, whether it was a successful completion and, if not successful, why not. The contents of the ID are set by the device reporting the interrupt at the time the interrupt occurs.

The JMP word is a jump instruction that specifies the first location of the routine that will be executed after interruption, and an indication of what interrupt status the machine will assume. Interrupt status means the ability of the system to accept interrupts. There is a field in the JMP instruction that defines whether all types of interrupts may still occur during processing of a current interrupt, or whether all interrupts are *enabled* except interrupts of the same kind, etc. There is a *fixed priority reporting relationship between interrupts* in that simultaneous interrupt occurrences will cause processor errors to be accepted before address errrors, before channel 1, etc. However, what interrupts may occur while others are being processed is a function of the JMP instruction in each three-word IDB entry.

When an interrupt occurs, the address of the related JMP word is placed in IC, the ID word is placed in MQ, and the contents of BR is placed in the base register of the processor. Processor errors and address errors cause the values in the IDB entry to be placed immediately in the processor registers. Channel interrupts await the completion of the instruction executing at the time of the interrupt. After IDB entry values are forced into the processor registers, the execution of JMP enters the interrupt handler.

Before the placement of values from IDB is accomplished, however, the status of the interrupted process is saved in a save area that is pointed to by the contents of the *SPR* (Stack Pointer Register) in memory location 12. The SPR always points to the next available save area. It is hardware-controlled so that it cycles around the three save areas. One of the problems facing an operating system designer in developing an operating system for this machine is developing a software method of ensuring that a saved S.V. is not overwritten. This is a problem existing in one form or another in all interrupt structures.

The full sequence of hardware events associated with an interrupt may now be described. We describe an *I/O completion interrupt*. At some prior time, a read of a device on channel 2 was requested by the running program. Let us assume that there is a simple "READ 2*n,m*" instruction that specifies the transfer of the next physical fixed block size record from a tape (device *n* on channel 2) into memory locations beginning at *m*. We assume that the hardware is such that the READ instruction has been passed off to circuitry such that the I/O transfer can occur while the processor is executing instructions that follow the READ. We also assume that there are components of the operating system that are responsible for coordinating the concurrent I/O and processor streams. We also postulate that the I/O circuits transfer data directly into memory without disturbing processor operations until the I/O operation is complete. Finally, we assume that there is hardware circuitry that synchronizes the references of the processor and the channels to memory such that a processor reference to memory is delayed a memory cycle when a channel wishes to place something in memory. All of our assumptions provide the enlarged concept within which an interrupt mechanism is meaningful: the ability of the processor to continue processing while an I/O transfer is taking place.

When the I/O operation is completed, the I/O circuitry sends a completion signal to the processor/channel interface, and sets the channel 2 ID word. This signal is used to change the immediate behavior of the processor. It is possible to construct a machine system that merely sets a bit to record the I/O completion. Processor response to the event of completion would occur on the execution of something like an I/O signal poll instruction.

The I/O completion event signal in the context of Fig. 1.3 causes an *interrupt sequence*. The S.V. is stored in the next available save area as pointed to by the SPR and the three-word IDB entry associated with channel 2 provides new contents for MQ, base register, and IC. The next instruction executed is the JMP to the routine that responds to the interrupt. This routine determines what device caused the interrupt, what the status of the READ operation is (*successful, device busy, device malfunction*), and does whatever else is associated with the completion of an I/O event in the system. Note that the routine may run with all *interrupts disabled* so that no interrupt can occur during its operation. It is probably encoded to run so that PE and AE interrupts can occur. If such an interrupt occurs, the S.V. of the channel 2 *interrupt handler* is itself placed in a save area.

Channel 1 interrupts may be allowed without elaborating the structure of the channel 2 interrupt handler because of the separate ID word. A particular detail of this hypothetical interrupt system is that channel 2 interrupts may also be enabled while processing a channel 2 interrupt without adding program complexity. This is because the ID word, which changes on every interrupt, is transcribed immediately into the MQ. *The usual reason for disallowing interrupts for some period of time is to prohibit the overwriting of a status word like the ID word until it can be saved.*

In the simple case of no interrupt occurring during the processing of the channel 2 interrupt, the program saved in a save area is returned to by execution of a JMP STACK instruction that places the contents of the save area (available by means of the SPR) in the S.V. registers of the machine. With the interrupted program restored to registers, it may now resume.

Interrupt mechanisms are an area of debate between hardware designers and software designers. The issue of hardware–software trade-offs in systems design is frequently joined at the time of defining the interrupt mechanism. Operating systems people are anxious to achieve a minimum interrupt handling time, and a minimum ''disable'' time. They prefer elaborate interrupt structures that reduce the number of instructions that must be used to save and restore registers and to analyze the reason for the interrupt. Hardware designers are concerned with circuit counts and hardware costs, and tend to prefer simpler structures that may cause the need for more elaborate interrupt-handling software. Out of this tension, various interrupt structures have emerged. The following list suggests some of the variations.

▪ Instead of a save area as discussed in Fig. 1.3, provide multiple sets of registers (more than one S.V.) so that no register save and restore is necessary if the interrupted program will be resumed immediately after interrupt interpretation and response. Some processors provide two sets of registers; others provide multiple sets.

▪ Provide only one I/O status word and rely completely on *software stacking* of ID-type words if I/O interrupts are to be allowed during I/O interrupt processing.

▪ Associate priority with interrupts by associating with a set of S.V. registers a set of interrupt areas each of which relates to a particular S.V. Each interrupt area is assigned to devices of particular priority.

■   Save only the IC in memory at interrupt time, and place new contents in IC without the necessity of a jump instruction.

■   Provide a separate interrupt enable mask that can be manipulated by a number of instructions.

■   Define more interrupt classes, for example, a parity error, an overflow error, an illegal operation error.

The reader should now be comfortable with the concept of interrupt and its variations. It is important to remark that an interrupt structure may have much more general use than is discussed here. For example, in machines with certain elaborate address formation schemes, certain interruptions called Segment Faults or Page Faults may occur when a program refers to an address that is not in storage at the time of reference. Similarly, multiprocessors may have interrupt locations in each processor that are associated with other processors and are used when one processor wishes to communicate with another.

Finally, interrupts cannot be fully understood without associated concepts of privilege and protection that are discussed in the next sections.

1.2.1.3   Instruction set

The operating system designer is interested in the instruction set of the hardware for a number of reasons. The designer, of course, uses these instructions to create an operating system. Although actual assembly language level encoding of systems has fallen from favor in recent years (for good reasons), the operating system developer must usually have a greater awareness of good and bad code than applications programmers must have. As a consequence of this, the high-level languages used to develop operating systems commonly provide closer access to machine structures than do applications-oriented, high-level languages. It is important for an operating system programmer to have a good feel for instruction sets in order to estimate how large programs will be and how long they will take to execute. Such appreciations will determine how rich in function the extended view the programmer creates can profitably be.

Another reason for interest in the instruction set is to gain an appreciation of the I/O structure of the system. Many of the details of operating system organization are responses to the specifics of the organization of I/O in the hardware of the system. The systems designer is looking for the richness and variety of I/O functions that can be performed. The systems designer is also interested in the distributions of functions between the processor and other intelligent units of the system and must understand functional richness and structure in order to determine what kind of interfaces to provide application programs and how to organize functions beneath the interfaces.

The relationship between an operating system and the underlying hardware is particularly affected by the concepts of *privileged operations* and of *supervisor state*. It is very common to define an architecture that has two fundamental states—a *worker program state* in which only a subset of the instructions can be executed, and a *control state* in which all of the instructions can be executed. This control state is variously called *Supervisor State* (IBM 370), *Master Mode* (Honeywell 6800), and similar names. In some systems, control state is automatically entered on the occurrence of an interrupt. In other systems, the architecture provides an option to enter or not enter control state on an interrupt. Entry into control state permits execution of the privileged operations.

An entry into control state is commonly provided by a particular instruction that forces an interrupt. The first instruction executed after this interrupt is executed in control state. The instruction is called *SVC* (Supervisor Call) in IBM 370 architecture.

The instructions that can be executed only in control state are usually the set of all I/O instructions, instructions that change the control or worker state of the machine without causing an interrupt, and instructions that can change the interrupt status of the processor.

1.2.1.4   Protection

The *protection mechanism* of a processor prohibits a program from referencing memory locations that are outside the range of memory allocated to the program. These mechanisms are designed to prevent damage to the operating system by an application program sharing memory with it, and to prevent damage to other application programs. An attempt to address outside of a defined memory space causes an interrupt and the invocation of the system.

There are various protection schemes. One method of constraining addressability is to set an upper and lower bound in a *memory bounds register*. Whenever an address is formed, it is checked to determine whether it falls within the limits. Another method is to associate each program with a *protection key*. Blocks of memory that may be referenced by the program have this protection key (a bit pattern of some length) written in bit locations not accessible by a program in problem state. Whenever a memory address is formed, the key of the program is compared with the key of the addressed location.

In "relocate" machines that provide an additional mapping from a formed logical address to a machine location, it is possible to combine the *addressing mechanism* with the *protection mechanism*. A full discussion of *relocation, paging,* and *segmentation* is provided later in the text. However, just enough of a relocate mechanism will be described here to show how address mapping and protection can be combined.

Consider Fig. 1.4. An instruction with a specified memory address of 1036 calls for the application of the contents of the IX to form an address. This address is 1058. Rather than referencing location 1058, the value is searched for in an

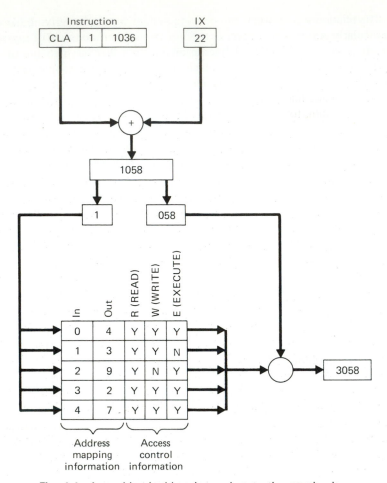

Fig. 1.4 A combined addressing and protection mechanism.

associative array called MAP. MAP represents the distribution of addresses 0000–4999 of the program across physical memory locations. MAP states that all program addresses in the 1000 range are physically located in memory locations 3000–3999. The memory location 3058 is the one actually to be accessed. The search of MAP with the value 1 (the high-order digit of 1000) produces 3000 to which 058 is added to form the relocated address.

Any program can reference only those memory locations that are represented on the MAP table. It is impossible to form an address that is not supported by a MAP entry and consequently impossible to address outside of the allocated area.

MAP also contains three bits called RWE. These bits define the kind of access permitted to memory area. Depending on the settings of RWE, a program may have some set of *READ, WRITE,* and *EXECUTE privileges.*

One use for MAP in addition to providing protection by constraining addressability is to extend the addressability of a program by providing longer machine addresses than are available in the address field of the instructions. Any particular program, for example, may be constrained to address in a 16-bit range, but a memory larger than that can be used effectively by a set of coexisting programs each referencing physical memory locations according to unique MAP settings. Thus the 16-bit range of any program may be extended by concatenating additional bits from a MAP.

It has been common practice when a machine is in control state to allow all memory locations to be accessible by the program in execution (normally a component of the operating system). Recently, however, mechanisms to constrain the addressability of programs running in control state have been attracting interest.

1.2.2   Structural Aspects of Hardware

In addition to box interconnection and processor characteristics, there are other hardware aspects that affect the structure of a system. The interface between hardware and software has been made more complex by the development of *firmware* methodology.

Firmware has added a dimension to the problem of what functions should be embodied in software and what functions should be implemented in hardware by providing levels of programmability underneath the apparent hardware architecture of the system. The development of microcode and the extension of the concept of memory hierarchy have had an almost revolutionary impact on the way machines and software may be organized and designed.

1.2.2.1   Microprogramming

The word *microprogramming* has a number of uses and sometimes causes confusion. Some authors use the word to mean any instruction set that is not revealed to a user of the system or even to software designers. This use stresses the aspect of nonvisibility and the concept of microcode lying beneath an apparent hardware architecture. Figure 1.5 suggests this concept. The top layer of apparent architecture contains a register population and an instruction set. Before microcode, the features of the architecture would be *hardwired,* defined in circuits and the result of the implementation of a logical design. This logical design would involve a description of the machine in terms of gates, flip-flops, matrices of various kinds, and signal encoding and decoding. The implementation of a LOAD instruction, for example, would involve a family of circuits designed to support a fixed logical flow of signals in the processor.

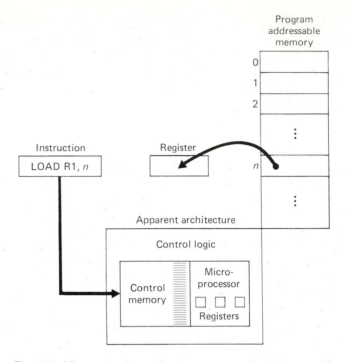

Fig. 1.5 Microcode beneath an apparent hardware architecture.

Microprogramming provides an alternate way of supporting an apparent architecture. The structure and functions are supported by a microprocessor with its own *hardwired instruction set*. This instruction set may be considerably different from the *apparent instruction set*. The memory of the microprocessor is physically and logically separated from the *program addressable memory* of the apparent architecture. No program running on the architecture can generate an address in the control memory of the microprocessor.

The instruction set of the microprocessor is used to interpret the instructions of the apparent processor. The LOAD instruction is defined by a subroutine in control memory that manipulates data flow in the hardware to give the effect of loading the programmer-visible register. Usually the instruction set of the microprocessor is simpler than the supported architecture so that a number of instructions are required to interpret and execute the higher-level instruction. For example, the higher-level architecture may support 32-bit words and the microprocessor architecture 8-bit words so that the loading of a 32-bit structure into a 32-bit register requires a routine of some complexity.

The extent to which the higher-level architecture is defined in microprocessor instructions depends on a number of economic and technological factors. There are price–performance goals and raw performance goals for various machines that indicate different balances of hardwiring and microcode support, and that indicate the speed and capacity requirements of the microprocessor. There has been a tendency for higher-performance machines to contain less microcode logic support than more modest machines do. This sometimes leads to the anomaly that more of the operating system can be embedded in microcode in smaller machines than in larger machines.

The idea of a small processor with a private memory hidden "underneath the hood" and executing higher-level macroinstructions is consistent with the idea of microprogramming being defined in terms of visibility. However, the word "microprogramming" is also used to suggest the instruction set of the microprocessor per se, regardless of whether or not it is visible to a writer of traditional programs. It is this use that sometimes causes confusion since one person may use microcode to mean a very simple instruction set, and another, hearing the word, assumes that the set must be "invisible."

The idea of microcode as a set of less capable instructions is made fully explicit in the phrase *vertical microcode*. This phrase suggests that functions are performed by executing down a list of instructions that looks reasonably like any instruction set. There is also a concept of *horizontal microcode* in which a word of microcode may look rather less like an instruction. The concept of horizontal microcode is easiest to understand if one visualizes a machine as having a set of registers and connections between them that form a network. A microcode word contains a bit for every point on the network that can send or receive a unit of information. If the bit is "on," the passing of data through the point is permitted. If the bit is "off," then the passing of data is prohibited. Thus the entire pattern of data movement in the machine is represented by the microcode word. This concept moves the idea of microcode away from programming and toward logical design.

The advantage of horizontal microcode is its potential for achieving a high degree of parallelism of function and the consequent speed that can be derived from this. In some systems, horizontal microcode is used to support vertical microcode instruction sets that in turn support apparent architectures. It is also possible to support apparent architectures directly in horizontal microcode.

1.2.2.2   Memory hierarchy and organization—cache memory

The idea of using a processor to define a processor at a higher layer is paralleled by the idea of various kinds of memory in different amounts and different speeds, accessible to various intelligent units of the system. A full treatment of the concepts of memory hierarchy would be a book in its own right. We will discuss the relation between primary, directly addressable memories and secondary memories in connection with our discussion of memory management. Here we will introduce some basic ideas about the kinds of memory that may be part of a system "beneath," rather than "above," primary memory.

By *primary memory* we mean the addressable array of locations commonly visible to the instruction set. This memory holds the programs and data objects referenced by the address formation mechanisms of the processor. The idea in its simplest form is shown in Fig. 1.6(a). This memory, regardless of its technology, has the attributes of being readable and writable on reference from a processor.

Figure 1.6(b) suggests a memory between the processor and primary memory. This memory is characteristically faster and smaller than the primary memory. It is still readable and writable on reference from a processor. It may or may not be visible. A perfectly visible memory would, in effect, become the primary memory. Addresses generated by processors would be to this memory, and a set of instructions to move from the larger memory would be provided. The larger memory would be used as a backing store approximately an order of magnitude or half an order of magnitude slower than the small memory. In the hierarchies defined on earlier UNIVAC 1100s, for example, or on the CDC 6600 there is this kind of perfect visibility.

The small memory may be completely "invisible." If so, it is often called a *cache* or a *hidden buffer*. Logic in the system becomes completely responsible for bringing referenced objects into the cache and managing the relationship between the cache and primary memory. The addresses formed by the system are primary memory addresses that will be translated to cache addresses if the objects referenced are in the cache. If they are not in the cache, the system will

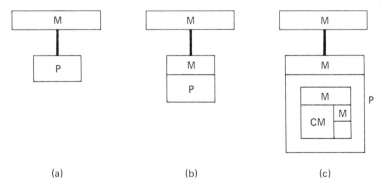

(a) (b) (c)

Fig. 1.6 Memory structures "beneath" primary memory. (a) Processor and primary memory; (b) processor and primary memory with cache memory; and (c) processor and primary memory with cache memory and a microprocessor with its own control memory, operand memory, and a small cache of its own.

bring them to it. Algorithms for the management of cache contents are represented in hardware logic or in microcode.

The cache memory may be partially visible. In such a design, addresses are still formed for the primary memory, but a set of contents management instructions are provided to increase the probability that referenced objects will be in the cache. Instructions that permit partial release or prohibit overwriting that might normally occur can be important to the performance of a hardware system. A modest increase in the percentage of time that an object is found in the cache can have a disproportionately large effect on the instruction execution rate of a processor. Thus if cache management instructions can increase the *cache hit probability* from 90 to 95 percent, it is conceivable that an increase of nearly 25 percent in instruction execution speed can be achieved for the processor.

As an example of this, consider a system that has a 500-nanosecond primary memory and a 50-nanosecond cache memory. Assume that the processor makes a single reference to memory for operands and a single reference for an instruction, and that if instructions and data are in cache, an instruction can be executed every 100 nanoseconds. If every referenced object is in the cache memory, then 20 instructions will be executed in 2,000 nanoseconds. The 20 instructions will involve 40 references to memory. If there is a 90 percent "hit," then four references will involve an additional 450 nanoseconds each to go to primary memory. Then 1,800 nanoseconds will be added to the time required to execute the instructions, for a total of 3,800 nanoseconds. If the hits can be raised to 95 percent, then only 900 nanoseconds are needed for two references to primary storage, and the 20 instructions can be executed in 2,900 nanoseconds. A disproportionate increase in instruction rate is achieved by a 5 percent increase in hit ratio. This would be partially offset, of course, by the addition of time for the execution of buffer management instructions.

Alternatively, cache hits can be increased by increasing cache size, but memory of this type is relatively expensive compared with the logic required to marginally increase its effectiveness.

1.2.2.3 ROS, ROM, PROM, etc.

In addition to layers of readable, writable memory, a system may have memories of various speeds and capabilities at various places.

The control memory introduced with the idea of a microprocessor supporting the apparent architecture may be a privately addressable memory of the usual read–write characteristics. However, it is possible that the memory containing the instructions supporting the apparent architecture is a *read-only memory,* a *ROM*. Such memories are useful because they can provide larger storage areas at greater speed for less cost. Since the apparent architecture is expected to be stable, the instructions used to support it can be "etched" into memory, and no ability to write that memory need be provided. The parameters needed to interpret a particular instruction may be left in main memory and made directly accessible to the microprocessor, or brought into a small writable local data memory.

Along the continuum from ROM to normally accessible memories, there are steps that define the difficulty of doing a write. Some memories may be written only by special instructions so that their contents can be changed from time to time but are not writable by the normal flow of STORE-type instructions found in the program stream. Writable control stores of this type are used by Burroughs in the B1700 to alter the apparent architecture of the processor to accommodate program structures generated by different compilers. Some memories (*electronically programmable read-only memories, EPROMs*) can be changed but only by a process external to the system that clears bit patterns and replaces them with new patterns.

Figure 1.6(c) suggests something of the richness of memory structure. The microprocessor has a control memory, a small operand memory, and a very small cache of its own. Beyond this, the microprocessor accesses the cache and primary stores of the apparent architecture.

The full complexity of memory organization can be guessed if one considers that there may be multiple microprocessors used to support an architecture, and that local buffering and local memories can be associated with hardwired units.

The reasons for using various kinds of memory organization come partly from the economics of technology and partly from considerations of system integrity. The *fragmentation of memories* into various types at various levels occurs because of the speeds at which some things need to be done, the relationships between the cost of logic and the cost of memory, and the costs of memories of various characteristics. In addition, it is the view of some designers that functions represented in a memory to which there is no physical path are more secure from erroneous change or malicious probing than are functions protected in a physically homogeneous memory by access control maps. Thus memory partitioning into physically separate memories in diverse technologies is an extension of ideas about write and access control.

1.3   THE HARDWARE–SOFTWARE INTERFACE

The issues at the hardware–software interface involve two essential questions.

- To what extent should functions be embedded in hardware?
- To what extent does hardware design imply constraints on software?

When the hardware–software choice is two-dimensional, in the absence of firmware, then the trade-offs lie in the degree to which hardware should be extended to support particular software operations. Classical issues of contention between hardware designers and software designers are the interrupt system, the protection mechanism, and the addressing scheme. We have already alluded to programmer goals associated with the interrupt system. There are similar issues with protection and addressing.

In general, programmers like to reduce the "granularity" of addressability and protectability in order to achieve the ability to give smaller amounts of memory space to programs and more closely match the actual space required to the allocatable unit. For example, if the protection mechanism applies a protection key to a block of addresses of 4K bytes, then it is impossible to allocate memory in units of smaller than 4K and still preserve protection. Similarly, the addressing scheme can define a minimum granule of addressability. Systems programmers are frequently concerned that the minimum granule will not be intensively used and that portions of memory that are truly free will be unavailable for allocation.

On the other hand, engineers are concerned about the length of registers, the width of data paths, etc., and the way extra circuits increase the cost of a machine. Thus they may resist enlarging registers to provide increased granularity of access. They may also be concerned with placing additional functions in hardware because the functions seem to make the machine slower for some accepted measure of hardware capability like millions of instructions executed per second.

What these comments suggest is that extremely parochial points of view on the part of hardware and software designers can lead to suboptimal design of a system, and that it is important for each group to attempt a common image of the system in order to make coherent hardware–software trade-offs. Systems architects are expected to be concerned with both hardware and software issues.

When microcode and memory hierarchy enter the design picture, issues of the hardware–software interface become considerably more complex. The ability to support an apparent architecture with an underlying level of vertical or horizontal microcode, the ability to use multiple memories of various types in the system, and the ability to use multiple microprocessors for various functions raise points of distribution of function, level of interface, and system structure of far greater complexity than the old two-dimensional hardware–software trade-offs.

1.3.1 Impact of Firmware

The ability to define an instruction set in microcode implies the ability to microcode functions at a level higher than the level of a traditional instruction set. There is the possibility that a higher-level language machine could be built that contains a COBOL or APL or PL/I interpreter so that compilation might be trivialized or even eliminated. Statements like $A = B + C(I)$ would be dynamically executed directly by the microcoded interpreter. A number of higher-level machines have been built for particular languages.

Short of a high-level language machine, it is possible to microcode all or part of the view of the system that is presented to a compiler. Those interfaces that are generally used by a compiler and that are either compiled into a program or provided by calling a resident program of the operating system could be supported by code in the control memory just as though they were machine instructions. In addition, certain control mechanisms of the operating system such as those that activate processes or handle interrupts of various kinds can be microcoded to execute more quickly and to free amounts of program-accessible primary storage. It is now common to find that some basic operating systems functions are provided in microcode. IBM's VM/370 operating system has been particularly aggressive in moving functions into microcode for models of the IBM System 370 processor family that have appropriate amounts of control memory available.

The considerations relevant to how much function to embed in microcode involve the generality of the interfaces and how well defined the algorithms associated with those interfaces may be. ''APL-machines'' may be reasonably constructed in microcode because the definition and the support of the language are well known. Whether more general-purpose machines can profitably be micro-coded to provide high-level support for many languages and many interfaces is a subject of some controversy. The IBM 5100 that provides BASIC and APL does not provide high-level interpretive support of those languages at a single level. It has taken an alternative approach of microcoding a 370 interface for APL and a S/3 interface for BASIC and running 370 and S/3 compilers on those interfaces.

Advocates of using microcode capability to extend the hardware interface and put more function ''under the hood'' no longer dominate advanced thinking. If it is possible to enhance an apparent architecture by microcode, then it is also possible to expose the microcode interface to the compilers and have the compilers create programs in the simpler instructions of the microlevel processor. Advocates of this approach contend that the lower-level instruction sets may be more efficient than the higher-level instruction sets. Many of the instructions in an instruction set of the S/370 level, for example, are not even generated by compilers. Given available technology with modest advancement in compiler methodology, very simple systems can be built that deliver enormous speed at very low price by having compilers generate lower levels of code directly.

1.3.2 Impact of Hardware Structure

Beyond issues of what should be in hardware, firmware, or software, current hardware technology also raises issues about the structure of the software layers.

With multiple processing units, and with varying kinds of shared and private memory in a system, the hardware–software issues must involve a determination of where to put what functions regardless of whether those functions are to be etched or loaded into memory. The structure of the operating system must be sensitive to the structure of the hardware. For example, if I/O is to be done on a specialized I/O processor in the system, and if queues associated with requests for service are placed in the devices themselves, then the modules that provide I/O service and the interfaces between those modules will look very different from those on a system with other attributes.

A partial view of this issue is represented in Fig. 1.7. Figure 1.7(a) suggests a system with a single memory and a single processor. The control state and the instruction set and register population available in control state are represented by C in the COMP box. The portions of memory addressable only in control state are represented by C in the MEM box. The P portion of memory is divided between various programs using the Problem (P) state of the COMP box in some interleaved fashion. P COMP can access only P MEM. C COMP can address C MEM and P MEM.

In this system, the coding and working space required to provide the operating system level view is all contained in a protected portion of main memory.

Figure 1.7(b) shows that some of the control portion of memory is actually in another memory, MEM2. This memory may be of the same technology and speed as the MEM1 memory or it may be a different kind of memory. Perhaps it is a control store that is "executable only" and invariant. The control left in MEM1 is working space, tables, and parameters. However, some control functions may be left in MEM1 if MEM2 is invariant. Certain programs that are to run in a control state, but that are not worth keeping in a primary storage at all times would be left in MEM1. The relationship between those programs and the programs in MEM2 is necessarily different from what it is when everything is in MEM2. The protocols for programs in different memories calling each other and passing parameters to each other would be different from the protocols for programs in the same memory. By reasonable inference, the distribution of function would reflect the two memories and the program packaging in Fig. 1.7(b) would not be the same as it is in Fig. 1.7(a).

In Fig. 1.7(c), a separate control processor is added to the system, and in Fig. 1.7(d), a family of control processors is added. There may be two I/O processors and a memory manager, for example. A detail of Fig. 1.7(d) is that the control processors cannot access MEM1. The concept of the I/O support, the memory management, and even the process relationship protocols between control and problem state are affected by the particular hardware structure of all of these systems. In fact, new concepts of software structure may emerge as a result of the new dimensions of hardware–software interface.

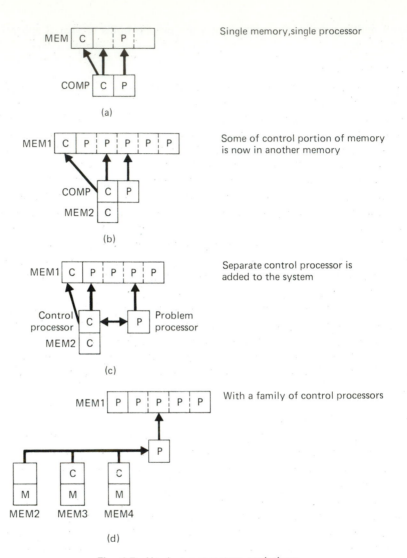

Fig. 1.7 Hardware structure variations.

1.4 CONCEPT OF OPERATING SYSTEM

If the fundamental interface between hardware and software is being unsettled by new hardware technology, it is only achieving a level of richness of design choice and function distribution that has always characterized the relationships between layers and/or modules of software.

We have a fundamental problem in defining what an operating system is and what it does. There are different opinions about what functions are applications functions and what functions are systems functions to be implicitly provided by the extended apparent architectural view provided by the operating system. We have various points of view about what components of a software package are part of the operating system and what are separately packageable products.

A software package contains various elements to reduce the cost of programming, enhance accessibility to the system, provide operational efficiency, and provide effective performance tuning, scheduling, and accounting. The goal of a software package is to provide economic benefit by increasing human and machine efficiency. To meet that goal there are programming languages, applications packages, database management systems, sorts, merges, schedulers, library systems, I/O control systems, linkage editors, and media conversion utilities. There are programmed functions available to reduce the cost of programming by reducing what must be programmed, or by reducing how much work is involved in writing a program. Similarly, there are aids for the operational and administrative functions associated with machine support.

In general, an operating system is a vague concept based upon tradition, hardware characteristics, the size of programs required to represent certain functions, and the distribution of functions among a community of application programs. Usually considered part of an operating system are

1. Those functions that involve an on-line interface with a *system operator* to support *device mounting, system reconfiguration*, and *system status modification*. This interface commonly allows an operator to *start a program*, to *stop a program*, to *inquire about the utilization of the hardware*, to *inquire about the rate of progress of a particular program*, to *inform the system of the association or disassociation of data sets with various devices*, etc.;

2. Those functions directly concerned with the basic I/O activity of the system. Particularly, programs that *manage queues of I/O requests, submit I/O requests to devices, handle interrupts from I/O devices*, and *allocate devices and channels for the use of particular programs or the residence of particular data sets;*

3. Those mechanisms in multiprogramming environments that control the patterns by which a population of active programs gains use of the processors of the system. The mechanisms used to enforce management policies about who should get what rate of service from the system are frequently thought of as part of the operating system, but may, at the highest level of policy definition, be thought of as extensions to the system;

4. Those mechanisms that provide the methods of access to the computational resource. For example, control stream readers/interpreters and interactive terminal command interpreters. These components interface with programmers (or

programmer surrogates) to accept requests for computational service. The control or command stream describes what kind of service is desired and qualifies the requestor as a legitimate demander of that service. These access components may also be thought of as extensions to the operating system, as subsystems that relate to the system almost as applications programs.

Programming language processors are not commonly considered part of the operating system. Examples can be found, however, in which they are so integrated into the system that no view of the system is possible "through" them. In the past, many functions that are now part of operating systems were part of compilers and delivered in the library of compiler modules. There is considerable flexibility at the compiler–operating system interface both in terms of function packaging and in terms of how applications programs receive space and services. In many single-language, on-line programming systems, the relationships between the compilation process and the allocation and control mechanisms are so intimate that it is difficult to see the edge of the compiler and the beginning of the operating system.

Whether a software element is part of the operating system is partly a matter of judgment, partly a function of the views of the system that are exposed, and partly a function of the history of the system. Many components of software packages are not considered part of the operating system because their functions emerged at a time after the underlying system was already fixed in structure with stable interfaces. Telecommunications and database management are good examples of this.

This text discusses the components and structure of operating systems, and presents various philosophies of what an operating system is. A reader attempting to develop mature perspectives will profit by considering seriously the observations about the amorphous nature of the concept of an operating system. The rate of progress from past to future is determined by the rate at which we can reorganize, recombine, and restructure our ideas about systems. Beginning with an alert that we are in an area of opinion and judgment should encourage the reader to peruse the text actively, and to ask continually if there might be other ways of structuring the functions and mechanisms that we describe.

ABBREVIATIONS, LANGUAGES, AND COMPUTERS

APL	CPU
BASIC	EPROM
CDC 6600	Honeywell 6800
CDC CYBER series	IBM 370
COBOL	IBM 5100

IBM VM/370   OS/MVT

Multics   PL/I

OS 1100   UNIVAC 1100

OS/MVS

BASIC TERMINOLOGY

application package   language processor specialists

application programmer   language specialists

assembly language   lexical analysis

channel   machine language

code generation   macroinstruction

code optimization   media conversion utilities

compiler   memory

computer operator   merge

control unit   parameter passing

data set   parity check

database management system printer

device mounting   processor

disk   programmer

double indexing   saving and restoring registers

drum   semantics

editor   software

hardware   sort

high-level language   syntax

high-level language machine tape

index register   telecommunications

indirect addressing   teleprocessing

instruction set   utility routine

interpreter

MORE ADVANCED TERMINOLOGY

addressing error   apparent instruction set

addressing structure   associative memory

backing store

base register

"black box"

buffer

cache "hit" probability

cache memory

command language

concurrent operation

control state

control stream reader

dynamic memory management

EXECUTE access

firmware

fragmentation of memory

hardware layer

"hardwired" instruction set

hidden buffer

input/output completion

interface

interrupt

interrupt handler

interrupts disabled

interrupts enabled

I/O control system

"level-of-view" concept

linkage editor

master mode

"megamachine"

memory addressing hardware

memory bounds register

memory hierarchy

memory management

microcode

microprocessor

microprogramming

multiprocessing

multiprogramming

operating system

page fault

paging

performance tuning

polling for interrupts

primary memory

privileged operations

program addressable memory

program library system

program structure

program visible registers

protection key

read, write, execute access

read access

read-only memory

relocation

scheduler

secondary memory

segment fault

segmentation

segmented addressing

software stacking of interrupts

supervisor call (SVC)

supervisor state

system reconfiguration

two-dimensional addressing

"visible" architecture

worker program state

WRITE access

EXERCISES

Section 1.1

1.1 In early computer systems, which did not have operating systems, compilers generated all of the machine language instructions necessary to run a program. Today's operating systems provide interfaces for compiler writers that reduce the amount of machine language instructions that compilers must generate.

    a) What functions, do you suppose, are implemented in these interfaces?

    b) Could these interfaces be used by assembler writers as well as compiler writers?

    c) Explain how these interfaces create a "megamachine" different from the underlying hardware.

1.2 Explain the differences between language specialists and language processor specialists. Which of these groups, do you suppose, is more concerned with operating systems?

1.3 It is not uncommon for a programmer to write a program in a "higher-level" programming language and then, at various points in the debugging process, to revert to lower levels, ultimately to machine-level dumps of memory.

    a) Why might it be desirable for a high-level language programmer to examine a memory dump?

    b) Why is it undesirable?

    c) How might operating systems be designed so that it would not be necessary for programmers to revert to memory dumps when debugging?

1.4 Computer operators view the operating system through the interface presented at the operator terminal or system console.

    a) Compare the operator's view with the programmer's view.

    b) Compare the operator's view with the compiler writer's view.

    c) Compare the operator's view with management's view.

1.5 The challenge of systems design is to create problem-solver interfaces of minimum contamination with computer concepts.

    a) Explain this statement.

    b) Why is this goal particularly important to computer users who are not familiar with the details of the computer?

    c) To what class of users is this goal not critical?

Section 1.2

1.6 The nature of a hardware system lies in the interconnection of packaged elements with varying degrees of autonomous operation and strongly distinctive attributes. Explain.

1.7 Explain the importance of each of the following hardware features to an operating systems designer.

    a) addressing structure

b) interrupt structure

c) instruction set

d) protection mechanisms

1.8 Explain in detail the operation of the interrupt mechanisms of a computer with which you are familiar.

1.9 Describe the full sequence of events normally associated with an I/O completion interrupt.

1.10 Why is it necessary to disable interrupts? Describe a computer architecture in which it is never necessary to disable interrupts.

1.11 Distinguish between the concepts of "worker program state" and "control state."

1.12 Describe two different schemes for memory protection.

1.13 What is microprogramming?

1.14 Distinguish between primary and secondary memory.

1.15 What is cache memory?

1.16 Discuss the concept of cache "hit" probability.

1.17 A modest increase in the percentage of time that an object is found in the cache can have a disproportionately large effect on the instruction execution rate of a processor. Explain.

1.18 Distinguish between ROM and EPROM.

Section 1.3

1.19 Give three factors that affect the decision as to what split of functions between hardware and software best achieves the stated objectives of a system.

1.20 If it is possible to enhance an apparent architecture by microcode, then it is also possible to expose the microcode interface to the compilers and have the compilers create programs in the simpler instructions of the microlevel processor. Explain.

Section 1.4

1.21 Name three software components that are included normally in an operating system. Name three software components that are placed normally in software packages considered to be independent of the operating system.

1.22 Briefly describe your notion of each of the following software components.

a) programming language translator

b) applications package

c) database management system

d) sort

e) merge

f) scheduler

g) library system

h) I/O control system

i) linkage editor

j) media conversion utility

1.23 The following functions are normally considered to be part of the operating system. Discuss each briefly. Each is discussed in detail later in the text. As you read the text, see how your understanding of these functions improves.

a) device mounting

b) system reconfiguration

c) system status modification

d) start a program

e) stop a program

f) inquire about hardware utilization

g) inquire about progress of a program

h) check association of data sets with devices

i) manage queues of I/O requests

j) submit I/O requests to devices

k) handle interrupts from I/O devices

l) allocate devices and channels to programs

m) decide which program gets an available processor

n) decide which program gets available memory

o) decide rates of service to programs

p) read control stream

q) interpret interactive terminal commands

1.24 In many single-language, on-line programming systems, the relationships between the compilation process and the allocation and control mechanisms are so intimate that it is difficult to see the edge of the compiler and the beginning of the operating system. Why?

2
Functions of Operating Systems

2.1 CONCEPTS

Various discussions of the major functions of operating systems have been
undertaken in the literature. It would seem like a relatively trivial task to list what
a product is supposed to do. In the case of an operating system, however, the task
is made difficult by various ideas about which components of a software package
are considered part of the operating system. A large view tends to include
functions delegated to utilities or other packaged programs, while a narrower
view excludes them.

A function such as "provide a command language for accessing the system"
is frequently considered an integral part of an operating system. However, it may
be thought of as an extension that is related to the operating system in the same
way as a compiler is related. For a particular function, some designers think that
mechanisms for the function are part of the operating system but that policies
that use the mechanisms are not. For example, the routine that suspends a
program from CPU use and replaces it with another may be thought of as a
fundamental mechanism. The routine that interfaces with installations to prepare
the schedule that will determine the basis of CPU use may or may not be part of
the operating system. Therefore, the listing of functions is complicated by issues
of "How much?" as well as by issues of "What?" Those who take a narrow
view of the functions of an operating system tend to create the following list.

- Manage the processor by *interleaving periods of CPU activation for pro-*
  grams. Handle interrupts, and *synchronize access to shared resources.*

- Manage the memory by *allocating to programs the memory they require*
  when they are using the processor.

■   Manage devices by *initiating I/O requests, maintaining queues,* and *reporting completions.*

■   Manage *program initiation* and *interprogram communication.*

■   Manage data by *supporting the creation, opening, closing, reading,* and *writing of files.*

An operating system contains a large number of primitive operations. These primitive operations may be grouped together in various ways to form structures. The large structures formed by the grouping of primitive operations form major components of the system whose names seem to define the major functions of the system. For example, in IBM's OS/MVT operating system there are three major functions of *Job Management, Data Management,* and *Task Management. Job Management relates to the activities associated with starting a batch job, Data Management relates to the activities associated with linking a program to data, and Task Management relates to the control of programs after they have entered the set of active programs sharing the resources of the system.*

The particular distribution of primitive operations between these major components is a response to the particular user environments that OS/360 designers anticipated in the early 1960s. In different environments, the definitions of these three major functions might or might not be meaningful. Take, for example, the sequence of associating a program with a data set. The act of *allocating the data set to the program (giving the program the permission and capability to use the data set)* is an act of Job Management. The acts of *opening the data set (preparing it to be referenced)* and *reading it* are acts of Data Management. The act of *allocating space for the file to be read into* is an act of Task Management. It is possible to conceive of permutations of these acts into different structures that lead to different categorizations of function.

An operating system may be thought of as a set of functions, a set of objects, and a set of mappings of functions on objects. The structure of the system depends on the concepts used to map functions onto objects.

Figure 2.1 shows a list of functions that may be performed upon "things" that exist in the system. These "things" are shown on the second list as data set objects, procedure objects, and device objects. This system can create, read, write, modify, destroy, and protect an accumulation of data sets, programs, and devices.

Figure 2.2 shows an organization of functions in which a module of function is packaged to perform all functions on a single object. Thus there is an operating system program that performs all operations on data set 1, another which performs all operations on data set 2, etc. The structure of such a system is shown in Fig. 2.2(b). The program running on the operating system CALLs the D1 manager for operations on D1, the D2 manager for operations on D2, etc.

Functions	Objects	
Create	Data set 1	Data set objects
	Data set 2	
Read	Data set 3	
Write	Device 1	Device objects
	Device 2	
Modify	Device 3	
Destroy	Procedure 1	Procedure objects
	Procedure 2	
Protect	Procedure 3	

Fig. 2.1 One-to-one mapping.

Such a structure is usable when the set of objects is small and may be efficient when the functions to be performed on each object are dramatically different.

Figure 2.3 shows a generalization of the concept of Fig. 2.2. If there are multiple instances of objects of a few basic types, then each manager module can be designed to perform all functions on all members of the object set. A similarity between Figs. 2.2 and 2.3 is that the location of procedure objects or device objects is information that is reasonably held within the managers. The

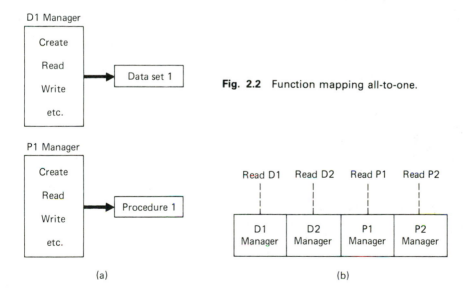

Fig. 2.2 Function mapping all-to-one.

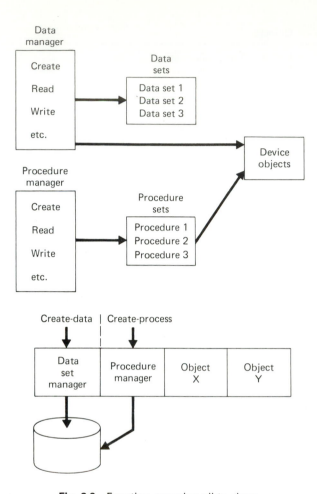

Fig. 2.3 Function mapping all-to-class.

system of Fig. 2.3 would necessarily contain more information since it needs device locations for all objects of the class.

Figure 2.4 introduces a notion of "stratification." In Fig. 2.4, there is a separate module for CREATE, DESTROY, READ–WRITE, and device handling. A program running on the operating system may call each of these modules independently (a hierarchy of function is introduced) and higher modules may call each other. This stratification permits the question: "What is part of the operating system?" When CREATE, DESTROY, and PROTECT are simple functions, they may well be packaged as operating system modules. When they are elaborate, as they may be for complex database management

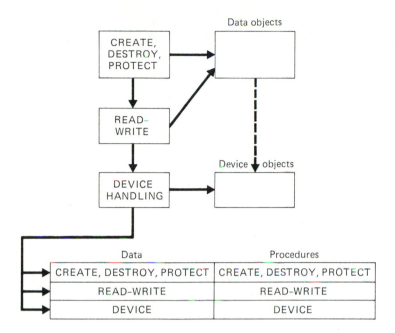

Fig. 2.4 Stratified mapping all-to-class.

environments, these functions may be packaged as part of a database manager. If this is done, then the database manager might run as a program on the operating system. The functions CREATE and DESTROY would not be operating system functions when they apply to data objects.

Figure 2.5 shows a conceptually different mapping of functions onto objects. This mapping creates a functionally specific module for each function and operates the module on all classes of objects. The READ must be coded to read all classes regardless of specific differences between the idea of reading a data set and reading a procedure. A number of essential differences between the earlier figures and Fig. 2.5 may be noted. For example, the location of objects must be commonly available to all the separate functional modules. Some table of locations, external to all functions, must exist in the system.

It is possible for stratification to occur in a system organized this way. Certain kinds of READs may be in modules in the operating system; others may be in modules packaged in database managers. For example, reading a logical record from a device when the logical record is identical to a physical record may be the extent of READ in the operating system. Reading a logical record that requires mapping into a set of physical records may be in a module in a database manager.

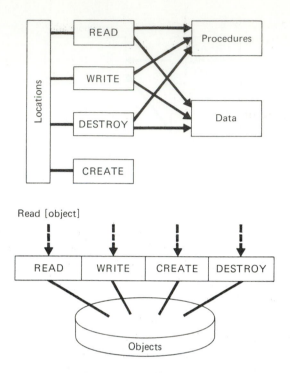

Fig. 2.5   Function mapping—one-to-classes.

The system of Fig. 2.5 "looks" and "feels" very different from Figs. 2.2 through 2.4. In one system we have modules called object managers, in the others we have modules called "readers," "writers," etc. Any particular general-purpose operating system will probably contain both kinds of mappings of functions and objects. Attributes of objects often determine whether functions applied to them are to be considered part of the operating system. Sometimes the occurrence of both is due to historical reasons and projects an unfortunate image of structural fuzziness and conceptual inconsistency on a system.

The essential structure and consequent efficiencies and flexibilities of a system depend heavily on *functional compartmentalization*. It is useful, however, to try to conceive of function independent of structure. Any list of functions does suggest structure and the reader is warned against the easy assumption that the four functions this text shortly presents imply four major components of the system. The functions used in this chapter intend to suggest in a very general way what operating systems do.

The most general statements of the functions of an operating system are that it

■ provides a set of apparent logical resources that are more easily manipulatable than underlying hardware;

■ provides mechanisms for access, sequentialization, and protection in an environment in which resources are shared.

There are so many variations permitted within these general statements that
the specific nature of abstractions and access mechanisms varies widely from
system to system, leading to different ideas of the specifics of operating system
functions.

The major characteristic of this chapter's list of functions is that it takes a
rather large view of function. This chapter discusses the functions of an operating
system that

■ define an environment for program creation and operation;

■ create a set of methods for accessing computer facilities;

■ create an interface for operations;

■ manage the resources of the system to achieve goals established by management.

The narrow list of five functions presented earlier is almost completely
embraced by the last item. This presents the view of the operating system as a
resource manager. This view still admits to various opinions about how extensively policy enforcement functions should be built into an operating system.

2.2   ENVIRONMENT FOR PROGRAM CREATION AND OPERATION

In this section we expand upon the program preparation hierarchy discussed in
Chapter 1.

A programmer wishes to (1) *state a problem solution in a convenient
language,* (2) *receive assistance with program testing and analysis,* (3) *be able
to partition his or her work,* and (4) *merge partitions at convenient times.* These
abilities are provided by *compilers,* various *testing and debugging components,*
linkage editors, and the *interfaces of the operating system that provide an
extended architecture.*

Certain support elements operate upon a program as data while preparing the
program for execution. These elements are the compiler and the linkage editor.
Although compilers are not normally considered part of the operating system,
linkage editors frequently are. *The function of a linkage editor is to combine
programs that have been written at different times* (*perhaps by different people*)
into a single program that will be treated as a structural unit. The output of a
linkage editor is loaded into memory by a *loader,* and receives resources from a
resource allocator.

When a program becomes active on a computer, it enters a *run-time environment*. It is this run-time environment that is represented by the operating system view of Fig. 2.6. It suggests that a particular program running on the hardware sees a system defined by the instructions of the processor, and a set of directly addressable memory locations from 0 to *X*. However, the program also sees a set of operations, in this example, *OPEN, GET, PUT, READ,* and *WRITE,* that are not part of the instruction set of the machine. These operations are defined by modules of the operating system that provide service as if GET, PUT, etc. were machine executable instructions.

What the running program does not see are the *privileged instructions* and *protected memory locations* that are hidden by the extended functions and from which the privileged operations are executed.

The motivations for the extended machine are to reduce the burden of compilation by providing a higher interface as a compilation target, and to reduce the amount of coding that must be done by programmers in machine language.

In an operating system context, these higher-level functions are conceptually part of the system. They are external to the application program. It is not absolutely necessary that the idea of providing these interfaces be associated with an operating system. A record advance routine, GET, could be part of the library of the assembler or compiler and included in a program whenever it calls for the function. *Macroassemblers* that do this are common. It is also common to place some coding for record advance into a compiled or assembled program even when there is an extended run-time environment.

Because of the concepts of control state, interrupts, and privileged operation, however, not all of the functions of a GET can be placed into a program by inclusion of an assembler or compiler library routine. Because the actual I/O instructions are privileged instructions that can execute only in control state, the

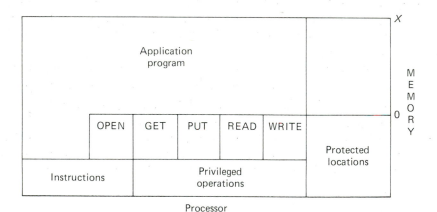

Fig. 2.6 Run-time environment.

program must at some point call upon services that cannot be compiled into it by the compiler. The operation of advancing a pointer to a next record in a buffer may be compiled into a program. When the buffer is empty, however, an I/O operation must be executed. In order to execute the I/O operation, an *SVC* (*Supervisor Call*) must be executed to put the processor into control state. The SVC develops an interrupt. The interrupt defined at this interface places the system in control state and the interrupt handler recognizes the SVC as a call for I/O.

Although we have spoken of GET, PUT, etc. as extended functions, it is actually more correct to think of them as language-provided pseudo-ops that may lead to the excitement of the extended hardware architecture through SVCs of Type 1, 2, 3, etc. Code provided by compilers translates from the pseudo-ops to SVCs. Assembly language programmers may use SVC calls directly if they choose.

Since the I/O either runs asynchronously with the requesting program or causes the requesting program to lose control of the processor, some mechanism in the extended machine must also perform the coordination of the program with its I/O or inform the program that its I/O has completed.

The sequence of events that involves moving from problem state to supervisor state to request I/O (and similarly when I/O completes) is conceived to support a multiprogramming environment in which more than one program is using the CPU and I/O subsystem. The concept of control state develops from the need to have a coordinating mechanism between programs that are not aware of each other's existence. The control state prohibits patterns of execution that may disturb the logic or integrity of *concurrent programs*. The idea of run-time environment, therefore, contains an idea of coordination and control as well as an idea of extending interfaces. It is for this reason that compilers cannot generate all functions into a compiled program in an environment of shared computer use.

Functions performed by programs may be common. Consequently, memory may be used more efficiently by defining mechanisms that *allow programs to share the same coding*. In this way the space required for duplicated functions may be minimized at the expense of coordinating mechanisms and some degree of generalization. The decision as to what functions should be compiled into a particular program and what functions should be provided by the extended machine is part of design judgment about the commonality of operations in programs. It is also an area of negotiation between compiler designers and operating system designers.

2.3　DEFINING AN ENVIRONMENT FOR ACCESS

A major function of an operating system is to provide support for interfaces that may be used to access the power of the computer system. The ease and convenience of accessibility greatly affect how intensely computers are used. The goal of those who believe that computer power can be offered as a kind of public utility serving heterogeneous populations with heterogeneous needs is to create usage interfaces and systems responses as convenient as those available on specialized systems while providing the flexibility and extended power of large systems.

For example, an APL programmer can get APL service from an IBM 5100 or other devices of that class. The programmer can also get APL service from a large system running APL on-line in a multiprogramming mix. The goal of the operating system designer is to provide interaction with APL on the large system on a basis as attractive as that available with the special-purpose APL machine.

The concept of views presented in Chapter 1 is relevant here. The view of an *end user* is a view of an application. *The end user is aware of a need for information and some set of procedures for getting it.* We wish to make those procedures as simple as possible with minimum intrusion of system "personality" or professional staff.

Similarly, problem solvers who require programming languages of some type to develop algorithms should have minimum awareness of aspects of the system that do not directly contribute to problem formulation.

Professional programmers also require convenient interfaces for application development, testing, and integrating larger software efforts. They require support in manipulating as well as creating programs.

There are several design issues associated with the modes of accessing a computer. The issues that this chapter focuses on involve the relationship between programming and the act of bringing a program to the machine for execution. We are interested in the relationship between a *control language* used to control execution, and a *programming language* used to describe a solution. We will be concerned primarily with views offered to a professional programmer or to a problem solver.

The act of creating a program is defined to be quite distinct from the act of running a program in most batch systems. Such systems will tend to have a control language that is quite distinct in syntax from the programming languages. This control language is an extension of the concept of an operator's language. An operator's language represents yet a third syntactical interface to the system.

To the extent that functional distinction can be made between the language interfaces, it is approximately correct to say that *the programming language describes a procedure and defines a data structure against which that procedure is to be applied. The control language associates the names of data collections with I/O devices and otherwise describes the resources that must be applied to a program for it to run. The operator language is used to manipulate physical configuration and system status.*

One of the problems associated with operating systems is defining the roles

of operators, programmers, and systems programmers in order to define who can
and/or who must say what to the system. Some systems treat all on-line terminals
like operator consoles, in effect combining control and operator functions. Some
systems merge the roles of the operator, programmer, and systems programmer.
Some systems assume that any programmer can acquire the skills required to
write all control statements. Some systems provide a general control/command/
operator language, and allow roles to be defined by associating credentials or
authorizations with specific commands.

To the extent that programming and requesting service coalesce as fully
interactive environments the awareness of a distinct control language and distinct
programming languages becomes less intense. Systems are presented so that verbs
like *EDIT, RUN, COPY, SAVE,* etc. seem to be extensions of the programming
language.

Certain structural issues are relevant here. It is possible to organize a system
so that the control language transcends the programming languages. A request to
run, a request for data sets, and a request to edit a program are the same
regardless of the programming language used. An example is the *TSO facility* of
IBM's MVS. There is a kind of *programmer's workbench* context. It is also
common to find each language encapsulated in its own command context. An
example of this is the BASIC subsystem in Multics. Some systems offer different
command control contexts and different compilers depending on whether access
is made through batch or on-line.

2.3.1 Origin of Control Languages

In early environments, *job setup,* the mounting of appropriate tapes and the
loading of the program, was accomplished by an operator under the direction of a
programmer or a *setup sheet* that contained directions for mounting program
start. Thus the programmer would create a list of tape unit and tape assignments
such as

- Mount tape labeled "master" on unit 3.
- Mount tape labeled "changes" on unit 4.
- Mount "scratch" tapes on units 5, 6, 7.
- Mount tape labeled "program" on unit 1.
- Mount tape labeled "overlays" on unit 2.

  Following the mounting instructions would be a start procedure.

- "1. Read 2 blocks from tape 1 into locations 0840-0960" and perhaps some
  "in progress" procedures like
- "2. On type out END FIRST MASTER mount tape master 2 on unit 3."

Important details of some early *IBM computers* (*IBM 650, IBM 704*) were that they lacked a *console typewriter* and that card readers were often used as the primary input source for programs.

The control languages for early operating systems necessarily were influenced by the card format medium. In addition, early systems allowed relatively little flexibility in associating devices and functions, and simple directives like "ATTACH a unit to perform a function" were not frequently used. Systems functions were distributed among devices in a fixed manner and no need was felt to allow a programmer dynamic definition of the system environment. Thus SYSLIB (the file containing the system), SYSOUT (the file containing system output), SYSUTi (work files) were preassigned. Changes in mapping functions to units were seen as operator functions with little or no meaning to a programmer.

Programmers, programming in FORTRAN supported by a compiler on the machine, or FORTRAN running as a compiler in the context of FMS (FORTRAN Monitor System) or IBSYS(7040 Operating System), experienced a rather small expansion of their efforts. The concept of a control stream was formed around operational aspects of machine control that did not much involve the application programmer. The programmer was asked to append to his or her FORTRAN deck a *JOB card* and a *DATE card*. Frequently the additional cards were prepared by operators and placed in an envelope taped to the side of a card reader. The idea of a JOB card was to allow a batch of job requests to flow into the system as a single deck with the request of one user separated from the request of another user by new JOB cards. The system could move from job to job without interruption, and an installation accounting routine could charge resource usage against JOBs.

The idea of a JOB as the essential unit of submission introduced the idea that multiple compilations, multiple compilations and executions, and multiple requests for execution of previously compiled programs could be serviced within the context of a single job. To support the automatic invocation of the compiler, a card was added that named the compiler and specified certain options such as compile or compile/load/go.

Because I/O device usage was largely fixed by convention, each JOB was assumed to occupy the whole machine, and the sequence of JOBs was defined by ordering the deck. Consequently the programmer had no need for many of the statements that characterize control languages in later and more flexible systems.

The concept of control of resources as an operator function led to the major syntactical variations between programming languages and control languages that are characteristic of batch control. As the expressive power of control languages increased to accommodate maturing concepts of *device independence* and *machine sharing,* control languages became more complex. They also became part of a programmer's work. The effort involved in creating control statements became a subject of some concern. We address this concern after a brief description of the batch job control language (JCL) for IBM's OS/360.

2.3.2 Batch Control

We will not attempt to give a comprehensive view of JCL, but merely to suggest its motivation and essential properties.

JCL is a highly horizontal language that permits a user to (1) *name a series of programs to be executed*, (2) *define the machine they will run on in terms of memory size and device population*, (3) *associate priorities with the programs to be run*, and (4) *associate particular data sets with particular system functions*.

The language is characterized as horizontal because of its small command set and its rich operand structure. An associated characteristic is the lack of procedural or flow attributes such as might be found in a programming language. These attributes involve conditional statements, parameter passing, nesting, etc.

The language contains three primary statements: JOB, EXEC, and DD. *The JOB statement defines the job structure, the EXEC statement names individual programs to be executed and the parameters for their execution*, and *the DD statement describes the data to be used by the program named on an EXEC*. The programs named on EXEC statements are called *job steps*.

A JOB may consist of completely independent job steps grouped together for convenience of accounting, or ordered steps such as *compile, link-edit*, and *execute* the resulting program.

The intent of the language is to provide a requestor of services with maximum control over the way the request will be serviced, and what resources the request will use. A control stream may contain embedded programs to be compiled and data to be operated on.

The operand structure is a keyword parameter list that follows no fixed column formats. The language has a set of keywords, like *PGM, DSNAME (data set name), DISP (disposition)* that *tells what to do with data sets after the job, DEVICE that tells what device or type of device to put a data set on*, etc. Each statement type has an associated set of keywords that are given in the form KEYWORD = with a parameter list of varying complexity. Certain of the parameters are also keywords with specific meaning to the system. Other parameters (such as program name or data set name) are the names of objects to be associated with the job.

The full power of an EXEC statement is suggested by some of its associated keyword operands. TIME provides a maximum time that the program should be allowed to run. REGION specifies the amount of memory that should be allocated to the program. DPRTY specifies the relative importance this program should have in a multiprogramming mix.

Data definition statements define the input and output datasets to be associated with the program running under the EXEC statement. DD parameters are provided to do such things as (1) *associate a device or a device type with a data set,* (2) *describe what should be done with a data set at the end of the job,* (3) *describe space needed on a disk device,* (4) *define label conventions,* (5) *define attributes of blocksize and buffering,* and (6) *define whether the data set is to be protected by a password.*

The richness, complexity, and oddities of JCL make writing control language somewhat formidable. In order to reduce this difficulty, the systems associated with the language provide mechanisms for providing preset parameters. These mechanisms are *default, cataloged procedures,* and *override.*

Default is a means of describing parameters to the system at another time, characteristically at the time an installation specializes the operating system for its own use. This time, called *SYSGEN* (i.e., SYStem GENeration) *time may occur before a system is shipped to a user, or at the user's installation.* If it occurs before shipment, what is delivered to the installation is a preparameterized "ready-to-go" operating system. If specialization occurs at the user installation, it is because the installation has reason to prefer private and unique parameterization.

SYSGEN, whether accomplished by vendor or at the time of installation, provides a time at which many of the parameters that are ordinarily specified on JCL can be provided so that they can be omitted from JCL statements. An unfortunate by-product of this, however, is that *a JCL stream cannot be taken from system to system without care that the default parameters on different systems are sufficiently similar so that the effect of JCL is the same on each of the systems.*

Another level of JCL simplification is the idea of the cataloged procedure. A *cataloged procedure is an entire JCL job stream, including EXEC and DD statements that can be summoned by a reference in an abbreviated stream.* The cataloged stream specifies JCL parameters. The JCL provided by the user merely calls for the application of the parameters of the named stream. For example, "//EXEC PLIFCLG" summons the cataloged procedure for executing a particular version of the PL/I compiler, and for loading and executing the compiled program.

For many standard service requests, the cataloged procedure may be summoned without change. In order to extend the usability of cataloged procedures the concept of *override* is defined. It is possible to call a procedure and to provide override statements that modify keywords on a control statement of the same name in the procedure. There are some conventions, however, that must be adhered to and that require that the user providing override know the sequence of keywords in the procedure in more detail than is desirable.

IBM's OS JCL is an example of a batch control language. All batch operating systems have a language of this general type with variations in the richness of the parameter set, the balance between required and optional parameters, and the syntax. OS JCL is a horizontal language. The control languages of *IBM's DOS* (*Disk Operating System*) and *UNIVAC's EXEC VIII,* for example, are somewhat more vertical. A more vertical language is one in which there are more verbs (commands, statement types) and simpler operand structures. A vertical language may also have a closer resemblance to a programmer language in that it may have some procedural attributes.

2.3.3   Command Language

In systems oriented to on-line use, the relationship between programming and requesting services from the system may become somewhat less distinct. The programmer at a terminal wishes to enter programs and summon services of the system during a single terminal session without experiencing dramatic changes in syntax or semantics. This desire may have two effects on the control language. First, its syntax may be more like that of a programming language, and second, its expressive power may be reduced. Reduction in expressive power is not, however, a universal problem with command languages.

Certain procedural properties of programs including looping, conditional statements, and computational capability may become part of the command language. The distinction between calling for a system function to allocate a data set and calling for an application function may become indistinct. Movement from command language to programming language statements may occur on a line-to-line basis.

Naturally, the underlying structure of the system reflects the relationship between the command language and programming languages. The compilation function may be brought into the extended machine to compile on a line-by-line basis (*incremental compilation*) or to act as an interpretive function.

A common characteristic of command languages is a loss of expressive power. Rather than allowing or requiring a user at a terminal to express resource requirements, the system establishes a set of conventions that describes a fixed environment within which the user will work. This environment typically includes a work space of a particular size in bytes, a set of available functions, and a library for functions that the user may define to the system for retention. While at the terminal, the user programs in his or her work space and saves and retrieves programs or data to and from his or her library.

A user finds such an environment simple and easy to use. An example of such a system is APL. As distinct from JCL-oriented operations, the conventions for using APL and for running programs written in APL are sufficiently standardized that the APL programmer does not have to define his or her environment for using the system. Commands such as COPY, LOAD, and START apply to the working environment of the programs or functions that the user wishes to manipulate. Partly because of the simplification of the command language, and partly because of the syntax of the APL language, the user has little sense of working with separate programming and control languages.

Other systems, intended more for the professional programmer than for the personal problem solver, allow simplified and standardized access to an on-line program entry and execution interface, but still provide a rich set of resource manipulation statements to ALLOCATE, ASSOCIATE, and COMBINE resources and programs. IBM's TSO and CMS are examples of such systems. The UNIX system similarly permits the use of a rich set of functions from a terminal. A goal of these systems is to simplify program entry and construction without restricting the expressive power of their command languages.

Perhaps the paradigm of on-line command systems is *Multics*. Multics was designed to support the concept of a *computational public utility*. The public utility concept provides for many different kinds of users making many different kinds of simultaneous demands on a system. The Multics command language is designed to permit program entry on-line, program editing on-line, and submission of jobs for *attended* or *unattended* (batch) *operation*. The system allows for any procedure known by the system to be called from the terminal, and it provides a structure for accessing any data collection from a terminal. A structure for defining the *access rights* of any user to any procedure or data object is provided in the command language. Many functions commonly accessible in other systems only to programs using the extended services interfaces of the extended machine are available (although in syntactically different form) as *terminal commands*. In addition, commands may pass values to each other, receive values by the invocation of procedures, and be organized into procedures (similar in concept to JCL cataloged procedures) summoned by a procedure call. Many of the features of Multics provide a conceptual basis for some of the attributes of command languages discussed in the next section.

2.3.4 Language Relationships and the Presentation of a System

There has been a good deal of discussion over the last decade about the nature of control and command languages. There have been conceptual and specific criticisms. The conceptual criticisms are more important because they address basic issues about how systems and the environment in which they live should relate to each other. An appreciation of the following discussion, although the discussion is philosophical in nature, does not require systems programming expertise. In fact, the reader should assume the mental role of someone responsible for organizing and running a computer facility, rather than that of a professional systems programmer.

1. The basic problem of what information is to be put to the system in control language form has never been seriously addressed. As a result, there are

parameters that must obviously be provided by programmers (such as buffering levels or data structure definitions), and parameters that seem to be legitimately providable only by surrogates of installation management (priority, device assignment). Many parameters imply procedures to discipline and control what is placed on the statements. The control languages of the last decade seem to represent an ad hoc intersection of operator languages, administrative languages, and programming languages in which the roles are not well defined.

2. Consistent with the above in that it reflects an uncertainty about various user roles is the criticism that the intersections of all major programming languages and command languages seem to differ from one another. The data-descriptive capabilities of PL/I, COBOL, ALGOL, and APL are sufficiently different from each other that the industry does not seem to have formed a defensible concept of what is a programming descriptive function or what is a request for service.

3. The languages are ad hoc and grammatically atrocious. They lead to errors in description of the resources and environments desired. They reflect convenience only to the implementors of the system who wish certain pieces of information in a form convenient to them.

4. The entire language structure has become too rich. Not only are there programming, operator, control and SYSGEN languages but there are also utility and service languages such as edit, link-edit, and sort with different syntax and semantics for similar functions.

5. The balance of "may" specify and "must" specify is wrong so that what is intended to be a service is likely to be a burden. In fact, the complexity of using control languages has defeated their fundamental purpose because the languages are, in fact, not used as they were intended. The intention was that a requestor of service would, for each instance of requested service, be able to describe precisely what he or she desired of the machine. This would enable the requestor to control costs by controlling the resources for which he or she would be charged. The intention was also to enable the system to maximize utilization of hardware by allocating to each requestor exactly what was needed. In fact, because of the complexity of the languages, control language statement groups that work tend to be used extensively. Not only will requestors not change their statements for different runs of the same work, which because of differing data may require different amounts of time and memory, but once there is a section of working control language, the requestors will use it as much as possible for all their work despite vast differences in resources required.

6. Because the control languages are so connected with the underlying systems design, they change as the underlying system evolves. Thus semantics change and the relationship between the extended machine and the control language

changes as more functions become available at run time. Thus whatever initial coherence the control language might have had is lost.

There are communities of users that wish to exert high degrees of control over the way they use the computing resource, and there are communities of users that do not. A user community happy to live within the constraints of a conventional resource and capability environment will view as a burden any mechanism that forces the community to describe the resources it requires, and the disposition of those resources. A community that values flexibility will view as a tool any requirement to describe environments. Richness will bother some; sparseness will annoy and constrain others. Surely, good syntax is preferable to bad, ease of learning is preferable to difficulty, crispness of semantics is preferable to ambiguity, but ultimately a control language will be viewed in terms of whether or not it accords with the users' image of how much they wish to control their own environment.

There has been much discussion about what to do with control languages in the future. Some people recommend that control languages be eliminated. Certain parameters might be moved into the syntax of programming languages. Other parameters might be moved into a system administrator's interface that would be used to define the privileges of various kinds of users, their absolute or relative importance, etc. Some feel that as systems become more and more on-line, the issue of control language will disappear and cleaner languages will naturally emerge.

One issue about control languages that is rarely addressed has to do with the way systems are presented to the world. Characteristically, in the past systems have been presented in such a way that the major interface has been the programming languages. Systems have been PL/I or COBOL or FORTRAN machines. With such a presentation, the idea cannot be avoided that control language definition is additional work to be undertaken after the real work of programming. Some designers now feel that the proper way to present a system is in terms of its control language. The control language is the primary interface to the system and the programming languages are cast as specialized subsets of the control language. The control language should be defined in such a way that applications can be planned using the commands of the control language. The utility services and applications packages appear as verbs of the language. It might well be that the functions provided by the commands will suffice to describe an entire application; that is, sequences of verbs like SORT, COPY, and SUMMARIZE will do all the application requires.

When a function is not provided, the user descends to the level of a programming language like RPG or PL/I to describe the particular function. The user then defines this function as a verb in the command language. The relationship between the command language and the programming languages is rather like the relationship between a higher-level language and a lower-level assembler language that can be "escaped to" for certain functions beyond the capability of the higher-level language.

Among the characteristics of this approach to systems presentation would be the following.

■   The command language stream is dynamically executable on a command-by-command basis or compilable into an unattended execution structure at user option.

■   The functions and services callable by programs through the extended machine, and the functions and services available to the command language should be identical. As underlying systems modify the balance between what is done before a program executes and what is done while it is executing, the change is not reflected in the control language.

■   Sufficient computational capability exists in the command language to minimize the need to drop into the programming languages.

■   The syntax and semantics of the language are as carefully studied as the syntax and semantics of any programming language. The language must allow selectable levels of power and subsets for various user communities.

The definition of good system interfaces naturally implies issues of system structure. To add a final touch to this topic, and for the sake of completeness, we observe that there are operating systems theorists who do not consider that the subject of control and command languages is fitting for a book on operating systems.

The definition of user interfaces, this school holds, is the job of those who know the characteristics of the user community. All that an operating systems designer can do well is to provide an operating systems structure and a set of building blocks so that people can build the interfaces they wish to build.

2.3.5   Types of Access

So far we have discussed the nature of control and command languages in their role as the vehicles for supporting access to a computing system. The following summarizes the various ways in which access to a computing system may be granted.

1. *Negotiated Scheduled Access.* Access of this type involves a human scheduler between the requestor and the system. It implies fixed periods of time during which the requestor will have absolute control over the machine. It was the earliest way of accessing machines and is still appropriate for projects that require special machine conditions. The development of a new operating system is an example. Testing of the new system implies a "clean" hardware base that precludes the operation of the current operating system. Current virtual operating

systems can provide apparently "naked" machines that can give the effect of negotiated access for system debugging.

2. *Local Batch Submission*. Access of this type removes a scheduler from the interface between system and requestor but probably includes an operator. Requests for machine service are made by sending physical media representing job control and programs to the machine room. Job completion effectively occurs when operators remove printed output from the system and put it at some accessible point. The operating system (1) responds to a queue of job requests placed typically in a card reader and (2) performs the jobs as they are sequenced by the operator. It is possible to have the operating system resequence job starts. This is common in third-generation systems. Job requests form an internal queue that is analyzed by a systems component called a scheduler. What a scheduler has available to schedule is determined by operator action, how it schedules is determined by its own algorithms, and what it schedules is determined by parameters describing priority and resource requirements in the control language.

3. *User-Directed Batch Submission* (*Remote Job Entry*). This access extends the operating system to the requestor and eliminates human intervention between the system and a user. Work stations with card readers and printers are made directly accessible to a user. A *communication protocol* between the work station and the central system is established such that, whenever a request for service is submitted, an element of the operating system becomes active to receive the request and place it on the queue of waiting jobs. The work station may be geographically remote or on site with the system. The important aspect of the access interface is the elimination of human operators both for accepting requests and distributing results. In effect, the operating system is extended beyond the limits of the machine room.

4. *Interactive Batch Submission*. Access of this type may clearly separate requesting from programming, but allows a requestor to dynamically form his or her request. On a keyboard with hard copy (or a tube), the requestor can undertake an interactive session with the job request elements of the system. Typically, the requestor has a simple *file manipulation language* and an available *library*. The requestor stores control language elements in the library, and perhaps some programming language elements. He or she can modify the library and form control stream. The requestor may be able to enter programming language statements and receive syntax validation line by line. When the user is ready to submit the job, he or she issues a statement that sends his or her control stream into the scheduling environment in which it becomes part of the batch *multiprogramming mix*. When the barrier between the conversational entry system and the batch execution elements of the operating system is crossed, the data sent over the barrier is not available from the terminal. An example of such an access capability is *CRJE* with IBM's *OS/MVT operating system*.

5. *Interactive Programming Access.* Access of this type may resemble (4) above very closely. All program entry is completed in a distinct step and then the RUN, a request for compilation and execution, is performed. Early BASIC systems were of this type.

It is possible, however, to intertwine acts of programming and execution so that programs need not be syntactically complete and instances of entry and execution intertwine. The command and programming languages may collapse into each other. A very old system called *JOSS (Johniac Open Shop System)* had characteristics of this type. Various *time-sharing systems*, systems that support multiple on-line terminals with various entry and execution events, make varying trade-offs between the relationship of programming, requesting, and executing.

6. *Network Access.* There is intense interest in increasing accessibility to computers to include intersystem interaction. Variously called *networking* or *distributed processing*, a goal of accessibility of this type is to allow a user to gain access to processes or data at computers other than the one to which the user is directly connected. There are various problems to be solved in the area of how much a user should know about where he or she is going to execute, in the area of determining when processes should go to data and when data should go to processes, and particularly in the area of making diverse operating systems talk to each other. *The next step in operating systems design will involve the discovery of suitable structures and interfaces for distribution and networking.*

2.4 CREATING AN INTERFACE FOR OPERATIONS

The *operational interface* of computing systems can be narrowly defined to mean the activities of *console operation* and *media mounting* and *dismounting*. It can also be broadly defined to include *tape librarians, systems programmers, schedulers, coordinators, keypunch operators*, and other entities that relate to the administrative and operational aspects of a system. This text takes a narrow view of operations on the principle that *one of the major problems with operating interfaces today is the lack of a clean distinction between operational and administrative functions. This lack of distinction enables operators at consoles to make essentially political and administrative decisions by manipulations of program status and priority.*

The job of an operator is not clearly defined for all systems. There are systems on which programmers assume the role of programmer/operators and systems on which the operator function is quite distinct from the programmer function. On systems that allow on-line user access, the distinction between command languages and the operator languages becomes somewhat arbitrary.

The operator language commonly provides the following capabilities to an operator.

- Change configuration.
- Start a job.
- Suspend or abort a job.
- Inquire about status of a job.
- Change priority of a job.
- Initiate and modify the system (i.e., "Initial Program Load").

In addition, the operating system provides a running log of events occurring on the system, reporting *job completions, malfunctions, enqueueing of outputs,* and *allocation of devices. Mounting* and *dismounting directives* are also printed (or displayed) where appropriate.

The capabilities listed above show the degree of administrative power that can be executed from a console. Many systems allow for the definition of roles in order to control the exercise of these powers. The parameters provided to the operating system at the time that the system is initially specialized may restrict certain functions to particular passwords or to specific consoles or terminals.

In addition to *specializing by authority,* it is also possible to *specialize by function*. For example, it is common to provide for multiconsole support such that messages relating to batch work go to one console and messages relating to terminal work go to another console. All messages representing terminal sign-on, terminal sign-off, and messages sent from terminal users to the operators would be segregated from the usual batch event dialogue that need not be so closely attended.

The operating system may also support remote specialized terminals in tape or disk libraries and sustain a flow of requests for delivery of data media to the machine room, or where appropriate, the mounting of media on devices in the library.

The specifics of the operational interface supported by an operating system are partially determined by the degree to which the operating system attempts to manage the system itself, and the extent to which it relies on operator directives. Some multiprogramming systems rely on the operator to establish the number of programs in the mix. Others are capable of dynamically determining appropriate multiprogramming levels within constraints set by systems programmers.

2.5   MANAGING A SYSTEM TO MEET PERFORMANCE GOALS

A central function of an operating system is to act as the surrogate of administrative policymakers who define a view of successful operation.

The operating system presents an interface to allow statements of how much importance is to be given to fast response time versus high utilization of equipment, and how various programs competing for resources are to be treated.

System definition parameters commonly provide biasing mechanisms for various classes of work, and policy statements to guide the algorithms of resource allocation for multiprogramming systems.

Among the more ambitious systems is *IBM's OS/MVS* that provides a set of parameters called *Installation Performance Specifications*. These IPS *parameters* define groups of work units and rates of service to be afforded each group. These work-load manager specifications are used with statements about resource utilization goals to guide a works manager, the *Systems Resources Manager*, during its dynamic control of the machine work load.

In general, an operating system

■ provides an interface to *administer the usage policies of the system;*

■ provides an interface to systems professionals to support *performance timing and tuning;*

■ provides an interface to describe *the importance of any particular job or terminal session in terms of its membership in a particular work group or class, a given deadline, or a relative priority*. This description is commonly done in the job control language.

■ provides an interface to *describe the resource consumption characteristics of a process*.

The task of the operating system is to manage the work to achieve the stated goals. It does this through its ability to *allocate or deny resources of CPU time, memory, access to devices,* and *access to collections of data*. Many larger operating systems inspect the system from time to time to determine whether or not goals are being achieved. They attempt corrective action if goals are not being achieved.

ABBREVIATIONS, LANGUAGES, STATEMENTS, AND KEYWORDS

ALGOL	DATE
APL	DD
ASSIGN	DEVICE
ATTACH	DISP
CMS	DPRTY
COPY	DSNAME
CRJE	EDIT

EXEC   READ
FMS   REGION
FORTRAN   RJE
GET   RPG
IBM's DOS   RUN
IBSYS/IBJOB   SAVE
IPL   SRM
IPS   START
JCL   SYSGEN
JOB   SYSLIB
JOSS   SYSOUT
LOAD   SYSUT
OPEN   TIME
OS/360   TSO
OS/370 MVS   UNIVAC's EXEC VIII
PGM   WRITE
PUT

BASIC TERMINOLOGY

attended operation   label conventions
batch job   loader
blocksize   macroassembler
close a file   open a file
compile/load/go   packaged program
create a file   patch
default parameters   read from a file
end user   setup sheet
file   software package
file manipulation language   systems programmer
incremental compilation   unattended operation
job setup   write to a file

ADVANCED TERMINOLOGY

abort a job

access rights

BASIC subsystem in Multics

batch control language

batch control stream

buffering

cataloged procedure

change configuration

change priority of a job

communication protocol

computational public utility

concurrent programs

control language

data definition statement

data management

device independence

device logical address

device physical address

distributed processing

initial program load

installation performance specs

interactive batch submission

interprogram communication

job management

job step

local batch submission

mechanisms versus policies

multiprogramming mix

negotiated scheduled access

network access

networking

on-line system

operations interface

operator language

password protection

primitive operation

program creation

program initiation

programmer's terminal

programmer's workbench

remote job entry

resource allocation

run-time environment

start a job

suspend a job

system generation

Systems Resources Manager

task management

terminal command

time-sharing

user-directed batch submission

EXERCISES

Section 2.1

2.1 Distinguish between mechanisms and policies for operating systems functions.

2.2 Discuss briefly each of the following functions of operating systems.

   a) interleave periods of activation of contending programs

   b) handle interrupts

   c) synchronize access to shared resources

   d) allocate memory to programs

   e) initiate I/O requests

   f) maintain queues of waiting I/O requests

   g) report I/O completions

   h) initiate programs

   i) handle interprogram communication

   j) support the creation, opening, closing, reading, and writing of files

2.3 What is a "primitive" operation?

2.4 Briefly describe the functions of Job Management, Data Management, and Task Management.

2.5 Discuss the concept of an operating system as a resource manager.

Section 2.2

2.6 Although compilers are not normally considered part of the operating system, linkage editors are. Explain.

2.7 Why, do you suppose, are I/O instructions privileged instructions that can execute only in control state?

2.8 Explain why, in a multiprogramming operating systems environment, compilers cannot (should not) generate all functions into a compiled program.

Section 2.3

2.9 The ease and convenience of accessibility greatly affect how intensely computers are used. Explain.

2.10 Distinguish among control languages, programming languages, and operator languages.

2.11 Describe briefly the functions of the JOB, EXEC, and DD job control language statements.

2.12 The richness of JCL makes writing control language somewhat formidable. Explain how default, cataloged procedures, and override help to simplify the task of writing control language.

2.13 Explain the concept of a computational public utility.

2.14 Discuss the concept of the "presentation" of a system.

2.15 Briefly discuss each of the following ways in which access to a computing system may be granted.

   a) negotiated scheduled access

   b) local batch submission

   c) user-directed batch submission (remote job entry)

   d) interactive batch submission

   e) interactive programming access

   f) network access (distributed processing)

Section 2.4

2.16 One of the major problems with operating interfaces today is the lack of a clear distinction between operational and administrative functions. This enables operators to make political and administrative decisions by manipulation of program status and priority. Comment on this problem.

2.17 Discuss each of the following capabilities normally provided to an operator via operator control language.

   a) change configuration

   b) start a job

   c) suspend or abort a job

   d) inquire about status of a job

   e) change priority of a job

   f) initial program load

Section 2.5

2.18 Many larger operating systems inspect the system from time to time to determine whether or not goals are being achieved. They then attempt corrective action if goals are not being achieved. What corrective action, do you suppose, might an operating system take if its thruput goals are not being realized?

3
Types of
Operating
Systems

3.1 TAXONOMY

The discussion to this point has described (1) those aspects of hardware that may influence the nature of an operating system and (2) the functions of an operating system in a general way. The discussion of functions has been general because of a broad idea of what is included in an operating system and because, until now, operating systems have been discussed as a genre. Actually, there are species within the genre, and the species have some quite distinctive characteristics. These characteristics are sometimes related to the functions that the system performs, and sometimes related to the essential structure of the system.

Systems differ in various ways. They differ in the assumptions they make about the professional competence of a user, the number of views they provide various specialists, the breadth of functions they provide, the elaborateness of each function, the degree to which they undertake self-management, and the degree to which they support program development activities. They also differ in their essential structure. A system organized to find and execute programs as the result of an external event differs in structure from systems that are organized to manage long-running batch programs in multiprogramming mixes. Finally, systems differ because the hardware bases that support them differ, and the environments of usage for which they are intended differ.

The classification of systems is not an easy task. There are a number of practical and conceptual difficulties in developing a taxonomy for objects that are defined only informally. Perhaps the greatest difficulty in identifying the various types of operating systems comes from the rate of change in the information-processing world. As hardware economics change, and as user desires mature, new systems emerge at an alarming rate.

The literature reveals a number of classification schemes. The size of the underlying hardware system is sometimes used directly to classify systems. There is a rough concept of a small-machine system and a large-machine system. The number, speed, and variety of resources imply what the profitable levels of resource management will be, and further imply the range and diversity of uses to which the computer facility will be put.

A large system is expensive, and there is reason to believe that its owners will be concerned about using it well. It will probably be the center of a consolidated work-load environment. This environment is characterized by the collection of independent jobs from a variety of sources. Because of the diversity of the work load, the scheduling and management of the system become major tasks. It is desirable to provide mechanisms that allow the system to participate in its own management. In addition, a variety of access techniques may be desirable, as well as a variety of very high-level services such as database management, inquiry, etc. The desire to use the large machine effectively in what is understood to be a "machine-cost intensive" situation tends to make the operating system very "general-purpose."

The large machine is itself a rather complex structure with asynchronous channels, possibly with multiple processors some of which are specialized, a wide variety of device types in large number, and an almost limitless variability in configuration. The techniques necessary to provide for the effective management of such systems are also complex and consume large amounts of time and storage space. The assumption of the operating system is that the total productive capability of the hardware will be increased by withdrawing nontrivial amounts of resource for system management. This will occur because the resources of the machine will be used more intensively.

Consequently, large-machine operating systems are characterized by extreme levels of *device independence, dynamic scheduling, resource allocation tactics,* and a *rich set of diverse interfaces.*

On the other hand, a small machine is "inexpensive." A less intense use of the resources does not cost as much as ineffective use of the resources of a large machine. The diversity of uses will be less because the hardware will saturate more quickly. There may be a greater tendency for the machine to be dedicated to a particular kind of access and use. Finally, the machine cannot afford the resources to support the richness of functions nor the intensity of management appropriate for a large machine.

The characteristics of a small-machine operating system reflect the limitations of small machines in a number of ways. One way is to limit the kinds of access that can be made to the system. Thus an operating system may allow only terminal access for conversational program development and the running of small programs in an attended mode. Alternatively, the system may offer only file management and limited data inquiry.

Another approach to the small system is to preserve its generality but to provide less support to users. The selection of devices for data sets may have to be done by operators or programmers rather than be allocated by the system. The system may allow some form of interleaved sharing of the processor, but restrict it to "multitasking" rather than to "multiprogramming." These phrases, as used here, reflect IBM 370/OS terminology for *asynchronous execution of routines of the same application (multitasking) as opposed to asynchronous execution of routines of different applications (multiprogramming). The difference is that in multitasking the application developer is responsible for planning and synchronizing, and in multiprogrammimg the system is responsible.*

When operating system design is dominated by machine size, an interesting phenomenon occurs in the relation between machines and operating systems. Over time, operating systems that were associated with very large machines are recalled to mind by the attributes of operating systems developed for newer small machines. It is a natural tendency to put function on small machines as soon as they can support it, but some ease of use and interface problems may result if the kinds of interfaces originally designed for the very select group of IBM 7094 users are presented to users who do not have that level of interest in computers as such.

Another attribute of a system that may be used to support a classification is the primary method of access to the machine that is provided through the operating system. We hear of conversational systems, real-time systems, and batch systems differentiated from each other by the way a user approaches the system.

Attributes of users may also be used to classify systems. *Programming systems, personal computing systems,* and *inquiry systems* are phrases that suggest some of the needs and characteristics of those who will be in direct contact with the system. Naturally, the external attributes of a system differ dramatically depending on the group that is expected to be the major user of the system.

Another method of classifying systems is by the relative sophistication of particular functions. There is a relationship between this and machine size, naturally. For example, a basic multiprogramming system suggests that the underlying machine is not sufficient to be profitably managed by advanced dynamic management tactics.

Traditionally systems may be classified as

- real-time operating systems,
- batch operating systems,
- time-sharing operating systems, or
- multipurpose operating systems.

This is not an entirely satisfactory classification scheme because the attribute of accessibility is used as the only differentiating measure. The variety of system characteristics available in time-sharing systems is as broad as the differences between the major classes themselves, and the concept of multipurpose cannot be crisply defined. However, the classification is as usable as any other as a structure for comments about the major characteristics of systems. Figure 3.1 reflects the relationship between machine size, access type, and system use. What it suggests is that programming development capability is independent of machine size and access type. Certain kinds of production environments, however, seem to require on-line access, although this access may be to a small or large system. Finally, there is a suggestion that real-time systems may well make up a unique class. A truly multipurpose or generalized operating system would provide the capability for all uses and all accesses. Presumably, the richness of support for each use and access would depend on the size of the machine.

The following sections discuss operating systems in terms of the previous list, but introduce the extra dimensions of Fig. 3.1. Finally, the emerging ideas of network operating systems and distributed systems are introduced. More discussion of issues relating to distribution is provided later.

Once more the reader is asked to be mindful of the fact that any classification of systems is imperfect at best, locked into naivete by an inability to see the future and by an inability to completely evaluate the past. Are these types of systems a natural phenomenon, such that they would all be found in some alternate universe, or are they accidents of the specific history of the industry? Is it necessary for all the types to continue into the future? Will new types emerge? Will they all disappear along with the very concept of an operating system, in the technology and design concepts yet to come?

Application	Type of access		Machine size	
	On-line	Batch	Small	Large
Programmer's workbench	√	√	√	√
Production systems				
• Transaction processing	√		√	√
• Database	√	√	√	√
• Personal computing	√		√	√
Real-time systems	√		√	√

Fig. 3.1 Operating system taxonomy.

3.2   REAL-TIME ENVIRONMENTS

The definition of a real-time environment that follows is largely due to Roy Herstand, author of the IBM manual for ACP (form # GH20-1473), the Airlines Control Program.

A *real-time environment* is characterized by processing activity triggered by randomly accepted external events. The processing activity for a particular event is accomplished by sequences of processing tasks each of which must complete within rigid time constraints. The external event will be the receipt of data or request for service from an on-line device that is characteristically not driven by a human operator. A response to the device may or may not be made. The interchange between the device and the system may be initiated by the system requesting status data from the device, or by the device that sends signals at a rate determined by its own requirements and design. The real-time system is a monitoring and control system with minimal requirements for intervention by human beings. Some intervention capability is provided, however, to allow human response when the computer elements of the system recognize the violation of set system limits, or when the computer elements of the system recognize a computer malfunction. Human intervention may also be allowed to reset parameters and adjust the mission of the monitored devices. Characteristically, *the computer system is completely dedicated to the control application and has been configured to guarantee on-time responses even at peak loads*. The environment is such that *utilization of equipment is less important than responsiveness to the environment*.

Real-time systems are used to monitor production lines, control continuous processes such as pipelines, monitor medical patients' critical functions, monitor and control traffic light systems, monitor and control laboratory experiments, and monitor the status of military aircraft. The devices that attach to them are as varied as the application of the concept. Characteristically, there is a need for specialized interfaces to be built between the devices and the computer system. These may take the form of analog/digital converters or of microprocessors embedded in the devices. The devices may be local to the computer in the sense that no telecommunications are involved in the interaction, or they may be remote so that some form of transmission across long distances is required.

The computer hardware base for such systems may be very small or very large depending on the needs of the application. There are numerous microprocessor-based, real-time systems. Processors of the general capability of a TI 990 or an LSI 11 (named as examples only) may be sufficient to support many industrial applications. The microprocessor-based system is particularly usable when the application requires little or no human intervention and when the system, once turned on, can run without change for long periods of time. In some real-time applications, the presence of a computer is not significant to the concept of the environment. The computer is almost invisible. A computer is used because it represents a convenient and inexpensive way to implement monitoring and control logic in a "black box." Instead of a hardwired solution, the algorithms of control are programmed into a standard microprocessor. The programming may be etched into ROM or PROM memory.

When somewhat more computer power and human interface are required, the application may run on a minicomputer such as an IBM Series I, DEC PDP-11, or Data General NOVA. These computers are able to support data processing peripherals that can collect historical data, support inquiry and parameterization from a terminal, produce reports, and perhaps even run data analyses in a multiprogramming background when real-time demands on the processor are low.

Rather large processors have been used for real-time when the data flow is very high and when significant data storage and computational requirements are imposed by the applications. Military command and control systems such as *SAGE Air Defense Command Control System, SACCS (Strategic Air Command Control System), BMEWS (Ballistic Missile Early Warning System)* used large systems specially designed for the application. Other real-time systems have used dedicated versions of standard processors or modified versions of standard processors.

The attributes of a processor that make it a good real-time processor lie mainly in its interrupt handling and analysis design, in its task-switching design, and in the power and flexibility of its interval timing and time of day capacity. It is important for the processor to be able to respond to external interrupts very quickly, to start processes very quickly, and to determine time intervals very precisely.

When there is a need for computational capability or storage capability that can be provided only by processors that may not have the interrupt structures ideal for real-time environment interfacing, a *front-end processor* may be used to handle responses to the real-time environment and to use a large, *back-end processor* as a *computational slave.*

The use of multiple processors or multiple computing systems is quite common in real-time environments. The multiplicity is used to achieve greater system reliability and/or to distribute functions across a network of related systems.

An example of a multiple computer real-time system is given in Fig. 3.2. The operational level of the system consists of three microprocessors that are physically close to a set of sensors that send data about an industrial or laboratory process. These processors may be in a hostile environment not suitable for human beings and consequently they run as unattended subsystems. Each processor is capable of making some control adjustments to the process it is monitoring. At a defined interval some form of summary data, or out-of-limit data, or trend data is sent up to the supervision-level mini. This computer

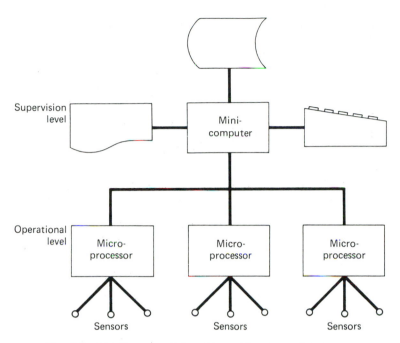

Fig. 3.2   Distributed real-time hierarchic micro-mini system.

supports an application monitor interface, produces printed reports, and stores accumulated data. From the mini terminal an operator can view and alter the behavior of the total system.

The variations on the theme of Fig. 3.2 are almost limitless. The operational level may be heterogeneous or homogeneous, the supervision level may be dedicated or shared, the operational level may have divergent amounts of local storage, local control, and local algorithmic power. The operation or supervision levels may be interconnected by loops, channels, or teleprocessing protocol lines.

Figure 3.3 shows a configuration more oriented to military command/control than to in-plant industrial process control. Radar stations and/or unmanned aircraft are sending signals to a front-end communications processor that immediately passes data to a designated primary control computer. This computer monitors the course of all detected aircraft and displays a picture of all aircraft on a large, status screen. The console at the primary is used to send messages to friendly aircraft to alter course and speed for intercept, to call for variations in display, and to call for simulations of the effects of possible decisions assuming various tactics on the part of hostile craft.

The SEC and TERT computers may be organized into the system in a

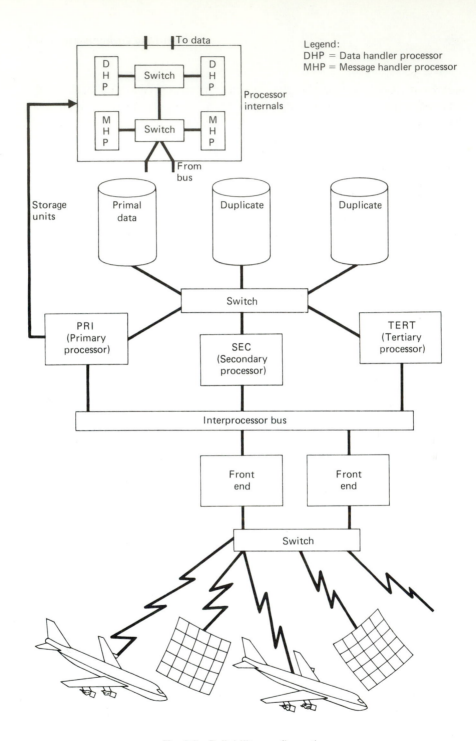

Fig. 3.3 Reliability configuration.

number of ways. They may be geographically dispersed on the assumption that the major reliability problem with the system will be due to hostile action rather than to computer malfunction. There may, of course, be duplicated processor power at the primary site. The configuration at the primary site may look like the configuration in the inset box. The local FE sends data to PRI/I whenever PRI/I is "up" and to PRI/II otherwise. PRI/I and PRI/II have access to the data and to the display screen.

If PRI, SEC, and TERT are geographically dispersed, it is possible for all three to work simultaneously so that each has the same current data regarding the status of air space. PRI is primary in the sense that only its output is passed on to manipulatable aircraft. This design is appropriate if large amounts of data are in fact necessary to develop response. It is necessary to replicate the data at all points in the system so that SEC and TERT can quickly assume command when PRI is out of the system. If it is possible to make responses with little data, then SEC and TERT need not receive data while PRI is operational. In an air-space monitoring application, for example, the data necessary to determine presence and course of all aircraft may be assembled within milliseconds, and no long history of tracking data is required for a center to assume command.

If PRI, SEC, and TERT are in the same center, or if there are multiple computers at a center, it is also possible to have positive checks of the system made by having the results of various computer calculations checked against each other to assure all computers are operational.

There are multitudinous variations on this theme. In the designs discussed so far, the operational capacity of the system must remain constant across a variety of component failures. It is possible to define failsoft environments in which degraded operation is acceptable for intervals of time. This degraded operation may be in the form of suspending certain background functions or in the form of doing things more slowly. Such environments may be appropriate for traffic control or civilian space control.

3.3 REAL-TIME SOFTWARE

Software for a real-time system naturally depends on the nature of the application, the nature of the processors actually used at a node and, if there are multiple nodes in the spirit of Figs. 3.2 and 3.3, the relationship between these nodes.

There are, however, a number of general characteristics of real-time systems that are present to some extent in all applications and in all nodes. A fundamental characteristic is what is called *queue-driven* design or an *event-driven* design. These are concepts related to the structure of the software. The underlying idea is that the system selects the programs to run as a result of receiving a message of a particular type. The idea is distinct from a *process-driven* design in which events happen on the system because of a pattern of program operation chosen for reasons of schedule or equipment utilization.

The real-time system has at its heart a queue manager that solicits and/or accepts messages from the outside, analyzes the messages, and calls for the execution of message processing programs. The message processing programs themselves may make references to data or they may have environments established for them by the queue manager when it calls for their execution. This will depend on how predictable the data required for any message is at the time the message is first identified.

Another common characteristic of real-time systems is that all data is on-line and that all processing programs are on-line in executable or nearly executable form. Because of the necessity to respond quickly, all or a major portion of processing programs may be resident in memory. If they are not resident, the memory management techniques tend to be fast and simple so that programs can be loaded and started with minimal delay.

There is a related tendency to keep processor management equally simple. Processing programs are allowed to run to completion or to the limit of set clock times and no attempt is made to balance channel, CPU, and memory usage by preempting and replacing programs on the basis of resource consumption patterns.

The application has control over the machine. Processing programs may release the processor voluntarily or at the end of the interval set by the queue manager acting as an application monitor. The application processing programs can guarantee themselves or be guaranteed contiguous intervals of control, can sample time, and can invoke subroutines with minimum overhead. Frequently, the application programs are closer to physical devices than is usual in a nonreal-time environment, and the application programming becomes responsible for system integrity, coordination, etc.

Many real-time systems are developed in dedicated applications-oriented environments in which hardware planning, applications planning, and operating systems planning are all accomplished together. There is frequently no assumption that the application will interface with a standard operating system.

Many aspects of dedicated real-time systems derive from the close interconnection between hardware, application, and systems development. Since all programs in the application are identified as part of design, and relationships between all programs can be determined, the loading levels placed upon the system in various circumstances can be determined, and sets of inputs and outputs can be completely designed. This means that many or all of the systems control activities that an operating system may undertake can be reduced or eliminated. For example, since schedules are planned as responses to certain events, there need be no generalized scheduling algorithms in the operating system. Similarly, there may not be need for the operating system to support generalized program-to-program communication conventions because all programs know about each other and can communicate with each other by negotiated specialized conventions if they choose.

The reader will recognize that concepts of control state and privileged operations may be burdensome to a dedicated real-time application. For example, if setting or reading a clock is important to some number of message processing programs and if reference to a clock is a privileged instruction so that each time a clock is referenced it is necessary to enter control state, then the requirement to enter control state may become a burden to the system. This may be overcome by running the entire application in control state. However, an architecture that abandons memory protection in order to make privileged operations available might present difficulties to a real-time application since protection against error or malicious problems would have to be sacrificed in order to reduce the control burden.

A last characteristic of real-time systems to be mentioned here is that programming and development of the system are separated from the operational system itself. It may be necessary to develop a programming development system as a prelude to building the application system or it may be possible to use an already existing operating system with a program development capability. It is not necessary that the system be developed on machines of the same architecture as that of the operational real-time system. *Cross-compilers* and *cross-assemblers* can be used to generate code for the operational system on entirely alien architectures. *A cross-assembler or compiler is one that runs on one machine to generate code for another. A meta-assembler is an assembler that can generate code for any architecture described to it.*

When microcomputers are used in a system, the use of a development system that runs on a very expanded version of the microcomputer system is rather common. The development system may itself be capable of etching read-only control memories after generating code.

The complete intertwine of the design of hardware, application, and system function is not a characteristic of all real-time systems. A rather low level of operating system interface may be provided for the application program in order to minimize the costs of application development. Some of the real-time systems allow more than one application to be run at the same time. It is possible to run two real-time applications, but it is more common to run a real-time application in the *foreground* and a batch application in the *background. Foreground and background represent the preferences for system control that the application is given.* A pure background application receives the processor only when there is no work for the foreground to do and loses the processor whenever work arrives for the foreground. In addition, devices are allocated to the background so that it causes minimum, if any, interference to foreground operations.

There are many generalized real-time operating systems available for large and small systems. These systems are not always used for real-time application development in the sense in which we have used the concept real-time in this chapter so far. The closely related world of *transaction processing,* which has many of the characteristics of real-time but with relaxed time constraints and with human terminal interfaces, may use operating systems with many real-time characteristics.

A typical minicomputer real-time operating system provides for a rigorous partitioning of memory into foreground and background partitions. There may be only one background partition, one area of memory that executes batch processing programs. The foreground partitions may be numerous (in the hundreds) in order to support the concept of the processing programs organized into a large number of tasks. Partitions are preset at system definition time. A task executes in a partition. *A task is a schedulable program unit that may be loaded into a partition.* On some systems, a set of tasks may be preassigned to partitions but it is becoming common to allow tasks to be loaded into any vacant partition. The operating system provides a set of activation and synchronization mechanisms between tasks. Tasks can pass parameters to each other and take interrupts on the arrival of parameters. Communication between tasks is accomplished through a common memory area itself defined as a partition. Routines from a library may be shared by being placed in a shared resident library partition.

The operating system may provide a simple run-time environment in which various user programs may be designated as control tasks or worker tasks. The control task designation is intended to allow an applications developer to provide special scheduling and control when they are required. The interface to the system may be at a very detailed level. By a detailed level interface one means that when a service is requested the application program must specifically form a request structure (or a control block) that describes the service required. To contrast a macrolevel interface with a detailed level: GET "A" tells the system that a record from file "A" is desired. The system has gathered information that tells it all about "A." It knows its record structure, it knows its device assignment, etc. A detailed level interface may call for the same function but must undertake to provide parameters of various kinds to supply required information.

It is common to find a command language associated with a system. This command language may be used to *direct the allocation of devices, start and stop tasks,* and *change priorities.* The existence of such a command language in small, real-time systems provides for some operational flexibility. The background partition is often intended to support program development compilers, text editors, and utilities so that some application development is possible on the real-time machines.

3.4 BATCH OPERATING SYSTEMS

The concept of batch comes from the mode of access to machine service. In its most precise meaning, batch alludes to the capability of a data center to accept job requests and to form streams of unrelated requests into batches of work that are submitted to the system at the convenience of the center. The concept of batching job requests comes largely from a short job or from a programming development environment. The speed of second-generation machines was such that setting up and tearing down jobs consumed large amounts of time relative to the expected duration of a job. Relatively long periods of system nonproductivity were caused by the time in minutes to mount and dismount tapes between jobs that themselves might take minutes.

The late 1950s' form of the *programmer's workbench* or *programming development system* was the extension of a compiler to undertake functions that would allow a programmer to send a card deck down to the computer center and receive results back from the center after some period of time. This time, *turnaround time,* might be measured in hours. *It was always best when it was short, of course, but it was most important that it be predictable.*

The programmer's control stream could call for various options of compile, compile/execute, dumps, traces, listings, decks, or whatever paraphernalia might aid the debugging process. The intent of batching was to increase the effectiveness of the system by smoothing job-to-job and intrajob transitions. It also eliminated periods of idle time while programmers stepped their way through programs, or shouted corrections to operators, during presystem debugging sessions. The effectiveness of programmers was thought to be increased by freeing them from attendance at the machine. The hope was that programmers would organize themselves productively during the turnaround period. There are still some who say that a fast, predictable batch turnaround system maximizes programmer productivity during debugging, particularly if every programmer cannot be guaranteed instantaneous access to a terminal. This might be particularly true of programmers who write out programs before approaching an entry terminal.

The control stream oriented batch system can also be used as a production system. Primitive versions of such systems instructed operators to submit decks and perform volume mounting according to a schedule. As batch systems have grown in sophistication, they have undertaken to start jobs without relying on operator initiation.

In general, the goal of a batch operating system is to facilitate the performance of various combinations of small and large jobs in such a way as to minimize overhead for job setup, breakdown, and job-to-job transition. Submissions may include requests for production runs, compilations, compilation and tests, tests, etc., in unpredictable combinations.

Batch systems are characterized by the elaborateness of their scheduling and resource allocation mechanisms. The systems reflect an attempt to create an environment suitable for the requirements of a large community of heterogeneous users where little is known at systems development time about the work-load, cost/performance, or responsiveness goals of a particular installation. We discuss three broad subclasses of batch systems.

- Single stream
- Basic multiprogramming
- Advanced multiprogramming

3.5 SINGLE-STREAM SYSTEMS

Batch single-stream systems are fading into the realm of the antique. Yet in looking again, after many years, at the manuals and articles about *FMS (Fortran Monitor System)* and *IBSYS-IBJOB for the 7094*, the authors were astonished by how sophisticated and elegant these systems were, how complete their concepts were, and how little they give the impression of being proto-dynastic precursors to modern times. They introduced almost all of the major concepts of contemporary systems—*control stream, I/O support at high macrolevels, program relocation,* and *device independence*—and they established the *concept of the "encapsulation" of a machine by its operating system and software package.*

They themselves were built on already solid programming concepts. By the late 1950s, increasing machine capability, increasing machine complexity, and an already serious concern with the cost of programming and the availability of programmers had caused some changes in what was considered profitable to do on and off the machine. Part of what had been considered a programmer's job had been absorbed by compilers, and scarce machine capacity was being used for program generation. FORTRAN and COBOL precursors were coming into general use. Macroassemblers (of sophistication still not surpassed today) were available with I/O control systems similar to current systems. Concepts of relocation had emerged because of the necessity for placing routines from I/O libraries and other libraries in different locations when used by different programs. There were interpreters, although they were in disfavor because of their slow speed when compared with compilation and machine-level execution.

The Autocoder macroassembler IOCS capability shows how conceptually advanced early languages were. The Autocoder supported macros GET, PUT, OPEN, CLOSE, SEEK, SCAN in ways similar to the contemporary meaning of such phrases. In addition, a set of JCL-like statements, submitted in assembler format, specified I/O devices, label definitions, and whether access to disk would be random or sequential. Each file used by a program was described for its work area, block size, record format (variable, fixed). The same kind of parameterization associated with contemporary systems was available with very early systems.

The *collecting loader* (also called the *linking loader* or *binding loader*) was a very early feature of software support. These loaders enabled programs that had been independently compiled to be formed into a single memory load, or library-provided subroutines to be linked with user application code. Before

these loaders were invented, it was necessary to assemble or compile routines together to form a single, executable core image. Compilers produced relocatable output with tables containing the addresses needing to be relocated. Relocation in this early sense meant the addition of some constant to address values as the program was being loaded.

3.5.1 FMS

The first systems attempted to organize the programming language, I/O support, and utility routines into some kind of organized whole. One of the earliest of these systems was the FORTRAN Monitor System for the 709. It is interesting because of the conceptual structure of the system, namely its view that the operating system was the backend of a compiler. The system was a single-language program development system that made minimum impact on the FORTRAN programmer. The programmer who knew FORTRAN could run under FMS after reading about ten pages of the manual.

Except for the limitation to FORTRAN, the system displayed most of the characteristics of a batch operating system. It allowed a series of consecutive compilations and a series of consecutive executions. It also allowed compile/load/go to appear as a unified process. It accepted rather sophisticated DEBUG directives defining desired dumps and the conditions for taking dumps. The stream was extremely simple.

```
ID
DATE
XEQ FORT CLG
FORTRAN source
DATA
data elements
```

In addition, there was a form of *overlay* control through a CHAIN command that enabled the definitions of overlays in the stream.

The elements of the system that supported the concept of batching were organized into the *monitor*. The monitor read the job stream and caused the compiler to be loaded when required. At the end of a compilation, the compiler would exit to the monitor that determined, on the basis of the next job stream element, whether the compiler was needed again or if the system was to be turned over to an object program load and execute phase. During the execution phase, no monitor functions were resident in the machine. The execution-time I/O support was defined by compiler library modules and there was no concept of coexisting unlinked programs in the system. Consequently, the executing program had complete control over the hardware. There was no concept of supervisor state or privileged operations that forced the user program and the I/O functions to be separated by a formal interface. The I/O device allocation was supported by a table in the compiler that associated logical and physical device addresses and provided a standard functional nomenclature. To change device assignments, a System Editor run was required. To provide flexibility, physical addresses were hardware dialable. An important aspect of the system was the concept of common job devices like SYSIN and SYSOUT. This reduced setup time by defining a common input and output stream used across jobs. The concept of common work tapes (SYSUTn) simplified set up by standardizing what tape units had to be mounted for each job.

3.5.2 IBSYS/IBJOB

IBSYS/IBJOB represents the mature, large, single-stream system of the early 1960s. This system generalized the capabilities of FMS by including a number of programming languages within its context and introduced the idea of a resident system nucleus acting as an extended machine. IBSYS, the basic monitor, contained resident basic I/O support, a dump capability, and an interface for the IBJOB monitor. The IBJOB monitor provided control stream services for FOR-TRAN, COBOL, MAP, a loader, and an IOCS library. In addition, programs not running "under" IBJOB could run directly on IBSYS interfaces. A picture of IBSYS/IBJOB structure is provided in Fig. 3.4.

IBSYS/IBJOB introduced many notions now common to many operating systems. The IBSYS control language included only two mandatory control statements, $JOB and $EXECUTE. $JOB defined the beginning of a work unit and caused the activation of a user-supplied accounting routine. It also restored the standard I/O environment. If any modifications to device usage occurred in a previous job (for example, the renaming of SYSOUT), these renamings were undone for a new job. The device assignment tables, embedded in FMS and accessible only to an Edit, became available to operator manipulation by control card under IBSYS. This was an important step to device independence.

The $EXECUTE card called for the execution of a subsystem or processor. The IBSYS supervisor called in the subsystem and transferred control to it. When $EXECUTE was read by a subsystem element and called for a program within that subsystem, that subsystem retained control. Otherwise the subsystem called the supervisor.

The IBSYS system contained a resident nucleus that was in memory at all times. This nucleus provided for subsystem/subsystem communication and provided an area for systems information such as the location of the start of the current subsystem, the location of the Unit Function Table, and the location of the Unit Availability Table.

The Unit Function Table contained pointers to entries in memory called UCBs, Unit Control Blocks. UCBs defined the status of I/O devices in terms of these loaders were invented, it was necessary to assemble or compile routines together to form a single, executable core image. Compilers produced relocatable output with tables containing the addresses needing to be relocated. Relocation in this early sense meant the addition of some constant to address values as the program was being loaded.

3.5.1 FMS

The first systems attempted to organize the programming language, I/O support, and utility routines into some kind of organized whole. One of the earliest of these systems was the FORTRAN Monitor System for the 709. It is interesting because of the conceptual structure of the system, namely its view that the operating system was the backend of a compiler. The system was a single-language program development system that made minimum impact on the FORTRAN programmer. The programmer who knew FORTRAN could run under FMS after reading about ten pages of the manual.

Except for the limitation to FORTRAN, the system displayed most of the characteristics of a batch operating system. It allowed a series of consecutive compilations and a series of consecutive executions. It also allowed compile/load/go to appear as a unified process. It accepted rather sophisticated DEBUG directives defining desired dumps and the conditions for taking dumps. The stream was extremely simple.

> ID
> DATE
> XEQ FORT CLG
> FORTRAN source
> DATA
> data elements

In addition, there was a form of *overlay* control through a CHAIN command that enabled the definitions of overlays in the stream.

The elements of the system that supported the concept of batching were organized into the *monitor*. The monitor read the job stream and caused the compiler to be loaded when required. At the end of a compilation, the compiler would exit to the monitor that determined, on the basis of the next job stream element, whether the compiler was needed again or if the system was to be turned over to an object program load and execute phase. During the execution phase, no monitor functions were resident in the machine. The execution-time I/O support was defined by compiler library modules and there was no concept of coexisting unlinked programs in the system. Consequently, the executing program had complete control over the hardware. There was no concept of supervisor state or privileged operations that forced the user program and the I/O functions to be separated by a formal interface. The I/O device allocation was supported by a table in the compiler that associated logical and physical device addresses and provided a standard functional nomenclature. To change device assignments, a System Editor run was required. To provide flexibility, physical addresses were hardware dialable. An important aspect of the system was the concept of common job devices like SYSIN and SYSOUT. This reduced setup time by defining a common input and output stream used across jobs. The concept of common work tapes (SYSUTn) simplified set up by standardizing what tape units had to be mounted for each job.

3.5.2   IBSYS/IBJOB

IBSYS/IBJOB represents the mature, large, single-stream system of the early 1960s. This system generalized the capabilities of FMS by including a number of programming languages within its context and introduced the idea of a resident system nucleus acting as an extended machine. IBSYS, the basic monitor, contained resident basic I/O support, a dump capability, and an interface for the IBJOB monitor. The IBJOB monitor provided control stream services for FORTRAN, COBOL, MAP, a loader, and an IOCS library. In addition, programs not running "under" IBJOB could run directly on IBSYS interfaces. A picture of IBSYS/IBJOB structure is provided in Fig. 3.4.

IBSYS/IBJOB introduced many notions now common to many operating systems. The IBSYS control language included only two mandatory control statements, $JOB and $EXECUTE. $JOB defined the beginning of a work unit and caused the activation of a user-supplied accounting routine. It also restored the standard I/O environment. If any modifications to device usage occurred in a previous job (for example, the renaming of SYSOUT), these renamings were undone for a new job. The device assignment tables, embedded in FMS and accessible only to an Edit, became available to operator manipulation by control card under IBSYS. This was an important step to device independence.

The $EXECUTE card called for the execution of a subsystem or processor. The IBSYS supervisor called in the subsystem and transferred control to it. When $EXECUTE was read by a subsystem element and called for a program within that subsystem, that subsystem retained control. Otherwise the subsystem called the supervisor.

The IBSYS system contained a resident nucleus that was in memory at all times. This nucleus provided for subsystem/subsystem communication and provided an area for systems information such as the location of the start of the current subsystem, the location of the Unit Function Table, and the location of the Unit Availability Table.

The Unit Function Table contained pointers to entries in memory called UCBs, Unit Control Blocks. UCBs defined the status of I/O devices in terms of

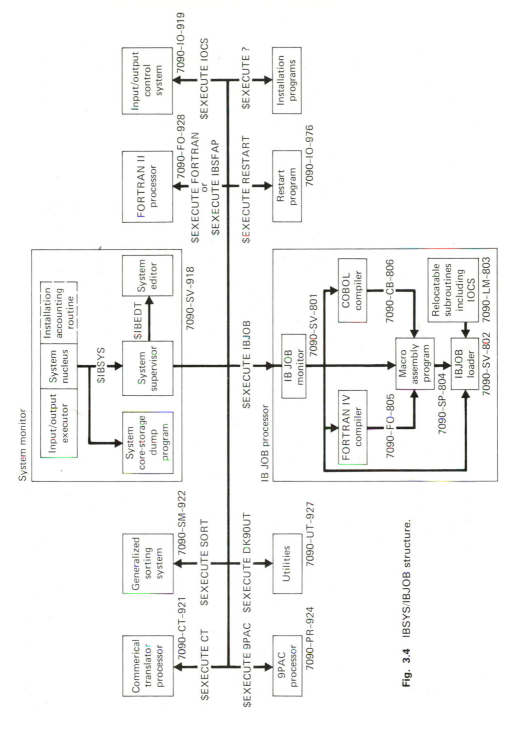

Fig. 3.4 IBSYS/IBJOB structure.

77

busy, ready, the address of the routine starting I/O, etc. A Unit Availability Table contained a unit available chain for each channel. These control blocks were needed for the allocation and use of devices. They formed the basis for the removal of certain I/O device control functions from the generated code of a user program and provided for flexibility in device assignment.

In addition to the nucleus, IBSYS contained an I/O executor that centralized I/O at a very low level of support. A family of services was provided that included interrupt handling, data conversion, punch and print support.

Interface to the I/O executor was at a very low level. The user had to determine if the device was free, and had to provide normal and abnormal return points. The reason for the low level was to provide a lowest common denominator for various processors and subsystems running on IBSYS. There was no concept of the coexistence of programs and consequently no need for privilege or protection.

The Supervisor portion of IBSYS was not resident. Its job was to sequence through the job stream and to provide an operator interface.

A Systems Editor was available for systems specialization and maintenance. The editing language provided for the modification, replacement, copying, and insertion and removal of systems elements. IBJOB provided an environment for the programming languages. It contained a loader, a monitor, and an IOCS library. The loader was responsible for allocating devices to a program as well as for loading a program and its system subroutines. In this function of allocation, the loader was a combined loader/allocator doing functions that are commonly separated in contemporary systems. It made sense to combine the acquisition of devices with loading because memory and devices were assigned to a program at the same time and no reason existed for separating the functions.

The I/O Editor provided an interesting capability. In addition to reading SYSIN and writing SYSOUT, the Editor encapsulated the language processors doing I/O on their behalf. Processors could be device-independent and give and receive records at a standard interface. This meant that input streams could come from multiple sources.

3.5.3 Spooling Systems

Single-stream systems began to take on some multiprogramming aspects reasonably early. By the end of the 1950s, a number of systems had *spooling* capabilities. *Spooling refers to the interposition of a fast I/O device or a random storage device between programs and slow I/O devices.* A program wishing to print a file might refer directly to a printer. The output support provided by the system, however, actually writes the print line to a faster device, perhaps a tape or a drum or a disk file. The print lines collected in a file are transferred to the printer at a time convenient for the system. (See Fig. 3.5.)

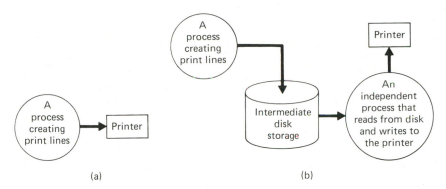

Fig. 3.5 Spooling. (a) A nonspooling system: As each print line is created, it is sent to the printer (a relatively slow device) and printed. Control is then returned to the program. A program rapidly generating print lines can run no faster than the printer can print the lines. (b) A spooling system: As each line is created, the print lines are temporarily written to disk (a device much faster than the printer). The program now runs to completion more rapidly. An independent process obtains the print lines from the disk and sends them to the printer. The printer operates at full speed simultaneously with the next job now processing.

The intent of spooling is to disassociate programs from very slow devices. The total running time of a program printing a file is characteristically determined by the time required for printing. The program is printbound and may use the CPU and faster input devices only very sparingly during its run. If a 50-page report is to be printed on a 600-line per minute printer (at 60 lines per page), it will take five minutes to print the report.

During the printing of the file, the tapes and processor are dedicated to the program even though they are idle for long periods of time. By putting the print file on an intermediate fast device, the running time of the program is reduced because the limiting device (the device that determines how long the program will run) is itself much faster. Thus more programs can be run on the system in any interval of time.

This approach to slow devices does not necessarily require software system support. The files to be printed can be taken from the main frame to an *off-line printer* or an *off-line satellite computer*. This mode of operation was quite common in very early systems. The UNIVAC had no on-line printer; early IBM 700s had satellite 1401s for off-line printing. When the printers are on-line to the main computer system, however, software must provide the mechanisms for disassociating the program from the slow devices, and for causing the printing to occur. There are several ways to organize these functions.

The operating system for IBM's 7070 included utilities for printing and punching as part of the basic system. The printer routine, for example, and the buffers required for it were part of a defined transient area of the operating system. The concept of a system output stream was associated with spooling so that print files were directed to the system output stream device. References to files associated with this device caused writing on the device by I/O support.

Printing of a file was accomplished by a printer utility that was multiprogrammed with the main chain, the user application program. The main chain had control of the system when the printer utility could not run. The printer utility gained control of the system whenever the printer became available for another line. The system would transfer control of the system to the utility that would prepare another line and then relinquish control.

A number of systems, including the UNIVAC III, had similar mechanisms. The multiprogramming capability was achieved by a minimal extension to the interrupt handler of the system. Whenever an I/O interrupt occurred, the I/O handler would determine if the spooling utility could run and would give it control. *Multiprogramming had its origin in this simple interleave between a utility and a main chain.*

A usual characteristic of spooling is that the file being printed belongs to a previously completed main chain. An assumption of spooling is that the spooling utility uses very little computer power and causes minimum interference with the main chain. The interference between main chain and utility comes when the main chain is denied the use of the processor or I/O subsystem because the utility is using it. Because of this denial, the elapsed time of the main chain is increased. Even when interference occurs, however, the main chain still completes more quickly than if it is attached to the printer. Interference is minimized when the I/O devices used by the main chain are on separate channels or, if on the same channels, the main chain is extremely CPU-limited.

There are two variations on the spooling theme. One variation, embodied in early OS/360, is to view the spooling utility as a worker program, itself a main chain. The concept of spooling is embedded in the generalized concept of multiprogramming. The spooling utility, a *writer,* runs on the same basis as any worker program. It is started in the same way, uses the same run-time environment interfaces, and competes for machine resources as part of the generalized multiprogramming mix. Another variation is found in UNIVAC's EXEC II for the UNIVAC 1107. *The significant attribute of this system (an attribute now found in later 1100 series systems and in IBM's MVS) is the ability to begin printing before the job creating the print file is complete.*

The UNIVAC concept involves the definition of a systems function called a *symbiont* because of its symbiotic relationship with a running user program. The main chain and the symbiont run together in a *producer–consumer relationship.* The main chain contributes records to a *shared buffer file,* and the symbiont prints records as they become available. This is a very particular use of a *message buffer* between two *cooperating processes* that we will discuss more generally later in this text.

The main chain interfaces with a function of the operating system called a *cooperative*. The main chain passes records to a cooperative that places them in a buffer area on a drum. When a cooperative determines that a buffer area is full, it calls a symbiont loader to load a symbiont into core and then places the symbiont on the *dispatching queue*. In this way the printing of a file is overlapped with the producing main chain.

Such a design intends to redress somewhat the strong thruput flavor of spooling. *Thruput relates to the number of jobs that can be put through a system over any period of time.* It is a measure of systems performance that contrasts with *turnaround, the length of time that it takes to return a result to a user of the system.* Obviously, the minimum time to a human usable result is achieved by letting a program use the slow devices directly. Any particular user would like to have his or her file printed as quickly as possible and may not mind using the system inefficiently. By interposing a fast device and collecting the file for printing afterwards, additional time is introduced into the turnaround sequence. If it would take 30 minutes to print a report without spooling, it will take 30 minutes plus main chain time to print it with spooling. Although more main chains may be brought to the system during an interval, the bottleneck may still be the printing capacity of the system as files to be printed enqueue on the utility.

While the symbiont concept cannot overcome the problem of print capacity bottlenecking, it can, under certain conditions, reduce the time until the printed output is available to the user. It allows main chains to proceed at a convenient rate and provides for an asynchronous software mechanism to print output. In some cases, the design will degrade to the unoverlapped design as, for example, when a printer is not available for allocation, but in some instances it maximizes the amount of printing that can be done while a main chain is running, introducing a turnaround improvement without serious damage to thruput.

3.6 MULTIPROGRAMMING SYSTEMS

An interesting phenomenon of the industry is that basic batch multiprogramming systems and advanced batch multiprogramming systems developed almost simultaneously as responses to different classes of machinery. A set of concepts had been waiting for machines large enough to support them. The machines of the third generation finally provided sufficient hardware. Particularly important to operating systems development was the emergence of disk in the late 1950s. *The emergence of disk storage affected systems in three fundamental ways.*

- *The device population became more varied and now included disks as well as tapes.*
- *There was a capacity for significant on-line storage and a need for organizing and managing this storage so that it could be conveniently used.*

- *The direct addressing capability of the storage presented new problems as well as new opportunities at the interface between a program and its I/O.*

In addition to disk storage, there was a general increase in system *asynchronism* and concepts of *interrupt, privilege* and *protection* emerged into hardware architecture. The third generation presented systems that not only required more management but could also profit from it.

3.6.1   Basic Batch Multiprogramming

The concept of a basic, as opposed to an advanced, multiprogramming system is naturally unsupported by rigorous definition. A full survey of multiprogramming systems developed since the early 1960s would show that there really isn't a simple continuum from basic to advanced multiprogramming systems. Yet there seems to be a rough instinctive judgment about a system that can be formed by observing

- The fundamental algorithms for memory management.
- The sophistication of CPU task-switching algorithms.
- The times at which data sets and devices can be acquired or released by a program.
- The degree to which the system participates in enforcing longer-range scheduling decisions.

In general, a basic multiprogramming system (1) requires a good deal of off-line scheduling, (2) manages memory conservatively so that partitions of memory tend to be defined or redefined by human operators and have long duration, (3) manages CPU multiplexing with only minimal attempts to balance resource usage, and (4) tends to associate data sets and devices with programs for the entire life of the program.

Commonly, basic multiprogramming systems are intended to run on smaller machines that cannot afford and will not profit from intense resource management, and that support work loads that are possible to plan. As machines increase in capacity from generation to generation, the basic systems take on more functions; they evolve naturally in the direction of larger systems as their machine base becomes more powerful.

IBM's DOS (*Disk Operating System*) is a typical basic multiprogramming system both in its general characteristics and in its evolutionary development. It is a general purpose operating system in that it can be used to support program development or production environments. It was originally intended for smaller members of the IBM System/360 line and is now commonly used on System/370s through the 370/148.

In its initial versions, the system allowed a fixed (and predetermined) number of programs to share a system in a very stable resource allocation environment. Memory was organized into partitions by decision of the installation staff, and these partitions were established as part of installing the system. The assemblers and compilers translated programs for particular partitions and could run only in those partitions. In effect, *the system defined multiple independent machines that were scheduled independently but could share devices and the use of the CPU.*

An important advance over second-generation (single-stream) systems was the idea, common to all multiprogramming systems, of an *internalized job queue.* Earlier systems relied upon operators to sequence jobs in a control stream. As the system progressed through the stream, the stream lived partly on a card reader and partly in a table. Alternatively, of course, the stream could be recorded on tape, but the idea that *the system undertook jobs in the order in which they were presented* was inherent in all systems. The arrangement of job sequences was done by hand or, perhaps, by a scheduling program that ran as an application program to form a "master schedule tape" containing the control stream in proper sequence.

The common use of disk devices permitted the job stream to be internalized in such a way that the scheduling function could be made part of the operating system. The job queue was made available to a scheduler that could search for the waiting job with the highest priority whenever a new job was to be started. This mechanism led to the establishment of a priority parameter in the control language. The capability of holding an internalized job queue considerably extended the participation of a system in its own self-management.

The operating staff, of course, still determined what jobs would be in the queue at any particular time. The number of jobs in the queue was limited by space and by the dynamics of job submission in the using enterprise.

In the highly stable "prepartitioned" system that was early DOS, a queue was created for each partition and the scheduling function was performed independently for each partition. Jobs on each queue, of course, were jobs that had been compiled or assembled for that particular partition.

A set of problems develops with such an approach. An underlying problem comes from the prepartitioning. Partitions are commonly defined to reflect an anticipated population of jobs to be run and commonly reflect the sizes required to run certain large jobs. If a partition of 64K is defined, it is in anticipation of a job requiring 64K. Similarly, partitions of other sizes are defined for the largest jobs aimed at those partitions. If the system has two 64K partitions and two 32K partitions, then four jobs may run on the system at any time. If there are two 64K jobs that will run all day, every day, and two 32K jobs that will run all day, every day, the planning and prepartitioning requirements do not cost anything in machine efficiency. This is also true if there is a set of jobs such that there are always two 64K jobs and two 32K jobs available to run in proper partitions. To achieve this, of course, an installation must not only undertake considerable planning but must also in fact have a stable, predictable work-load environment. If this is true, then the inflexibility of the system presents no problem and the costs inherent in flexibility would present no advantage.

However, the prepartitioning may lead to serious underutilization of the system if the large partitions commonly run jobs that are considerably smaller. To the extent that 32K jobs are run in the 64K partitions, for example, in a 192K system, fully one-third of the memory of the system is unused. This may not be a problem if the system is not memory-limited. However it will be a problem if the system is. *Memory-limited means that there is ample reserve power in the I/O subsystem and the CPU to handle the additional load that might come from additional programs in memory.* This means that more work can be done on the system without serious decay in responsiveness if more programs can be fit into memory.

A problem associated with prepartitioning is an implied increase in programming costs and decrease in programmer productivity. Any particular application must be aimed at a particular partition. Depending on the distribution of program sizes already running on the system, a new application may be directed to a partition of a size such that fitting it into the partition will either distort the program structure of the application or increase the difficulty in programming any particular program, or both. Distorting the structure means that the distribution of function among programs in the application is done for reasons of memory size rather than to accommodate a natural flow of function.

The increase in difficulty in creating any particular program comes from the need to make the program fit into a specific amount of memory. There is ample evidence that programming costs increase dramatically when it is necessary to constrain programs. Indirectly, this leads to further underutilization of the machine because application designers structure applications in such a way as to minimize the possibility that particular programs will not fit. That is, if they are aiming at a 32K partition, they will distribute function into programs they feel will be around 20K. To the extent that they succeed, the 32K partition will be underutilized.

Beyond the underlying problem of prepartitioning, an additional exposure to bottlenecking and underutilization of memory space comes from a system that preassigns programs to particular partitions of a certain size and schedules each partition independently. It is possible that a 32K job will be waiting for a 64K partition, but a 32K partition is inactive. Because the job was compiled for the addresses of a particular partition, it cannot be switched into an available partition of appropriate size.

Other features of early DOS reflected its assumption of a stable, well-known, highly partitionable working environment running highly separated units of work.

Each partition had its own SYSIN and SYSOUT stream. The control language provided minimal support of the concept of device independence characterized by the association of systems symbolic functions with specific devices through ASSIGN statements. In addition, certain functions could be performed only from certain partitions. For example, compilation could be done in a background partition and teleprocessing from a foreground partition only. The concept of foreground and background (introduced in connection with real-time systems) relates to a set of priorities associated with a partition. Each partition has a priority that is used to determine its power to acquire the CPU. The CPU is always given to the partition of highest priority that is ready ro run (i.e., the program in that partition is not waiting for an I/O request to complete).

The inflexibility of such a system comes from an image of the machine and from an image of the working environment. There is a strong desire to keep the operating system small and to minimize the time that the system spends managing itself. An operating system of the general capability of early DOS might require in the neighborhood of 10,000 to 16,000 bytes of resident function. As memories have increased, and as general machine capacity has increased, the properties of low-level batch systems have expanded. One important expansion has been the undertaking of the support of work that is not batch. Capability for handling on-line databases has been added to systems like DOS. We will discuss the attributes of on-line systems in later sections. In addition to the generalization of access capability, largely through the provision of subsystems that run on the base of the initial batch system, small systems have grown in underlying sophistication of function. Among the particular advances of small batch systems are

■   *Operator-driven partition redefinition* that allows an operator to redefine partition sizes from an operator console.

■   *Relocatable assembly and compilation* that allow any program to be run in any partition of adequate size. This eliminates the bottlenecks of rigidly defined distributed scheduling and begins to approach the concept of the total system as a dynamically allocatable pool of resources.

■   *Symbolic device assignment* that allows control stream requests for device by class or type, and allows the operating system to assign devices at program start time.

■   For DOS, in particular, *the ability of an application program to be organized into a structure of tasks* in the spirit of real-time systems. This structure permits a program in a particular partition to ask the operating system to schedule asynchronous programs to run in the same partition and to support synchronization between multiple programs running in the same partition.

■   The support of the concept of *virtual memory,* as in DOS/VS. Virtual memory allows the definitions of partitions whose total size exceeds the amount of main memory available to the system. Mechanisms in the run-time environment associated with *paging* and *segmentation* essentially relieve the programmer from planning overlay structures by mapping virtual memory addresses into real memory locations and providing for the movement of referenced virtual locations in and out of storage. The defined virtual memory space lives on direct access devices organized to represent blocks of real memory locations. The techniques of virtual memory are discussed in detail later in the text.

■   *The development of enhanced operating support and scheduling mechanisms that provide centralized spooling capability through operator initiated spooling utilities, for example, DOS POWER.*

In discussing the extension of capability of a basic batch operating system over time, one runs directly into the taxonomy problems alluded to in the opening paragraphs of this chapter. Many of the new attributes are associated with systems that have grown out of their batch orientation to some extent and many newer small systems are not, in fact, batch-oriented in the original meaning of the term. Most small systems of today are small multipurpose systems that allow a variety of access modes. A more detailed look at the underlying structure of a system is required to gain an appreciation of the system's primary application. For example, a batch system may run a program in a partition that allows conversational access to compilers or even to on-line application programs. This system may exhibit properties very similar to a time-sharing system.

Contemporary thinking has caused us to reconsider what is meant by batch. Among the modes of access discussed in the last chapter is *conversational entry* and *closed execution.* A programmer or a user goes to an on-line terminal to develop a control stream for the execution of a program. At one point, the user types a "SUBMIT" command that causes the control stream to be enqueued on the job queue. It may be possible to name the terminal printer as the output device and receive printed results at the terminal at the end of the job. Such a method of operation will look more or less like a time-sharing system depending on the average size of the job queue and the average size of a job. What is important is that the program, while in execution, is completely removed from association with the submitting terminal, and runs as an unattended program. This concept of "unattended" has always been central to batch operations. However, the word "batch" no longer need imply card deck or tape submission, nor the intervention of operational staff between a user and the system. The distinction between on-line and batch operation has almost been reduced to a concept of the length of the requested execution. As we will discuss later, *some systems treat a program as a terminal-oriented unit of work until it has run for a certain length of time without making a terminal response. After that time it is treated as an unattended job in a background partition reserved for unattended jobs.*

3.6.2 Advanced Batch Multiprogramming

The large-scale batch multiprogramming system is distinguished from its small relative by the degree to which it undertakes management of the resources of the system. It was developed to support large machines for use in consolidated work-load environments of unpredictability and diversity of use. In the early to mid-1960s, when systems like *OS/MVT* or *OS/MFT, GECOS, SCOPE, MCP*, and their like were conceived, these systems were considered to be general purpose. They were, in fact, intended as the glory of their times, capable of handling consolidations of programming development and production work loads in such a way as to maximize the effective utilization of equipment. Equipment utilization was a preoccupying concern because the realization of the economies of scale then generally thought to be inherent in large machines depended on using the hardware at high-utilization levels.

In addition to providing greater degrees of resource management, the large systems provided considerable richness and flexibility in program support functions. More varieties of *data organization* and *methods of accessing data* were provided in order to increase the probability that higher-level interfaces would be usable by applications programmers. Control languages were considerably expanded in expressive power and allowed the kind of flexibility associated with JCL as described previously.

Systems differed from each other in details of *memory management, processor management, I/O management,* and richness of function, but they were similar in intent and concept. Among the common features were:

■ Some degree of *dynamic memory management.* This includes an ability to give just as much memory as was requested by a program at the time of its start. This feature distinguished the advanced systems from smaller partition-oriented systems. In addition, some concept of dynamic growth and contraction was supported. OS/MVT, for example, allowed a program to issue *GETMAIN* and *FREEMAIN* macros during run time. The effect of these macros, however, was to organize and grant accessibility to space that had already been allocated as part of a program's region when the program was initiated.

■ Some capability for *sharing code* other than in the operating system by the nomination of special areas where, for example, *blocking* and *deblocking* or *buffer control routines* could be made resident and sharable by multiple programs.

■   Considerable *elaboration of library systems* involving mechanisms for the *cataloging of on-line data sets* and other functions in support of *disk devices as on-line repositories of data.*

■   Considerable *elaboration of the structure for job submission.* The simple monitor of single-stream batch systems becomes a *reader* and a *scheduler* so that the acts of reading a control stream and scheduling a job become quite distinct. In OS/MVT, a reader transfers a compressed form of control stream to the job queue. An *initiator* inspects the queue at some rate independent of the operation of the reader.

■   *A residual reliance on operators for large amounts of system control despite an elaboration of scheduler sophistication.* An operator has the power to *determine the multiprogramming level, change the priorities of jobs, abort jobs*, and *hold them on the job queue.* One aspect of further development in these systems is an *attempt to decrease reliance on operator activity.*

■   A continuing *elaboration of the mechanisms for CPU allocation,* including the introduction of *heuristics* to make the systems more responsive to the instantaneous patterns of resource usage exhibited by a mix.

As concepts of generality began to include various kinds of on-line usage, the large multiprogramming systems began to address the problems of their use in on-line environments. Consequently, they were extended with specialized *telecommunications* I/O support functions, and with the *on-line programming interfaces such as TSO (Time-Sharing Option). IBM's top-of-the-line operating system, OS/MVS is not perceived as a large batch multiprogramming system but as a general host of batch, on-line programming, and database management systems.* The degree to which success in attempting such generality may be achieved is a topic for the end of the book, but most designers believe that the secret of success is hidden somewhere in structural concepts.

The true successor to OS/MVT is not OS/MVS but OS/VS1. OS/VS1 essentially extends the concept of batch multiprogramming to a virtual memory machine by extending memory management to map a virtual 16 megabyte address space onto a smaller physical address space with a minimal perturbation of the structure and interfaces of the earlier system. This is probably the end of the advanced batch multiprogramming generic line.

3.7 TIME-SHARING SYSTEMS

Time-sharing alludes to a system whose major intention is to distribute computer power among a set of users at terminals in such a way as to support the illusion that each one has a dedicated computer supporting his or her requests for service. The user may be a programmer developing a program or an end user requesting the execution of a program.

The essential goal of a time-sharing system is service and responsiveness to the on-line user. In achieving this goal, the system may sacrifice effective utilization of hardware. Although there are many similarities in the techniques used in batch multiprogramming systems and in time-sharing systems to *multi-plex* the processing units, there is a fundamental difference in goals. *The goal of a batch multiprogramming system is machine utilization.* The goal of a time-sharing system is to provide rapid response to user requests.

There are also differences in the nature of the work that is given to the system. Time-sharing systems are most effective when each interaction with a user results in a short unit of work that can return some form of response to the terminal in a few seconds. Batch multiprogramming systems are most effective on long jobs with some significant slack in their required completion times.

Work-load mixes for batch multiprogramming systems are best when they display maximum heterogeneity with regard to their use of computer resources. This is because the system can best achieve resource use balance with a large amount of different kinds of load. *Time-sharing systems respond best to work loads of high homogeneity of functions used and time required.* This is because repeated use of a function minimizes the effort of the system to fetch the function and make it available to a terminal. Homogeneous populations require less system management in order to sustain the appearance of simultaneous service.

There are many varieties of time-sharing systems, ranging from systems that offer only a single programming language (Dartmouth BASIC) to large, multi-language, fully supported systems like IBM's TSS/370, and Multics. There are systems that are oriented to program development and systems that are closed production systems used by agents of a business.

3.7.1 Programmer's Workbench

The early work in time-sharing systems concentrated upon the use of a terminal as a kind of workbench for program development. The early systems included *QUICKTRAN,* the *SDC Q-32 Time-Sharing System, CTSS at M.I.T.,* and *Dartmouth BASIC.*

QUICKTRAN provided a fully conversational FORTRAN capability from a terminal with an added ability to call application programs, for example, COGO. Dartmouth BASIC provided on interactive entry capability to BASIC.

In both of these early systems, the programmer at the terminal had only one programming language available. The systems differed in that QUICKTRAN was more truly conversational, providing syntax responses for each entered line, and dynamic redeclaration of arrays. BASIC accepted lines passively until a

RUN command was given, at which time a compilation of the entire entered program was undertaken.

Since the early systems, on-line programming, testing, and execution have become available in a number of ways. There has been a proliferation of small time-sharing systems and a number of larger systems provide on-line program development capability through various subsystems. A distinction is beginning to be made between *programmer's workbenches* and *personal computing*. IBM's TSO capability with OS/MVS operating system is a programmer's workbench in intent. It provides a very full range of programming language and command stream capabilities. On the other hand, *IBM's VSPC*, for example, is intended for problem solvers not interested in using the terminal for the development of large systems.

In general a *programmer's workbench* must include

- A set of commands for the activation, testing and modification of programs.
- A file system with mechanisms for protection, sharing, and maintenance of collections of objects in the files.
- One or more programming languages.
- A run-time interface that may intersect with the command language.

A programmer's workbench need not be associated with a time-sharing environment. Characteristically, however, the underlying system provides for multiple simultaneous access to the system.

Among the features of contemporary programmer's workbenches that are generally thought to be convenient and desirable are the abilities

- to extend and reform the command language to form "working dialects" for specialized users
- to call any program in the system from the terminal
- to pass arguments from one command to another
- to define sharing rights among project teams to control access to the files in the system
- to specify unattended operation for any program

A contemporary system receiving much attention is a system developed for the *DEC PDP-11* called *UNIX*. UNIX is a small system with an on-line file system, a text editor, and an array of programming languages. It can run on a machine with 50K of 16-bit PDP-11 words but can itself occupy up to 42K when full I/O device buffering and support are used. The system is much like Multics in the capabilities it presents to a using programmer.

3.7.2 Transaction Processing Systems

There are several on-line application-oriented operating systems that share the characteristics of pure real-time systems and time-sharing systems. They are like real-time systems in that they are event-driven with relatively lean resource management algorithms. They are like time-sharing systems in that each transaction entering the system comes from a human operator at a terminal. It is quite common for the human operators to be lay people.

The computational aspects of the applications running on many systems are reasonably trivial. Processing commonly consists of the receipt of a message from a terminal, analysis of the message, scheduling of a message processing program, some number of references to an on-line database to receive information needed for responding to the message, and the scheduling of a response to the terminal. Because the time constraints on responsiveness and the penalty for failure to respond within a certain time are less critical than those associated with real-time systems, the levels of interface provided to an application programmer are commonly higher than on real-time systems. The structure of supervisor state/problem state is less burdensome for a transaction processing application than for real-time.

These systems are not necessarily time-sharing systems in the strictest sense. Time-sharing suggests that a form of system-imposed multiplexing is imposed upon a population of active programs. This time division attempts to limit the amount of continuous time that any particular terminal receives service from the processor. In a transaction system, it may be common to allow the processing of a transaction to run to completion or to run for a specified period of time. If processing is not completed, the transaction may be aborted rather than suspended and serviced at a later time. While a transaction is running, the operating system may interrupt to accept I/O completion messages but it will typically return to the interrupted transaction program after servicing an I/O completion. This is in contrast to an advanced multiprogramming system that commonly uses an I/O event completion as a time to determine what program should be run.

A typical transaction-oriented operating system is *IBM's ACP, Airlines Control Program*. Although it has a history in airlines reservation systems, the system has also been used by many banks for various on-line teller applications. The system has a number of general characteristics that distinguish it from a batch or multiprogramming system.

■   *Close integration of telecommunications capability into the underlying operating system*. The communications control program handles all aspects of teleprocessing as an integrated part of the basic system.

■   *Close integration of database handling with a simplified set of system recording conventions.* The system provides ordinal number record allocation into fixed size areas on disk. In addition, the system offers simple space allocation management of record spaces.

■   *The system offers no control language nor programming development capability in its fundamental elements.* However, an extensive set of testing tools for the debugging of programs in simulated on-line environments is provided.

■   *The heart of the system is a CPU loop program that inspects Ready, Input, and Deferred Queues looking for work.* The Input Queue receives transaction messages. The other queues contain program control blocks that represent programs doing low-priority work, and notices of I/O completions for processing programs. The activity of the CPU loop, looking for work, is started by an interval timer.

■   *A simple run-time environment is provided for invoking the operating system and describing data records.*

■   *Memory allocation is done on demand in fixed-size memory blocks.* Three sizes are available. Provision is made for maximum sharing of code and data by active processing programs.

The system may cohabit with OS/VS through a "*hypervising*" technique that essentially partitions the system into an ACP front end and an OS/VS background system. The ACP interrupt handlers are able to recognize interrupts related to programs running under OS and invoke the hypervisor program to receive them. Control always remains with ACP until the CPU loop has nothing to do. At this time, control passes to the hypervisor that runs OS/VS like an application program. The cohabitation with OS enables ACP to permit concurrent program development in a manner somewhat similar to the background partition of DOS and other small on-line systems.

3.8   MULTIPURPOSE SYSTEMS

During the discussion of the evolution of multiprogramming systems, we encountered the taxonomical problem of the evolution of systems originally designed to be batch systems but that have grown out of their classification in various ways. Thus OS/MVT at the time of its maturity offered on-line database manipulation, conversational program development, and even integrated transaction processing. These capabilities were added to OS/MVT by subsystems that provided specialized run-time environments for programs running within them. Thus OS/MVT provided an extended machine for *TSO* or *IMS* or *CICS* that, in turn, provided extended machines for application programs running in their context. In effect, a series of specialized monitors extended the capability of the batch multiprogramming system. In a sense, MVT became a general-purpose system in this manner. When we discuss concepts of structure in more detail, the problems associated with such extensions will be mentioned.

Within the current meaning of the term "multipurpose," a system must have the attribute that any method of access and any use is supported by the underlying system in a similar manner with similar efficiency. According to this definition, there are probably no truly multipurpose systems. However, there are systems that seem to come close to being multipurpose by virtue of their original design if one excludes database management at the very high DL/1 language level and relaxes the requirement that the system does everything equally well at the same time. Thus OS/MVS is capable of supporting time-sharing (through TSO) and batch in a highly integrated structure controlled by basic elements of the system rather than by specialized monitors. It does not do this, however, for IMS.

Within the concepts of their time, excluding real-time and database management, *UNIVAC's EXEC VIII, IBM's TSS/360* and *Multics* probably come closest to being true multipurpose systems. EXEC VIII even had some features that suggested that the system designers anticipated joint on-line program development (demand processing), transaction processing, and fast turnaround batch usage. All three systems introduced new levels of dynamic resource management, and Multics and TSS introduced concepts of virtual memory as a collection of objects (*segments*) that a program had various rights to address. TSS viewed memory as an *enlarged linear address space* for each user of the system. Both TSS and Multics were primarily intended for on-line use, but each allowed unattended operation in a straightforward manner. EXEC VIII did not introduce virtual memory, but integrated the control of various classes of use (demand, real-time, batch) with an attempt to sustain a policy-driven proportion of systems services going to each class.

The concept of a multipurpose operating system may imply less function rather than more function. Some designers feel that a set of common basic building blocks, each representing a defined primitive operation, should be made available for end users to construct operating systems of various kinds, avoiding, if possible, fixed structural relationships in these building blocks.

What is probably most useful about the concept of general-purpose or multipurpose is the way we have failed to achieve it. However fast our ambitions grow, the new kinds of demands grow more rapidly. This is not a small problem in the real world of systems development in which decisions must constantly be made about how to market systems, when to extend old systems, when to restructure old systems, and when to undertake new ones. Given requirements of performance, efficiency, and function on one side, and of compatibility on the other, in the constant atmosphere of change and competition, choices of design are not easy to make.

Section 3.9 introduces a new set of considerations for operating system designs, and Section 3.10 summarizes those factors that influence design.

3.9   NETWORKING AND DISTRIBUTION

The concept of *networking* or *distributed computing* was introduced in the discussion of real-time systems. A system composed of multiple *computing nodes* is common to such environments. The multiple computing nodes may exist solely to provide reliability, or each node may be allocated a particular set of application functions that together form the total application. A characteristic of the pure multinode reliability system is that the operating system at each node, the application programs at each node, and the data at each node are essentially replications of these elements at another node.

When functional specialization is designed into a real-time system, it is possible that the hardware at each node will be configured to give optimum support of the local function. These configurations may be such that different operating systems are required at each node. This may be because a node is too small to support a full operating system, or because each node contains hardware from different vendors. In application situations in which all functions are well known and predefined, the communication between nodes may be thought of as an application responsibility in the same way that interprocess coordination may be thought of as an application responsibility in a single node. In more general environments, however, it becomes desirable for operating systems to talk to other operating systems and to provide system-to-system interaction functions for applications running on more than one computer.

Both transaction-oriented systems and batch systems may become involved in networking situations or in multicomputer distribution of function. An alternative to the close integration of teleprocessing support found in ACP is the *MVS/NCP* structure of IBM 370/168s and other IBM processors of that class (3033) running OS/MVS. In these systems, the concept of *network control*, the interface to remote terminals or satellite controllers (e.g., IBM 3790s) is removed to a front-end processor (3704, 3705) which offloads from MVS the requirement for physical control of remote devices. The 370x runs under a small monitor called *NCP* (*Network Control Program*) that has a specified interface to a teleprocessing handler function of MVS called *VTAM,* the *Virtual Telecommunications Access Method.* The essence of this arrangement is the offloading of certain functions from a host system onto an associated support machine.

This concept can be extended, of course, so that the front end becomes considerably more powerful than a *network controller.* It would be possible to provide a variety of operating systems services in a front-end machine including spooling, time-sharing services such as program editing and compilation, system scheduling, and even some application functions. Similarly, it is possible to conceive of back-end machines that offload data management functions to data management operating systems. All of the permutations of function suggested earlier when we discussed various microprocessor and microprogram support of operating systems are conceivable in the relationships between complete computer systems. There is the added dimension that application functions, data, and various degrees of local and system control can be distributed geographically between systems.

Batch systems may also be organized into networks that permit a job submitted anywhere in the system to be sent to a node in which appropriate data exists or in which there is greater availability of computer resource. IBM's *JES* (*Job Entry Subsystem*) extensions to its operating systems provide such networking capability.

There is a subtle and not always easily recognized difference between networking and distributed processing. In general, networking suggests a high degree of autonomy between computers. It implies that each computer is a multipurpose system capable of stand-alone operation that

■   offers specific functions to users of the network, serving as a point where particular kinds of processing functions are performed (for example, particularly fast vector arithmetic at a node in the network occupied by an ILLIAC IV class machine);

■   offers a load-balancing capability for a collection of processors;

■   offers a particular kind of service, such as fast FORTRAN compile/load/go.

Distributed computing or distributed processing suggests that a single application has been organized to spread across a family of computers such that some computers perform only certain application functions, or specific partitions of data are allocated to each computer. In general, the relationship between computers is closer, the instances of interaction more frequent, and the reliance of one system on another more intense. Actually, the industry lacks a rigorous taxonomy for distinguishing between systems of computers and distributed computer systems.

There are several fundamental operating systems issues associated with networking and distribution. At this moment, the questions of system-to-system communication have been answered primarily by adding communications executives to existing operating systems that allow them to talk to replications of themselves or to specific selected operating systems usually produced by the same vendor. Thus, for example, *DEC's DECNET* provides for communication between various DEC operating systems running on PDP 11 architectures. Hewlett-Packard provides for communication between RTE A, RTE B and RTE II to form a multipurpose time-sharing, real-time, and high-function central system in a hierarchic structure.

Some workers in the field suspect that the requirements of distribution and networking will eventually cause serious changes in the underlying structure of operating systems. This will occur in order to provide an environment for applications that will relieve them of the necessity for knowing where in the distributed system a particular piece of data is or where a particular program is. In order to provide this kind of transparency, run-time macros like OPEN or GET will require an ability to go to geographically remote locations to retrieve requested data. The question of what an operating system is is made more complicated when a total single system concept is spread across multiple machines. These issues will be addressed again later.

3.10   INFLUENCES ON DESIGN

We have suggested that hardware architecture influences the design of operating systems. Concepts of memory addressing, privilege, protection, interrupt handling, and microprogramming affect a designer's view of what operating systems function and structure might be appropriate for a hardware system. Again, in this chapter, the issue of richness of function as a response to machine size has been raised. In the face of so many kinds of operating systems, it might be useful to discuss the influences on design with a little more detail.

The job of operating systems design is to present a machine to users. In order to do this a designer must

■   determine the nature of hardware and develop ways to correct hardware weaknesses and enhance strengths;

■   understand the environment in which systems will be used, including the nature of using organizations, their missions, and the demography of users;

■   understand the state of the art of the time during which the system will be used in order to provide orderly extensibility and growth. Particularly, the designer must be aware of what the universities and competitive vendors are undertaking.

3.11   UNDERSTANDING A MACHINE

An unavoidable question is: To what extent should software design influence hardward design? Some idealists claim that software should be specified first and then hardware developed to run the software well. Since software defines the user interfaces that make a system desirable, it is obvious, to some, that software should define the system that is to be brought to the market. In doing this, it will be possible to negotiate proper hardware/software trade-offs, avoid undersupport of software function, and avoid irrelevant overdesign of hardware. An example of overdesign is the implementation of instructions that will never be generated by the compilers of the software system.

Such an approach is very difficult in general-purpose systems because of the difficulty of crisply specifying general-purpose interfaces, and the difficulty of determining the feasibility of function when no hardware base has been defined. There tends to be a kind of *software lag* in systems design. Even when developers wish to coordinate hardware and software development, the hardware invariably gets ahead. The result of this is that software designers are usually confronted with a reasonably solid hardware design to which they must react. There will invariably be some negotiation, particularly in areas of interrupt definition, task switch support, memory management, and the splits between firmware and software.

3.11.1 Checklists

The following checklists of hardware attributes are useful in trying to assess the nature of a machine.

Interrupt Mechanism

- Does the interrupt mechanism suggest the machine will be efficient in event-driven environments because of multiple interrupt levels or multiple entry points at the same level?

- What is the requirement for register save/restore for each interrupt?

- How much time does it take to determine the cause of any interrupt?

Answers to these questions will indicate to what extent this system should be oriented to application environments with high interrupt rates, and to what extent the system itself can or should use the interrupt mechanism in going from function to function on an event or timed basis.

Instruction set

- Does the machine have a general-purpose instruction set suitable for commercial and scientific use?

- Is there some bias in the set that implies a particular use such as a communications controller?

- Is the instruction set sufficiently high level so that a particular programming language and its syntax and semantics are implied by the machine?

- What are the details of privileged and nonprivileged instructions?

The instruction set implies what the nature of good applications for the hardware will be and what programming languages will be appropriate for the machine.

Cost/Performance

- Is this system sufficiently expensive so that it is desirable to support consolidated work-load environments?
- Will typical applications fail to consume significant resources of this system?
- What percentage of the resources of the system can profitably be withdrawn in the interests of advanced resource management?

Distribution

- How many things can go on at the same time? I/O-CPU overlap, multiple I/O overlap, multiple CPU-I/O overlap, specialized processor overlap? To what extent should the system be viewed as a set of asynchronous functions?
- Are I/O and storage management clearly distinguished on the machine? Does a class of I/O device become visible, or may all storage devices be treated in a single-level hierarchy?

Configurability

- What is the minimum system that must be supported?
- What is the maximum system?
- What techniques for parameterization and/or version definition are suggested by variations in configuration? Should there be a family of operating systems?

3.12 KNOWING THE USER

An understanding of the environment involves answering the following questions:

What kinds of work loads are to be brought to the machine? large jobs of high value? small jobs of high value? jobs of low individual value? What kinds of access capabilities will be desirable?

What kind of support will surround the system? Will it be in a large data processing center? Will it be associated with an operational department lacking professional expertise? Will it be closely linked to other machines?

What kinds of professional expenses are permissible? Will there be professional operators? professional systems programmers? How much money can be spent for training?

What compatibility requirements exist for previous machines or for coexisting machines? Is it necessary to read each other's data? compile same languages? preserve Job Control Language? preserve run-time interfaces?

3.13 THE STATE OF THE ART

An appreciation of the state of the art involves a knowledge of what competitors and universities are doing. Particularly, we need to know whether (1) competitors have announced new capabilities that imply new insights into market definitions. Have they developed a new kind of operating system? (2) Have competitors combined functions in a way that implies some different concept of systems structure? (3) Does university literature indicate some advance in concepts of structure or design methodology? (4) Have new insights into classical trade-off problems been achieved? (5) Have extensions of function previously thought not to be feasible been shown to be feasible?

The interplay of machine influence, user environment, and state of the art will determine what kinds of operating systems will exist at various times, and what the general nature of each kind may be. The emphasis will change over time. New functions will emerge; new structures will be undertaken. There will be periods when the products are stable and attention is focused on design and implementation methodology. Undertaking the design of a major operating system is an enormous task. The task of designing an operating system with a working life of more than five years over which it must service thousands of users is awesome.

ABBREVIATIONS, MACHINES, LANGUAGES, STATEMENTS, AND KEYWORDS

ACP	DOS POWER
Autocoder	DOS/VS
BMEWS	FMS
CHAIN	FORTRAN
CICS	GECOS
CLOSE	GET
COBOL	IBM 370/168
COGO	IBM 709
CTSS at MIT	IBM 1401
Dartmouth BASIC	IBM 7070
Data General NOVA	IBM OS/360
DEC PDP-11	IBM Series I
DECNET	IBM System 7
DL/1	IBSYS/IBJOB for 7094

IMS	SCOPE
IOCS	SDC Q-32
JES	SEEK
LSI 11	SYSIN
MCP	SYSOUT
Multics	TI 990
MVS/NCP	TSO
OPEN	TSS/370
OS/MFT	UCB
OS/MVS	UNIVAC III
OS/MVT	UNIVAC 418
PUT	UNIVAC 1107
QUICKTRAN	UNIVAC 1108
SACCS	UNIVAC EXEC II
SAGE	UNIX
SCAN	VTAM

TERMINOLOGY

advanced batch multiprogramming

asynchronism

back-end processor

background

basic multiprogramming

batch operating system

batch single-stream system

binding loader

blocking/deblocking

buffer control

collecting loader

cooperating processes

cooperative

CPU multiplexing

cross-assembler

cross-compiler

device independence

disk storage

dispatching queue

distributed computing

dynamic memory management

encapsulation of a machine

event-driven design

fixed length records

foreground

Fortran Monitor System

front-end processor

hypervisor

industrial process control

inquiry system

internalized job queue

interrupt

I/O interrupt

I/O management

Job Entry Subsystem

linking loader

main chain

main frame

memory limited

memory management

memory partition

message buffer

meta-assembler

military command/control

monitor

multiprogramming mix

multipurpose operating system

multitasking

Network Control Program

network operating system

networking

off-line printer

off-line satellite computer

on-line

operator-driven partitioning

overlay

paging

personal computing system

prepartitioning

print-bound

privilege

process-driven design

processor management

producer–consumer relationship

programmer's workbench

protection

queue-driven design

real-time environment

real-time operating system

record format

relocatable assembly

relocatable compilation

relocation

resident in memory

segmentation

software lag

spooling

symbiont

symbolic device assignment

task

thruput

time-sharing operating system

transaction processing system

turnaround time

Unit Availability Table

Unit Control Block

Unit Function Table

utilization of equipment

variable length records

virtual memory

Virtual Telecommunications Access
    Method

EXERCISES

Section 3.1

3.1 Distinguish between "large" machine and "small" machine operating systems.

3.2 Distinguish between multitasking and multiprogramming.

3.3 Discuss briefly each of the following types of operating systems.

   a) real-time

   b) batch

   c) time-sharing

   d) multipurpose

Section 3.2

3.4 What is a real-time environment?

3.5 In a real-time environment, utilization of equipment is less important than responsiveness to the environment. Explain.

3.6 Discuss five applications of real-time systems.

Section 3.3

3.7 Distinguish between queue-driven design and process-driven design.

3.8 What is a cross-assembler? What is a meta-assembler?

3.9 In a real-time system, what applications tend to be run in foreground? What applications tend to be run in background?

3.10 What is a task?

Section 3.4

3.11 What is batch?

3.12 Discuss briefly the following classes of batch systems.

   a) single stream

   b) basic multiprogramming

   c) advanced multiprogramming

Section 3.5

3.13 Briefly discuss each of the following concepts of contemporary systems.

   a) control stream

   b) I/O support at high macro levels

   c) program relocation

   d) device independence

   e) "encapsulation" of a machine by its operating system

3.14 What is a collecting loader?

3.15 Discuss spooling.

3.16 What is a "main chain"?

3.17 A usual characteristic of spooling is that the file being printed belongs to a previously completed main chain.

    a) Explain the statement above.

    b) How does this characteristic of spooling affect job turnaround time and thruput?

    c) Suppose it is desired to be able to print a file as it is produced by a running main chain. What design changes might be needed in the operating system? How would job turnaround and thruput be affected?

3.18 Discuss each of the following in the context of spooling systems.

    a) OS/360

    b) EXEC II for UNIVAC 1107

    c) IBM MVS

    d) symbiont

    e) producer/consumer relationship

    f) shared buffer file

    g) message buffer

    h) cooperating processes

    i) cooperative

Section 3.6

3.19 State three ways in which the emergence of disk storage in the late 1950s affected operating systems development.

3.20 Explain each of the following attributes of basic multiprogramming systems.

    a) a good deal of off-line scheduling is required

    b) conservative memory management
      i) memory partitions defined by human operators
      ii) memory partitions have long duration

    c) CPU multiplexing managed with only minimal effort at balancing resource usage

    d) data sets and devices tend to be associated with a program for the entire life of the program

3.21 Explain the following statement in the context of IBM's DOS (Disk Operating System).

    "In effect, the system defined multiple independent machines that were scheduled independently but could share devices and the use of the CPU."

3.22 How did the emergence of the concept of "internalized job queue" affect the development of basic multiprogramming operating systems?

3.23 Explain how prepartitioning memory can result in significant waste of computing resources.

3.24 What does it mean for a system to be "memory limited"?

3.25 Briefly describe each of the following advances in small batch systems.

    a) operator-driven partition redefinition

    b) relocatable assembly and compilation

    c) symbolic (or "generic") device assignment

    d) the ability to organize an application program as a structure of tasks

    e) support of virtual memory

    f) centralized spooling capability

3.26 Discuss each of the following capabilities of advanced batch multiprogramming systems.

    a) dynamic memory management

    b) sharing code other than in the operating system

    c) support of disk devices as on-line repositories of data

    d) elaboration of the structure for job submission

    e) decreased reliance on operator activity

    f) elaboration of the mechanisms for CPU allocation

Section 3.7

3.27 What is the essential goal of a time-sharing system?

3.28 Why is effective utilization of hardware less important in time-sharing systems than in batch multiprogramming systems?

3.29 What is a "programmer's workbench"?

3.30 Briefly discuss UNIX.

3.31 What is a transaction processing system?

3.32 Discuss each of the following characteristics of transaction processing systems.

    a) close integration of telecommunications capability into the underlying operating system

    b) close integration of database handling with a simplified set of system recording conventions

    c) no control language

    d) no programming development capability

    e) heart of the system is a CPU loop that looks for work

    f) simple run-time environment

    g) memory allocation on demand

3.33 What is hypervising?

Section 3.8

3.34 What criteria do we ascribe to multipurpose systems?

Section 3.9

3.35 What are the differences between networking and distributed processing?

Section 3.11

3.36 What aspects of a machine's interrupt mechanism indicate how useful the machine will be in environments with high interrupt rates?

3.37 How does a machine's instruction set influence the choice of applications for the machine?

3.38 Can high-level language programming ultimately disguise inadequacies in a machine's instruction set?

4
Structural Issues in Operating Systems

4.1 SYSTEMS CONCEPTS

At this point in the text, it is useful to explore the abstract notion of a system before continuing with the discussion of operating systems structure. *A system is a set of objects and a set of relationships between the objects.* The properties of a system are derived from the attributes of the objects, and the nature of the relations between them.

The various systems of the human anatomy form a single larger system, and there are relationships among systems so that they are properly subsystems of a single larger structure. A common criticism of medical practice is its general naivete about the relationships between the classically defined subsystems of the body.

A system may be defined by a particular attribute that one desires to study. Thus from the complex set of objects and relationships involved in a system called an ''urban center,'' special systems such as ''traffic flow'' and ''educational services delivery'' can be defined and studied. The problem with defining special systems for study is to make sure that all of the relevant objects and relationships have been selected and well defined so that the system is well defined. Systems dynamics and ecology stress the system view of the world in a way that stresses the discovery of the interrelationships among objects.

An operating system is a set of objects and a set of relationships among the objects. The description of objects and relations is a description of the structure of the system.

As with any system, care must be taken to select the right objects into the foreground. If this isn't done, important attributes of the system may be excluded from view. What is particularly true of operating systems is that there is no generally agreed upon set of objects, and no generally agreed upon set of relationships. However, there are many common elements that enable one to explore operating systems as systems.

4.2   A TIME-DIVISION APPROACH TO OPERATING SYSTEMS STRUCTURE

A useful way of observing the structure of an operating system is by monitoring the flow of a unit of work through the computer. There are definite stages. Consider the following "times."

- *request time*
- *select time*
- *compilation time*
- *combination time*
- *activation time*
- *run time*
- *postrun time*

These times may be associated with all types of operating systems whether batch or on-line. The specific events associated with each time, the number of discretely defined times, and the visibility of various times affect system flexibility. In effect, they define the flow of work into, through, and out of the computer.

4.3   SYSTEMS SERVICES AND WORKER PROGRAMS

Any operating system has a set of systems services that operate in order to prepare for the running of a particular program. The control stream processor invokes functions that prepare a program to operate and prepare the system for the operation of the program. On the other hand, the run-time services are summoned through the run-time macro languages. The strong division between prerun-time and run-time systems services is emphasized by two different language interfaces.

The programs that provide the prerun-time services may be organized into components that operate as independent *worker programs*. This is characteristic of compilers and also of linkage editors that organize independently compiled programs into a single program. As independent programs, each of the prerun-time service programs has the loosest kind of association with the operating system. They are not often included as operating system functions by workers who think of operating systems as sets of programs that have specially designed relationships with each other distinct from their relationships with user programs.

4.4   REQUEST TIME

It is worthwhile to inspect the times we have defined in a little more detail. *Request time is the time at which a user requests the attention of the system.* On batch systems, it is the time that a control deck is entered into the system. To the user, request time is the time that the deck is submitted to the data center. The relationship between the user, the data center, and the machine system may be such that there is a delay between submitting work to the data center and submitting work to the machine system. Contemporary operating systems commonly provide some form of direct submission through a remote card reader or through a terminal. If request is made through an interactive terminal, there are a number of structural details that determine whether the moment of request is the moment of signing on to the system or a later moment when a stream of work is submitted during a terminal session.

4.5   SELECT TIME

Select time is the time at which the system determines to postpone or grant attention to the request. It may grant or deny service because of competing priorities or because of some appreciation of the load on the system. The input to the select mechanism is the output of the request mechanism. In a third-generation batch system, requests are handled by a request receiver that forms entries on an internal queue. This internal queue is the input to the select mechanism. The receive mechanism is commonly called a *reader* or a *command interpreter*, the select mechanism is commonly called a *scheduler*.

4.6   COMPILE TIME

Compile time is, of course, the time during which a source program is merely data input to a mechanism that translates it into a form closer to that required by the run-time mechanisms of the system. The output of a compiler is input to a program combiner. Other inputs to a program combiner are already compiled programs selected from a program library and the *combiner control language*. The combiner control language specifies what programs are to be combined with the program just compiled, and where these programs can be found. The output of the combiner is a structure that is ready for activation.

4.7   ACTIVATION TIME

Activation time is the period during which actions are taken to start a program. These actions may include the allocation of devices for I/O, the allocation of data sets, and the allocation of memory locations. Perhaps more than any other "time," activation time determines the flavor of a system in terms of its flexibility, complexity, and the relationship between prerun-time and run-time concepts. To the extent that allocation decisions are moved forward, a system becomes less flexible. To the extent that allocation decisions are delayed, perhaps even moved to run time, a system becomes more flexible, but at the expense of potential overhead in the run-time environment.

4.8   RUN TIME

Run time is the period during which the program is said to be active in the system. In single-stream batch systems, run time is a contiguous interval in *wall clock time* during which the program performs its operations until conclusion. In multiprogramming systems and time-sharing systems, run time is the interval during which a program is represented in the system by a formalized system element representing the status and capability of program. This element is formed by the activator to represent the program in the system. It is called, variously, a *TCB* (*task control block*), *control point, process activation record, process control block,* etc. It represents the existence of the program in the system and its ability, desire, and (sometimes) history of use of the system. In multiprogramming and time-sharing systems, there are periods of time between activation and completion during which the program is not using any resource of the system, or is not using the CPU resource. In time-sharing systems, this system element may not represent a particular program but rather a particular terminal user.

It is during run time that a program is a user of the operating system's extended machine, the collection of services made available by components of the operating system most commonly understood to form the system. It is the internal structure of the *run-time environment* itself that attracts the bulk of interest from workers in the operating system design area.

4.9   POSTRUN TIME

Postrun time is the period during which the system undertakes to ''flush'' a completed program. The resources used by the program are retrieved from it and made accessible to other programs. In some systems, it is the time during which output produced by the program is printed or punched.

4.10   SYSTEMS SERVICES AND PRIVILEGE

There is a problem with our definition of times, and in the concept of prerun-time services being themselves worker programs. If the compiler is a worker program, it itself must experience the sequence of request, select, combine, activate, run, and postrun times. This leads to the simple observation that compile and combine must be deletable times in the sequence of times. This must also be true, of course, because there will be programs already compiled and/or combined that a user wishes to request, select, activate, and run.

A further problem exists. If the request, select, and activate functions are themselves merely worker programs, how are they to be requested, selected, activated, and run? One solution to this problem, of course, is to have an operator who forces selection and activation of the request, receive, select, and activation mechanisms so they are then continuously represented by an activation record in the run-time environment. They may be dormant until a programmer control stream becomes available to the system, but they are ready to run when work arrives. This is a common solution, and basically what is meant by *starting a reader* or *starting an initiator* in IBM's OS systems.

But it is also common to perceive that request, receive, select, and activation are truly systems-wide functions that have a relationship with the total system differing somewhat from that of the compiler and combiner. This different relationship is reflected in the need for these mechanisms to have access to tables and files that are not accessible to any worker program. These special rights of accessibility derive from the need for these mechanisms to know what resources of the system are available, and to gain access to queues that worker programs cannot be allowed to manipulate. This different relationship can be reflected by not permitting programs other than these mechanisms to access certain key system files; that is, no other program can ask for allocation of these files or perform OPENs and GETs to them. The special relationship may be reflected in more important ways such as always guaranteeing core space for them, or running them at special systems-level priorities, or even providing them greater privileges in the run-time environment. These extended privileges might include the ability to directly refer to memory locations not allocated to user programs, or to enter the service functions at lower levels to avoid some of the overhead of common entry. This overhead includes, for example, checking the correctness and legitimacy of a request submitted by a program.

The difference in status between a compiler and activator is commonly reflected in the control language. A control stream explicitly calls for the execution of the compiler or combiner, for its own problem programs, and for a set of utilities like sort or copy. It usually receives the services of request, receive, select, and activate implicitly because of the mere submission of the control stream.

4.11 SINGLE-TIME SYSTEMS

Since the prerun-time services may be made implicit, they can be performed at a number of different points along the path to entering the run-time environment.

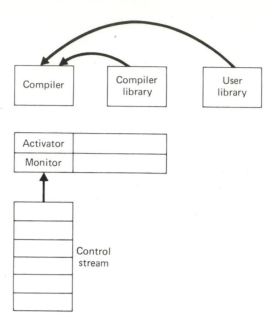

Fig. 4.1 Simplest times in simplest structure. Monitor recognizes control stream. Compiler processes data and device requests. Activator calls in first record; the rest is "self-loading."

Consider the simplest conceivable environment in which an operating system hardly exists at all.

It is possible to collapse nearly all the functions of all the times into a compiler. Request time might be serviced by an operator or by a simple resident monitor program that calls a compiler or a user program depending on whether the control stream names a compiler for a worker program. The compiler is capable not only of making all memory assignments but also of making all device assignments in such a way that real fixed memory addresses and real fixed device addresses are compiled into the program. The output of such a compiler would be directly executable. Necessary waits for mounting could be compiled into the program and even all run-time functions could be compiled into the program. Programs that are to be combined with the program to be compiled might be combined by recompilation, or by giving the compiler access to a library of precompiled routines used in much the same way as most compilers use the libraries of functions made available through the compiler languages. Activation is merely the act of loading a program put into absolute machine form by the compiler. "Self-loading" decks or files were a common feature of early systems. Figure 4.1 shows the simplicity of such a system.

The disadvantages of such a system, of course, lie in its inflexibility, and in the inability of programs written in one language to be combined with programs in another. The inflexibility comes from the early assignment of devices and memory. In order to overcome this, the concept of separate times expanded into what we are used to now. It is interesting to speculate about the structural evolution of operating systems if the concept of relocatable paging mechanisms had been developed sooner. It would be perfectly possible to multiprogram and time-share without all of the times and distribution of function that are currently employed if early designers understood that absolute code produced during compilation could be relocated by run-time mechanisms making it reasonable to go directly from compile time to run time.

4.12   UNIVERSAL COMPUTER-ORIENTED LANGUAGE

The idea of distinct "combine–activate" time (or link and load time) as a significant and definable time emerges from the desire to delay the *binding* of programs to devices, data sets, and memory locations and to facilitate the combining of programs written in different languages.

There is an interesting stop along the way. Part of the motivation for separate combine–activate time is to allow combination of programs from different source languages. The idea of having the compilers reduce programs to a common form that agrees about such things as *register conventions, subroutine linkages,* and *parameter passing procedures* was first represented by the idea of an *UNCOL,* a *Universal Computer-oriented Language.*

UNCOL represented an attempt to define an intermediate compiler form at which all compilers would aim. The UNCOL form was to be translated into machine form by a single translation mechanism. The motive behind this, of course, was to facilitate the construction of compilers for new or specialized languages. There was an associated idea of being able to develop languages for new machines by simply writing an UNCOL back end for any new architecture.

An initial approximation of the UNCOL idea was the use of the system assembler as the target for compilation. The attraction of this idea was in the use of an assembler library for I/O functions, and other routines. The dream of a common library for all programming languages has never been achieved, and each compiler still has an associated private library of functions unique to it. The use of the assembler as an intermediate point simply does not work efficiently in the dynamics of compilation and assembly. Also, a truly general UNCOL has never been achieved.

4.13 LOAD TIME

An early division of times was the emergence of a significant *load time*. Load
time initially included selection time and activate time.

Selection time was the first occasion on which the monitor saw a call for
execution or was notified of the completion of the compiler. The loader was
summoned to load the object program into memory. As part of loading, the
program was allocated, and devices and previously compiled programs were
linked to the program being loaded.

Programs included in a compiler library were moved into the loader library
and the loader became responsible for supplying basic I/O device handling
routines.

A feature of the loader was *relocatability, the ability to place a program in
any selected set of contiguous locations in memory*. The loader had to be able to
combine separately compiled programs as part of a continuous linear space. In
addition, the I/O support routines had to be relocatable since they would occupy
different locations depending on exactly what I/O devices were being used and
the size of the user program.

Compilers now produce relocatable programs and symbolic device assignments. The compiler output includes a set of load directives indicating what
programs are to be combined at load time, and what symbolic I/O files need
device assignment. The final stage of loading places the program in memory, and
transfers control to it.

The existence of a loader of such functions requires the elaboration of the
monitor so that it includes a set of tables representing available system resources,
and a set of control blocks representing the association of symbolic file names
with real device names. Although the resource availability tables might be kept
in a file for reference only during load time or postrun-time cleanup, the control
blocks are part of run time. Whenever a program references an I/O file, the control
blocks must be referenced in order to obtain a specific device address.

4.14 LINK–EDIT TIME

A further development of prerun-time structure came from elaboration of load-
time functions to include a distinct *link–edit time* (combine time) preceding
activate time. The user program combine capability was extended so that a set of
programs could be combined independently of allocation and activation. The
capability of a combiner was extended to include more sophisticated part selection and inclusion functions. Only the output of the link editor is submitted to
activate time.

Activate time itself became more than load time. The allocation of data sets
and devices was separated from the allocation of memory locations. The alloca-

tion of memory locations was separated from loading a program into selected memory locations.

4.15 ALLOCATORS

The need for an allocator function developed in the presence of a wide variety of different kinds of resources. The allocation function may be kept simple with the notion of an activator that receives a program from a scheduler and assigns resources to it. When allocation is accomplished, the program is turned over to the loader.

There is an alternative notion that involves a concept of a set of allocators each associated with a particular kind or class of resource. Activation time then becomes the time that it takes to execute all of the allocators on behalf of a program. Thus a program moves from *data set allocation* to *device allocation* to *memory allocation*.

Each one of these allocators must have access to tables reflecting the availability of particular resources. The idea of a program with ''arm's length'' relationship to the operating system decomposes into the idea of a set of transient allocation functions running as extensions to the monitor.

Two questions come to mind. If the allocators are a family of monitor functions, who calls them? If they can be called, then can they be called at any time? The answer to the first question addresses the issue of the relationship of select time and activate time. The select mechanism, after determining which program it wishes to start, is a likely mechanism to call for allocation for the selected program. This design collapses select time and activate time into a single time. The structural relationship between initiators and allocators in OS/MVT is defined in this way.

Between a system that makes all allocation decisions at the front end and a system that makes no front-end decisions, there are many choices. In any particular system, designers must choose when it is appropriate to bind a program to another program, to bind a program to devices, and to bind a program to particular memory locations.

4.16 SUBSYSTEMS

Certain prerun-time systems services may be combined into conceptually distinct subsets of capabilities, i.e., *subsystems*. A compiler, for example, may have a particular editor, a particular combiner, and a particular loader associated with it. The user of that compiler views the computer system through this collection of associated elements. The BASIC subsystem in Multics is such a subsystem.

Any set of prerun-time services may be organized to form a subsystem. For example, request receipt, spooling, selection, and activation may be combined

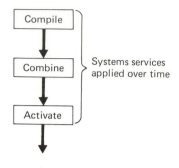

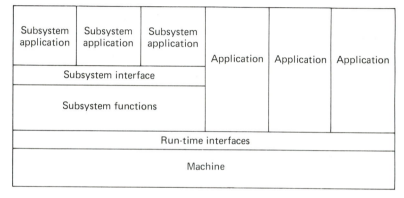

Fig. 4.2 Subsystems and systems services.

into a single component distinct from the run-time environment. JES (OS) and POWER (DOS) are subsystems of this type.

The concept of a subsystem also intersects with the concept of the run-time environment. A subsystem may present an enhanced set of run-time interfaces. This is a unique set of enriched macro services packaged to facilitate running programs that require them without burdening programs that do not require them.

Figure 4.2 shows a conceptual structural overview at the level of discussion so far. The figure suggests a mix of application programs that interface to the run-time environment, and that have been staged through a sequence of times. In addition, there is a set of programs that are using specialized interfaces associated with a subsystem that has been brought into the machine in order to service the programs compiled for, or written to, the subsystem interfaces.

TERMINOLOGY

activation time   allocation of I/O devices

allocation of data sets   allocation of memory locations

BASIC subsystem in Multics

binding programs to devices

combination time

combiner control language

command interpreter

compilation time

control language

control point

control stream

"flush" a completed program

link–edit time

load time

parameter passing procedures

postrun time

process activation record

process control block

program combiner

program library

reader

register conventions

relocatability

request time

run time

run-time environment

scheduler

select time

"self-loading" deck or file

starting a reader

starting an initiator

subsystem

system

TCB—Task Control Block

UNCOL

wall clock time

EXERCISES

Section 4.1

4.1 What is a system?

Section 4.2

4.2 A useful way of observing the structure of an operating system is by monitoring the flow of a unit of work through the computer. Discuss the various stages in the flow of work through a batch single-stream system.

Section 4.3

4.3 Why are prerun-time service programs such as compilers and linkage editors often not categorized as operating system functions?

Section 4.4

4.4 Discuss request time in the context of a time-sharing system.

Section 4.5

4.5 Distinguish between request reception and selection.

Section 4.6

4.6 When a user submits a request to a computer system for execution of an already compiled program, compile time is deleted from the sequence of times through which a unit of work flows. Comment on the validity of this statement.

Section 4.7

4.7 Perhaps more than any other "time," activation time determines the flavor of a system in terms of its flexibility, complexity, and the relationship between prerun-time and run-time concepts. Explain.

Section 4.8

4.8 What is a process control block? List several items of information that might be placed in a process control block.

Section 4.9

4.9 What does it mean to "flush" a completed program from a computer system?

Section 4.10

4.10 Why do systems services normally have more privileges than worker programs?

Section 4.11

4.11 Discuss how it is possible to collapse nearly all the functions of all the "times" into a compiler.

Section 4.12

4.12 What is an UNCOL?

4.13 Why, do you suppose, has the UNCOL idea never been achieved?

Section 4.13

4.14 Why do I/O support routines, and library routines in general, need to be relocatable?

Section 4.14

4.15 Explain the advantages of having a distinct link–edit time.

Section 4.15

4.16 What is an allocator?

Section 4.16

4.17 What is a subsystem?

5

The
Run-Time
Environment

5.1 THE NATURE OF THE RUN-TIME FUNCTION

This chapter discusses the structure of the *run-time environment*. It introduces the notions of *processes, primitives,* and the relationships between application programs and the run-time environment. In this section we discuss the nature of the run-time environment and the sources of its functions.

In the run-time environment, a set of capabilities not defined in the operation codes of the machine is made accessible to running programs almost as though these capabilities are part of the operation codes. In addition, there are functions that support the coordination of programs in multiprogramming or time-sharing environments. These functions include *privileged operations* and *memory protection.*

The elements of the run-time environment can be characterized in a number of ways. Some elements are explicit and others are implicit. An *explicit element* is one that operates because it is explicitly called for by a program. The GET macro is an example of this. An *implicit element* operates without a formal call because of the need to coordinate the *multiprogramming mix.* For example, the decision to take processor control away from a program because a system clock has run down is an implicit function of the run-time environment. Certain underlying functions may be both implicit and explicit. They may operate at the request of a program, as the indirect result of a program request, or at the discretion of the system. For example, the function *WAIT,* which causes a program to lose control of the processor, may be made available to a program that wishes to voluntarily release control. It can operate because a GET statement finds a depleted buffer and the system decides to put the requesting program to *sleep,* or it can operate because the system decides to help meet its scheduling goals by quieting a running program.

Another characterization of elements of the run-time environment is by the permanence of residence in storage. This reflects the observation that even within those elements that have been brought into run time, there are differing levels of intensity of use and need for fast accessibility. Just as the dynamics of a system can be inferred from what is available at run time, a finer appreciation of dynamics can be inferred from what functions are permanently in storage, what functions are *transient* but preallocated to particular memory locations for fast load, what functions are relocatable within a particular area, and what functions are relocatable anywhere in the system. Those permanent, *wired-down* elements of the run-time environment that are sometimes called the kernel are really extensions of basic machine architecture and are dropping into microcode in recent hardware designs.

Closely related to residence is the basis upon which functions run. This concept has two components, *contiguity* and *initiation. Initiation refers to the way the function is started.* A function may be started by direct transfer such as a branch or subroutine link. A function may also be started by enqueueing it on a queue of active programs representing the multiprogramming mix. Some systems provide a special fast service queue for operating system run-time functions. Those functions that are truly time critical are characteristically resident and startable by direct transfer. This direct transfer must be from another routine in the run-time environment that has the necessary privilege to make the transfer.

Contiguity concerns the degree to which a function is guaranteed control over the system. Some critical functions must be *uninterruptible.* This means that the interrupt mechanism of the hardware cannot operate until the function decides to allow it. Certain kernel functions run in this manner because it is necessary to guarantee contiguous control over the machine to assure quick completion or because an interrupt before completion may disrupt the integrity of the system. In general *it is wise to design in such a way as to minimize the time that a system is disabled for interrupts*.

A final interesting categorization of run-time functions is by their source. Three general kinds of run-time functions can be perceived.

- Those functions common to several application programs.
- Those functions brought into the run-time environment from systems service components in order to increase flexibility.
- Those functions appropriate to the multiprogramming environment and beyond the ken of an individual program.

Using a hardware machine analog, the functions taken from programs might be thought of as extensions to the instruction set, and the multiprogramming

functions as extensions to the control mechanism of instruction counter, instruction register, etc. The operating system sequences through programs as a
machine system sequences through instructions.

5.1.1 Functions from Application Programs

There are certain operations in programs that seem to be common. The recognition of those common functions led very early to the definition of *macros* that
eliminated the need for programming the functions, and provided selected or
generated elements from a library to perform the functions. Early systems caused
these contributed functions to be generated into the program, enlarging the
program's requirement for space, and requiring the function to be loaded
whenever the program was loaded. By defining a very basic set of common code,
and making it resident in the machine, compilation, linkage, and load times
could be shortened. The concept of a resident package in a single-stream
machine derives from this ability to shorten front-end processes.

In multiprogramming and time-sharing systems, the existence of a set of
shared common functions suggests that each program will be smaller since one
set of code will be shared by many programs in the mix. As a consequence, *more
programs or larger programs can share the machine.*

Which functions should be brought into the run-time environment and which
functions should be generated into a program? In general those functions that
have the greatest commonality, and consequently the greatest probability of
being used by more than one program in a multiprogramming or time-sharing
mix, should be brought into the run-time environment. Those functions that will
coordinate the use of resources shared between programs that are not aware of
each other's presence must be brought into the run-time environment.

5.1.2 Functions from Systems Services

As systems have enhanced their objectives for flexibility, many functions have
been moved into the run-time environment from the prerun-time environment.
This is particularly true of the relationships between a program and resources,
and a program and other programs.

The movement of function represents a delay in binding time, a postpone-
ment of allocation decisions, and a repeatability of allocation decisions through
the life of the program.

Consequently, programs have run-time macros that permit requests for the
acquisition of additional memory space, the execution of completely independent
program modules that have not been combined by compilation, linking, or
loading, and the dynamic acquisition and release of files and devices.

The flexibility of program/physical resource, program/software resource,
and program/program interaction supported by these macros implies that a good

deal of information that might be incorporated into code in a user area in less flexible systems must now be represented in systems tables organized to be easily modifiable to reflect systems changes.

There are rather complex table and control block structures in operating systems that have high degrees of flexibility. A compiler translating a READ statement may select a device and generate code to allow the reading of that device. When the device is not to be assigned until run time, or when it is assigned at some allocate time just prior to run time, it is necessary to show the relationship of programs to devices in some table structure. At any time, the I/O, memory, and data set assignments of the system's population of programs must be reflected in a family of tables that also may be used to reflect the status of the resources.

5.1.3   Global Functions

The tasks of the *global functions* are to *coordinate resource usage* and *enable sharing* in an environment in which programs may be unaware of their joint use of the machine system. Examples of global functions are:

- Switch the attention of the CPU.

- Fetch portions of a program from a backing store to primary memory.

- Collect statistics about the utilization of components of the system.

- Measure the rate of progress of jobs in the system and make adjustments where necessary.

5.2   STRUCTURE IN THE RUN-TIME ENVIRONMENT

Just as the prerun-time environment decomposes into a set of programs with various distributions of function, the run-time functions of an operating system can be organized in various ways. The packaging of functions can differ, the mechanisms for communicating between programs thought to be part of the run-time environment can differ, and the selection of functions to be performed during run time will differ from system to system.

A great deal of attention has been paid to the structure of run-time environments over the last decade. Much of the interest has been motivated by those interested in *structured programming,* and in the development of higher-level languages suitable for the implementation of systems programs as opposed to application programs. The motive of a large group of workers has been to show that operating systems concepts can be regularized, structured, and understood in terms of an aggregation of relatively simple algorithms with a defined set of interrelationships.

There are questions about whether or not a set of general design principles has truly been discovered and whether the natural structure of a system has been revealed in a general way. If such a set of design principles existed, then the development of operating systems in the future could be guided by them, and resulting systems could consequently achieve goals of consistency, extensibility, and coherence beyond those achieved in current systems.

After devoting an entire chapter to different kinds of operating systems, it would be wonderfully relieving if one could now show that there is considerably more sameness than difference, or that by recombining essentially identical modules into different structures one could transform one system into another. Although many common abstractions have been defined, and many fundamental ideas about structure have matured, we are still a long way from being able to apply a usable set of design principles that transcend machine structure. What this chapter attempts to do is to describe some major notions of structure appearing in the contemporary literature, and then talk about the functions of a run-time environment in a very basic way.

5.2.1 Hierarchy

A very fundamental notion of the structure of the run-time environment is the concept of the functions being packaged in well-defined layers. Just as we opened this text with a discussion of the concept of a computing system as a hierarchical structure in which the operating system was one element, it is possible to look more deeply into the operating system and see more discrete levels. The fundamental notions of this structure were presented by Dijkstra in his description of the T.H.E. multiprogramming operating system. It is that concept of hierarchy that will first be discussed here.

The functions of the run-time environment are defined to be those that enable the sharing of hardware resources among a community of users. The two fundamental operations associated with sharing involve a mechanism to multiplex the attention of the CPU(s) among a set of programs, and a mechanism to coordinate the use of all resources of the system between contending users. Consequently, the lowest level of systems function contains a *dispatcher* and a *locking mechanism*. (Both of these concepts will be discussed in detail later.) What is important to understand at this point is that a mechanism exists that takes the processing unit away from the control of one program and gives it to another. This transfer of processor control is undertaken by the system without any logical direction on the part of a running user program, although most systems include a means for driving the dispatcher at the request of a running program. The dispatcher may transfer control on a timed interval basis or in response to some other event exterior to the logic of a running program. Such an event may be the completion of an I/O operation or a demand for attention from a console or terminal operator. The existence of such a mechanism was mentioned earlier in

connection with spooling and multiprogramming. The dispatcher allows programs that are not aware of each other's existence to share the use of a single
processor (or group of processors) in an interleaved fashion.

The dispatcher operates from a queue of *activation records* that contains an
entry for each program. *An activation record is a formal structure of the system
that represents a program to the dispatcher.* Every program that may receive
control is represented by an activation record used as a repository for status and
capability data about the program.

*The locking mechanism is used to sequentialize requests for systems re-
sources other than the processor.* At various times, programs at higher levels in
the hierarchy will operate to acquire or release certain resources on behalf of user
programs. It is necessary that during an interval of time when certain critical
tables are changed (for example) that the system can guarantee that processes
are sequentialized with reference to these operations. For example, consider a
multiprocessor system in which program A running on processor 1 wishes to
have an additional 64,000 words of storage and program B running on processor
2 wishes to have an additional 16,000 words of storage. Both of these programs
may summon the use of a system memory allocator program. This program may
run on both processors more or less simultaneously. At one point, the memory
allocator will reference a table of available memory to determine from where to
take 64,000 (or 16,000) additional locations. While the memory allocator running on behalf of program A is inspecting and modifying the available memory
table, it is necessary that the memory allocator running on behalf of program B
be denied access to the table. In order to accomplish this, a *lock is associated
with the table so that when the lock is set no program requesting access to the
table may proceed.*

These locks are called *P- and V-semaphores* by Dijkstra. P and V have
become widely accepted as the names of lock manipulation operations. In the
lock's simplest form, there is a single location, the semaphore location, that is
able to take on the values 0 or 1. When a program wishes to access a resource
protected by a lock, it performs a *P-operation* on the semaphore, setting it to zero
and indicating the resource is not available. When the program is through with
the resource, it performs a *V-operation* setting the semaphore to one indicating
that the resource is available.

If the memory allocator running in the service of program A reaches the
critical point first, it sets the semaphore to zero indicating the available memory
map may not be referenced. When the memory allocator running in the service of
program B reaches the point at which it desires access to the table, it attempts a
P-operation on the semaphore. However, it will find the semaphore already set,
and will not proceed to use the table. Assume it will "spin on the lock," that is, it
will continue to attempt the P-operation. Eventually, the allocator running for

program A will execute a V-operation, releasing the resource and the allocator running for program B will proceed to gain access to the table.

In the multiprocessing situation, it is desirable that the P- and V-operations be unified in order to prevent the following possible phenomenon: processor 1 has referenced the semaphore and is in the process of setting it to zero and storing the change in a semaphore location. Between the time that processor 1 has first referenced the semaphore and the time it stores its changed value in memory, processor 2 references the semaphore. It will find its unchanged value and itself undertake to grab the lock. There are software algorithms for handling this problem, but *most multiprocessors have an instruction that treats a reference, change, and store to a location as a single unified event.* A processor referencing a location used by a *test and set* or *compare and swap* in the program of another processor is denied access to the location until the completion of the semaphore sequence. In this way the integrity of a P- or a V-operation is guaranteed by hardware.

In single-processor designs, the P- and V-operations are still meaningful because of the dispatching mechanism and the interrupt mechanism. It is possible for a program to request the allocation of a resource whose manipulation involves sequentialization. The resource manager running on behalf of the requesting program may lose control of the processor while it is still holding the lock, during the interval between the P-operation and the V-operation, because of an interrupt and the subsequent operation of the dispatcher. A successor program may request the resource and it will find the lock held. The resource protected by the lock may not be in condition for manipulation because the program that obtained the lock has left it in some partially altered state so it is proper to deny the second program access. Some operating systems will undertake to start immediately the holder of the lock at this point. Some locks are held only by programs that do not allow themselves to be interrupted. Of all of the details of operating system design, the lock structure is perhaps the one that varies most from system to system. But regardless of details and the policies that are enforced around the lock structure, some underlying idea of program synchronization and sequentialization is universal.

In the Dijkstra structure, the memory management functions are on the level above the dispatcher/lock level (Fig. 5.1). These functions are present in the run-time environment when either or both of the following capabilities exist.

■　The user program (or any program) can request an additional allocation of memory space by the issuance of run-time macros.

■　The user program (or any program) can receive additional allocations of real memory space by virtue of a mechanism that maps "virtual" space onto "real" space. These concepts are discussed in detail later. What is sufficient to

Level 4	Job managers	1. User processes 2. Read control language
Level 3	Device managers	1. Logical/physical device mappings 2. Buffering
Level 2	Console manager	1. Operator interaction 2. Manages system console
Level 1	Page manager	1. Memory management 2. Implements virtual memory
Level 0	Kernel	1. Implements processes 2. Synchronization primitives

Fig. 5.1   Levels in the T.H.E. operating system.

understand here is that it is possible for a program to form an address that refers to instructions or data not in memory. The memory manager will be triggered by a hardware mapping device that recognizes when the referenced address is not in memory.

The memory manager on level 1 is a user of the functions at level 0. In a clean and perfect hierarchic structure, no function at level 0 can ever require the services of level 1. By inference, the P- and V-mechanisms and CPU dispatch mechanisms on level 0 must be resident in memory at all times since they cannot call upon the services of a memory manager. The memory manager, as we have seen, may use the P- and V-mechanisms to lock the memory availability table while it is doing allocation.

Memory management at level 1 may run as a "process," represented by an entry on the dispatching queue serviced by the dispatcher. It is synchronized, using the P- and V-mechanisms, with the behavior of the drum used as a backing store for memory elements flowing to and from the system. Running as a process distinguishes this level and all higher levels from the "primitives" in level 0.

The third level (level 2) in the T.H.E. structure provides for support of operator interaction. The programs at this level provide an impression for all programs at level 3 and above that they have a dedicated console. The console level allows for the acquisition and release of the console. Since this level is above the memory management level routines, it need not be resident but may call for storage or the paging mechanism.

At the next level (3) resource managers for I/O devices are provided. These programs map symbolic device names onto real device names and provide buffers for input and output streams. The functions at this level are also implemented by processes that run as programs on a dispatching queue serviced by the dispatcher. This level is a user of the function provided by level 2 (to report, for example, malfunction), of level 1 for memory management, and of level 0 for synchronization.

The highest level of hierarchy contains "user processes" that call upon the lower levels to provide a context of resources. The idea of the hierarchy is to define an environment of apparent resources for a user process, and to deny it a view of real resources that underlie the apparent resources. Thus a user program sees the reader, punch, and printer through the interface provided by the level 3 processes. The level 4 and level 3 processes may see the console support at level 2. All processes and functions may use the memory mapping capabilities available from level 1 and the underlying P and V and dispatching mechanisms at level 0 to coordinate all activities.

There are two fundamental concepts in the development of the hierarchic structure. The first is that a program at any level may only use the services of a program at a lower level, the second is that the time required to perform functions at each level should be smaller as one moves inward toward level 0. The need for a program at a higher level to invoke a lower-level service must not introduce unacceptable delays in the progress of the higher-level program.

The ability to decompose the functions of the system into a strict hierarchic structure has a number of advantages for the development of systems because of the possibility of developing levels independently, and because of the resultant ability to prove the correctness of the system under development.

The essential notion of the T.H.E. hierarchy is the idea of a higher level as a user of the services of a lower level. An important idea is the independence of the user and "usee" as regards their individual internal structure.

In general, the principles of hierarchic design involve the following basic concepts.

■   Each level treats the level below as if it is a hardwired invariant function that it accesses across rigidly fixed interfaces.

■   Each level has direct access only to the level directly beneath it and has no knowledge of deeper levels.

■   Information "hiding" is perfect in that the data structures known to a level may be manipulated only at that level. Concepts relevant to data at a level are also enclosed in that level. Thus a deblocking routine knows nothing about buffering, a buffering routine knows nothing about devices, etc.

The notion of hierarchic structures has attracted a good deal of attention since it was first explicitly described. To some extent, it may be true that all operating systems are inherently hierarchic and that the mere notion of hierarchy is not sufficient to guide the design of a system. Difficult decisions must still be made about what functions are appropriate at what level, how levels communicate with each other, and how programs at the same level communicate.

There may also be some confusion between the general benefits of *modularity, the division of a system into well-defined programmed units with known inputs, known outputs, and a reasonably limited set of possible variations in function,* and notions of hierarchic relationships. In addition, there are some problems with strict hierarchic structures that may lead to special cases that break out of the clean pattern intended for the system. Another problem with the concept is that it has been strictly applied only to the development of relatively small systems. However, the fundamental need to introduce some organizing structural concept into the run-time environment makes the idea of hierarchy very useful and important.

There are several variations on the hierarchic concept based on uses presented in the literature. It is possible to define the lowest layer as a CPU monitor that contains only the dispatcher and all interrupt handling. Process synchronization is moved into a higher level that performs more sophisticated synchronization than what is available through the basic P- and V-mechanisms of T.H.E.'s lowest level. All coordination between all programs in the system, including sending messages to one another, signaling events, and waiting for events is handled at this level. User programs, as well as higher-level systems programs, have access to these coordinating functions.

Another variant places only all basic I/O device handling in the lowest level. This is particularly appropriate in hardware systems (for example, some microprocessors) in which a good deal of code is required for very basic hardware operations. The placement of device code at the lowest level is also consistent with real-time applications in which CPU dispatching is not a properly assumed basic operating system extension of the machine.

Madnick and Donovan generalize level 3 of the hierarchy to a process management level. This is the level at which the control blocks representing programs are created and destroyed and at which programs (as processes, i.e., as things represented by a control block) communicate with one another. This level may require memory management that remains at level 2. Level 4 manages physical I/O, while level 5 manages files. Alternatively, some workers prefer to see I/O, process management, and memory management exist at the same level.

If the creation of a process requires memory allocation, then an intralevel call of the memory manager by the process manager is permitted.

These variations are attempts to address specific needs of various systems without violating hierarchic structure. There seems to be a set of problems associated with any particular hierarchic structure based upon the idea of fixed services available only at a given level. The general solutions seem to be duplicating services at various levels and/or allowing intralevel service calls.

Consider a problem with the idea that CPU dispatching is performed at level 0 and memory management is performed at level 1 in the context of a very simple time-sharing operating system. The nature of this system is that there is a fixed number of terminals being serviced and each terminal is represented by an entry on a dispatch queue. Only one terminal's work space is represented in memory at a particular time. The act of dispatching (giving control to a particular terminal) involves writing out the work space for the terminal whose active time has just expired and reading in the work space for the terminal next to receive service. The dispatcher at level 0 cannot call upward to achieve the write and read of work space associated with the dispatching event. In order to overcome this problem, it is necessary to provide a higher-level dispatching function above the memory management level. The higher-level dispatcher can be activated by the lower-level dispatcher and it, in turn, activates user processes.

A similar kind of problem exists in the relation between an I/O process and a memory manager process in a paging machine. In such a machine, a process may refer to an address that is not in main memory. In order to bring it into main memory, a memory manager must use a drum or disk manager. The drum or disk manager, however, may also respond to traditional I/O operations such as READ and WRITE. When a read is being done it is necessary to *pin a page to memory*. That is, it is necessary for the I/O process to call upon the memory manager to take action to assure the system that a page of memory serving as the target of an I/O operation will remain in memory throughout the operation. We have, therefore, a situation in which the memory manager uses an I/O manager and the I/O manager uses the memory manager. This requires putting memory management and I/O management at the same level and allowing intralevel calls.

Another fundamental problem of hierarchy has to do with the specifics of interrupt handling on particular machines. It is possible to conceive of an interrupt system in which appropriate interrupts are handled at the appropriate level. For example, there might be 16 levels of interrupt with a possible control state and problem state at each level. Clock interrupts would be handled at interrupt level 0 that corresponds to hierarchic level 0. I/O interrupts might be handled at, for example, level 2.

What such an underlying hardware structure would provide is the ability to enter a level directly without the operation of a "first-level interrupt handler"

(FLIH) that would necessarily exist at a given level in the hierarchy. A *first-level interrupt handler is the routine that immediately responds to an interrupt*. If all interrupts are handled at level 0 by a single FLIH and, as a result of an interrupt, an activation record must be created, then it is not obvious how an upward call to a higher-level CREATE PROCESS could be avoided.

Hierarchies differ in the rules by which levels can be crossed. In the strictest hierarchy, each level must go through all intervening levels on its way down. Some structures, however, allow for a continuum of restrictiveness. Lister and Sayer, for example, permit only hierarchic access to the lowest layer (dispatcher and interrupt handler) from the process monitor and resource manager, but permit any level to access the resource managers.

In general, there is a concept of transparent hierarchy in which all lower levels are accessible to higher levels. The idea of transparent hierarchy is one that is useful, for example, at the interface between a user program and various levels of I/O support. Depending on whether a user wishes *deblocking (record by record receipt and placement), block-level management (in which logical blocks are presented to a program)*, or only *device handling (physical block management and interrupt handling)*, the user may enter the support hierarchy at the appropriate level. If the three levels of I/O support are thought of as representing three layers, then deblocking calls upon block management and block management calls upon device management are necessary. A user program wishing the highest level of support may enter with a GET macro. A user wishing lower levels of support may enter with READ or *Execute Channel Program*, bypassing the function of the higher level.

It is possible to organize a single interface such that the user program always calls upon that interface with the same macro. A routing mechanism at the interface then determines how many levels to bypass by an examination of the attributes associated with the file being referenced.

An example of such a design comes from the DPPX operating system for the IBM 8100. The application program wishing I/O services issues a SEND or RECEIVE (DPPX equivalents of PUT and GET) to a standard interface called the ESS interface.

Beneath the ESS interface are various layers of I/O services that are well structured into replaceable modules. A user wishing blocking–deblocking level services will pass from the ESS layer into the PS (Presentation Services) layer and then, when necessary, down into MS (Media Services) for buffering control, and into IOAS when physical I/O is required.

The passage through layers is under the control of a router that is formed at the time the referenced file is "connected" (DPPX equivalent of OPEN). A file is connected at a certain level of service and the layers associated with that service are defined at that time. When a receive is issued, the ESS layer determines that the RECEIVE macro is well formed and then passes the request "downward" on the basis of the routing table associated with the connection of program to file.

If a program does not wish deblocking, then the ESS, through the routing table, will direct all RECEIVEs to an MS layer. The RECEIVE macro does not change.

An interesting aspect of the DPPX structure is that it is possible for users to replace specific layers and it is possible to add new services beneath the ESS interfaces. Additional I/O services, in the spirit of a database manager, may be added to the system beneath the ESS layer without disturbing the application program interfaces.

Hierarchic structures may differ in the degrees of option that a process at a higher level has in its movement downward. It is possible to restrict a process in any level so that it can use only one process in a lower level. In this way a single unique path from any level down through the hierarchy can be defined.

5.3   PROCESSES AND PRIMITIVES

Among the programs of the operating system, some are organized as extensions of the architecture and others as service functions. In making a distinction between two types of programs, one is referring to the nature of the way the program assumes control of the processor.

5.3.1   Primitives

There are various ways of transferring control to a section of code. Within a single program element there are, of course, simple branches. A running program can transfer control within itself by executing a branch instruction. This has no external effect upon the system. There is no change in any table or queue of the system that occurs as a direct result of the transfer of control.

In more complex program structures there is a more formalized transfer of control called a *subroutine call* in which a program element is invoked by another program element. The invoked program element may be part of the same program structure as the invoker. In the simplest of the relations defined for a caller and a callee (the callee as part of the same program structure as the caller), parameters are passed in registers or shared memory addresses, and the callee runs under the activation record (entry on dispatch list) of the caller. There are considerably more complex relations between callers and callees in certain systems that will be discussed later.

The important idea in both the direct transfer and the simple subroutine call is that the code transferred to begins to execute immediately without the support of any mechanism of the system. The caller, in effect, ceases to exist and either is never reestablished because it has no structural identity (direct transfer), or is reestablished by the action of the RETURN from the callee. This reestablishment occurs as a result of the callee executing some kind of a return jump that places a designated return location in the instruction counter of the machine.

A completely sequential relationship exists between a caller and a callee. As a result of the sequential relationship there is no need for any synchronizing mechanism. Such a sequential relationship may be appropriately established between programs in the operating system and user programs, or between operating system programs at different levels of hierarchy. The relationship is useful when there is no meaningful work that a calling program can do until the called program has completed. Effectively, the called programs operate as "long" instructions in the caller.

Consider a user program that desires the allocation of additional real memory. Suppose that the system provides a GETMAIN macro that can be issued during run time and that this GETMAIN is effectively a call upon the memory manager. Further assume that the memory manager operates in control state. A usual way of designing this relationship is to place some code in the user program that will issue an SVC to place the system in control state and force a service request interrupt. Interrupt analysis will transfer control to the memory manager that will then allocate the requested space and alter whatever is necessary in the caller's activation record to reflect the allocation. The memory manager is started by direct transfer from the interrupt analysis function that is entered by the SVC interrupt. The relationship between the calling user and the memory manager is conceptually identical to the relation between a caller and a callee. Parameters are passed, and a return is made. The memory manager runs without an activation record as a primitive operation of the system. In order to do this, it may be necessary to inhibit all interrupts so that the memory manager can assure itself that it has continuous control over the machine until it completes. Because the memory manager runs in control state, it would usually have the power to inhibit interrupts while it runs.

The operating system functions at the bottom of the hierarchy frequently are designed to run in this manner. The first-level interrupt handlers and the dispatcher, the synchronizing programs (P- and V-operators), and the memory managers are commonly among them; while they are running, the activation records of the higher-level programs need not reflect a dependency on their completion because there is a perfectly sequential relation defined.

5.3.2 Processes

A program may call upon another program by requesting that the called program be scheduled for subsequent operation. In the simplest situation, the caller and callee are part of a single combined program structure so that there is no need for allocation. The calling program and its callees share the resource environment created by allocation to the caller or to some conceptually higher structure that contains both the caller and its callees.

Figure 5.2 provides some structural basis for the concept of schedulable programs sharing the same resources. In Fig. 5.2, the higher-level structure is an "environment." At allocation time, prior to the run-time environment, an environment block is formed that holds pointers to the memory locations allocated, to devices allocated, and to the files. In addition, a list of program elements that may run as part of the environment is formed. After allocation, an activation record is created for the first program to run on behalf of the environment. This activation record is placed on the dispatching queue. At some later time the dispatcher gives control to this program, and the program may call for the scheduling of another program associated with the environment. It does this by calling the *create process level of the operating system*. There would now be two activation records on the dispatch queue. The actual execution of the programs depends on the action of the dispatcher.

It is common, in current literature, to call a program with an activation

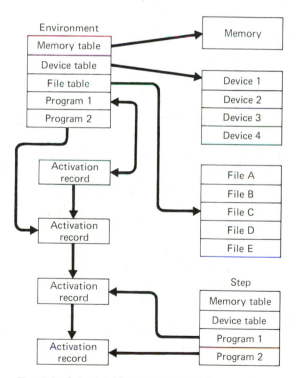

Fig. 5.2 Schedulable programs sharing resources.

record representing it in the system a *process*. The reader must be careful, however, in perusing different systems because the notion of a process is not identical in all systems, and there is some inconsistency in a terminology that includes words like task, subtask, procedure, and process. Notions of process will be discussed in more detail later. Most of the non-IBM literature uses the term *process* to denote the system abstraction that is dispatchable and synchronizable in a system. IBM's 360 and 370 operating systems use a *task* as the manageable structure. There are vastly different notions about the ownership of resources involved in notions of process and task from system to system.

At this time, we need this notion only to point out that a function of the operating system may be run as a process, with an activation record. Earlier, when we discussed prerun-time services and "times," it was clear that the compiler and linkage-editor ran as processes. All of the prerun-time service functions, including scheduling and allocation, run as processes. These functions are clearly prerun-time functions when they run as processes that complete before the program they are scheduling or allocating itself becomes a process; that is, before it has an activation record formed and placed on the dispatching queue. Their functions are summoned by statements external to the text of the program they are processing.

Certain of the prerun-time services may be brought into the run-time environment to be summoned by macro call, as we have seen with GETMAIN. But, unlike our GETMAIN example, they may be run as processes. As mentioned earlier, the operating system programs that exist at upper hierarchic levels tend to be run as processes and not as primitives (although it is not unusual to find processes running at very low levels of the structure).

An operating system process may be scheduled for a number of reasons. It is possible for the dispatcher to schedule a global operating system process at timed intervals or in response to a specific event. An example of a global operating system process is a program that may be summoned to perform an analysis of the level of utilization of various resources (CPU, memory, channels) in a system, and the rate of progress of the programs in a mix. Such a program might merely collect statistics or it might actually reorder or modify the dispatching queue in order to improve system performance. Since the program does not provide a particular service to a particular program in the mix, and provides no prerun-time service, it can be summoned only by the dispatcher. Since it may be a program of some duration, it may not be desirable to run it as a primitive, but as a process that may be interleaved with other processes.

When an operating system process is summoned by a user program, it may be used synchronously or asynchronously. That is, it may be summoned as a subroutine or as a "cooperating" process. Some differences in structure and implementation of the relationship between the calling user and the called function occur depending on whether there is a sequential or an asynchronous relation.

The sequential relation is operationally identical to running the operating system program as a primitive in that the calling program is quieted until the function completes. However, because the operating system program is to be run as a process, an activation record must be created and placed on a dispatching queue. The call to the operating system differs from a user process activating another user process in an environment (the example of Fig. 5.2) in an important way. The rights of the operating system process may be considerably greater than the rights of the calling user process. As a consequence, its activation record must differ in some way. In particular, it may be able to address locations unavailable to the calling process and it may be able to execute instructions not available to the calling process. It may run in control state from locations not available to the calling process. The notion, introduced earlier, of multiple activation records sharing a resource environment may not apply, because the called program may not be mapped into the table of resources available to the environment (that is, the operating system program is not named as a callable program), and the resources used by the called program may not be allocated to the caller.

The activation record of the operating system process may be identified as a special type of activation record having all rights to all resources. It is also possible to associate the activation record with a different environment table permitting greater resource accessibility but not total accessibility. This would conform to a notion, implicit in hierarchic concepts, that each lower level of the operating system has greater rights than each higher level.

On a call to a synchronous process, the activation record of the called process effectively replaces the activation record of the caller on the dispatch queue. Figure 5.3 illustrates the concept. The dispatch queue is the list of blocks named PROGRAM A, B, C, etc. Each of these blocks represents an activation record. Figure 5.3 shows the association of processes with their environments. Note the complex structure involving D, E, and OPERATING SYSTEM. This structure is a LIFO (last-in—first-out) stack that can actually occur at any node in the dispatch chain. At the top of the stack, an activation record for OPERATING SYSTEM is associated with a master environment that defines the resources available to OPERATING SYSTEM. Because OPERATING SYSTEM is at the top of the stack at this dispatching node, whenever the dispatcher visits that node it is OPERATING SYSTEM that will receive control. If, for any reason, control is taken away from OPERATING SYSTEM, it will be returned to OPERATING SYSTEM when the node is visited again by the dispatcher. When OPERATING SYSTEM completes, it will have its activation record destroyed and PROGRAM E will exist at the top of the stack.

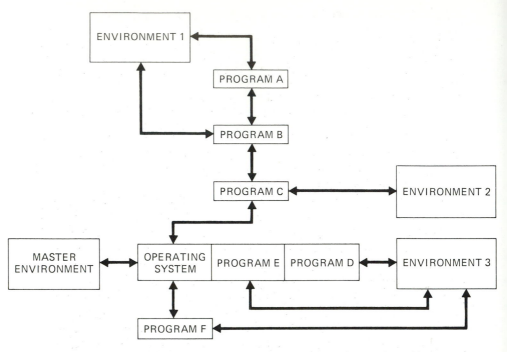

Fig. 5.3 Dispatch queue, activation records, and synchronous stacking.

There is a terminology problem associated with these concepts and with Fig. 5.3. Some would say that OPERATING SYSTEM, E, and D are not processes but instead are procedures running on behalf of a process that is totally represented by the stack. The definitional problem of what is a process concerns divergent concepts of whether the process is the stack of records representing program activations, or a program activation. In systems in which programs share resources held by a higher structure, the concept of process usually is built around the structure that owns the resources. In systems in which each invoked procedure can own a private set of resources, the concept of the individual program as a process begins to intrude. In general, it is most common to think of the stack of invoked procedures as the process.

Although the effect of a synchronous call to an operating system function is much like a call to a primitive (in that the caller loses any possibility of regaining the system until the callee is complete), there are several important differences between the two phenomena.

■   The operating system function operates as a process with an activation record so that it can be interrupted and resumed at the convenience of the system.

A primitive, with no activation record, must run to completion before it can be left.

- The operating process may have a quite distinct set of rights and attributes from the caller but it can take on some of its characteristics. For example, it may assume the dispatching priority (position in dispatch queue) of the caller.

- Running as a process, multiple activation records for a single operating system function may exist. As a result (particularly true in a multiprocessor), the same service may be given more than one caller at the same time with synchronization provided by P- and V-mechanisms. The rate of service for each caller is determined by the dispatcher.

It is possible to schedule an operating system process on a special dispatching queue that is always given preference for service. Thus whenever there is an activation record on the special queue that can use service, the dispatcher gives that record the processor. Processes on the preferred queue may be ordered by priority of their requesting programs.

The use of a special queue for functions of an operating system time is part of MVS design. In this system a distinction is made between an SRB and an ASCB/TCB. The usual dispatcher, process create, and process suspend rules apply to called application processes. However, a set of specialized operating system functions can be called for by privileged subsystems and scheduled on a special SRB (Service Request) queue. These SRBs have the property that once they run they are deleted and must be rescheduled to run again. This facility is intended for the use of specially authorized programs, running with extended privileges, to provide enhanced control over system events.

5.3.3 Asynchronous Processes

There are conditions in which a process that calls another process may be able to continue to operate while the other process exists. Depending on the actions of the dispatcher, both processes may receive intervals of processor service. We discuss here the very simple case of a process calling a program that becomes a process only as the result of that call.

Consider a program that wishes to write a record to an output file and that is perfectly capable of doing additional processing while the WRITE is going on. Assume that a call to WRITE results in an interrupt that eventually causes an activation record to be formed for a WRITE process. Assume further that there is a buffer into which the calling process has put records and from which the WRITE process takes records. Also make the simplifying assumption that the buffer area is commonly addressable by both processes.

After the activation record for the WRITE process has been put on the dispatching queue, both the calling process and the WRITE process may be activated by the dispatcher that is insensitive to the relationship between them. As a consequence of this, some synchronizing mechanism must be defined so that the WRITE process and the calling process are properly behaved.

The two processes must share some common communication mechanism beyond the buffer itself. A way of establishing this mechanism is for the caller to include among the parameters of its call for WRITE the address of a location that the WRITE will use to record the completion of its operation. This location must be checked by the caller before it can place additional output records in the shared buffer. This location may be in its activation record or it may be a uniquely defined location called, in IBM's System/370 operating system, an *Event Control Block* (ECB). A macro, frequently called CHECK, may be provided to a using program for the purpose of determining if the WRITE process has completed. At any time after the call, *CHECK* may be used to determine if the WRITE is complete. If the WRITE is not complete, the process may go on to do other work, or it may spin on the CHECK if there is nothing for it to do.

When the WRITE process completes, it may directly *POST the completion* of its function or it may, as part of the act of termination, ask a lower level of the operating system to POST the completion on its behalf. *The act of POSTing is the recording of some value that, by convention, the CHECKer recognizes as notification that it may proceed past the checkpoint.*

The reader will recognize that the POST action and the ECB concept are similar to the P- and V-concept in which a lock is established on a resource to which access must be sequentialized. Its use here differs from P and V as earlier described in that it is not uninterruptible, and its coordination does not occur at the lowest level of the operating system. It is common to allow synchronization at higher levels so that processes can send messages to each other without the use of the lowest P- and V-level of the system.

The structure that involves two activation records, a shared buffer, and a shared communication mechanism may also be used to synchronize sequential processes. A first instance of such use may be seen as a response to a failed CHECK. If the CHECKing process has nothing further to do until the WRITE is complete, it may issue a WAIT. *The issuance of a WAIT directs the elements of the operating system to (1) record in the activation record of this process an inability to continue, and (2) take the processor away from the process.*

Many operating systems have forced WAITs associated with specific calls for processes of the system. For example, a call for a WRITE may result in the operating system assuming the calling program cannot continue and recording an "unable to continue" in its activation record. This may also happen as an indirect result of a call to the system. For example, a record advance PUT may find a full output buffer at which time the PUTting program will be suspended.

The concepts of process synchronization are considerably richer than the concepts we have discussed here. Ideas of coordinating continuing processes, coordinating processes sharing the same code, and the use of queues for synchronization will be explored further later in this text.

5.4 VERTICAL AND HORIZONTAL SYSTEM STRUCTURE

The idea of hierarchy suggests a notion of horizontal system structure in which layers lie upon each other and particular functions are performed at each layer. Rather formal rules for passing from layer to layer may be applied and supported by hardware mechanisms. However, there are some vertical notions that also exist in the organization of an operating system. The design of a particular system actually reflects a kind of tension between horizontal and vertical concepts.

A vertical notion is mapped on top of a horizontal notion in Fig. 5.4. The vertical notion is that there is a family of *handler processes* for each of the I/O devices associated with a system. Thus a user may enter at different points for different I/O devices. What is vertical about the notion are two concepts—first, the availability of multiple peer functions at the same level—second, the idea of the depth of service that may be provided within a level. Figure 5.4 suggests that the I/O processes may call upon process management, memory management, and lock management and are subject to the dispatcher. What is vague in Fig. 5.4 are issues about the relationship between the ideas of interrupt, device management and interface, the relationship between vertical functions in reader, etc., and horizontal functions in the underlying layers. We discuss these concepts in this section. We make the simplifying assumption (addressed in later sections) that a using program wishing any level of I/O service issues a macro that calls a process of the operating system.

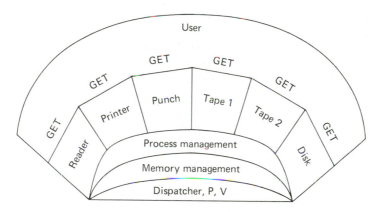

Fig. 5.4 Horizontal and vertical structure.

Consider the usual levels of I/O service, GET, READ, CHANNEL, and DEVICE (Fig. 5.5). *GET is an internal function that moves a record to a designated program area or provides a pointer to a record in a buffer.* The function may also inspect the availability of records. When there are no records available in a buffer, GET may call READ. *READ is concerned with buffer management and the association of logical blocks with memory spaces.* READ depends on *CHANNEL that maps physical blocks onto logical blocks.* For example, a logical block may be constructed from several physical blocks that are discontiguous on a physical device by use of a chain of transfer words that define the gathering and selection of discontiguous device words into a contiguous area in memory. *DEVICE concerns itself with the physical eccentricities of the unit being read or written, its timing, signal, and control protocols, etc.* Not all levels exist in all systems. On some hardware, the CHANNEL and DEVICE levels coalesce into each other. Design in this area is very sensitive to hardware details.

We will use these four levels of I/O service to explore various notions of horizontal and vertical function organization.

A purely vertical concept would organize the entire flow from GET through the various levels to I/O device manipulation as a single module with only intraprogram communication.

A considerably more horizontal notion would associate each of the levels of I/O service with a structural layer. The special requirements of record advance would be wholly contained within the highest level. Similarly, the special requirements of *block handling* and *buffer control* exist at the next level. A movement from level to level involves some form of program-to-program communication and synchronization.

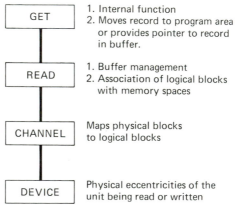

Fig. 5.5 Four levels of I/O.

Figure 5.6(a) illustrates a pure notion of vertical organization, and Fig. 5.6(b) illustrates a rather horizontal organization. What is particularly important about Fig. 5.6(b) is the crossbar arrangement between the levels. This suggests that regardless of the entry point at the deblock level, any kind of block level management can be undertaken and regardless of the block level management, any kind of device handling can be undertaken. This crossbar is associated with the idea that no device characteristics are represented in any way at the buffer management level and no buffer management characteristics are represented at the deblocking level.

The special advantage of such a horizontal organization is that new devices can be supported by the addition of handler level programs without any perturbation of programs at higher levels. This, of course, is a fundamental characteristic of any layered or hierarchic approach. A potential disadvantage of the layering is the time that it takes to move through all the layers. Since each layer is packaged to be independent of any other layer, a formal call of some complexity will be required. There is also some unavoidable absurdity in certain combinations. It will be necessary, for example, to define semantics for REWIND printer or BACKSPACE punch.

The advantage of a strongly vertical organization of function is the degree of functional integration that can be achieved, and the programming efficiency that may accrue because the code for record advance can rely on some known characteristics of underlying block and device characteristics. Another advantage is the ability to think of a certain class of device as an entity whose characteristics can be defined and handled in a unique and integrated way without concern for

Fig. 5.6 (a) Vertical and (b) horizontal structure.

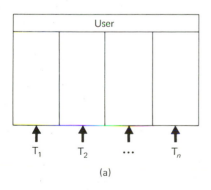

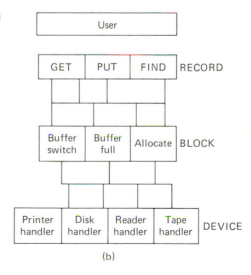

(a)

(b)

the eccentricities of other device classes. An important use of this separation is for device classes (such as communications devices and storage devices) whose characteristics are very different. If one applies the concept of DB/DC, so that DB (database management), processing, and DC (data communications) are three quite separable functions, then a vertical DB manager including an integrated disk manager and a vertical DC manager including integrated network, terminal, and message handling is a reasonable design.

The DPPX operating system, whose horizontal layers were referenced before, has, in fact, some vertical aspects in that there are really two parallel layers, one for storage class devices and one for communication class devices.

Classical vertical designs, however, do not show the layering of DPPX and are highly integrated structures. A disadvantage of vertical organization is that a module contains functions that may reflect peculiarities of devices at a rather high level. This may lead to great difficulty if new devices of a particular type present themselves for support because it is necessary to inspect the vertical structure across its entire body in order to determine how characteristics of the new device may be integrated into the module. Of course, in the most extreme vertical design, each device has its own vertical module so the support of a new device involves the creation of a new module responsible for all transformations along the path from a device to a usable image in memory accessible by a user process.

A possible feature of vertical design is the exposure of unique semantics for each vertically integrated function. Thus, for example, a set of macros that would be used for disk drives would differ from those used for tapes or for telecommunications functions. This specific peculiarity is common among operating systems that have placed access methods at very high levels in the system structure and embedded them in application code.

5.4.1 Access Methods, File Types, and Structure

In the discussion so far, we have ignored specific mention of a level of I/O service that one might call *file level*. The idea of file level derives from the fact that a system may offer various kinds of structures within the context of the concept of a file. Thus a file may have (1) *fixed or variable-size records,* (2) *sequential or indexed accessibility,* and (3) *direct accessibility.*

A file with sequential accessibility allows a reference to the next record based only upon an idea of a physical order on a device. A file with indexed accessibility allows the idea of "nextness" to be associated with an *ordering key*. The file structure is expanded so that there is an *index* (or a hierarchy of indices) that defines the location of a particular record within a file. The indexing used by IBM's OS/360 operating system (for example) involves a *master index* that points to a set of *cylinder group indices*. Each entry in the master index points to a cylinder group entry that contains all records with keys equal to or lower than the master index entry's key value. Thus if a file is spread across many cylinders, there would be multiple master entries pointing to entries in a cylinder group index. Figure 5.7 shows a master index that indicates that the file is spread across four cylinder groups such that cylinder group 1 contains all records with keys up to and including 1000. Cylinder group 2 contains all records with keys up to and including 3000, etc. The cylinder group index indicates that this particular cylinder group contains four cylinders, and that each cylinder contains records up to and including the key values indicated in the entries. The rest of the story is reasonably easy to infer. Each cylinder pointed to by a cylinder group entry has a *track index* that defines the records contained on each track.

A *track* represents an area on a disk (or a drum) accessible to an arm or read head during a revolution of the spindle while the arm/head is stationary. A *cylinder* represents the characteristic of most disk units in that there are multiple READ/WRITE heads associated with an arm, and that when an arm is set in a position, a number of surfaces are available to the arm. The cylinder concept also is dependent on the fact that the arm mechanisms use only one of the READ/WRITE heads at any time and therefore are not capable of parallel reading of various surfaces. In view of the ability of an arm to read from only one platter, and in view of the relatively long time it takes to move an arm across the surface of a disk platter, the idea of a cylinder as an allocation unit for a file has emerged. *A cylinder is a collection of tracks available to an arm on all surfaces.* It is interesting to speculate how disk file organization might change if all heads on an arm might read in parallel.

Indexed access permits a user to reference records by the concept of next "in order" where order is independent of physical order. It is relevant to disk and drum devices because it allows degrees of freedom in the use of physical space and permits insertion and deletion of records without changing the logical idea of "nextness."

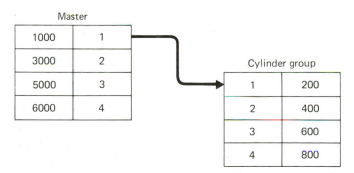

Fig. 5.7   Master/cylinder group mapping.

Direct access introduces the idea that a program can ask the system for a particular record in any sequence by its name. It relieves the system of imposing order on the records and places the responsibility for determining what record is "next" on the calling program. The "name" of a record may be its address or its record number in the file. Direct access may or may not be supported by indexing of various types.

The ideas of level of I/O service and of various file types are directly involved with notions of vertical and horizontal functional organization, and a discussion of the intersection of notions of service level, device type, and file type sheds a good deal of illumination on the tension between horizontal and vertical organizations of the functions of an operating system.

IBM's OS/MVT and its cousins and successors have the notion of an *access method*. There are multiple access methods that represent intersections of concepts of how functional elements should be arranged. The access methods provided by IBM include (or have included at one time) *Basic Sequential (BSAM), Queued Sequential (QSAM), Basic Index Sequential (ISAM), Queued Index Sequential (QISAM), Direct Access (BDAM), Basic Telecommunications (BTAM), Queued Telecommunications (QTAM),* and various others. Two rather important methods, *VSAM* and *VTAM*, are evolutionary replacements for various earlier methods. VSAM provides combined functions of ISAM, SAM, and BDAM. VTAM provides enhanced telecommunications function supporting the *SNA* (*Systems Network Architecture*) protocols.

The most obvious vertical design notion that is apparent in the family of access methods is the partitioning of the device world into two classes of devices: terminal/telecommunications devices addressed by the various TAMs, and non-terminal devices addressed by the others. The second vertical notion is the not-so-perfect partitioning of devices into random access storage devices and sequential access devices. ISAM, QISAM, and BDAM are appropriate only for use with disklike devices. SAM may be used on a random access device but is intended for use on devices such as tapes, card equipment, and other document-oriented peripheral equipment.

Any access method can get to any named device within its device class, and there is some ability for access methods to refer to files created by another. *The "Q" methods represent buffered deblocking versions of the "B" methods (no deblocking or buffering).* However, SAM files cannot use DAM files or ISAM files. Thus there are many file types that are subject to manipulation only by appropriate access methods.

The vertical notion integrates the ideas of level of service, file type, and device type. There is a horizontal notion in the design of the access methods in that there is an ultimate base, common to all, called the *I/O supervisor* that operates at the channel–device level. Above this level, however, are vertically integrated programs representing a complex of paths to files of various types at different service levels with large amounts of integrated device dependent code. *The contribution of VSAM is to allow the establishment of a more general systemwide access convention that reduces the number of system file conventions and provides multilevel service.*

The highly vertical design of the original IBM access methods seems to reflect a preoccupation with device type and the kinds of operations that are possible on different types of devices. A difficulty with this preoccupation is the evolution of devices themselves and the proliferation, over the life of an operating system, of functionally similar devices of various attributes. A further difficulty may emerge as there are evolutionary conceptual changes regarding the usefulness of the compartmentalization of storage or terminal-like devices. There is also a burden on the system because a user program referencing a file of a common type without buffering must use a different access method than a program referencing the same type of file with buffering. So, although two programs in a multiprogramming mix may share ISAM (using techniques shortly to be discussed), if another program using an indexed file wishes buffering, QISAM must exist in the memory of the system. Finally, there is no ability for common buffering or *buffer pooling* across buffers to be controlled by different access methods.

There is a need for a technique to find good balances of horizontal and vertical slicing and packaging of function in any application and particularly in operating system design. The decomposability of functions has received attention from various schools of interest in the computing community. Those concerned with parallel processors, with structured programming, with distributed processing, and with operating system design have investigated methods for the isolation of *modules* and the definition of *interfaces* between them. It is possible that the underlying bias toward vertical or horizontal functional definition is less important than the quality of program packaging techniques used as the basis for system implementation. These packaging techniques will increase the alterability, maintainability, and extendability of vertical structures by defining compact self-contained modules that retain identity even when integrated into vertical components. Thus it is perhaps not the idea of hierarchy that is important, or of layers, but the idea of clean modularization that can underlie any structure.

Yet the call for modularity is not new. At the time of conceptualization of the large general-purpose operating systems that now are allegedly difficult to maintain, difficult to alter, and difficult to test, modularity was a recognized requirement. No one counting the modules of a large system would conclude that the system was insufficiently modularized. Actually, the number of modules seems to increase the complexity because of the tremendously large set of relationships that can exist between the modules, and the impact that changes in one module can have in another.

It is not clear whether the secret lies in enhanced techniques of function distribution, in notions of "top-down" programming, in enhanced machine support through microcode, in less ambitious concepts of what a system should do, or in yet undiscovered techniques for analyzing program structures or enforcing program discipline.

5.5   OTHER NOTIONS OF STRUCTURE

The notion of hierarchy and the notion of structure have become very much intertwined in the literature. The single direction of flow of call, as established in T.H.E., is not a requirement for all modules. There are various structural ideas that are intertwined with considerations of resource allocation and protection and security that may or may not be hierarchic. The reader should now be aware that there is by no means general agreement about what constitutes coherence in an operating system, how structure should be perceived, and whether a proper motivation is performance, maintainability, or protection.

   Some designers are interested in the extent to which features of security, integrity, and debugability may be achieved without hierarchy. If information hiding is carefully applied, then carefully written modules might be addressed from various points in the system without compromise.

5.6   INTERFACE DEFINITION

In the previous sections of this chapter we have discussed some ideas relating to how certain functions associated with operating systems may relate to each other, some introductory ideas of processes and process relations, and we have expressed some concerns about ideas of structure. The rather simple idea of what the run-time environment looks like to an application program will now be directly addressed.

   The comment has been made a number of times throughout this book that the run-time environment presents a functionally enhanced "megamachine" that has had its basic instruction set extended by a set of macro instructions. Regardless of the underlying structure of the programs in the run-time environment, a running application program receives a specific service from the system by issuing an instruction or set of instructions that puts the system in control state. While in control state, certain memory locations may be referenced and certain instructions may be executed that are not properly referenced or executed by application programs.

   Control state is entered in a number of ways. It is correctly entered as a result of an SVC-like call or as a result of an I/O or clock interrupt. It is unintentionally entered by an attempt to execute a privileged instruction, by an impermissible memory reference, or by recognition of a hardware malfunction. This section concerns itself only with permissible intentional entry to control state. Uniprocessors may be either in control state or problem state at any one time. The issuance of an SVC, in effect, invokes another machine that has an expanded register population, instruction set, and addressing capability. Over a given period, the system will experience alternations between being in problem state and being in control state.

The observation that any processor may be thought of as two processors—a problem processor and a control processor—suggests that part of the design of an operating system must address the issues that always arise when there are two or more functional units existing as elements of a system.

- What function is performed on what unit?
- Who is the "master"?
- What are the protocols for communication between the units?

To a large extent, the underlying hardware architecture determines the basic decisions of what functions will be performed on what unit. In a machine that has input/output instructions defined as privileged operations, for example, it is necessary that all I/O device handling be performed by the control machine. Similarly, if modification of the memory bounds registers, or manipulation of clocks are privileged instructions, those functions must be performed by the control machine. The definition of a minimum set of operating systems functions must necessarily include those functions that can be performed only in control state.

This statement should not be construed as suggesting that a designer searching for a minimum set of operating system functions has finished design when the basic interrupt-handling, lock-setting, and device-starting functions have been defined. The search for the definition of what functions should be placed in the operating system must include considerations other than privileged operations, but certainly a starting point for defining what functions go into the control machine is provided by the privileged operations.

Certain systems provide hardware organizations that are not in accordance with the simple ideas of a two-state uniprocessor. The PDP-11, for example, is a three-state machine that supports a concept of control state, monitor state, and problem state. Designers of Multics have proposed machines that would support a concept of numerous levels of protection rights so that programs operating at different levels have differing rights to manipulate collections of data, and an extended hierarchy of rights is defined between programs operating at different levels. Even a nominal two-state machine such as the IBM 370 has an inherent third state defined by running *"enabled" (interrupts allowed) or "disabled" (interrupts not allowed)* while in control state.

Similarly, multiprocessors of various kinds allow a system to be in problem state and control state simultaneously, and consequently must provide synchronizing mechanisms of more complexity than those required by the simpler notion of an SVC putting the system into control state and suspending problem state operations.

The influence of a multistate machine, or of a multiprocessor, is to provide the requirement that more elaborate decisions be made about the functions of the operating system and about the structure since the distribution of function across more than two machines involves a wider decision space than the distribution of function between two machines.

The choice of what functions to place in the operating system is influenced by a concept of the relationship between problem programs and the system. A basic question to be answered is "Who is to be master?" A basic decision must be made about the kind of power a problem program is allowed to have. Earlier in this chapter, the concept of synchronizing processes using the macros CHECK, WAIT, and POST was introduced. In that discussion, there was an early assumption that a process could call upon another process, and then itself determine when the called process was completed. During the execution of the called process, the calling process did more or less what it wanted. It could go on to other work. It could release the processor. In general it was very much the master of its own acts and status. This notion is perfect if the called and calling process are each running on an independent processor so that each may, in fact, proceed in parallel. On a uniprocessor, however, the notion is meaningful only if there is some underlying multiplex function that interleaves processor service between the caller and the callee. This multiplex function may be provided in hardware (e.g., Honeywell 800 with time division multiplexing between eight programs), or by a clock-driven software dispatcher. The existence of the underlying multiplexed level suggests that the running program is not in as absolute control of its own rate of progress as the defined logical relation between caller and callee suggests. That is, there are intervals of time in which the callee and caller are not actively progressing that have nothing to do with their declared intention to wait or their desire to continue.

We mentioned earlier that it is possible to design the relationship between a problem program and the operating system in such a way that the notion of who is master tilts very much in the direction of the system. Consider the situation of a problem program desiring to write a block and issuing a call for this service to be performed. In a system in which the operating system is master, the operating system may take it upon itself to assume that the calling program has no meaningful work to do, and effectively put it in a WAITing state until the WRITE is completed. During the interval of the WRITE, the calling process is denied CPU service. The right to determine logically when it may remain a candidate for dispatching is taken from the problem program and vested in the operating system. This notion may be constrained to calls to those functions that are part of the set of operating systems functions, or may be generalized to all interprocess relationships including any call or reference to a function or data object that is defined by the conventions of the system to be "outside" the calling program.

In designing a system, it is important to decide just what program–program and program–data relationships require operating system intervention, and what kinds of decisions the system may make when it is invoked. To what extent is it desirable, for example, (1) to allow a problem program to assure itself continuous, uninterrupted control of the system; (2) to maximize interprogram communication without operating system intervention; or (3) to maximize what data (systems or other) a program may look at without the intervention of the operating system?

Systems concerned with the efficient performance of a single application may tend to maximize the prerogatives of a program. These systems will also tend to put minimum function in the run-time environment and maximize the notion of what application function is. Systems very concerned with maximizing the sharability of a hardware base among many users with different levels of cooperativeness will tend to search for minimum cost ways to exert control over an application program.

In many operating systems, MVS among them, the issue of who is master and who is slave is addressed by defining two levels of interface to the operating system. One level is for application programs that are not authorized. This level leaves essential control to the operating system. Another level of interface for authorized programs shifts the balance of control back out of the operating system. This interface is intended for subsystems or major application packages written by sophisticated programmers.

Another aspect of the interface between a problem program and the operating system involves the syntax and semantics of the invocations of the operating system by the problem program. In raw form, a problem program executes a supervisor call instruction that causes an interrupt. The SVC commonly denotes a function to be performed. Each of the specific services the system will perform can be associated with a numeric code so that SVC 01 is a request for more memory, SVC 02 is a request to read a file, SVC 03 is a request to write, etc. In real-time operating systems that assume a maximum amount of user function, it is common for programmers to write coded SVCs directly. In environments in which assembly level coding is permitted (or required), and in which the assembler is low function, the coder writes function into the application, using SVCs to call for specific services.

In many systems, the programming languages, and associated libraries, even at the assembly level, provide a higher-level semantic and functional interface between the problem program and the operating system.

5.6.1 Function Sharing

The programmer writing ALLOCATE, GET, PUT, READ, and WRITE is exercising a higher-level interface. The macro that is generated by use of a macroinstruction instead of an SVC may make only a trivial contribution to the interface. For example, if it is necessary to support any particular SVC by loading parameters into registers or particular locations, a macro may be used that will attend to the bookkeeping operations. Instead of writing a sequence of loads to define a parameter set, and then writing the SVC, the programmer writes a macro with a parameter list of some type and the language processor develops the linkage. This level of interface support contributes no additional function at the interface. Its only purpose is to smooth the linkage coding and guarantee the formal correctness of the invocation. The generated macro may include a run-time check of the correctness of the parameter list, but this kind of check is usually left to the called service.

The use of macro-supported linkages with the operating system introduces the possibility of providing more service in the macro than only linkage support. Once more the GETs and READs can serve as examples. The deblocking and block-handling services provided by a system may be thought of as a higher-level service of the operating system. They may also be thought of as contributed extensions of a running application program. Some system designs permit an installation to decide whether the higher-level functions are part of the operating system or part of user programs. The possibility of embedding higher-level functions in the operating system also suggests that there may be elements of the run-time environment that do not operate in control state.

There are many possible variations in the application program relationship with the higher functions. Consider a vertical structure that contains two Integrated Access Methods. Integrated Access Method 1 supports blocking and deblocking of a sequential data set on any device. Integrated Access Method 2 supports only block-level services on the same kind of data set. IAM 1 and IAM 2 are delivered as part of a system library. It is possible to design the system in two ways.

■   IAM 1 and IAM 2 are permanently resident parts of the run-time environment so that the GETs to IAM 1 and the READs to IAM 2 cause the linkage to operating system code for deblocking or block movement. Any buffers associated with IAM 1 or IAM 2 are defined in systems space, and neither code nor data is addressable by the running program.

■   IAM 1 and IAM 2, when used by an application program, are compiled into the address space of the program. All record and block management and all buffering are considered part of the application program. The operating system is invoked only at the bottom access method when actual I/O is required.

These two possibilities represent extremes of design (1) in which all record handling is external to an application program and (2) in which no record handling is external until control state is required. The distinction between them is important in multiprogramming and time-sharing systems in which more than one program will be in memory at the same time and in which more than one program may be doing similar operations.

Design 2 would cause a maximum replication of code for programs performing similar operations because it would provide private copies of essentially duplicated procedure and private buffers for each program. However, the path through the code might be minimized since each private copy could be specialized to the particular needs of the running program (as regards record length, block size, etc.), and formal linkages might be reduced. Design 1 would cause a minimum replication of code since a single copy of each IAM would reside in memory, and that copy would be used by all programs. On the other hand, each user of the common code would be required to pass parameters describing its particular requirements. These parameters would require interpretation and some form of insertion, and more formal linkages might have to be undertaken since presumably, for example, there are more instances of GET than of device level I/O. In addition, IAM 1 and IAM 2 would be resident at all times regardless of whether or not either or both were being used.

It is obvious that there are work-load circumstances in which design 1 is superior and work-load circumstances in which design 2 is superior. Design 1 would be superior when, for example, there are characteristically four programs in a mix and each program uses IAM 1 and IAM 2 across two kinds of devices. Design 2 would be superior when there are two programs in a mix and one program uses IAM 1 and the other uses IAM 2. Obviously there are circumstances in which it is very difficult to decide, and also circumstances in which time and space must be traded against each other.

In order to resolve the difficulties in deciding between them, many operating systems undertake either one or both of the following approaches.

- Allow an installation to decide on the level of shared function by specifying an area in which common function will reside, and making this area accessible to running programs.
- Define a mechanism by which shared functions may be forced to reside in memory when they are being used, and allowed to leave memory when they are not being used.

The first notion is represented in IBM 370 systems by the idea of a *link pack area* in which frequently used routines can be made resident. The second notion is represented by the idea of a systems transient area in which functions can be loaded when they are required. The sharing of common code requires the imposition of run-time parameter passing and interpretation, and the possible expansion of the size of the shared code itself since it may be written with generality and universality of use in mind. But beyond this there are other characteristics of shared code that relate to concepts of isolation and serialization. A fundamental notion is the idea of *reentrant* code.

Reentrant code is invariant code that does not change as a result of use. Each user must provide parameters and return points in such a way that the shared functions can use them without incorporating them into its structure. For example, parameters might be passed in a work space within the application program.

Code that is perfectly reentrant can be interrupted in the midst of serving one user's request, serve the request of a preempting user, and return to the first user when complete. *It is not necessary that all shared code be reentrant. If a shared routine is guaranteed to always complete service to a user before servicing another, then a preliminary restoration phase would allow the code to be shared.* Such code is said to be *serially reusable*. Reentrant code is preferable because it allows more flexibility. It is required for multiprocessing and for interleaved use in multiprogramming.

Some shared functions may be called directly as with GET or READ. Other shared functions are called indirectly by means of requests for the service that are enqueued on behalf of the caller. The idea of a queue is rather important in operating systems design and is a casual form of process coordination. Consider a program that has entered one of our integrated access methods in a shared situation. The GET code may eventually recognize a need to perform I/O. Since the execution of an actual I/O involves access to a device that may be shared by many programs, and since the time to perform the I/O may be long, the GET code will characteristically call a program (an I/O supervisor) to undertake the task of actually submitting the I/O. This program will determine if the device is free and, if the device is not, the program will characteristically ENQUEUE a request for the use of the device. The act of ENQUEUEing a request involves placing an element describing the request in a queue of such elements. At some later time, the queue will be investigated for service rendered by some queue-ordering discipline.

The idea of a queue is so important in coordinating programs that the ability to define queues for sending messages between all programs, including application programs, is frequently made one of the services of the run-time environment. Many elements of the operating system themselves use ENQUEUEing of requests for the services of other elements.

5.6.2 Forms of Requests for Service

Beyond issues of whether certain functions should be placed in the operating system, placed in user space, or shared in a third level of common storage,

CALL	Transfer control to a program that will operate as part of the process of the calling program.
LOAD	Load a program into memory. The operating system will locate the requested program and allocate storage to it.
WAIT	Do not dispatch the issuer of the macro until an indicated event (or events) has occurred.
POST	Set an event to the status of having occurred.
ENQ	Place a request for use of a serially reusable resource on a specified queue.
DEQ	Release a resource previously held.
STIMER	Set Interval Timer.
ATTACH	Create a new process to run as a child of the issuing process.
DETACH	Delete a process.
GETMAIN	Allocate storage.
FREEMAIN	Release storage.
WTO	Write to operator.
SNAP	Dump specified storage area.

Fig. 5.8   Macros from OS/VS Release 1.

there are many different possibilities for the definition of run-time services macros. These are not dissimilar in substance from issues concerning the definition of command languages. A fundamental decision is whether the macro language will contain many simple directives or fewer directives that require more parameterization. Commonly, the run-time macros are grouped into major functional areas such as I/O, load-module control, synchronization, and storage allocation. The specifics of the groupings will, naturally, reflect the structure as well as the function of the operating system and will also reflect how various concepts of resource management are approached in the system. The specific commands will also reflect ideas of who is master by defining what functions a program can call upon and what information it is allowed to have.

Figure 5.8 contains a partial list of macros taken from IBM's OS/VS Release 1 operating system.

The parameters associated with macros of this type are commonly addresses of systems structures that contain data about programs to be loaded or that are used to POST completion of events. Commonly, the called service will return a value in an indicated location that will tell the calling application program whether the service was performed as requested.

Another notion associated with the macro language is connected to ideas related to hierarchies. Using the I/O macros GET, READ, etc., one can demonstrate the connection between macros and layers of service. It is possible to provide a single I/O interface macro called, for example, SEND (for output) and

RECEIVE (for input). It is possible to specify as parameters of SEND/RECEIVE exactly what level of service is desired. The operating system defines a transparent hierarchy and routes the SEND/RECEIVE to a deblocker, block handler, or channel manager as appropriate. This routing may also be determined by a routing structure independent of parameters in the SEND. For example, when a data set is OPENed, it may be OPENed at a particular level of service. It is also possible to determine the level of service from control language statements. If a control block is built for each file either at allocate time or open time, then the SEND can be interpreted as a GET or READ without parameters associated with the issuing of SEND.

It would be possible to define relationships within the context of SEND so that not only I/O but also program-to-program communications could be supported by use of the same macro. A SEND using a name of an object defined to be another program would cause a placement of a request for execution on a queue associated with the named program. A SEND could be used as a form of ENQUEUE, or as a form of ATTACH.

The general power of a particular macro is associated with the amount of interpretive power a designer is willing to associate with the procedure that will process the macro call. A problem may occur in systems that have grown over time whether or not a transparent hierarchy is provided. For example, suppose a system initially offered GET, READ, and EXCP (execute channel program) either as multiple named entry points to an integrated access method or as independent modules. As the system grows in function, the time associated with service at various levels may expand and may become unacceptable to some users. There may be a need for a lower-level entry point to I/O service for users who wish particularly fast return and who are willing to provide code for function down to starting a device. Such an entry point might be called (as in OS/MVS) SIO.

The addition of SIO is going to be no easy task in any system because it will involve either a new macro or new parameters, a set of device modules perhaps previously intertwined with EXCP, and perhaps changes to macros that open files. But regardless of the difficulty of providing a new level, the real difficulty occurs when, later on, one wishes to move programs to a new operating system. When an interface is provided and applications use it, the interface is enshrined in perpetuity, and it may be necessary to provide compatibility with interfaces long after they are meaningful or useful in new environments. This problem reflects a very real design tension between the desire to provide fast, efficient, low-level interfaces that maximize user control, and the desire to avoid being committed to low-level interfaces that may become cumbersome as concepts in systems structure change.

The function and generality of any level of service affect how many levels of service must be defined. The ideas of how general and powerful a GET macro should be are by no means fixed. The more powerful the GET, the lower the use of a READ may be. There is, of course, an ironic counterargument to this that suggests the more powerful the GET, the higher the use of a READ may be. We will conclude our discussion of interfaces by inspecting these contradictory ideas.

The idea that it is possible to reduce the use of a lower-level service by increasing the power and generality of a higher-level service comes from the observation that lower levels are used when a higher level cannot be used. The argument may be made that the reason one used READ is because the record level functions available in GET are inadequate to support a particular need. The definition of the structure of a record, for example, may be distributed in such a way that the provided GET cannot advance a record. The provided GET may, for example, advance a pointer only by a constant, or physically move a contiguous set of locations from a buffer to a defined work area. Users of the READ interface have descended to that level because they must provide their own unique record advance. The way to eliminate the need for the lower service level is to so enrich the capability of a higher service level that descent to a lower level is never necessary. The more function at the higher level, the less recourse there will be to lower levels.

The counterargument is that by enriching the higher level to include every conceivable kind of record advance, it will become so large and slow that fewer, rather than more, programs will use it. Recourse will be taken more and more to private implementation of all services, and the pressure for simpler lower levels will increase until it is irresistible.

These arguments are endless but they reveal the essence of design tensions between ideas of richness of function and performance efficiency, between allowing applications programs maximum prerogative and providing maximum service, between notions of choice and release from choice that characterize every operating system design.

ABBREVIATIONS AND COMMANDS

ATTACH	DEQ
BDAM	DETACH
BSAM	DEVICE
BTAM	ECB
CALL	ENQ
CHANNEL	FLIH
CHECK	FREEMAIN

GET

GETMAIN

ISAM

LIFO

LOAD

Multics

OPEN

POST

PUT

QISAM

QSAM

QTAM

READ

RECEIVE

SEND

SIO

SNA

SNAP

STIMER

SVC

T.H.E.

VSAM

VTAM

WAIT

WRITE

WTO

TERMINOLOGY

access method

asynchronous processes

Basic Direct Access Method

Basic Sequential Access Method

Basic Telecommunications Access Method

blocking/deblocking

buffer management

caller/callee

compare-and-swap

contiguity

control state

cooperating processes

cylinder

device-handler process

direct access

direct transfer to code

dispatcher

Event Control Block

execute channel program

first-level interrupt handler

global functions

Index Sequential Access Method

indexed access

initiation

I/O supervisor

kernel

last-in–first-out stack

lock

locking mechanism

"long" instructions in caller

memory protection

modularity

P and V

"pin" a page to memory

posting completion of I/O

primitive

privileged operation

problem state

procedure

process

process synchronization

proving correctness

queue of activation records

Queued Index Sequential Access
Method

Queued Sequential Access Method

Queued Telecommunications Access
Method

reentrant code

resident in memory

resource usage

run-time environment

semaphore

sequential access

serially reusable

shared common functions

simple subroutine call

"spin" on a lock

subtask

Systems Network Architecture

task

test-and-set

Virtual Sequential Access Method

Virtual Telecommunications Access
Method

"wired down"

EXERCISES

Section 5.1

5.1 In the run-time environment, a set of capabilities not defined in the operation codes of the machine is made accessible to running programs almost as though these capabilities are part of the operation codes. Explain.

5.2 Distinguish between explicit and implicit elements of the run-time environment.

5.3 Why are certain elements of the run-time environment "wired down"?

5.4 In general, it is wise to design in such a way as to minimize the time that a system is disabled for interrupts. Why?

5.5 Explain the importance of function sharing in a multiprogramming environment.

5.6 What factors influence the decision as to which functions should be brought into the run-time environment and which functions should be generated into a program?

Section 5.2

5.7 Discuss Dijkstra's concept of hierarchy as implemented in the T.H.E. Operating System.

5.8 Give an example of the need for a locking mechanism.

5.9 What does "to spin on a lock" mean?

5.10 When a process spins on a lock, it consumes valuable CPU cycles. Some designers prefer to avoid this type of "busy wait" by removing the process from contention for the CPU until the lock clears. In what circumstances might this alternative design actually yield worse performance than simply spinning on a lock?

5.11 In a clean and perfect hierarchic structure, no function at level 0 can ever require the services of level 1. Explain.

5.12 What are the two fundamental concepts in the development of Dijkstra's hierarchic structure?

5.13 What is modularity? Are hierarchic relationships inherently modular?

5.14 What does "to 'pin' a page to memory" mean?

5.15 What is a first-level interrupt handler?

Section 5.3

5.16 Discuss each of the following methods of transferring control to a section of code.

   a) simple branch

   b) subroutine call

   c) request that the called program be scheduled for subsequent operation

5.17 Discuss the differences between a synchronous call to an operating system function and a call to a primitive.

Section 5.4

5.18 Discuss the following usual levels of I/O service.
   a) GET

   b) READ

   c) CHANNEL

   d) DEVICE

5.19 Briefly discuss
   a) sequential access

   b) indexed access

   c) direct access

5.20 What factors have influenced the emergence of the concept of cylinder as a natural allocation unit for disk files?

5.21 Comment briefly on the general nature of each of the following access methods.

a) BSAM	b) QSAM	c) ISAM
d) SAM	e) QISAM	f) BDAM
g) BTAM	h) QTAM	i) VSAM
f) VTAM		

5.22 Read the following statement. Then comment on how modules of a large system should be designed.

> Actually, the number of modules seems to increase the complexity of large systems because of the tremendously large set of relationships that can

exist between the modules, and the impact that changes in one module can have in another.

Section 5.6

5.23 Describe five different ways in which control state may be entered.

5.24 Multiprocessors of various kinds allow a system to be in problem state and control state simultaneously, and consequently must provide synchronizing mechanisms of more complexity than those required by the simpler notion of an SVC putting the system into control state and suspending problem state operations. Explain.

5.25 Discuss process synchronization using the macros CHECK, WAIT, and POST.

5.26 Comment on the desirability of the following proposed goals of operating systems design.

    a) Allow a problem-program to assure itself continuous, uninterrupted control of the system.

    b) Maximize interprogram communication without operating system intervention.

    c) Maximize what data (systems or other) a program may look at without the intervention of the operating system.

5.27 What is reentrant code?

5.28 What is serially reusable code?

5.29 Briefly describe the functions of each of the following macros taken from IBM's OS/VS Release 1 operating system: CALL, LOAD, WAIT, POST, ENQ, DEQ, STIMER, ATTACH, DETACH, GETMAIN, FREEMAIN, WTO, and SNAP.

5.30 It is possible to reduce the use of a lower-level service by increasing the power and generality of a higher-level service. Ironically, this may cause an increase in the use of the lower-level service. Explain.

6
The Kernel of the
Operating System

6.1 THE BASIC KERNEL

The kernel of an operating system consists of that body of code that is intensively and commonly used by all programs at higher levels as if it were an extension of the machine. It contains, commonly, an apparent extension of the instruction set and an extension of the sequencing mechanisms of the hardware. A fundamental design issue in the development of an operating system is the choice of what functions to put into the kernel. Another design issue is the extent to which ideas of structure should be applied to the design of the kernel itself.

Operating systems differ widely in the size and nature of their kernels. Some workers hope to restrict a kernel to fewer than a thousand locations. These designers are often influenced by the need to design a base for a very wide variety of systems' uses extending from large general-purpose systems to very small specialized applications. The base for such a range would necessarily need to be limited in those functions that existed at the lowest level and would tend to move as much function as possible to the upper levels of the run-time environment.

The smallest kernels may provide only limited information about a running process's set of accessible programs or data objects. More ambitious kernels may monitor the relationship between called and calling processes, providing a check to guarantee the protection of objects in the system. Even more ambitious kernels handle process synchronization, resource allocation, and systems directory management. The kernel for one version of the Multics operating system takes approximately 44K words and handles dynamic linking of processes to each other, virtual memory management, and controls the accessibility of objects in the system to running programs.

To some extent, the design of the kernel of a system involves the decision about what functions are to be placed in *level 0 of the hierarchy*. The level 0 functions have the following attributes.

■   They are *resident in primary storage*. Although not all functions in an operating system that are resident are part of the kernel, functions that are part of the kernel tend to be resident. This is because they must be accessible in the shortest possible period of time. In some structures, the kernel functions are resident because memory management lies above them in the hierarchy, and upward calls to memory management services may not be made. Some systems, for example, the HYDRA kernel, do not impose the upward call restriction, but even when services at higher levels can be used, elements of the kernel tend to be resident. Larger kernels that include richer functions may tend to have less wired-down primary storage than leaner kernels.

■   They tend to *run in control state as uninterruptible primitives,* and are consequently able to guarantee themselves contiguous intervals of time.

■   In systems in which a mechanism for protection exists beyond that of the distinction between control or problem state, the elements of the kernel tend to *run at highly privileged protection levels*. For example, Multics has the concept of a number of levels of accessibility privilege called *rings*. There are eight implemented rings in the Multics system. (See Fig. 6.1.) Each Multics *segment* (*collection of data or procedures*) is associated with a particular ring or rings through an entry in the directory system in which all segments are *cataloged*. The right to read a particular segment, for example, may be recorded in the directory for processes that are running in ring 3, the right to read or write may be accorded to processes that are running in ring 2, etc. Various processes running at various ring levels consequently have different rights to access various bodies of code and data.

The kernel interface is kept low in order to avoid imposing unnecessary richness and consequent path length upon an implemented higher-level interface. Since the developers of the subsystems are themselves expected to be systems programmers, they are competent to attend to the increased programming sophistication involved in dealing with minimum kernels. HYDRA defines the kernel to be that set of basic functions that can be used to build higher-level constructs representing database systems, command languages, schedulers, etc.

It is, perhaps ironically, the perception of increasing variety and complexity in the systems environment that has tended to make contemporary workers think in terms of smaller and less ambitious kernels. When an operating system run-time environment is explicitly intended to interface with application programs and application programmers directly, there is strong motive for rich function and well-supported interfaces. As usage has become so complex that application programs characteristically use very specialized kinds of service for

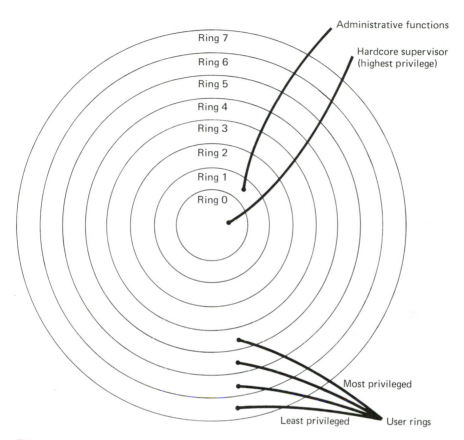

Fig. 6.1 Concentric protection rings in Multics. Rings 0 through 3 are used for supervisor and administrative segments. Rings 4 through 7 are user rings. The concentric ring concept is a generalization of the "supervisor state" and "problem state" dichotomy. A procedure in ring i may reference, during its execution, any procedure or data segment in rings $\geq i$. A procedure in ring i cannot reference data segments in rings $< i$, and may call procedures in rings $< i$ only through carefully controlled entry points called "gates."

interactive programming and for transaction processing, it is sensible to retreat somewhat and provide less function in the underlying module. In a way, the design of a kernel is not unlike the design of an instruction set for a hardware processor. As more and more variety of use is expected for a machine, the instruction set naturally tends to become more primitive, and the system relies more on the intervention of a compiler. As use becomes more homogeneous, the instructions can be made functionally richer because there is a higher probability that rich instructions can be profitably used.

In early designs, the structure of the kernel was considerably less formal than it is now in good contemporary designs. The binary world of "in control state" and "not in control state" was intended to protect the system from applications programs, but not to provide protection for elements of the kernel from each other. The kernel was a completely trusted user, any element of the kernel could address all of memory, and any table used by the system could be reached by any element of the kernel.

This early simple idea led to operating systems structures that were difficult to debug and particularly difficult to modify. Very complex interdependencies, and surprising loci of reference to system data contributed to difficulties in guaranteeing the modifiability of the system, and even the integrity of system data. Recently, ideas have emerged that impose some kind of structure within the kernel itself, and that constrict the rights of elements of the kernel to collections of data appropriate to carefully defined functions. Thus a kernel routine that manipulates tables reflecting the allocation of memory space would have no more right to access a queue of I/O requests associated with an I/O handler than a user application program would have. This notion of functional privacy may or may not involve hierarchy in the Dijkstra sense.

The following sections describe the functions that are commonly found in the kernel of an operating system. Among them are traditional elements such as *interrupt handling, I/O support, dispatching,* and some more recent candidates such as a *generalized call facility,* and *basic file system.* Many elements of an operating system, such as the *high-level schedulers, intermediate-level schedulers,* and *advanced memory managers* are discussed in detail later in the text. The elements described in this chapter are chosen because they are frequently thought to be fundamental and because they provide simple vehicles for describing the use of some fundamental data structures used by an operating system.

6.2   INTERRUPT HANDLING

Since entry to the kernel is characteristically associated with an interrupt, some resident capability to respond to an interrupt is a requirement for the kernel. The exact nature of the interrupt-handling routines is very sensitive to the design of the interrupt hardware. The IBM 370 architecture provides a number of interrupt types, for example, *SVC (supervisor call), I/O, program check, external/timer,* and *page fault.* Each type of interrupt has an associated *FLIH (First-Level Interrupt Handler).* When a FLIH gains control, it normally prohibits further interruption until it reaches a "safe" point. A safe point is the location in which status information that existed at the time of the interrupt is stored so that it can be retrieved.

An important interrupt associated with the 370 architecture is the SVC. The SVC interrupt is received by an SVC FLIH that identifies the requested service and determines whether the service routine that will perform the requested functions is resident. If it is resident, if it will itself use no service routines, and if it will run with interrupts *disabled (permitting no interruption),* then the SVC FLIH passes control directly to the service routine.

In effect, service routines that have these characteristics run as primitives. Service routines that are not resident, that may be interrupted, or that may call upon other service routines must run as processes. The possibility of having to summon a routine into memory suggests the requirement that an area allocated to the operating system must be organized as a *transient area* into which service routines may be overlaid. A further requirement is the existence of a program-fetch function of some sort that can bring transient elements into the transient area. This small loader must have the capability of locating the referenced program on a storage device and of bringing it into main memory. The capabilities of the loader may be quite basic, involving no relocation capacity (ability to choose exactly where in memory the summoned routine will be placed), and access to only a small specialized library of programs in absolute code. The loader may itself be resident or only partially resident so that its first function is to call in additional portions of itself.

It is possible to extend considerably the concept of a small, special purpose, service routine loader to the point at which it develops into a file system responsible for loading, locating, and linking all routines that are referenced by any running process in the system.

The specific action that an interrupt handler first takes depends on what is required to secure the necessary checkpoint of system status at the time of the interrupt. In many machines, it is necessary to store register status and condition codes on each interrupt. Some machines have two sets of registers so that the contents of the problem state registers need be stored only if the interrupted problem state program is going to be replaced by another program as a result of the interrupt. The interrupt handler and whatever operating system routines run use an alternate set of registers whenever the machine is in control state.

A common place for storing machine status is the activation record of the interrupted process. This activation record contains a fixed space for the insertion of machine status at the time the process loses control of the machine. It is necessary that the interrupt handlers have some way of accessing the activation record in order to store the required information if they store it in the record. This does not present too much of a mechanical difficulty since the address of a current activation record can be made available in many ways. It can always be placed in a fixed location in memory, for example. However, since the dispatcher or some other routine that restores save contents must also have access to save areas, some care must be given in systems design to the basis upon which save areas or activation records can be referenced.

It may be desirable for the interrupt handler to store registers in a private place (system save area) and then, if necessary, pass values to the dispatcher. This is an important design issue that occurs whenever a collection of data is needed by two or more elements of the system. While no one suspects a system-provided interrupt handler of maliciousness, some designers feel that careful control should be applied whenever a critical system data collection is to be shared. A bug in an interrupt handler can destroy the system's ability to continue working on any process if it erroneously accesses the set of activation records. Similarly, if for some reason the structure of an activation record changes, it is desirable to limit the effect of the change by minimizing the number of referencing elements that must be modified. It is a matter of judgment whether or not a particular shared collection of data should be directly accessible from different elements, or whether all referencing elements must use some single element whose only function is to protect that data. Part of the judgment involves performance issues, vulnerability, and the degree to which routines are trusted and known.

After taking whatever action is necessary to assure the resumability of the interrupted process, the FLIH determines what service is requested and activates it.

6.3 DISPATCHING

We have referred to the existence of a *dispatcher* and a *dispatch queue* throughout this chapter. This section discusses these elements in more detail.

Dispatching is the act of deciding which process will run next and of establishing in the instruction counter of the machine the address of the next instruction to be executed. Associated with this act is the establishment in registers of the machine those values associated with the process about to begin, so that if the process had been previously *suspended,* it resumes under the same conditions that existed when it was suspended. The value placed in the instruction counter is the instruction that would have been executed had the process not been previously interrupted. The dispatcher may also be called upon to save the status of a displaced process in a save area if that status information had not been previously saved by, for example, an interrupt handler. It has been usual to consider the dispatcher a fundamental element in an operating system and in the kernel. It is, however, possible to design a kernel that does not include a dispatcher, and leave the mechanisms of process switching up to a higher level or to the application programs themselves. Whether or not a dispatcher is part of the kernel is influenced by whether programs running as applications are assumed to be known to each other, and the degree of system control that is to be given to the application.

A brief description of how a set of programs could share a machine without a dispatcher is useful in introducing the fundamental ideas of dispatching. Figure 6.2 shows three programs that share a common set of locations in which there is a

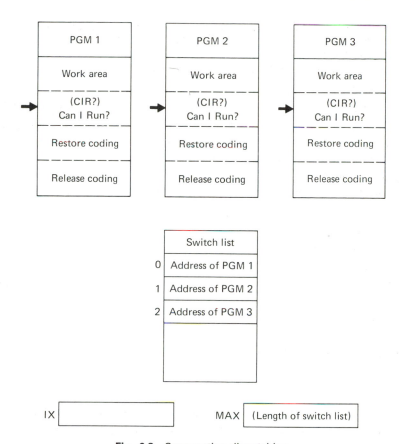

Fig. 6.2 Cooperative dispatching.

switch list. This switch list contains an entry for each program representing its entry point. The entry point is the first instruction that it will execute when control is passed to it. In each program, the entry point is the first instruction of a routine that determines if the program can run. This routine is called the "Can I run?" routine, and it may be placed at any arbitrary point in the program.

Control is passed from one program to another by execution of the *release* coding. The release code stores whatever the program wishes in its work area and performs a JUMP INDIRECT to the switch list. The address of the JUMP INDIRECT is the origin of the switch list. The full indirect address is formed by adding the value of an index register to the origin of the switch list. The value of the index register comes from IX in the common area. IX is initially set to 1. As part of release, the running program loads an index register with IX. It also tests to see if IX + 1 exceeds MAX (MAX = 3). If IX + 1 does not exceed MAX, then IX is set to IX + 1. If IX + 1 does exceed MAX, then IX is set to 1 and the index register is set to 0. The reason for the IX–MAX manipulation is to allow PGM3 to release to PGM1. Thus PGM1 will always find IX = 1, set IX = 2, and release by jumping indirectly through the second location on the switch list (ORIGIN + 1) because the index register still equals 1. PGM2 will always find IX = 2, set IX = 3, and release by jumping indirectly through the third location on the switch list (ORIGIN + 2). PGM3 will always find IX = 3 and IX + 1 = 4. Therefore, it will set IX = 1 and the index register to 0 and jump indirectly to PGM1 through the first location on the switch list (ORIGIN + 0).

The indirect jump through the switch list allows any entry point address to be placed on the list so that any program in any set of locations with any entry point can be reached by a JUMP INDIRECT. The number of programs can be increased by anyone manipulating the value of MAX. Making entries on the switch list is not normally a dispatching function even for a generalized dispatcher, but part of creating a process.

Each program has complete control over what it saves in its work area, where it puts its *CIR routine,* and how exactly it encodes its release. The CIR determines whether or not the program wishes to run at the time control is passed to it. It does this by inspecting indicators in its work areas that are set or not set. Each indicator represents something meaningful to the program. A program can establish any reason for not desiring to run when transfer is passed to it. Remember, *the program is not being called by the releasing program, it is just being given a chance to run.* There is no logical functional relation between the three programs that are being executed in a *round-robin* way.

A valid reason for not running is that, prior to releasing, the program issued an I/O and the I/O is not complete. Assume the I/O hardware is accessible to the programs, and that for each device there is a location in the interrupt handler that is set to 0 when the device is free, and set to 1 when it is busy. In the work area, there is a pointer to the device status location. CIR accesses the location to see if the device is free or busy. If it is free, the I/O operation has completed. If it is busy, the operation has not completed.

This kind of operation can be made plausible if devices are not shared, and each program submits I/O only to specific preallocated devices. If CIR finds no reason not to run, then *restore* code is executed to reestablish the machine to the conditions of the time of the last release, and the program does its function, running until it decides to release.

If an I/O interrupt occurs while a program is running, register contents are saved in a private interrupt save area and restored when interrupt handling is complete. Various extensions to the scheme could allow time-driven control and other elaborations.

What we have undertaken is to separate the notion of dispatching from the notion of a dispatcher by introducing the elements of CPU sharing within the context of a "dispatcherless" system. *The essential elements of dispatching provide ways to*

■ record the status of a program that is going to lose control so that it may be resumed;

■ select a successor program;

■ determine if a program can run;

■ reestablish (or establish) a program in the machine.

In systems in which there is a dispatcher, each of these elements becomes formalized. The work area of a program becomes a control block variously called an *Activation Record, Incarnation Record, Dispatch Control Block, Process Control Block,* or *Task Control Block*. The contents of this block depend on the specific system. Among the common elements in this structure are

■ name or program identifier of some type

■ save area

■ pointers to structures representing I/O allocation

■ memory locations assigned

■ status data indicating ability to run

■ priority

■ pointers to structures representing particular programs running for this process

These process control blocks are created for every program structure that is to be treated as a process. We will think of a *process as the schedulable element of the system*. The process control blocks may be kept in a kernel area or placed in program spaces.

Regardless of how they are allocated, the control blocks as a group represent a switch list or dispatching queue, or some number of switch lists or subqueues. Because the control blocks represent a list, there is often provision made for indicating predecessor and successor blocks, sometimes by more than one criterion. For example, a pointer may define the next control block, another set of pointers may point to a chain within the list ordered by some classification scheme indicating various associations of processes or preferences to be given. Later in the text we discuss dispatching policies and the use of various queue structures to support goals associated with dispatching.

Any particular process can be in one of a number of states. A process that is actually executing is said to be in the *running* state. A process that is able to run is said to be *ready*. A process that cannot run until some event occurs is said to be *blocked*. Some systems have an additional state called *hold* or *out* or *suspended* indicating that although the process may be ready, it should not be dispatched. Frequently a separate queue, managed by a system element other than the dispatcher, is used to represent held processes that are not to be dispatched for some interval regardless of their ability to run.

The blocked or ready states are indicated in the control block. *A process may become blocked for a variety of reasons. It may be waiting* (1) *for the completion of I/O,* (2) *for a lock to be released,* (3) *for any process on whose output it depends,* or (4) *for a paging operation* (on a paging machine). In selecting a process to be activated, the dispatcher must select from among only those that are ready. Usually, mechanisms other than the dispatcher modify the data in a control block that indicates ability to run.

In addition to recognizing ability to run, the dispatcher must have some notion of the desirability of running any particular program. This desirability is a reflection of some policy established by some person or element of the system responsible for scheduling. There is quite a bit of variation among systems regarding how much participation in policymaking the dispatcher should have. Those who hope to keep kernels small and to impose as little bias as possible in the way a system operates feel dispatchers should not be responsible for deciding what processes are preferred.

An established policy can be represented to the dispatcher in several ways. One way is to have a process that runs at intervals to order the dispatching list by any criteria it chooses, and have the dispatcher always select the next ready process encountered on the list after a process is quieted. A second way is to provide a table whose entries reflect policy that the dispatcher enforces. A truly table-driven scheduler was implemented for later versions of TSS/360 and exists in TSS/370. Its use involves a highly intelligent dispatcher, however, that is truly a combined scheduler/dispatcher, responsible for moving processes from the eligible (hold) queue to the dispatch list.

If desired, a dispatcher can do more than merely pick the next ready-to-run process. For example, each control block may have an explicit priority, and the dispatcher may have the responsibility for scanning the entire dispatch list to find the highest-priority job. A dispatcher may also be asked to make choices between selecting a process belonging to a particular chain or a separately defined subqueue. Thus a subchain of I/O-bound processes may be woven through the dispatch list, or multiple lists may be established for processes with various degrees of I/O-boundedness, and the dispatcher includes an algorithm that determines how much preference to give to I/O-bound processes. Various dispatching tactics are discussed later in the text.

One way of controlling the effect of the dispatcher on the system is by controlling the conditions under which dispatching will occur. *A dispatcher can be entered when*

1. an application process decides it no longer wishes to run, and issues a WAIT, blocking itself or merely releasing control;

2. an element of the operating system determines that an application process can no longer run, blocks it, and requests the dispatcher to replace it;

3. a clock has run down, and in consequence a period of time during which a process is allowed to continue has completed; and

4. an event that changes the blocked status of some process occurs, and the dispatcher is asked to assure that the highest-priority ready process takes control of the machine.

If only condition 1 is used as a reason for entering the dispatcher, then application programs have maximum control over how they use the system. The only occasion for task switch is "*politeness reentry*" or "*voluntary release.*" If conditions 1 and 2 are used, then the system takes a little more control, but there is still a strong sense of a process running to a convenient stopping point. When conditions 3 and 4 are used, there is a strong element of preemption in the system in which processes are switched at intervals completely disassociated with their own status. Some ways of balancing the strongly preemptive nature of 3 and 4 are to

■ *Set clock values sufficiently high so that processes tend to complete before the clock runs down.* This is effective in transaction environments in which one knows about how long a typical transaction takes, and sets the clock to some reasonable value that will allow the transaction processor to effectively complete in one dispatching interlude. It is particularly effective when conditions 1 and 2 do not occur. Conditions 1 and 2 would not occur on a very simple time-sharing interactive programming system in which a user works within a preloaded work area and cannot reference I/O devices. The idea is especially appropriate when transactions are single messages requiring a single response.

■ *In the control block of each process, record an indicator that determines whether or not the process is preemptible.* This will insulate certain designated processes from condition 4.

It is possible to have more than one dispatcher in a system. This may come about because a subsystem is given authority to dispatch between its own private set of users. The system dispatcher grants an interval of service to the monitor of the subsystem that is represented by a control block on the dispatching queue. The monitor, using a private dispatching queue, apportions this time among its own users. The monitor dispatcher would not, of course, be part of the kernel.

In machines with various interrupt levels associated with various applications, it is possible to use multiple FLIHs and multiple dispatchers. Depending on one's point of view as influenced by the construction of the system, the dispatchers would or would not be considered part of the kernel.

In comparing the descriptions of a simple dispatcherless system and of a dispatcher, we see that the basic differences lie in the formalization of the idea of a work area, and in the removal from each program of the responsibility of saving and restoring status. In addition, the will of the system can be imposed upon the program in the form of a decision about who is to run next and for how long.

6.4   I/O SUPPORT

I/O functions have been alluded to frequently throughout the text as examples of interfaces, hierarchic organization, and as the basis for discussing design issues from various viewpoints. This section discusses a common element of the kernel called an *I/O supervisor* or *I/O control program*. The fundamental function of this element is to manage the population of I/O devices by submitting I/O requests to channels and devices, and by responding to signals from the devices notifying the system of their status. There are two conditions under which the I/O control program is entered: (1) from a higher-level module of the run-time environment or an application program seeking to perform I/O, (2) from the devices themselves seeking to give notification of a completed operation or of some error condition. We will discuss each of these entries in turn.

6.4.1   Request for I/O Service

In order to satisfy an I/O request, it is necessary to have a good deal of information. The amount of information and the way the information is supplied depend on the structure of the hardware and on the nature of the allocation mechanisms associated with other elements of the operating system. This discussion will assume that the I/O control program is not responsible for allocating devices or files to various programs but merely for servicing references to files and devices already allocated by some other mechanism.

The information required to undertake an I/O operation is basically

- the address of the device

- the function to be performed

- the address of the data

On a system with no concept of channels, with fixed block sizes, and with no multiprogramming, nothing more is required to do any I/O. As the I/O hardware structure becomes more flexible, and as concepts of device independence and device sharing enter the operational environment, more information is required. For example, information is needed to specify a channel address, to describe the format of the block to be read in terms of its size and other characteristics, and to associate the request with a particular process so that information about completion can be POSTed and the process unblocked. Information describing the allocation of devices to files and files to programs is required. A rather elaborate set of tables, parameter lists, and control blocks of various kinds is needed to sustain even a reasonably flexible I/O support system.

The I/O request service element uses this complex of data structures to determine if the request is valid, and if the device and channel are available. If the I/O hardware is free and the request valid, the I/O request service element starts the device. Otherwise it either enqueues the request on a queue associated with the hardware or it returns directly to the requesting program with a notification that the request has not been accepted.

All of the information required to submit an I/O request can be compiled into a program if all file characteristics and device assignments are expressed in the programming language. It is more usual for device assignment directives and file–device associations to be made in the command language, or to be maintained in a system catalog. As part of the shift to on-line operations, a larger percentage of referenced files are preallocated files with permanent assignments. A *catalog* or *file system* maintains a record of preallocated files and provides specifics about device assignment. Programs wishing to refer to these files need make no statements about device assignment in the command stream. When a programmer wishes to use a noncataloged file, the programmer may specify a class of device rather than a specific device.

Our earlier discussion of JCL did not address any specifics of device–file assignment. In order to provide a fuller picture of I/O support, we will inspect some of the parameters on DD statements that are relevant to I/O service. The DD statement is used only as an illustration of the kinds of information that can be collected in support of a highly flexible I/O system.

The DD statement provides a *data set name* and associated parameters. Among these are an allocation parameter called UNIT that may specify a specific device, a type of device, or a group of similar logically equivalent devices. Thus a specific unit, a type of direct access device (e.g., 2319), or any direct access device can be requested. The DD statement also allows specifications of the DISPosition of the data set after completion of the program (KEEP, PASS). A good deal of information about the file can also be provided, for example LABEL, RETention period, and library membership.

The parameter set of major interest to this section is the DCB (Data Control Block) set. These parameters may be provided through the programming language or through the command language. The DCB parameters describe the nature of blocks and records in the file. For example,

- block size
- organization (direct access, indexed sequential, physical sequential, etc.)
- length of a logical record (actual or maximum)
- type of logical record (fixed length, variable length)
- length and position of a key
- encoding
- buffering technique

The information provided about allocation, file structure, and record structure is used by the allocation mechanisms and by OPEN to establish tables and control blocks required for ongoing I/O reference service. Various operating systems will, depending on when and how allocation is done, split the specific functions of allocation and OPEN differently. It is almost universal in existing systems to define an *allocate time* and an *OPEN (connect) time*, but it is not clear that there must be a logical break between these functions in all environments.

The acts of allocation are the association of a file with a device (or the recognition that the association already exists), the association of a device with a program, and the association of a file with a program. Allocation is based upon a set of tables prepared by the command language interpreter. Using as an example a simplification of the IBM OS/360 MVT operating system, for each DD statement a JFCB and an SIOT (Job File Control Block and Step Input/Output Table) are created by the DD statement processor. The JFCB contains all of the descriptive data about data set name, buffering, history, blocking, and logical records given in the DD statement. In addition, it contains information about disk space requirements. An SIOT contains information about allocation requests for device types or names. For each DD statement within a step, there are therefore a JFCB and an SIOT describing the data set characteristics and the allocation requests. These blocks are linked to each other and to other JFCBs and SIOTs for the EXECUTE statement defining a step. The allocator associates devices by constructing for each JFCB and SIOT pair a TIOT (Task Input/Output Table) that contains (essentially)

- job name
- step name
- pointer to JFCB representing the DD statement for which allocation is made
- pointer to UCB representing device allocated

Allocation is the act of inscribing a pointer to a UCB in the TIOTs constructed for a task. A UCB is a control block that exists for every device in the system. UCBs are created when the system is established or when the device population changes. They are a resident, protected collection in the kernel's space. Each UCB contains (essentially)

1. physical unit address of the device represented by the UCB
2. an index to a table that describes the location of I/O coding that is unique to this device type. Thus for each kind of device (direct access, tape, etc.) there is a basic device handler pointed to from a device table that is pointed to from the UCB
3. the location of an error handling routine for device errors
4. unit symbolic name

5. device characteristics

6. address of system element representing the last user of this device

7. status including indications of whether or not
   a) the device is busy
   b) the associated control unit is busy
   c) the device is transferring data from a disk
   d) the device is seeking data on a disk
   e) an error condition occurs

8. associated files (if any) and space available on disk device

9. associated users (if any)

10. channel association of device

The allocation process uses a search of UCBs to locate an appropriate device or space on a device, and once selecting a device inscribes its UCB address in the TIOT. The allocator is interested in UCB entries 10, 9, and 8. The I/O control program is interested in the remainder of the entries.

When a program issues an OPEN macro during run time, the OPEN services use the TIOT and JFCB to construct and/or complete control blocks that are required for referencing the file. The two essential control blocks are the DCB (Data Control Block) and the DEB (Data Extent Block). A DCB structure for each file referenced in a program is built in the program's space by the language processor. It is the function of OPEN to complete the DCB with information in the JFCB that was collected from the command language.

The DCB contains information that is interesting primarily to GET and PUT. The information in the DCB is largely that JFCB information pertaining to record, block, and buffer definition. While constructing a DCB, the OPEN routine determines which access method will be used to reference the file, and provides for the establishment of that access method in user space. OPEN, in this IBM structure, is not a part of the access method but a transient service of the run-time environment reached through an SVC. In other systems, OPEN is placed with GET, PUT, READ, and WRITE as part of the I/O support package.

There are some fields in the DCB of interest to the I/O control program. They have to do with (1) certain error conditions and represent a way of communicating errors from I/O control to a DCB, (2) the address of the DEB that is associated with every DCB, and consequently with every opened file.

A DEB describes the allocation of a file on a physical device. It points to a UCB to identify the allocated device. It points to the TCB (Task Control Block—the dispatchable unit in the system) to identify the process to which the file has been allocated. It contains a series of addresses in the access method at which control is to be passed under certain conditions of I/O error. It describes the addresses on a disk occupied by this file. The DEB is constructed in part from the JFCB (from which it gets its device layout) and from the TIOT (from which it gets its UCB addresses).

We have now mentioned a great many control blocks in passing from DD statements to an opened file. As a matter of fact, we have not mentioned all associated blocks covering all circumstances, and we have made a number of simplifications. The creation of a DEB, for example, involves execution of special routines in an access method, etc. The blocks that are available and relevant to referencing a file are the DCB, DEB, and UCB.

Finally, after allocating, opening, and reminding the reader of access methods, we are ready to read a block using the I/O control program. With the exception of the UCB, none of the functions or structures we have discussed are part of the basic I/O control program in the kernel. However, the flow from control language statement, through allocation, through OPEN, until the first operation on the file is basic to an understanding of what is involved in a complete conceptual design, and demonstrates the relationship between various elements of the system. It may also suggest the points at which various design decisions need to be made.

In order to operate on an open file, it is necessary to submit a referencing command that contains enough information for the I/O control program to associate the request with the control blocks. In the IBM systems that serve as the basis for this discussion, the request for I/O is made through the mechanism called an IOB (Input/Output Block). This IOB contains the address of the DCB, the address of a channel program, and the address of a storage area for the I/O control program to use in POSTing the completion of the I/O request. The channel program address is a particular feature associated with the I/O hardware architecture of IBM 360s/370s. It represents the mapping of logical structures on physical layout through the use of lists of channel command words that describe functions and locations of various elements of a logical record. It is this program that enables "*scatter write*" and "*gather read*" *data-chaining* to devices. This list is generated by OPEN. All we use of the concept is the fact that there is a set of I/O commands existing in the user space whose address must be passed to the I/O control program.

Entry to the I/O control program is through an SVC executed by an EXCP (execute channel program) macro instruction. The EXCP can be used by an access method or by an application program. On entry, the I/O supervisor has a pointer to the IOB; through the IOB it can access the DCB, through the DCB it can access the DEB, and through the DEB it can access the UCB. Thus it has access to all information it requires to submit an I/O request. The initial action of the I/O control program is to check the validity of the control blocks and to set error conditions to an initial status.

At the end of validity and initialization processing, the I/O control program forms a *request element* that will be used to represent this I/O request in the system. The request element contains the addresses of the control blocks that define the I/O service. Thus, the request element contains

- the address of the TCB (associating a process with this request)
- the address of the UCB (associating the request with a device)
- the address of the IOB (associating the request with a channel program)
- the address of the DEB (locating space on the device for the data set)

The I/O control program now attempts to determine if the device is available by an inspection of the UCB. A device may be unavailable because it is busy, because its control unit is busy or, for a disk device, because the arm is engaged in seeking. If the device is available, the availability of the channel is inspected. Finding the availability of a channel involves a test of the availability of the channels indicated in the UCB as associated channels. A unit may be accessible through more than one physical channel. The physical channels that provide alternate paths to a device are called *logical channels*. A table in the system associates logical and physical channels. The address in the UCB is an address to the table defining the logical channel. The I/O control program issues an instruction to physical channels attempting to find a path to the device. When the device and the channel are both available, the I/O operation is started.

The starting of the I/O operation, of course, is very specific to the hardware of a system. In IBM 370 architecture, I/O is started by the issuance of a SIO (start I/O) instruction that has an associated set of channel commands in user space. The address of the channel commands is in the IOB; the address of device specific code is in the UCB. When the I/O is started, the request element representing the I/O request is marked *active*. As a conceptual simplification, consider that the system keeps a list of all active request elements (elements whose I/O is in progress).

If a channel to the device cannot be found, or if the device is busy, the request element is marked *enqueued* and is placed upon a queue associated with the logical channel. There is a queue for each logical channel defined to the system. These queues may be ordered in various ways, either FIFO (first-in–first-out) or by priority of the requesting program.

There is an interesting detail here that relates to disk devices. There is a concept of "stand-alone" seek in the IBM systems wherein an arm on a disk is sent off to find a cylinder. This seek is issued by the I/O supervisor without reference to the command list in user space. The seek can proceed while the physical channel is transferring data from some other arm associated with the channel. In addition to the channel queues, a set of seek queues is maintained by the system. These seek queues are ordered by the address of the seek so that the arm is kept moving in an efficient manner. Thus at any time the arm is known to be at a particular cylinder address. The seek queue contains stand-alone seek requests for addresses equal to or greater than the current position, and seek requests for addresses less than the current position of the arm. The current position of the arm is in the UCB and the seek position required is determined from the DEB. The arm is kept moving in a single direction reflecting the seek queue that is ordered by address. The stand-alone seek command is issued and completed before a data transfer operation is given to the channel. The actual enqueueing on a logical channel queue is not done until the stand-alone seek is given.

When the I/O is successfully issued by the I/O control program, the request element is dequeued from the seek queue or logical channel queue and placed on the list of active elements. As we will see in the next section, the attempt to submit an I/O can be triggered as a result of an I/O interruption as well as by the receipt of an IOB from the SVC mechanism. When an I/O interruption occurs that frees a device or channel, the queued elements are inspected and a queued element is submitted to the I/O system. On submission of an I/O, the I/O control program makes appropriate modifications to the UCB to indicate that the device is now busy. In addition, the address of the related active request element is placed in the UCB.

6.4.2   Completion of I/O Service

When an I/O operation completes, an interrupt occurs that causes the operation of the I/O FLIH. The I/O FLIH operates in control state, with interrupts disabled. It transfers control to the interrupt supervisor of an I/O control program. The primary functions of the interrupt supervisor are to determine the nature of the interrupt, to POST the completion, and to submit a successor I/O request to the channel/device population from the queue of waiting requests. A major part of interrupt analysis and response involves the handling of error conditions. This error analysis response involves accessing vendor-supplied device dependent error routines, trying the I/O again, and/or accessing elements in a user routine or access method for a response to various error conditions. The discussion of I/O in the kernel has been restricted to correct hardware responses and legitimate I/O requests. In the real world, a tremendous amount of effort must be invested in designing for error conditions. One particular danger of design is that the design is biased for worst case so that code is inefficient except when errors occur.

On an I/O interrupt, the hardware will surely provide the reason for the interrupt and the address of the interrupting device. The interrupt routine must find the UCB associated with the interrupting device. If the hardware provides no direct method, the UCB must be located through a system table that associates the channels with related UCBs. When found, the UCB provides the address of the associated request element. From this request element, all associated blocks can be found.

The analysis of the interrupt involves the inspection of an interrupt status word that indicates the status of the channel/device pair at the time of interrupt. We consider what happens only when the status word indicates the successful completion of an I/O request. This status word must be moved from its primary hardware location before the system can be enabled for further interrupts. It is moved, in OS, to a location in the IOB that was used to initialize the request.

The IOB provides a location in which the successful completion of the I/O should be recorded. The interrupt supervisor calls upon the system POST routine to make appropriate recording. If the process is blocked WAITing for this I/O to complete, this POSTing unblocks the process and makes it available for dispatching when the dispatcher next executes.

The I/O interrupt supervisor maintains the load on I/O channels by inspecting channel status looking for channels that can be activated. At the end of I/O processing, the FLIH determines whether the process interrupted by the I/O interrupt should be resumed, or whether the dispatcher should be entered.

The compressed flow that we have described omits one detail of importance in the relationship between the I/O supervisor and the program that requested the I/O. The access method or the user program must provide certain code to handle certain kinds of interrupt status. This code, in IBM systems, is provided in appendages to which the I/O supervisor gives control under certain interrupt conditions. These referrals to higher-level code are intended to allow running programs to provide specialized responses to specific conditions. Some of these are error conditions, but others relate to situations reflecting the particular organization of the data used. There is, therefore, throughout normal submission and interrupt handling, a number of references to code not in the supervisor but in a user area. A program that wishes to provide function for certain conditions can code the appendages and provide addresses to them. This program would issue EXCP macros directly to the supervisor. Programmers who do not need to concern themselves with status at this level can rely on those interfacing modules that allow higher interfaces to the I/O control program.

6.5 MEMORY CONTENTS MANAGER

Memory contents management is a function frequently found in the kernel. In most systems, the concept of allocating and de-allocating storage at run time is represented in some form. Various approaches to the organization and management of memory are discussed later in the text. This section describes a simple mechanism for controlling the contents of main memory in order to introduce the kinds of functional elements that are involved in a simple kernel. The assumptions of this section are a nonrelocate, nonpaged, nonvirtual-memory system in which all of available memory is allocatable to any program. This implies that all memory management is done as a result of an explicit request for additional storage. This explicit request can come from a running user program directly in the form of a GETMAIN, or can come from a higher-level service of the run-time environment that in the process of servicing a request or loading a program recognizes a need to acquire storage.

The fundamental data structure required for memory management is a *memory contents table*. This table is chained so that each entry actually resides in the first locations of the memory block it is describing. Each entry contains the following information.

- The condition of the area of memory. For example, (1) the area is *free*, (2) the area is *used and not freeable* (program or data), or (3) the area is used but freeable (program or data)
- a pointer to the preceding memory area (area with lower addresses)
- a pointer to the succeeding memory area (area with higher addresses)
- the size of the area
- a pointer to the process using the area if the area is being used
- if the area is free, a pointer to the preceding and succeeding free areas

This kind of contents chain is used by Burroughs' Master Control Program (MCP) and by IBM's OS/MVT. Although these systems differ in details, the concept of a chain of area definitions is common to both.

This chain may be used to represent all of memory or only that part of memory that is allocatable to processes not in the kernel. If the entire memory is represented, then the kernel areas are marked "used and not freeable" so that kernel functions will never be overlaid in memory. There may be other elements in memory that are marked "nonfreeable." For example, in MCP those areas of memory allocated to the Program Reference Table (PRT) of a running process are marked "nonfreeable." The PRT is the fundamental unit of a running process that contains scalar variables used by a program, and pointers to its routines and data objects. The intensity of use of a PRT by a running process requires that a PRT be made resident. If the kernel locations are represented in the memory table, then some distinction must be made between these per-manently "wired-down" functions and those elements of a program that should be kept resident while a process is running or while it is on the dispatching queue(s) in nonHOLD or OUT status.

When an area of memory is requested, the memory manager is given the size of the area required, whether or not the area will be overlayable or resident, and a means of determining the identity of the requestor. The memory manager searches its list of free space looking for an area that will fit the given size. When it finds one, it carves the amount of space requested from the area, creating an entry representing the allocated space and an entry representing the residual free space of the area used for allocation. The allocated entry contains an indication of whether or not it may be freed, a pointer to the process control block of the using process, and appropriate pointers to predecessors and successors on the memory chain. The new free entry contains pointers to the free areas preceding and succeeding it, and a notation of its size.

Memory management, like dispatching, has a problem in the policy versus mechanism area. The manner in which the memory manager searches the list of memory areas reflects a *memory management policy*. This policy contains elements of the balance between desires to use memory effectively and desires to give good service to certain programs. There are two ways to control the allocation of space in real memory. First, one can control who can call the services of the memory manager. Second, one can control what kinds of decisions a memory manager makes by making various distributions of functions between a basic memory manager and higher-level routines. These higher-level routines may be viewed as object managers that handle the allocation of logical structures to processes in the run-time environment. Thus a running process refers to a table or file or another program by use of an object manager. The object manager then tells the memory manager what is required in the way of primary memory for the referenced object. The policies of memory allocation are implemented in the object managers and the memory manager does only what it is directed to do.

A purely neutral memory manager may need to be told a number of things, and would be entered only when a requirement for allocation or de-allocation has already been determined at a higher level. For example, a request for more storage from a running process would be handled by an allocation manager that might make a determination as to whether this request should be honored, depending on the priority of the requesting program, the amount of space available, and other issues of system balance and component utilization. Such an allocation manager would ask the memory manager how much free space is available, ask the Process Control Block how much space this program already has and its priority, and then determine whether to request more space. If it decides to request more space, it tells the memory manager whether this space should be marked "nonfreeable," whether it should be taken from space already used by some other program of lower priority in the dispatch queue, or whether additional space should actually be allocated to the requesting program. In certain circumstances, the allocation manager tells the memory manager to make space by rearranging storage, or by eliminating certain areas. Another function of an object manager might be to determine whether an object referred to by a process is already in storage, and to inform the memory manager to inscribe a pointer to the requesting Process Control Block. By imposing a level of object management above the memory management level, and structuring the run-time environment carefully, it is possible to build a highly flexible operating system that can implement various allocation strategies and tactics on top of a basic mechanism. This mechanism, since it is neutral, small, stable, and simple, might be implemented in microcode without risk.

6.6   OTHER ELEMENTS IN THE RUN-TIME ENVIRONMENT

Beyond the basic elements of the kernel, there may be any number of functions in the run-time environment. Higher-level services, in and out of the run-time environment, will be discussed in subsequent chapters. Additional functions associated with resource allocation strategies and tactics will also be discussed later. The reader at this point has a reasonably complete basic idea of the functions, structure, and associated design considerations of a run-time environment, and should find the literature reasonably comprehensible. Privilege is reflected, for example, in the PDP-11 that has three levels of operation, (1) a kernel state, (2) a monitor state, and (3) a user state. The notion of monitor state may be used to support the idea that the underlying subsystem program is a kind of monitor that requires additional privilege and greater accessibility to system data than would a normal user program. A subsystem monitor that has responsibility for resource allocation among its users may require access to systems tables not usually accorded.

The degree of integration of a subsystem is a resource management design issue. It is possible to fully integrate a subsystem behind its unique user inferfaces. Such an integrated subsystem would be fully managed by the base system. For example, the central base system dispatcher and scheduler would dispatch and schedule each individual running program regardless of the subsystem context. That is, users, not subsystems, would be represented on the dispatching queue. This is the relationship that exists between the TSO (Time-Sharing Option) and the MVS operating system. Similarly, memory assignment for all users is managed by a central memory management mechanism. The advantage of this is the maximizing of flexibility and balancing of service to users across all subsystems. This is important because it is the user, after all, and not the subsystem that must receive significant service.

ABBREVIATIONS, STATEMENTS, AND COMMANDS

DCB	GECOS
DD	GET
DEB	GETMAIN
EXCP	HYDRA
FLIH	IBM's OS/MVT

I/O FLIH

IOB

JFCB

LABEL

MCP

MVS

OPEN

PRT

PUT

READ

SIOT

TCB

TIOT

TSO

UCB

UNIT

WRITE

TERMINOLOGY

activation record

basic file system

blocked process

Burroughs' Master Control Program

"Can I run?" routine

catalog

channel command word

channel program

channel queue

checkpoint of system status

control state

data-chaining

Data Control Block

Data Extent Block

device independence

dispatch control block

dispatch queue

dispatcher

"dispatcherless" system

dispatching

DISPosition

execute channel program

external/timer interrupt

file system

first-level interrupt handler

gather read

generalized call facility

"held" process

incarnation record

Input/Output Block

interrupt handler

interrupts disabled

I/O-bound process

I/O completion interrupt

I/O interrupt

I/O supervisor

I/O support

Job File Control Block

kernel

"level 0" functions

logical channel

memory contents table

memory management policy

memory manager

page fault	scatter write
paging	"schedulable" element
physical channel	scheduling
POST completion of I/O operation	seek queue
primitive	segment
process	"stand-alone" seek
process control block	Step Input/Output Table
process synchronization	suspended process
program check interrupt	SVC interrupt
Program Reference Table	switch list
protection ring	Task Control Block
ready process	Task Input/Output Table
request element	Time-Sharing Option of MVS
RETention period	transient area
round robin	Unit Control Block
running process	

EXERCISES

Section 6.1

6.1 Although not all functions in an operating system that are resident are part of the kernel, functions that are part of the kernel tend to be resident. Why?

6.2 Kernel functions run as uninterruptible primitives. Explain.

6.3 Briefly discuss each of the following functions that are commonly found in the kernel of an operating system.
  a) interrupt handling
  b) I/O support
  c) dispatching
  d) generalized call facility
  e) basic file system

Section 6.2

6.4 What interrupt types are mentioned in the text?

Section 6.3

6.5 Explain how a set of programs could share a machine without the use of a dispatcher.

6.6 Discuss each of the following essential elements of dispatching.

a) a way to record the status of a program that is going to lose control so that it may be resumed

b) a way of selecting a successor program

c) a way of determining if a program can run

d) a way of reestablishing (or establishing) a program in the machine

6.7 Discuss the need for each of the following items normally included in a Process Control Block.

a) name or program identifier of some type

b) save area

c) pointers to structures representing I/O allocation

d) memory locations assigned

e) status data indicating ability to run

f) priority

g) pointers to structures representing particular programs running for this process

6.8 Explain the purpose of each of the following process states.

a) running

b) ready

c) blocked

d) hold

6.9 Give four reasons why a process may become blocked.

6.10 How does the dispatcher determine the desirability of running any particular program?

6.11 Four situations in which a dispatcher can be entered are

a) when an application process decides it no longer wishes to run, and issues a WAIT, blocking itself or merely releasing control;

b) when an element of the operating system determines that an application process can no longer run, blocks it, and requests that the dispatcher replace it;

c) when a clock has run down, and by consequence a period of time during which a process is allowed to continue has completed;

d) when an event that changes the blocked status of some process occurs, and the dispatcher is asked to assure that the highest-priority ready process takes control of the machine.

Discuss several ways of balancing the strongly preemptive nature of (c) and (d).

Section 6.4

6.12 What information is required to undertake an I/O operation?

6.13 A rather elaborate set of tables, parameter lists, and control blocks of various kinds is needed to sustain even a reasonably flexible I/O support system. Explain.

6.14 The Data Control Block parameters describe the nature of blocks and records in a file. What information is contained in the DCB?

6.15 The Unit Control Block (UCB) is a control block that describes the attributes and status of a particular hardware device. Discuss the items of information contained in the UCB.

6.16 What is a "stand-alone" seek?

6.17 During execution of a program, a READ operation is issued to obtain the next record of a sequential disk file, and to place this record into a given area in main memory. Describe the precise sequence of events that ultimately causes the record to be read properly. Mention all relevant systems programs and control blocks involved.

6.18 What is an I/O completion interrupt?

6.19 One particular danger of the design of error processing routines is that the design is biased for worst case so that the code is inefficient except when errors occur. Explain.

Section 6.5

6.20 Describe the organization of a typical memory contents table.

7

Systems
Services

7.1 THE CONCEPT OF SYSTEMS SERVICES

Earlier chapters mentioned that there is some controversy about what portion of the systems software constitutes the operating system, and what portion should be considered a set of utilities that runs on the operating system base. Even within the context of an operating system, functions may be divided into prerun-time and run-time functions. We have seen that the design goals of a system can alter ideas of what are appropriate functions to perform ''on a program'' or ''for a program,'' and what are appropriate functions to perform during the program's stay in the run-time environment. Beyond this, there is the idea that even within the run-time environment there is structure, and some functions are considered part of the kernel while others are considered to exist as extensions to the kernel as specialized macrocallable services.

It is very difficult to define the idea of a *system service* precisely since the notion includes both elements of the run-time environment not in the kernel, and large programs that run as part of the prerun-time environment. The functions performed are sometimes in the run-time environment and are sometimes not. A designer places the functions within the system according to judgments about how frequently the services are to be provided, how large the programs representing the services are to be, and what balance between flexibility, burden, functional richness, and operational efficiency seems appropriate for the goals of the system.

Systems services discussed in this section are services that are control stream callable. They are structured as large independent modules of the system that run on or for a program before or after it is committed to the run-time environment. There are three major types of such systems services.

- prerun services to programs such as *compile, combine and edit*, and *allocate resources*

- postrun services to programs such as *de-allocate resources*, and *print output*

- services to the system including *control stream reading*, and *high-level scheduling*

Certain auxiliary services such as system definition may also be thought of as system services.

7.2   THE CONTROL STREAM READER

We have frequently mentioned the concept of *job control languages* or *command languages* that provide vehicles for requesting program execution. These languages provide statements that describe items such as

- the name of the requestor

- the name of the program and, if necessary, where it is

- the data required for the program and, if necessary, where it is

- the disposition of data after program completion

- the devices required

- the estimated running time for the program

- the estimated amounts of primary storage

- the priority or deadline

This *control language* is combinable into *control streams*. In interactive systems there is a tendency to execute each control statement as it is presented. In batch systems, they are collected and executed as a group.

A *reader* program may be started at the choice of an operator who wishes to submit a control stream. A reader may also be started by an element of the run-time environment that reacts to an interrupt from a device known to be a source for control stream.

The function of the reader program is to place the control stream onto some internal storage mechanism. The physical device is commonly a disk or other DASD device. The logical output of the reader may be onto a spooling buffer or directly onto the waiting job queue. The use of a buffer area before placement onto the job queue is common when the stream comes from a remote or teleprocessing interconnected stream source.

The reader characteristically transforms the stream into a more compact internal format and may modify, append, or expand the stream using systems-stored collections of stream. The reader may also check the stream for correctness.

The modification or expansion of stream is common when the submitted stream can be written in a shorthand form that provides for simple requests. The shorthand must be expanded into the real control language that will be processed by subsequent schedulers and allocators. For example, in IBM's OS systems it is possible to place a control stream in a procedure library and name each control stream element. A full call for FORTRAN execution involves a total description of work-space and device requirements. A FORTRAN user, however, may submit a single simplified statement that names the FORTRAN compiler. The control stream reader will recognize the FORTRAN reference, go to the procedure library to find the full FORTRAN call stream, and use this stream as its output.

Checking the accuracy of the control stream is a common reader function. However, in some systems (e.g., IBM OS/VS1) this function is placed in the job-scheduling mechanism. If the time delay in reporting control-stream errors is not critical, and if maintaining source device operation at rated speeds is important (and not achievable unless reader function is minimized), then the delay of checking is an acceptable design.

The relationship between the reader and the scheduler is an important design decision. If the system desires to accommodate high-priority jobs without operator intervention, then the reader must recognize a high-priority job and be able to call immediately for the operation of the scheduler. If this capability is critical enough, then the reader and scheduler may be combined.

The need for a reader derives from the concept of new job submission of heterogeneous jobs with diverse priority and resource usage characteristics. Real-time systems that prohibit submission of jobs not predefined to the system do not require submission vehicles that must be processed by a control-stream reader.

7.3 LOCATION ASSIGNMENT AND LOADING

There are two fundamental activities associated with program preparation for execution that are normally performed after compilation. These activities involve (1) combining programs that have been independently compiled and (2) associating programs with machine locations.

Earlier, we discussed the existence of various "times" in the progress of a program toward execution. This progression of times is easily seen in the choices available as to when to *bind* a program to machine locations.

A program may be assigned locations at the time of its creation. The programmer does this by coding in absolute addresses. A program may be assigned locations during compilation. Some assemblers associated with real-time operating systems have allowed this as an option in the past. The motive was to eliminate the burden of *relocating* the program each time it was called, and was appropriate for systems that did not have hardware support for quick relocation.

Historically, the concept of *static relocation,* the ability to place a program anywhere in primary addressable storage, involves the creation of a relocatable module by the compiler and the existence in the system of a *relocatable loader.* This relocatable loader defines a time called *load time* that has had historic significance in operating systems evolution.

In contemporary systems design, as we will see in the resource management chapters, the allocation of data and devices to a program is quite separate from the allocation of primary storage. The act of relocating a program, or associating an *address space* with a *location space,* may be performed many times upon a program that may move in and out of primary storage into different locations each time.

The act of *loading* is very much a part of the implicit run-time environment in virtual memory systems. The loading of a program, in the sense of a first-time association of locations, if it conceptually exists, is an act of placing a program into *virtual memory space* (memory space mapped onto DASD devices). The loader in such systems tends to lose identity as a major systems component, and collapses into the run-time environment in which it may decompose into program fetch and memory management.

However, in earlier systems the relocatable loader was frequently designed to play the role of a scheduler/allocator and was a major system component running as a system service.

The loader accepted as input a relocatable file created by the compiler and a limited loader directive language that described I/O devices required, file buffer requirements, and system subroutines to be used with the program. The loader allocated all resources and had a library search capability for finding referenced compiler or I/O subroutines. A limited program combination capability existed in order to provide addressability to the systems provided routines. The reader, curious about the evolution of systems, will find the description of the relocating loader for IBSYS/IBJOB in the *IBM Systems Journal* (1963) a treasure of conceptual material. At a time when operating system structure is of such concern, a perusal of older systems often reveals lost arts.

The actual act of relocation depends on the machine structure. There are two aspects to this; first, to find a suitable set of locations and second, to actually bind. Finding suitable locations may be done by a simple counter that records the number of locations already assigned. Each time a routine is placed, the counter is bumped by its size, and therefore represents a pointer to the first free location.

Binding a program to locations may involve modification to the addresses of the program. The language processor appends to each instruction a set of *relocation bits* that indicates whether or not the address field of the instruction should be modified by the loader. Shift instructions or immediate instructions, for example, would be marked *nonrelocatable* because it is not meaningful to modify these values by the offset of the program in memory.

Machines may use index registers as *relocation registers* or have a distinct set of relocation registers. On such systems, the loader does not physically modify addresses (except in certain instances to effect program combination or to resolve constant addresses), but places a value in a relocation register that is added to the address field to form a location address. The programmer or compiler must provide a map of the registers that a particular relocatable section will use as an address offset.

7.4   PROGRAM COMBINATION AND LINKING

Programs may be combined at various times. They may be combined before they are submitted for compilation. This may be done by hand, actually concatenating decks to form a single compilation unit, or by some library utility that places named program units onto an input medium for the compiler. Programs may also be combined by the compiler itself in response to directives in the language such as CALL, procedure definitions, function references, etc. The compiler may have a precompilation library to combine referenced modules from a provided library and from its own library. Some of these modules may be in a language form associated with compiler output so that the compiler need not compile the entire stream.

Programs may also be combined at load time by a relocatable loader with a collection capability. Finally, programs may be combined dynamically in run-time environments wherein a reference to an exernal routine causes it to be located, allocated, linked, and executed in response to the call.

The systems service described in this section defines an additional time when programs may be combined. It is a time between compilation and loading called *linkage-edit time. The linkage editor is a systems service run as a program with a set of programs as input. It outputs a combined program in (usually) relocatable form. A distinction between a collecting loader and a linkage editor is the detail that a collecting loader creates a memory image in place and a linkage editor creates a named data set or file for subsequent loading into memory.*

The inputs to a linkage editor are a collection of programs to be combined, the locations of these programs, a designated output medium, and a set of linkage directives that may describe sections of the programs to be included in the linkage and sections to be modified in some way. The input language used to describe the linkage function is commonly a specialized language submitted after the job control language call for the linkage editor.

The work of the linkage editor is to take a set of independent linear address spaces and combine them into a single linear space. This enables a program to reference an independently compiled program directly.

In addition to the input stream directives, the linkage editor relies upon an addendum to a program called an *external symbol dictionary*. The external symbol dictionary is created by the compiler to represent references made by the program to labels or variable names not internally defined, locations specified by the program as external references, and any areas defined as common areas by the program.

The linkage editor creates a single combined program by resolving the cross-program references represented in the external symbol dictionary.

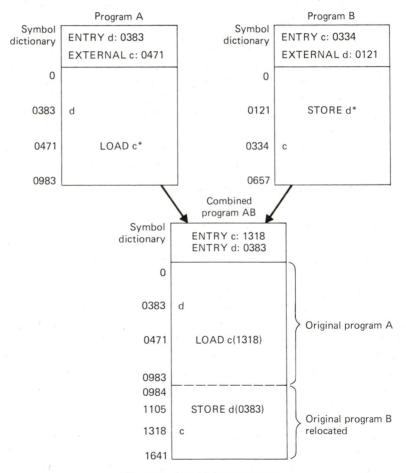

Fig. 7.1 Combining programs.

A somewhat simplified description of the process is as follows: Figure 7.1 shows a very simple conceptual control stream call for linkage editing with programs A and B to be combined into program AB. Program A has an external symbol dictionary that records an unresolved external reference to a symbol c occurring at relative location 0471 and a symbol d at relative location 0383 that is an entry point to the program. Program B's external symbol dictionary records an external reference to a symbol d occurring at relative location 0121 and an entry point symbol c occurring at relative location 0334. Both programs are compiled to relative locations beginning at 0.

The linkage editor combines the two programs initially by concatenating them into a single structure. Program A has locations 0 to 0983, but new locations for Program B go from 0984 to 1641. All references in it must be adjusted to reflect the change in relative address space.

The external symbol dictionary of Program A is inspected for external references. The undefined reference to c is found, and program B's dictionary is searched for a corresponding entry. There c is found and it is then associated with relative location 0334. Its new position in the concatenated space, however, is 1318. The LOAD c at 0471 is now completed as a reference to relative 1318.

Similarly, Program B's dictionary is searched for external references, and the reference d is found. Program A's dictionary shows a corresponding entry definition at location 0383. The STORE at Program B's 0121, which is now at relative 1105, is completed to read STORE 0383. The external dictionary for Program AB contains no unresolved references, but does contain an adjusted externally referencible table indicating the new locations of c and d.

This new program, although combined, is still in relative address form and a loader operation is still required to associate the address space with real machine locations.

7.5 THE HIGH-LEVEL SCHEDULER

In batch systems, the function of selecting a job to run and, perhaps, acquiring a set of resources for it is performed by a systems service component called the job scheduler. The selection of jobs from a queue of submitted jobs in the batch environment supposes a preliminary reader function as described earlier. The scheduler operates relatively infrequently because changes to a batch program mix occur over relatively long intervals. Scheduling at more frequent intervals in order to maintain system goals dynamically is the function either of a dispatcher that runs as part of the run-time environment, or of an intermediate between the high-level scheduler and the dispatcher that may be called a *dynamic allocator* or a *systems resource manager*. Sometimes the name scheduler is given to a routine at this level. This is particularly true in real-time or time-sharing systems in which the function of initial start selection may not be distinctive enough from periodic restarting of a process to merit a distinct systems component.

The scheduling function may be represented in a distinct service component whose task is to select a candidate and pass it on to allocation. Scheduling and allocation may be combined into a single service module. The reader, scheduler, and parts of allocators may be combined into a composite systems service called a *job entry subsystem*.

The scheduler may run at the request of an operator or at the request of another systems component. The run-time environment may request the operation of the scheduler when sparse resource use is observed in order to increase the utilization of system components. The reader may request the operation of the scheduler in response to a "hot job."

The scheduler inspects the job queue to determine the next job to start by certain criteria that balance concepts of priority and resource usage. A scheduler may be biased to select highly I/O-bound jobs in preference to CPU-bound jobs or jobs that will best fit in memory. A scheduler may also be biased to select high-priority jobs or shortest jobs. Commonly, schedulers select priority within resource usage pattern, or preferred resource usage pattern within priority by some bias built in or provided as a parameter.

Upon selection of a candidate for startup, the scheduler calls upon allocation mechanisms. Systems differ in what resources are allocated by a front-end, startup process, and what resources are allocated during the run-time environment. This is discussed in detail in the resource management chapters.

In less ambitious batch systems, a conservative approach to resource management tends to increase the resources that are initially allocated. This is consistent with stable environments assumed by such systems. When all allocation (other than CPU and channel use time) is done at scheduling time, then the allocation mechanisms tend to be part of the scheduler. The allocation mechanisms maintain lists of available resources, and accomplish allocation by reducing the available resource count and establishing ownership of the resource. This is commonly done by a set of tables associated with the system and a table associated with the program. These tables combine to reflect the facts that Program A can access file 3, that file 3 is on device 7, and that device 7 is on channel 4, for example. The tables are used in order to disassociate program structure from resource environment, and achieve some degree of flexible resource allocation.

In more flexible systems, allocation may occur at times other than system scheduling time, and hence become a part of the run-time environment. The scheduler then invokes the allocation mechanisms as service macros. It is common to divide allocation by resource class. The allocation of a data set, for example, may be accomplished only at schedule time, and that function may be accessible only by the scheduler. The allocation of core may be dynamic through

GETMAIN macros accessible to the program as part of the run-time environment.

7.6 SYSTEM GENERATION

One of the tasks associated with many operating systems is the definition of a specific version of the system from a collection of modules that is delivered by a vendor to a particular installation. This process, commonly called *SYSGEN* (*System Generation*) involves

- the selection of various modules to form a specific system
- the description of the physical placement of modules in a complex of storage areas
- the description of the physical population of devices and storages that define the machine configuration
- the establishment of particular parameters that represent scheduling policies and resource management goals
- the establishment of various table sizes, buffer size limits, etc.

The specifics of the SYSGEN process are influenced by many of the ideas that influence whether or not a service should be made part of the run-time environment. The same desire to increase flexibility has moved some of the system definition statements commonly associated with SYSGEN time to another time called *IPL* (*Initial Program Load*) in which an operator can use the operator language to alter or provide certain SYSGEN-like parameters. For example, in IBM's early DOS, the partitions of memory were defined at SYSGEN time so that a repartitioning of memory required the generation of a new system. As the system matured, partition redefinition became possible at IPL time. The IPL process involves those activities that "bring up" a system from a dormant state.

Another consideration that influences the SYSGEN process is the operating system vendor's view of how the system should be marketed. There are two rather different approaches to the marketing of an operating system. At one extreme, there is an *OEM* (*Original Equipment Manufacturer*) approach in which many individual components are separately defined and priced, and a user constructs a system tailored out of components. At the other extreme is a completely structured, predefined system with either minimum parameterization or complete parameterization provided by the vendor. Within these extremes, different operating system offerings strike different balances between the desire to provide highly configurable, optimizable systems, and the desire to constrain the expense and effort of creating a running system. By and large, system designers are influenced by trends among user organizations. A current trend is toward a reduction in the effort to generate a system, and a willingness to pay the price in optimization. A manifestation of this is IBM's *IPO* offering of the OS/MVS operating system that provides preparameterization and reduces the SYSGEN process to a relatively trivial effort. The widespread acceptance of this offering indicates that users feel the cost of flexibility is too high.

In its simplest form, the SYSGEN process involves a complete representation of all of the modules of an operating system and a system generation language. The statements of the system generation language are read and interpreted by a SYSGEN processor that applies the directives against the total set of modules in order to create a customized version of the system. This process is commonly undertaken by the user installation, and involves writing generation directives, and then executing the statements under the control of a SYSGEN processor. The creation of libraries of control language statements and the establishment of data dictionaries or user profiles is then undertaken to establish a meaningful running system.

Another dimension of this effort involves the possibility that major components of a system may be generated separately so that establishing a large multicomponent system involves a number of individual generation processes. Finally, an aspect of SYSGEN that has been troublesome to some users is the need, in some systems, to regenerate as a result of what they view to be trivial changes in systems configuration, such as, for example, the addition of a terminal device. This problem is eased somewhat by *partial system generations,* the ability to regenerate only portions of a system, and of course by moving definitional capability to IPL time.

The SYSGEN process is interesting because it is so closely related to the notions of structure and scope fundamental to the design of the system. A contemporary concept of system generation brings the process on-line and almost eliminates the existence of SYSGEN time as a unique and separate set of tasks. SYSGEN becomes initialization of a delivered functional base system that is already in an operational form. The system contains a package of preset parameters that are applied by an initialization process that can be run from a terminal device. Changes to the parameter list are accomplished by use of the system editor and changed parameters are applied by the initialization process. The command language of the system is used to redefine configuration, extend itself to form new functions, add new (perhaps user-created) functions, and specify resident functions. The concept of system creation has moved from a concept of generation as an off-line process to the use of the system to build itself.

Another issue that has been associated with the SYSGEN process is the nature of new releases or new versions of an operating system. It has been traditional for vendors to periodically supply new versions of systems in the form of complete replacements of an old system. Thus one might be running OS Release 21 or OS Release 22, etc. and the installation of a new release would involve a major effort. The movement from one release to another was motivated by the unique availability of support for a new storage device in the new release, or of a new teleprocessing function, or of a considerable improvement in the performance of the system. Additionally, there was the overhanging threat that the system supplier would withdraw maintenance services from older versions as of a certain date.

This pattern could sometimes disrupt applications development in an installation because of the effort involved in moving from one system to another. In order to break this cycle, IBM developed the notion of *Selectable Units* that is intended to allow an installation to choose various degrees of stability or rates of change. The concept of the Selectable Unit is the partial optional replacement of a portion of the system that leaves other elements of the system undisturbed. The success of this approach depends on the degree to which design has minimized the number of interdependent modules in the system so that areas of clean functional partitions can be defined.

Although different in approach, the Selectable Unit and preparameterized concepts both are trying to address the issue of how much effort is involved in establishing and maintaining a current operating system.

7.7   SYSTEMS SERVICES AND THE RUN-TIME ENVIRONMENT

The decision about what functions to place in the run-time environment and what functions to exclude from that environment is driven by a number of systems concepts. On-line interactive systems present a much less distinct view of "times" than do batch systems, and the distinctions between prerun, postrun, and run-time functions begin to blur. In the future, all services may be presented within the concept of a terminal session that involves the intertwined issuance of commands that cause services to be performed, and commands that cause application functions to be executed. Multics and other systems already provide a certain overlap between commands, run-time macros, and many properties of programming languages in the command language. There is a developing feeling that command language should be optionally executable on a verb basis or compilable.

The structure of current systems reflects their evolutionary growth. Contemporary partitions of function between prerun-time services, basic kernel, and run-time services often reflect a desire to avoid perturbing an old structure when a systems service is brought into the run-time environment. Sometimes structure represents the political organization of the people who created the system. Certain interfaces are appropriate for groups working across long distances, and other interfaces are possible when people are working closely together.

In general, as machines become more powerful, one may expect enrichment of the run-time environment, and as on-line work becomes the dominant method of access, we will see a more cohesive approach to the language structures that are used to request computer services.

TERMINOLOGY

address space
basic kernel
batch program mix
bind a program to locations
"bring up" a system
collecting loader
command language
control stream reader
dynamic allocator
dynamic linking
external symbol dictionary
high-level scheduler
"hot job"
IBM's IPO offering of OS/MVS
IBM's TSS/370
IBSYS/IBJOB
Initial Program Load
IPL
job control language
job entry subsystem
linear address space
linkage-edit time
linkage editor
linker
linking
load time

loading
location space
memory space
OEM
Original Equipment Manufacturer
paging management
partial system generation
prerun-time services
program combination
reader
real memory
relocatable loader
relocatable module
relocation
relocation bits
relocation register
run-time services
scheduler
Selectable Unit
static relocation
SYSGEN
SYSGEN processor
system generation
system service
systems resource manager
virtual memory space

EXERCISES

Section 7.1

7.1 Give several examples of prerun-time systems services to programs.

7.2 List several examples of postrun-time systems services to programs.

Section 7.2

7.3 Briefly discuss the need for each of the following items normally described by control language statements.

a) name of the requestor

b) name of the program and, if necessary, where it is

c) data required for the program and, if necessary, where it is

d) disposition of data after program completion

e) devices required

f) estimated running time for the program

g) estimated amounts of primary storage

h) priority or deadline

7.4 The logical output of a control stream reader may be onto a spooling buffer or directly onto the waiting job queue. Discuss the advantages and disadvantages of each of these dispositions for control stream.

7.5 How would you implement the ability for a system to expand abbreviated control stream into the full-control language statements needed by schedulers and allocators?

7.6 Real-time systems that prohibit submission of jobs not predefined to the system do not require submission vehicles that must be processed by a control stream reader. Explain.

Section 7.3

7.7 List the various times at which a program may be assigned to specific memory locations.

7.8 Discuss the operation of a relocating loader.

Section 7.4

7.9 Discuss the various times at which programs may be combined.

7.10 Distinguish between a collecting loader and a linkage editor.

7.11 What items are normally input to a linkage editor?

7.12 What is an external symbol dictionary? How is it used by the linkage editor?

Section 7.5

7.13 Discuss each of the following criteria used by a scheduler in selecting the next job to be run.

a) What is the job's priority?

b) Is the job I/O-bound?

c) Is the job CPU-bound?

d) Will the job fit into an available slot in memory?

e) Which available job will run for the shortest time?

Section 7.6

7.14 Comment briefly on each of the following functions of system generation.

   a) the selection of various modules to form a specific system

   b) the description of physical placement of modules in a complex of storage areas

   c) the description of the physical population of devices and storages that define the machine configuration

   d) the establishment of particular parameters that represent scheduling policies and resource management goals

   e) the establishment of various table sizes, buffer size limits, etc.

7.15 A current trend is toward a reduction in the effort to generate a system, and a willingness to pay the price in optimization. Comment on this.

7.16 What is a partial system generation?

7.17 Explain IBM's concept of the Selectable Unit. What attribute of systems design is extremely critical to the success of this concept?

8
Subsystems

8.1 CONCEPTS OF SUBSYSTEMS

The word "subsystem" is used to mean many things in the literature. In this section, we introduce some common ideas and some contrasting perceptions about subsystems.

A subsystem is a set of functions that are organized so that they form a package that is perceived as a conceptual entity. A subsystem defines an environment for the use of the system that has well-defined limits and provides a set of services to a specialized set of users. The services provide support for the complete processing of user tasks through the system.

This definition of a subsystem suggests that certain large systems subcomplexes currently referred to as subsystems are not subsystems. As an example, the *Job Entry Subsystem* of IBM's OS operating system would be excluded by the definition because it does not provide a context for the complete processing of user work but is merely a job submission mechanism. We classify this package as a system service.

A true subsystem provides an extension to the run-time environment that provides higher-level services of a specialized kind to programs running within the context of the subsystem. In addition, a subsystem may provide a "monitor service" for the control of resources allocated to it by the system. The subsystem may take responsibility for granting memory, processor time, and files to programs running under the subsystem. A subsystem may provide a private command language, a set of programming languages, and an assortment of utilities that are operable only as programs within its context.

A possible distinction between a systems service and a subsystem is that a systems service tends to be generally but infrequently used by most (or even all) users of a system while a subsystem tends to be intensively used by a group of users, but its users represent a (possibly small) fraction of all the users of the computing system.

The perception of the nature of subsystems is related to one's view of what an operating system is, and to the evolution of operating systems. The growing awareness of different groups of users with vastly different requirements has led to a desire for easy extendability and modifiability that is changing notions of what functions should be in the operating system and what functions should be in subsystems.

The concept of the subsystem is closely related to the evolutionary development of operating systems. An early use of the idea of providing and packaging more than one level of interface was the definition of IBM's IBSYS/IBJOB operating system.

There was a desire to extend the operating environment for a new set of programming languages and to maximize the sharing of certain systems functions between the new languages. Each language compiled to a common run-time environment with common I/O interfaces and with common linkage conventions.

There was also, however, a need to preserve historical run-time interfaces for FMS and other earlier packages. The joint need was met by the development of a low-level IBSYS interface usable by older programs, and a higher-level IBJOB environment supporting richer interfaces for new user languages. There was, therefore, a basic operating system environment with limited interface support, little shared function, a subsystem for the new COMTRAN (an early COBOL-like commercial programming language), and FORTRAN compilers.

Subsystems generally emerge during the life of an operating system because the underlying system structure is set and should not be disturbed. As the industry progresses, new needs emerge (such as the need for telecommunications support, the need for database management, etc.), and the most efficient way to meet these needs is often to impose a set of enhanced interfaces upon an older structure.

Even if it is reasonable to modify the older structure, many new embedded functions might impose performance burdens on programs that run under the system, but do not need the new services. The design trade-offs are whether a new set of functions should be imposed on an old interface, whether the old interfaces should be extended to provide richer services, or whether new interfaces should be provided to bypass the old interfaces.

Consider a system with a simple "GET NEXT" service that advances to the next record. A database management capability is to be defined that allows a statement like "GET all instances of key = 13976" to be presented to a service macro. The enriched GET may be designed to use the underlying GET with no modification to the underlying GET. The enriched GET may be a unit package that goes directly to devices without use of the old simple GET.

If the enriched GET is implemented by expanding the original GET's capabilities, the database management becomes part of the underlying operating system. Programs may use the GET for simple record advances or complex searches. This approach avoids the definition of a new interface at the possible expense of increasing GET processing time for all programs. Since the GET has more functions, it will take more time to analyze what each program requires.

A subsystem approach is to provide a new "GET COMPLEX" macro that is available only within the context of the database management package and usable only when the DBM is "on." One way of implementing the enriched GET is to have it call upon the old GET. The subsystem is a user of the underlying system in this case. This may lead to some inefficiencies. Alternatively, the new GET could be in a unique package that uses devices directly.

Subsystem requirements may be anticipated by operating system designers who create a set of specialized interfaces between the operating system and subsystems. These interfaces may allow a subsystem special privileges like operating in supervisor state or using supervisor state capabilities. For the GET example used above, an entry point well within the old GET, perhaps at the device start point, might be defined for privileged use by subsystems.

In effect, subsystem interfaces are exposed to a subsystem, but these interfaces are not exposed to usual application programs. These interfaces enable a subsystem to operate more efficiently.

An extension of the view that a subsystem rests upon a basic system leads to a more contemporary view of subsystems. The term is now used frequently to mean any set of functions that is not part of the kernel or the basic control program. Organick, in his discussion of Multics, refers to the subsystem writer as any author of a service not delivered by the Multics kernel and Basic File System. The HYDRA designers talk about the construction of subsystems using basic kernel functions in a manner suggesting that the command language of an operating system, any specific directory mechanisms, schedulers, etc. are subsystems.

In contemporary thinking, the notion of subsystem becomes intertwined with notions of process hierarchy, and the difference between a user process and an operating system process is seen to be one of jurisdiction only, the extent of the rights that a process has to reference objects in the system. Thus the basic operating system provides a context for programs running under it. These programs, in turn, can provide contexts for programs running under them. A family of operating systems, each providing a particular context for user programs, emerges as a result of each level in the system providing an interface for a lower level.

Figure 8.1 shows this notion as described by Brinch Hansen. The top node(s) of the tree represents the basic operating system that is the initial owner of all resources. S creates A, B, and C to which storage and other resources are allocated. A, B, and C provide a pool of physical and logical resources and a set

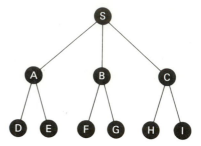

Fig. 8.1 "Tree" of subsystems.

of interfaces for D and E, F and G, and H and I, respectively. Each level in the tree imposes a set of allocation strategies upon its progeny processes. The basic system imposes the requirement that a process allocates a subset of its own resources only to its progeny, and that a process can start, stop, or eliminate only its own descendants.

In RC4000, as described by Brinch Hansen, CPU time is provided by a time-driven dispatcher in the basic operating system regardless of a process's position in the tree, and all processes can communicate with all other processes. It is not necessary, however, that this be true. It is possible to impose hierarchic selection of processes to be run, as well as to restrict communications between processes to those processes running within a subsystem. An idea closely related to this hierarchic notion is the idea of a process running within a resource environment. An environment is like a subsystem in that it represents a pool of resources, but it does not represent a set of unique interfaces to programs running within the environment.

Those who feel that the basic kernel of an operating system should contain only a small set of functions tend to the view that a user program should run in the context of intermediate interfaces that provide services meaningful to the application, and strategies and policies for resource use. These intermediate levels are called subsystems or operating systems. The idea of restricting the services of the lowest level is related to the ideas that first drove IBSYS/IBJOB, but represent considerably more complex perceptions of the varieties of use and access to which a computing system may be put. The advantages of a primitive operating system used as a base for hierarchically structured subsystems may be stated as follows.

■   The burden of generalization in the system base is minimized. If the system is to be used in a variety of ways, then it is better to provide specialized services in specialized contexts rather than to try to generalize a base set of services.

■   For any set of users of a particular type, optimization can be achieved by dedicating a computing system to the operation of a particular subsystem or operating system with the minimum base system providing a minimum burden.

■ New ways of using a system, including highly specialized interfaces, can be implemented as new operating systems or subsystems. The major use of the primitives of the basic operating system, in fact, is to provide a set of subsystem building blocks so that subsystem designers can create specialized subsystems with minimum effort. A strong extension of this approach, coming from HYDRA, insists that the basic operating system functions must not only be devoid of policy and embedded strategy but also be devoid of rigid structure. That is, a function that is hierarchically above another function in one subsystem might be conveniently lower in another subsystem.

The danger of general functions lies in the burden they impose on users who do not need the generality. The danger of the structure of the rich, underlying system is that it might, over time, become inappropriate, and extensions to the system must then build a scaffold around inappropriate structures. Therefore, it is better to provide minimum base systems, and place more functions in subsystems that are running on top of them.

There is an interesting analog between the design of an operating system and its subsystems, and the design of a machine instruction set and compilers. If a machine is being aimed at a well-defined set of users whose requirements are well known, then the instruction set can be biased toward those users and can be functionally rich. If only PL/I programmers are to use the machine, then the machine organization may have a set of instructions that closely approximate PL/I's notion of machine organization. There might be a CALL instruction, an ALLOCATE, a machine concept of STATIC storage, a machine algorithm for subscript checking, etc. If a machine is being aimed at a more general market, then the rich PL/I mechanisms might not be effective, and would represent a burden on the machine.

Similarly, if an operating system is being aimed at a set of users whose characteristics will vary, then the functions required for all these users might well be embedded at low levels of the operating system. As user differences become more intense, and as specialized user groups become well defined, it is perhaps better to minimize the common functions. The instructions of the basic mechanism become less rich, and specialized functions are moved into higher levels and specialized, well-isolated environments. The contemporary approach, then, is to design for subsystems as an inherent structural concept, rather than to design for a basic operating system to undertake all environments.

There is an interesting continuum that relates notions of subsystems to notions of virtual machines and mininets and multiprogramming. Figure 8.2 shows five sets of concentric circles. Each set has four rings defining application, monitor, kernel, and hardware layers. Figure 8.2(a) shows a simple single-thread system in which a single application program runs on a services/monitor level that in turn is interfaced to the operating system kernel resting on the machine. Figure 8.2(b) shows a multiprogrammed machine in which several application

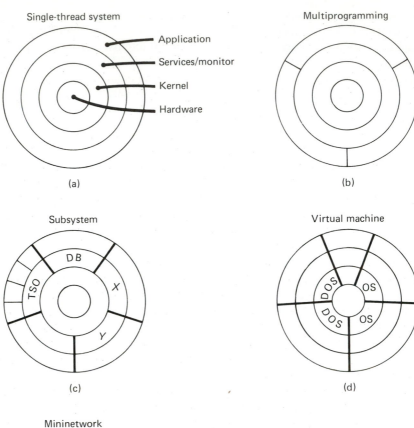

Fig. 8.2 Continuum of sharing.

programs interface to a single monitor. Figure 8.2(c) shows the subsystem concept. Here a set of applications programs runs on a set of monitors/services
(subsystems). Two of the subsystems are time-sharing and database. The difference between Figs. 8.2(b) and 8.2(c) is the availability of the independent
interfaces and the specialized services associated with each one.

Figure 8.2(d) extends the dividing line one level lower and suggests that the
subsystems themselves run on different operating systems. For example in Fig.
8.2(d) there are two instances of OS and two instances of DOS. The difference
between Figs. 8.2(d) and 8.2(c) is that even the kernel of the operating system is
not being shared. The operating systems are running on a minimal basic kernel
called a *virtual machine interface*. The notion, fundamentally, is to provide a
mechanism whereby users who have developed subsystems or applications
within the context of a particular operating system can share a machine. Figure
8.2(e) shows a mininet in which even hardware is no longer being shared. The
interesting continuum described by Fig. 8.2 is that the transition from a single-
thread system, through multiprogramming, through subsystems, through virtual
machines, to mininetworks is a continuum of choice about how much function is
to be shared, and how much is to be specialized in separate and parallel contexts.
The concept of a subsystem is a step in the direction of special-purpose instru-
ments. It is meaningful in an economic context in which the benefits of sharing
underlying hardware and basic operating systems functions outweigh the incon-
veniences of contention and performance perturbation.

8.2   SUBSYSTEMS AND THE USER COMMUNITY

We have stressed that the subsystem is a partitioning concept. The fundamental
advantage that a user community receives from subsystems lies in the amount of
knowledge that is required to use a subsystem.

For end-users, a simplified interface can be devised within the context of the
subsystem so that knowledge of system conventions can be minimized, and the
user can behave as if a system is dedicated to the user's needs. Systems
programmers can develop systems skills only within the context of the subsystem, and application programmers need learn only those interfaces that are
relevant to programming applications on a particular system.

The packaging of functions in well-defined partitions may constrain the
burden of evolution of both the underlying system and the subsystem. Because
the underlying system contains fewer functions, it may be stable for longer
periods of time. Because a subsystem is more specialized, and also more isolated
from hardware characteristics, it may be easier to evolve and modify with less
sophisticated systems skills.

Finally, the simplification of underlying structure may make performance
prediction easier than it is in systems that attempt to handle diverse user functions

in a single context. One interesting aspect of partitioning at a time when there is growing interest in various kinds of networking and distribution is the possibility of vesting professional skills associated with maintaining particular subsystems in the user departments.

But any partitioning technique may also introduce problems. A set of unique interfaces defining specific contexts for computer use is valuable when the interfaces are in fact considerably simpler, and when users need learn only one interface. This imposes a requirement that the users of any subsystem stay within their boundaries. If the users of the system tend to move from one interface to another, then the total learning requirement for a user may go up as the user is required to learn several systems interfaces. In addition, each interface may provide similar functions; for example, editing a file may be a function provided in subsystem 1 and subsystem 2. If there are different semantics and somewhat divergent conventions for editing depending on subsystem context, a user may experience considerable annoyance.

The partitioned environment may inconveniently constrain availability of functions, and make it impossible, for example, to reach certain libraries or programs from one subsystem because they are encased in another. Some of the unfortunate aspects of contemporary systems that have developed time-sharing programming subsystems on a batch system base are the inability to reach data sets cataloged for the batch system from a terminal, or to reach data sets in the terminal subsystem from the batch stream, or to reach data sets developed in one subsystem when operating in another. In order to assure coherence for the programming development community, it is desirable to organize a programming development subsystem as a single structural entity regardless of the method of access the programmer is using and regardless of the programming language.

A final difficulty that may lie in imperfectly developed subsystem environments is a performance burden imposed because of a need for communication between subsystems that was not perceived at the time the subsystems were conceived. In order to overcome systems boundaries, intercommunication mechanisms are grafted onto a structure not designed to support certain kinds of communication. This is very often a consequence of a system becoming a subsystem. That is, a system conceived as an operational whole at the time of its design comes to be viewed as only a part of a greater whole as systems concepts grow. Thus a database management subsystem operating on a single-processor system may find it necessary to talk to similar systems running on other processors. Or a database system with a particular set of data format and structure conventions may encounter a new requirement to pass and receive information from a database system of very different conventions. In order to provide communications, it is necessary to devise and impose on the systems new services that establish interaction protocols, and means of translating between the conventions private to each independently developed system.

Certainly, no criticism can be leveled at the initial design and subsystem definitions that failed to perceive forthcoming requirements for intersystem or cross-subsystem communication or, if perceiving them, considered that these requirements were sufficiently remote so that current design could not be legitimately burdened with them. However, in determining what functions to place in a base system and what functions to place in subsystems, designers must be aware of the exposure. If the base system is minimized in order to provide the benefits of maximum compartmentalization, a price in new subsystem communications mechanisms may eventually have to be paid. These observations apply particularly to the design of partitioned systems for networking and distributed processing hardware structures.

8.3 SYSTEM–SUBSYSTEM SPLICE LEVELS

A fundamental decision in designing the relationship between a system and its subsystem is what functions are going to be defined as global functions operating on, or on behalf of, all subsystems, and what functions are going to be made local to a subsystem. This exercise is essentially the same as defining the functions of a kernel, or defining the minimum set of base system services. However, there is a difference since certain global functions provided for all subsystems may be by no means simple primitive operations. For example, a general directory and catalog maintenance service may be provided by the basic system for all subsystems, or a telecommunications-handling service may be provided by the base system for use by all subsystems. A subsystem can provide its own set of utilities or share systemwide utilities of various kinds including editors, linkers, loaders, and programming languages.

When interfacing a subsystem with a base system, it is possible to use only the standard run-time interfaces available to any program that is to run under the base system. It is possible, however, to provide a specialized set of more privileged subsystems interfaces that allow a subsystem to enter at lower levels of the base system, to reside in storages reserved for the base system, and to have expanded privileges not commonly allowed normal worker programs. The notion of expanded subsystem privilege is reflected, for example, in the PDP-11 with its three levels of operation: a *kernel state,* a *monitor state,* and a *user state.* The notion of monitor state may be used to support the idea that the underlying subsystem program is a kind of monitor requiring more privilege and accessibility to systems data than a normal user program. A subsystem monitor with responsibility for resource allocation among its users may require access to systems tables not usually accorded.

The degree of integration of a subsystem is a resource management design issue. It is possible to fully integrate a subsystem behind its unique user interfaces. Such an integrated subsystem is fully managed by the base system. For example, the central base system dispatcher and scheduler would dispatch and schedule each individual running program regardless of the subsystem context. That is, users, not subsystems, would be represented on the dispatching queue. This is the relationship that exists between the TSO (Time-Sharing Option) and the MVS operating system. Similarly, memory requirements for all users are managed by a central memory management mechanism. The advantage of this is the maximizing of flexibility and balancing of service to users across all subsystems. This is important because it is the user, after all, and not the subsystem who receives significant service.

Conversely, it is possible to make a subsystem responsible for resource management within a set of resources that are allocated to it. The central dispatching queue of the base operating system would have no knowledge of the processes running under the subsystem. Only the subsystem itself would be represented as a receiver of CPU time. Within the time periods granted by the central dispatcher, a private subsystem dispatcher would operate to allocate time to users of the subsystem enqueued on a private subsystem dispatch queue. It is possible to prepartition memory among subsystems, and allow each subsystem to control the allocation of space among its users. Fundamental allocation mechanisms of the base system might be used by subsystems to acquire or release resources even if responsibility for allocation decision making is vested in the subsystems.

Some care must be taken in the design of the resource allocation structure to make sure that the behavior of the system is consistent. A possible design of the subsystem–base-system interface is to vest dispatching in a subsystem monitor, but to leave memory management as a global function. This might lead to situations in which the memory manager has insufficient information about running processes to make the best decisions about memory allocation based upon patterns of memory use.

In determining how to apportion resource management functions, it is necessary to balance considerations of performance, required levels of resource sharing and allocation flexibility, and the complexity of the underlying system. In addition to issues of the functional relationship between subsystems and underlying systems, there are some interesting questions about how extensive and general-purpose a particular subsystem can be. There are common notions that an interactive programming subsystem is a meaningful concept and that a database management system is a meaningful concept. But these are still very broad concepts admitting to the possibility of various kinds of use with varying requirements. Some designers feel that the notion of a database management system is too broad a notion in that the parameterization required to support various users is too extensive. A better notion is "any number of database management subsystems" each specialized for the needs of a particular set of users.

The effort required to build specialized systems might not be more than the effort to parameterize more general structures if a proper set of subsystem building blocks can be constructed from a set of base system building block functions. Any particular subsystem is a construct of the basic building blocks that rests upon a very elemental kernel. Thus if certain users wish a relational database system of certain characteristics, they should be able to build one. If other users desire a hierarchic structure, they should be able to build their system. Then the notion of all users desiring database management support out of a single structure becomes unnecessary.

8.4   DATABASE MANAGEMENT SUBSYSTEMS

This section is not intended as an introduction to database concepts but merely as a discussion of the general nature of database subsystems.

Minimally, a database management system consists of a *data description language* for specifying the logical structure of units of data, and the relationship between units of data. For example, a collection of data items may be named as a record, and a description of the format of such a record provided to the system as a *record prototype* through the data description language. In addition, a relationship between one type of record and other record types may be described. Thus a description of a record type DEPARTMENT may be provided to the system, as well as a description of a record type EMPLOYEE. A relationship between DEPARTMENT and EMPLOYEE may be described such that the EMPLOYEE record type is understood to be a progeny of the DEPARTMENT record type, and the membership of employees in departments becomes understood by the system. The actual representation of the relationship (an instance of a hierarchic relationship) may be represented in the system by a pointer from the prototype record of a department to the prototype record of an employee. Various database management subsystems allow various relationships to be formed, allowing or not allowing, for example, networks of data relationships or constructing relationships to well-formed hierarchic trees. Similarly, it is possible for a system to provide a set of relationship types or to allow various relations to be named and described by a user.

The intent of the data description language is to provide a logical view of data in the database. One interesting system relationship is that between the data description features of various programming languages, and the views of data developed by the data description language. There are two possible viewpoints to be taken about this relationship. One viewpoint is that data descriptions provided in the programming language must conform to logical organizations of data as described in the data description language. An extension of this point of view follows the argument that programs wishing to refer to data in a database should be relieved of data description responsibility entirely. Compilers for such programs should have available to them the database system dictionaries containing all necessary data descriptive elements. Consequently, a mechanism should exist in the database system for providing descriptions of data structures that the algorithmic portions of a program may reference.

An alternate point of view is that the data description provided by a programming language is a description of the view of data that a particular program wishes to use while it runs. This local data organization should be created by the database system for the use of a program by mapping the system's logical view of data into the program's view whenever a data reference is made. Thus an additional function of GET, for example, is field formatting and structure building so that objects described by the program come into existence on behalf of the program.

Another mechanism of the database subsystem is the relating of descriptions of prototype records to actual instances of a type of record in the database so that a program can reference actual occurrences of the records. This involves a mapping of logical views of data onto physical allocation of actual records.

In addition to the basic data mapping mechanisms, a database management subsystem must contain a run-time language for data reference supported by various run-time services involving complex data-searching macros, formatting macros, and presentation macros. Beyond the run-time macros supporting program references to data in the database, the subsystem may also provide an on-line inquiry language allowing inquiries of various types to be made against the database from a terminal. This language would be supported by a language interpreter that would reduce it to the run-time macros used for database reference. Inquiries may be restricted to a set of planned requests or the on-line user may be allowed to form requests of varying complexity.

The database system may rely upon the basic data macros and the device support of the underlying system. It may have an incorporated terminal support interface or use a general systems telecommunications access method for talking to terminals referencing the system. Commonly, the database subsystem is responsible for scheduling transactions through itself once they are received at its interface. This interface may be a master process that summons particular transaction processes when various types of inquiries are received. The management of systems buffers and the scheduling of processing programs are commonly part of the subsystem that may use underlying services to perform these functions.

The variety of database management subsystems is rather large. On the one hand there are programs that are little more than report writers, and on the other there are systems of the functional richness and complexity of IBM's IMS. There are also various schools of database design with various preferences for hierarchic, network, or relational database concepts. Some of the problems of database management become particularly complex in the context of distributed processing when it is desired to locate related data structures at different geographical locations in physically partitioned computer systems. There is a vast literature on database management systems that addresses issues of data structure and concepts of data quite apart from ideas about the structure of a system and its relationship to an underlying operating system. As a starting point the reader is referred to C. J. Date's book, *An Introduction to Database Systems,* in Addison-Wesley's *The Systems Programming Series.*

The trend to on-line data management and the dedication of computer systems to database activities have many implications for systems design. New concepts in machine organization are emerging in response to database concepts. For example, there is interest in "search engines" or "back-end minis" or "database machines" specifically designed for efficient manipulation of storage and formatting, and interceding between a computational processor and a storage mechanism. The I/O-oriented services of an operating system would be removed from the operating system of the computational processor and each high-level data reference macro would be passed on to the back-end machine for analysis and execution. The computational processor would receive information as requested and be entirely relieved of data search and formatting responsibility. Figure 8.3 represents this idea with the added notion of a front-end engine responsible for interfacing to an on-line terminal network.

Figure 8.4 represents another idea about systems organization. Here several

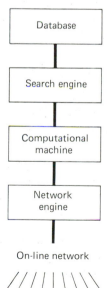

Fig. 8.3 "Fragmented" system.

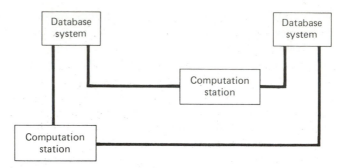

Fig. 8.4 Network of computational and data management stations.

processors are connected by teleprocessing lines or high-speed channels to form a network consisting of computational stations and data management stations with each data management station handling some partition of system data. References to the database would be appropriately routed to the proper data management station by the local operating systems of the computational processors. Some designers interested in subsystems and virtual machines feel that logical equivalents of this kind of network can be achieved by subsystem or virtual machine definition with relationships between subsystems designed to give, on the same physical machine, the operational structure of a physically dispersed network.

The problems associated with such concepts are numerous and not yet entirely understood. Among the issues under current investigation are whether or not a program or a user at a particular station needs to know where the data is located, or whether the system should undertake to locate data referenced by name only. Further, there are issues of reference synchronization and network optimization problems that are concerned with when data should be moved to another station for processing, and when processing should be done where the data is. Distributed database management is the current edge of the art.

8.5   INTERACTIVE PROGRAMMING SUBSYSTEMS

The common elements of an *interactive programming subsystem* are

- a command language and interpreter
- one or more programming languages and associated compilers
- a general editor and file management component
- a mechanism for distributing computational power and storage space among users

The Time-Sharing Option (TSO), offered as a subsystem of IBM's OS/MVT and OS/MVS operating systems, is a useful example of an interactive programming subsystem in the context of a larger system. It illustrates the problems that have to be addressed *and* the problems that result when one large system is merged with another. The design of the system had an imposed requirement to preserve compatibility with OS file and access method conventions, and a requirement to provide the same run-time services for user programs that would be available to any program developed to run under OS. In addition, the TSO capability runs concurrently with the OS batch environment or other subsystems.

The TSO subsystem consists of a command language that provides the capability of entering and retrieving data at a terminal, or entering programs and requesting execution within the time-sharing environment or outside of the context of the subsystem in the batch environment provided by the basic system. The command language for the subsystem is unique to the subsystem in that it is not the job control language associated with the basic operating system.

However, when a program developed within the TSO subsystem is to be executed outside of the context of the system, JCL statements may be placed in a data set defined at the terminal and associated with a SUBMIT command that forms a full request for batch execution, and passes the generated batch job to the scheduling queue of the batch system.

In addition to passing jobs to the background, a user can also summon services into the foreground. Any compiler, for example, that can run under OS can be invoked to run in the context of the TSO subsystem. Actually, any module of the operating system that exists in load module form (ready for loading) can be invoked at a terminal by use of a CALL command that loads the module into the subsystem area and gives it control. In this way, the subsystem is able to provide access to the services of the basic system while providing certain services that are unique to terminal operation.

The unique terminal services are provided for a programmer by an element called ITF (Interactive Terminal Facility) that supports BASIC and a subset of PL/I. ITF PL/I program development can be done on a line-by-line interactive basis, with each line executed as it is entered, or by collecting entire programs into complete statements of problem solution before execution. In addition, other language processes are available. Associated with the programming languages are elements called prompters that provide for the invocation of a compiler without the usual JCL "wrap" by automatically undertaking allocation for a compiler invoked by a RUN command. An interactive debug capability is also provided with certain FORTRAN, COBOL, and PL/I language processors.

A programmer at a TSO terminal uses the EDIT command to create a file that represents his or her program in any programming language. The EDIT command can specify line-by-line syntax checking for the ITF provided languages (BASIC, PL/I Subset, FORTRAN) or any of the languages associated with a prompter.

When the programmer completes the entry of a program, the programmer can choose to

- execute one of the compilers associated with a prompter and foreground operation to produce a compiled version of the program;
- call one of the background compilers into the foreground for compilation;
- send the program to the background.

Each of these choices involves a different level of understanding of the underlying system. To execute a prompter-supported compiler in the foreground requires a knowledge of only the TSO command facility. To execute a background compiler in the foreground requires some knowledge of the allocation requirements and resource use of the compiler and appropriate ALLOCATE statements in the command language. To execute in the background requires a knowledge of JCL statements used by the background allocator and scheduler. Executing a compiled program after a foreground compilation is accomplished by issuing a LOADGO command.

The TSO command language also provides commands for the definition and allocation of data sets, listing user data sets, listing user characteristics, and some simple data utilities. Beyond the programmer interface, there are operational and operator commands that allow for the inspection and modification of system status.

The TSO system is an extension of the basic system that involves a number of components and interfaces.

- A *message control program* provided by the systems telecommunication access method. This is used to interface with remote terminals.

- A *time-sharing control task* with subsystemwide responsibilities. The function of this element is to respond to an operator action calling for the activation of the time-sharing subsystem. It obtains required memory space for a control region from the basic system, and it builds control blocks. While the system is running, the "TSC" is responsible for memory contents management and for the swapping in and out of memory of the spaces used by active terminals.

- A *region control program* responsible for the management of each foreground region. The notion of a region as it occurs in OS/MVT relates to an area of memory allocations associated with a particular job stream. The idea of foreground and TSO operation relates to the definition of some number of regions available for the specific use of TSO terminal users. Each region may have multiple terminals associated with it. Each region has a region control task (a process sharing a single copy of region control code). A region control task operates as a process under the time-sharing control task. The function of a region control task is the suspension and restoration of terminal user processes running within the region. When a user has been selected for swap, the RCT must suppress and save outstanding I/O requests and then restore these requests when the user is swapped back in.

■ *LOGON Scheduler*. A LOGON scheduler runs in the foreground region and is responsible for processing LOGON messages from terminal users. The function of LOGON is to interface a user to the system by inspecting his or her user profile and constructing a stream of JCL statements that are used by the basic system to allocate resources needed by the user. A particular user is made to look like a STEP of a JOB to the basic system. In this way resources outside of the subsystem context that are used by a foreground user are coordinated with resource requests being made from outside the subsystem. Actual allocation of data sets, spaces, and devices outside of the space used in the foreground is accomplished by the basic system allocators and initiators so that the subsystem requires no private allocation mechanisms.

■ *Terminal monitor program*. The program named on the EXEC statement of the JCL that LOGON creates to submit to the control reader of the basic system is the terminal monitor program. The terminal monitor program operates as a kind of private operating system for each user. Whenever a command is received, the TMP loads the command processor and activates it. When the command is finished, the TMP deactivates it. TMP also is responsible for error handling for errors that occur as a result of command processing.

■ The *command processors* and *associated service routines*. The set of command processors provides the functions called for by the TSO command language. Although unique in function, the command processors perform many similar actions such as parsing and scanning a statement for syntax errors, receiving and sending messages from terminals, and receiving command lines from files of commands. In addition, those commands that relate to compilers in the system must use allocation routines to acquire resources for those compilers when invoked in the foreground.

■ A *system driver*. The elements so far discussed provide a structure for time-sharing operation by providing a hierarchy of programs running on a system base and using system services. The particular degree of integration or separation of terminal services from the rest of a using population is defined by the nature of a component in TSO called the time-sharing driver.

TSO under OS/MVT is less integrated into the operating system than TSO under MVS because of the existence of the time-sharing driver in the MVT system and the integration of its functions into MVS in the MVS system. We will discuss the nature and function of the driver in the MVT environment in which TSO is more conceptually a subsystem.

The driver is a module responsible for the allocation of systems service between time-sharing users. The driver has available to it several parameters describing the way an installation wishes to see its system used. The driver also has available to it current data about the status of the system and each user in the system. On the basis of the goals defined in the parameters and the status of the system, the driver determines the pattern of processor and memory usage of the system.

We have mentioned that the resources of the system may be allocated directly to individual programs within a subsystem by the base system, or the base system may allocate resources to the subsystem for apportionment to individual running programs. In the relationship between OS and TSO, the task control program acquires memory space, and region control programs manage the residence of user programs within that space at the direction of the driver. Other resources are allocated to programs by the allocation mechanisms of the basic system. The CPU resource is managed for the entire system by the TSO driver that effectively becomes the scheduling mechanism for all programs on the system—foreground and background. The driver adjusts the order of the dispatching list to define a priority for running user programs and uses parameters to resolve competition among all running regions on the system.

Splicing TSO onto MVS involves tailoring a message control program to run with the telecommunications access method. This involves a SYSGEN-like process using JCL to describe terminal types, lines, terminal addresses, data encoding, and line protocols. JCL must be provided for the support of the invocation of the control task and message control program at startup time. Also, a set of user profiles must be provided by the user installation and system parameters must be provided to the control task and the driver. The control task must be given the maximum number of users, and the number and size of the foreground regions. The driver must be told about installation desires for region and queue management, and the calculation of service intervals for running programs.

TERMINOLOGY

back-end minicomputer	EXEC
Brinch Hansen	FMS
command processor	hierarchical structure
COMTRAN	HYDRA
database machine	IBSYS/IBJOB
database management subsystem	interactive programming subsystem
EDIT	Interactive Terminal Facility

ITF

JOB

Job Entry Subsystem

LOADGO

LOGON

LOGON scheduler

message control program

Multics

operating system process

prompter

RC4000

region control program

RUN

search engine

STEP

subsystem

system driver

systems service

terminal monitor program

time-sharing control task

time-sharing driver

Time-Sharing Option of IBM's OS

TMP

TSO

user process

EXERCISES

Section 8.1

8.1 Define subsystem.

8.2 Distinguish between the concepts of systems services and subsystems.

8.3 Subsystems generally emerge during the life of an operating system because the underlying system structure is set and should not be disturbed. Comment on this.

8.4 Discuss the relative merits of each of the following means of embedding new functions in a system.

  a) Impose a new set of functions on an old interface.

  b) Extend old interfaces to provide richer services.

  c) Bypass old interfaces with new interfaces.

8.5 Discuss the advantages of using a primitive operating system as a base for hierarchically structured subsystems.

8.6 The danger of general functions lies in the burden they impose on users who do not need the generality. Explain.

Section 8.2

8.7 Why are neatly packaged subsystems attractive from the standpoint of
  a) the user?

  b) the systems programmer?

  c) the applications programmer?

8.8 Discuss several problems that may be introduced by the partitioning technique of subsystems.

Section 8.3

8.9 It is possible to fully integrate a subsystem behind its unique user interfaces. Such an integrated subsystem is fully managed by the base system. Comment on how dispatching and memory management are handled in this situation.

8.10 It is possible to make a subsystem responsible for resource management within a set of resources that are allocated to it. Comment on how dispatching and memory management are handled in this situation.

Section 8.4

8.11 What is a database management system?

8.12 The trend to on-line data management and the dedication of computer systems to database activities have many implications for systems design. Discuss several of these implications.

8.13 What is a "search engine"?

Section 8.5

8.14 What are the elements of an interactive programming subsystem?

8.15 Discuss briefly each of the following components of the TSO subsystem.
   a) message control program
   b) time-sharing control task
   c) region control program
   d) LOGON scheduler
   e) terminal monitor program
   f) command processors
   g) system driver

9
Resource Management

9.1 THE NOTION OF RESOURCE MANAGEMENT

Central to all of the various ideas of operating system function and structure is the concept of *an operating system as a manager of resources*. This concept has two aspects. First, there is the notion that the operating system provides mechanisms that allow the sharing of the resources of a computing system by protecting resources and by resolving contention for their use. Second, there is the notion that certain resources are defined by the operating system or through use of the operating system. These resources are conceptualizations of abstract structures. Thus while a physical memory has a set of hardware-defined locations, an operating system presents a view of an extended address space or a collection of objects in a name space. While a disk is a set of physically defined *tracks*, the operating system supports concepts of *cylinders, data sets, catalogs,* and *libraries*.

The concept of *resource management* itself contains three essential ideas. First, of course, is the idea of a *resource*. Second, there is an idea of a *goal to be achieved by resource management*. Third, there is a relationship between the resources that are managed and the nature of programs that are allocated or denied resources. We will address a resource, the idea of policies in resource management, and the interface between operating system resource management and programs.

9.2 THE NOTION OF A RESOURCE

In early-systems thinking, the resources of a computing system were considered to be the *processor*, the *memory*, the *I/O channels*, and the *devices*. Contempo-

221

rary thought has generalized the ideal of what a resource is. A resource has become an abstraction that is defined to the system and given a set of attributes relating to the accessibility of the resource and its physical representation in the system. Thus a set of software resources, subject to system management, may be defined to a system as objects to which access must be controlled.

There is the idea of some object that may be given a certain type of identity and is managed by an object manager responsible for the objects of a certain type. Common types of objects are *files, libraries,* and *programs.* In HYDRA, any kind of object may be defined by naming a type of resource and then associating objects with the named type as instances of the object accessible to processes. *A process,* as we have seen, *is a procedure in execution. A procedure, a collection of computer code,* on the other hand, is only an object in the system. The function of the operating system is to define an abstract machine composed of abstract resources that are conveniently manipulated by processes to protect the use of resources, to assure coherence, and to impose policies of economic use.

9.3   POLICY

Given a set of resources, the use of those resources must be guided by a *policy.* A policy is a statement of the goals of an enterprise as regards the successful operation of an information system.

A major influence on the design of operating systems over the last 15 years has been the desirability of allowing the *shared use of computer resources.* The concept of a "consolidated work-load" machine system located within the context of a highly skilled, centralized, data processing agency has been basic in medium to large-scale systems designs. The concept is based upon economies of scale of hardware, economies in centralizing professional skills, and relatively expensive equipment. To a degree, some of these underlying assumptions are weakening, but as economic motives for sharing memory and processors decline, economic motives for sharing data increase, and the fundamental mechanisms of access and allocation maintain their importance.

The fundamental building block of resource management is a management policy. Without a clearly formulated policy, no software algorithm or human procedure can be deemed effective or be measured against goals. The essential decision that management makes is whether maximum profitability of the data processing resource comes from its responsiveness to work requests or its highly efficient use. We will demonstrate later that there is a *response–utilization dichotomy,* that certain scheduling and location decisions are made to maximize responsiveness, and that other decisions are made to maximize levels of utilization of the machine. This is true whether these decisions are made by human schedulers or by algorithms in an operating system. Policy may be stated as a set of *scheduler objective functions* that

- minimize average flow time
- minimize number of late responses
- minimize maximum late response time
- maximize utilization of hardware
- maximize utilization within the constraint that no response is greater than a certain time limit
- service work of class A at a given rate, work of class B at a given rate, etc.

These policy decisions may then be given to a professional staff to use in planning the pattern of work submitted to the system, or (ideally) policy decisions may be given to the system itself. An important interface of an operating system is its relationship with the *policy-formulating mechanisms* of its environment. Ultimately, policy should be expressible directly to a system in the terminology of nontechnical policymakers. Some contemporary systems provide a policymaker's interface that represents a considerable extension of an operating system into the area of policy support. IBM's OS/VS2 (MVS), for example, provides an Installation Performance Specification that essentially accepts policy statements about rates of service, and balances between utilization and work-load objectives. This interface, however, assumes a rather high level of technical competence.

The interface between the operating system and the management of an installation also involves an issue of how much preliminary planning must be done before work is presented to the system. Systems that are more flexible require less planning for *work flow* and *mix formation*. This means less work for scheduling staffs but more work for the system itself.

There are currently some problems at the interface between the policymakers and the operating system. There are those who feel that the distinction between policymaking and operations is not clearly drawn in current operating systems interfaces, and that many functions operators perform are really policy functions since their effect upon the system goes beyond keeping the system operational. For example, an operator's ability to change the priority of a job represents an administrative decision, and an operator's ability to resolve resource contention is similarly a policy decision that should not be made on the "floor." This criticism concerns itself with the potential economic effect on an enterprise of decisions about programs that are to produce valuable information for enterprise use. These designers believe that there is inadequate control over operator behavior and an overreliance on operator action. Some years ago, a survey of installations of a major computer manufacturer indicated that operator action had considerably more effect on the productivity of a system than did the algorithms of the operating system.

Another concern about policy interfaces involves the necessity to interpret policy in terms of systems parameters meaningful only to professionals, and whose effect upon the actual performance of complicated systems could not be well understood. Thus while the idea of describing the rate of service a particular program should receive from the system is important, it unfortunately involves rather abstract technical concepts. An installation manager wishing to describe a policy about one-second response time for department A, and never more than one-half hour late for the batch of department B, cannot do so in direct terms. The interfaces that the operating system presents require an understanding of technical notions of *rates of service* and *queueing disciplines* to be applied to various queues in the system. This requires the interposition of technical staff between a policymaker and the system.

In addition, there is some concern about the consistency of various mechanisms for describing policy to a system. Over the years, as older systems have matured and been extended in their resource management capabilities, multiple interfaces have been developed for the expression of policy. These interfaces do not always contain identical concepts, nor do they interface with each other to form a coherent policy-enforcement mechanism. Thus an interface may exist in a subsystem for describing when jobs are to be started, and an entirely different interface may exist to describe what kind of preference a started process should receive after it has entered the multiprogramming mix. The existence of two distinct interfaces with possibly different terminology and different syntax makes it more cumbersome to describe exactly and consistently what policy is and to determine just how a system will behave under certain work loads given a set of policy parameters.

These problems relate to issues of ease of use and complexity that are of major concern in the operating system area. Some feel that systems have gone too far; others, that they have not gone far enough to support policy expression.

9.4   PROGRAMMING STYLISTICS

If the effectiveness of resource management is dependent on proper *policy formation and expression* on one hand, it is constrained by issues of *programming style* on the other. A programmer has certain techniques available to fit a program into a machine. It is unavoidable that these techniques result in programs of particular shapes and resource consumption attributes. The stylistics of programming constrain the effectiveness of resource management by defining an object that uses resources in a way that may be difficult or expensive for the system to control. For example, the way programmers plan the use of buffers to balance program flow will affect the behavior of the mix in which the program runs. Other program stylistics, such as memory addressing patterns and page layout and packing, will affect the performance of a system in ways substantially beyond the ability of an operating system to control, or will involve very complex mechanisms for the operating system when it undertakes to control them.

The operating system may penalize or encourage programs with certain characteristics. It may even allocate or de-allocate resources to emphasize or neutralize, but the system cannot reach into the basic structure of a program in order to modify its own performance or the way it will perform with other programs in a mix. It is not always bad programs that represent problems to an operating system. It may be the good program that has achieved a local optimization that provides the greatest problem for a system trying to optimize a mix of programs on a more global basis.

Programming style determines the size of a program and consequently the amount of resources a particular program will use. The length of time a program will hold resources and the variation of the intensity of use of resources during program life are also functions of the essential shape and mass of a program.

The expected size of programs can affect resource management strategies in very basic ways. Consider a population of very small, short programs. Since each program is small, the amount of resources it uses, and the amount of time it holds the resources, represent small loads on the system. The allocation of resources may be made to each program and the system may make the reasonable assumption that resources allocated will be intensively used while the program is executing. The divergence between nominal utilization and real utilization will be small enough so that the system need not monitor resource use at a level below that of allocation for a process.

Now consider that these programs have been link-edited together to form a single considerably larger program. The resource requirements of this program will be considerably larger than the individual requirements. It may become profitable for the system to undertake one or both of two possible strategies. The first strategy is to grant resources only when they are specifically required. That is, allocation is moved into the run-time environment and requests for resources are made and honored on demand rather than at process-creation time. The second strategy, which is called *dynamic heuristic resource management,* undertakes to monitor the way the process is using resources and to enlarge or constrict the resources as a result of the resource usage pattern. The system makes the assumption that during the life of a large program there will be significant divergence between real and nominal utilization, between the resources actually being used over a short interval of time (*real utilization*), and the resources used by the program by prerun-time or run-time requests (*nominal utilization*). The system attempts to retrieve idle resources for use by other processes.

This strategy is based on the assumption that individual programs will be sufficiently large so that there is significant variation in the way they use resources during their incarnation as processes, and so significant *resource recapture* can be achieved. The resources that may be managed in this way, of course, are only the *preemptible resources,* those that can be given to and taken from a process without logical effect. Real memory and CPU allocation are the only obvious examples. The preemptibility of a resource is also determined by the relative expense of allocation and de-allocation.

9.5   FUNDAMENTAL ECONOMICS OF RESOURCE MANAGEMENT

It is important to put resource management policies and strategies in a meaningful context with respect to the effective use of computing systems. We consider here ideas of value and cost.

The value of computing lies in the economic benefit that accrues to an enterprise because of computing. Value may be derived from reducing the cost of creating, manipulating, and storing data; increasing the productivity of users and of professionals associated with the system; providing information of better quality on a more timely basis; providing an increased ability to correlate data from different agencies of the enterprise; and providing more sophisticated business planning methodologies. The cost of computing includes hardware costs, professional staff costs involved in developing applications and maintaining data and programs, and costs associated with actually using the system.

Some fundamental changes in underlying economics have occurred over the last decade. These changes have had a profound effect on certain ideas associated with resource management in computing systems. In essence, the economic changes revolve around the related phenomena that hardware represents a diminishing percentage of the total costs of a system and that labor costs are increasing at dramatic rates. Therefore, the preoccupation of the 1960s and early 1970s with the effective use of computer hardware is being replaced by the desire to make systems maximally responsive to user needs, and to provide fresh information of high quality when it is needed.

The desirability of achieving maximum utilization of a machine system is limited by the desire to guarantee good responsiveness. *The value of a computer system should be measured by the value of the information it produces.* Some information is very time sensitive with steep losses in value if it is late. The cost of lateness may be many times the cost of underutilization of the machine. A real-time system tracking a rocket, for example, must interact with the rocket at a certain rate. Since the value of the rocket is much higher than the value of the machine system, the computer may be kept lightly used in order to guarantee its ability to respond appropriately under all load conditions. The economics of computer use suggests that the computer be allowed to be underutilized for important intervals.

Conversely, if there is a population of work units, each of low individual value, each of which maintains the value of its information for long periods of time, then utilization-enhancing mechanisms are important to reduce the machine cost of processing the work units. For example, if there are five batch jobs, each of which produces information worth $5,000 to the enterprise, and this value remains stable during the course of a day, then it may be important to maximize utilization of equipment. Consider that the cost of the system is $1,000 an hour and that each job will utilize 60 percent of the system while it is running. If the system is serially dedicated to the batch jobs for ten hours, the total cost of producing $25,000 worth of information will be $10,000 for a "net profit of computing" of $15,000. Imagine the pattern of use to be as shown in Fig. 9.1. Since, over the ten-hour period, the economic value of the information will remain stable regardless of when the information becomes available, there will be no economic loss if all jobs complete at 7:00 P.M. This suggests that programs may have their completion times delayed.

Each of these programs utilizes 60 percent of the system while running. If two programs are run together in a multiprogramming mix, they may tend to delay each other. It is possible for them to get into each other's way so badly that each will take longer to complete than if each runs alone. However, for this example we will assume that we will not encounter worst cases; that is, profitable mixes can be formed. *The idea of a profitable mix is that a set of programs sharing a machine will in fact make more effective use of the machine than if the programs run serially.*

If we group job 1 and job 2, they will finish jointly at 12 P.M. This represents a one-hour delay for job 1 and a one-hour speedup for job 2. The delay occurs

	Duration	Effective utilization	Cost	Cost per value
Job 1	9 A.M.–11 A.M.	60%	$ 2,000	$ 5,000
Job 2	11 A.M.– 1 P.M.	60%	2,000	5,000
Job 3	1 P.M.– 3 P.M.	60%	2,000	5,000
Job 4	3 P.M.– 5 P.M.	60%	2,000	5,000
Job 5	5 P.M.– 7 P.M.	60%	2,000	5,000
			$10,000	$25,000

Fig. 9.1   Pattern of use—five batch jobs.

because the total demand on the system exceeds 100 percent while job 1 and job 2 are running together. In fact, they represent only a marginally satisfactory mix. No economic value loss or benefit derives from the rearrangement of completion times. However, the total system cost of running job 1 and job 2 has been reduced to $3,000. Information worth $10,000 has been made available for $3,000 rather than $4,000. Note also that additional work can be done during the day to increase the economic product of the system. This is all shown in Fig. 9.2.

Consider a startling contrast. Suppose that the economic value of job 1 is $30,000 at 11 A.M., but 0 at 12 P.M. The value shown in Fig. 9.2 would be $27,500 minus $10,000 or $17,500 of net benefit. The value shown in Fig. 9.1, however, would be $50,000 minus $10,000 or $40,000 of net benefit. This simple example shows how important it is to form a proper understanding of value and cost in planning system use. The policies we discussed in an earlier section are necessarily based upon this kind of appreciation.

The time of engineers, programmers, and information seekers is becoming as expensive as the hardware of rockets. It is now clearly perceived that the economic cost of an overloaded machine can be as high as or higher than the cost of an underloaded machine if, because of overloading, the economic productivity of on-line terminal users becomes disrupted. A system interacting with 40 working design engineers and giving less than one-second response time to each engineer but running at 70 percent equipment utilization can be considerably more effective to an enterprise than a system giving unpredictable response times in the range of three to five seconds (for example) with the equipment running at 99 percent utilization. This is because the engineers will produce less, will find that

	Duration	Effective utilization	Cost	Cost per value
Job 1	9 A.M.–12 P.M.	120%	$ 3,000	$ 5,000
Job 2	9 A.M.–12 P.M.			5,000
Job 3	12 P.M.– 3 P.M.	120%	3,000	5,000
Job 4	12 P.M.– 3 P.M.			5,000
Job 5	3 P.M.– 6 P.M.	120%	3,000	5,000
Job 6	3 P.M.– 6 P.M.			5,000
				30,000
Job 7	6 P.M.– 7 P.M.	60%	1,000	2,500
			10,000	32,500

Fig. 9.2 Reducing cost.

the system behavior disrupts their thinking patterns, and may generally experience frustration and stress that will affect the quality of their work adversely.

9.6 WHEN RESOURCE DECISIONS ARE MADE

A relationship exists between an operating system's resource management components and a community of people who form policies for use based upon perceptions of cost and value. An important part of this relationship involves the extent to which the operating system participates in forming and enforcing policy. Earlier, we mentioned that the contrast between basic and advanced multiprogramming systems is based primarily on the notion of how much planning must be done in order to use the system. Even if a system allows minimum planning, it is not always profitable to rely upon the resource allocation mechanisms of the system.

One view of a computing facility is that of a system as a *continuous process mechanism*. If one thinks of the system as a pipeline from input to output and wishes to minimize human scheduling, then the system will manage the pipeline dynamically. Over any time interval, some portion of system capacity will be consumed by resource management in order to assure that pathological conditions are not occurring in the mix, and that the mix is running well. It is analogous to a pipeline with measuring devices, temperature gauges, and other kinds of analysis equipment constantly monitoring what is flowing through the pipe. In most current computing systems, this monitoring process (which inspects for gross imbalance of resource use, programs seriously behind schedule, etc.) actually constricts the flow of work, in effect constricting the pipeline. The process of controlling the work flow is a burden on the flow itself. The burden is legitimate for either of two reasons.

■   There is no alternative. The nature of the environment is such that no significant planning can be done, and dynamic management interspersed or concurrent with real work flow is the only way to get significant loads on the system.

■   The amount of flow smoothing actually achieved by dynamic, on-line management actually exceeds the investment in such management. There is a net profit to intensive management.

These two conditions can occur when there is maximum "surprise" in the work load itself. If patterns of use and load cannot be predicted, then it is necessary to rely upon resource management mechanisms of a very dynamic nature that are sophisticated enough to adapt resource usage patterns to a constantly changing work load.

Another view of a computing facility is that of the installation as a *plannable production facility*. The important difference between this view and the continuous process view lies in a characteristic not of the system, but of the work load. There are environments in which it is feasible and profitable to plan. To the extent that the resource consumption patterns of the work load are known and stable, that the work load is repeated, and that units of work tend to cluster in known patterns, planning becomes effective and economical. There are two reasons why. The planned scheduling process can be applied to choices and combinations that are not reasonably available to a dynamic method trying to make fast decisions. Perhaps as important, planning relieves the load on the system so that work in process continues with minimum perturbation due to global analysis.

The front-end scheduling process can itself use the scheduling support provided in a program. There have been ''off-line'' macro schedulers available for some years. In effect, the approach is to ''front-end'' the scheduling load, taking system time to plan so that less load is imposed while the work is in process.

How much front-end planning and scheduling should be done and how much dynamic scheduling should be done depend on what is known about the work load. The danger of overplanning is that there may be misinformation or insufficient information, and the system may become committed to an unrealistic schedule it cannot achieve. The danger of underplanning is that pathological conditions beyond the capability of dynamic resource management may occur. There is an interesting danger in running stable work loads on dynamic systems.

Consider the payoff in dynamic scheduling. This payoff is the avoidance of gross system underutilization on the basis of continuous monitoring of system use and schedule status. This payoff is minimized when stable populations of work not representing pathological mixes are run on the system. If a mix that has been running well, for example, on a previous version of the system is brought to a new system with much enhanced dynamic resource management, there is a real danger that the thruput of the system will actually go down. This may occur even if the mix is running on a faster version of the architecture. Since the mix is initially well formed, there is tolerable contention between the programs and acceptably balanced resource usage. If 0 percent of machine time was previously used to manage the mix dynamically, any increase in that percentage must run the mix better than it was run before. If, on the new system, 20 percent of system time is invested in dynamic resource management, then a more than corresponding improvement in performance must be achieved. But on a well-known, preadjusted, well-formed mix there may be very little imbalance to smooth out, and the additional investment in on-line resource management may bring poor returns.

The current state of the art includes many resource management and scheduling mechanisms. Since the operating system can manage only what is brought to it, mechanisms are necessary to schedule work load in a macroscopic way. It is necessary to form some kind of schedule on a daily or weekly basis. Schedules representing shift loads can be brought to the high-level scheduler that then decides when to submit work to the system. Contemporary designs of large systems often include an intermediate-level scheduler that does some degree of dynamic scheduling of work introduced by the high-level scheduler.

It is important not to confuse the issue of how much work should be done by human beings and how much by the machine operating system with the issue of planning versus dynamics. The level of human effort associated with proper definition of the objectives and biases of a dynamic resource manager can equal the level of human effort associated with planning.

9.7 THE LIMITS OF RESOURCE MANAGEMENT

The degree of resource management on a system, the intensity with which the performance of a system is monitored, the variety of binding times available, and the flexibility of allocation and de-allocation are limited by the nature of the machine hardware.

A machine with a very rich set of different kinds of resources, each of which has an ability to be used on a shared basis, and that can run concurrently, is more likely to profit by intensive management than a machine with a sparse set of resources that have little concurrent capability.

It is possible to both overmanage and undermanage a system. For example, consider a machine A with operating system OPA that runs at a nominal thruput of 1. Now postulate a machine B that is four times faster than A. OPA running machine B achieves a thruput of only 1.6. The inference that can be drawn is that OPA is undermanaging B. It is not sufficiently sophisticated to find instances of underutilized B resources and find suitable uses for these resources. This may be because it does not allow sufficient flexibility in allocating and de-allocating B's resources, or it does not inspect system status often enough in sufficient detail.

Similarly, consider an operating system OPB that runs B at a thruput of 3.7. Running on A it reduces thruput to .5. OPB is overmanaging A. The time OPB is taking to determine how well A is running is consuming too much of the resource A.

The fundamental assumption of resource management is that the consumption of resources will enable the net remaining resources to sustain greater loads. The argument is that, given a 3-MIPS, 8-megabyte, 16-channel machine, the withdrawal of 300 KIPS, 2 megabytes, and 4 channels will allow the remaining 2.7-MIPS, 6-megabyte, 12-channel machine either to be more responsive or to do more total work than it could do in its "raw" configuration. This argument is based on the notion that individual programs will not load the machine, and that a significant load cannot be placed on the machine unless there are management facilities available to enable sharing.

The proper level of resource management is important. There is a dispute in the industry as to whether or not there are economies of scale. It used to be commonly held that if one doubles the price of a system, one quadruples the thruput of the system. Although this notion has never really been formalized and tested, it supports the idea that there are economies in one large system rather than two small ones. It is not clear, any longer, how true the notion is, or why it might or might not be true. However, it is clear that in order to be cost effective a large machine must be reasonably well utilized. Given a constraint that responsiveness should always be given the first consideration, a large machine must sustain reasonable utilization levels in order to achieve economies of scale. Therefore, proper resource management facilities are absolutely essential on a large system.

TERMINOLOGY

"animated spirit" of a procedure

contention for resources

continuous process view

cost of computing

cost of lateness

demand resource allocation

dynamic heuristic resource management

dynamic scheduling

"front-end" scheduling

Installation Performance Specification

nominal utilization

plannable production facility

preemptible resource

procedure

process

programming stylistics

real utilization

resource

resource as an abstraction

resource management

resource management policy

resource sharing

response–utilization dichotomy

responsiveness

value of computing

EXERCISES

Section 9.1

9.1 An operating system provides mechanisms that allow the sharing of resources of a computing system by

a) protecting the resources;

b) resolving contention for their use.

Discuss several operating systems mechanisms that perform the above functions.

9.2 Certain resources are defined by an operating system to be conceptualizations of abstract structures. What does this mean?

9.3 Comment on each of the following essential ideas of resource management.

a) the resources

b) the goals to be achieved by resource management

c) the relationship between the resources that are managed and the nature of programs that are allocated or denied resources

Section 9.2

9.4 The function of the operating system is to define an abstract machine composed of abstract resources that are conveniently manipulated by processes. Comment on this.

Section 9.3

9.5 A major influence on the design of operating systems over the last 15 years has been the desirability of allowing the shared use of computer resources. Discuss five ways in which operating systems design has been affected.

9.6 The essential decision that management makes is whether maximum profitability of the data processing resource comes from its responsiveness to work requests or its highly efficient use. Explain.

9.7 Discuss each of the following scheduler objective functions. How do they relate to (or conflict with) one another?

a) Minimize average flow time.

b) Minimize number of late responses.

c) Minimize maximum late response time.

d) Maximize utilization of hardware.

e) Maximize utilization within the constraint that no response is greater than a certain time limit.

f) Service work of class A at a given rate, work of class B at a given rate, etc.

9.8 An important interface of an operating system is its relationship with the policy-formulating mechanisms of its environment. Policy should be expressible directly to a system in the terminology of nontechnical policymakers. Discuss several items you would consider in the design of a policymaker interface.

9.9 There are those who feel that the distinction between policymaking and operations is not clearly drawn in current operating systems interfaces. Explain.

9.10 Some years ago, a survey of installations of a major computer manufacturer indicated that operator action had considerably more effect on the productivity of a system than did the algorithms of the operating system. Discuss several reasons why this might be true. Do you consider this desirable or undesirable? Why?

Section 9.4

9.11 It is not always bad programs that represent problems to an operating system. It may be the good program that has achieved a local optimization that provides the greatest problem for a system trying to optimize a mix of programs on a more global basis. Explain.

9.12 What is dynamic heuristic resource management?

9.13 What criteria make a resource preemptible? List several resources that are preemptible. List several resources that are not preemptible.

Section 9.5

9.14 Discuss each of the following items contributing to the value of computing.

 a) reducing the cost of creating, manipulating, and storing data

 b) increasing the productivity of users and of professionals associated with the system

 c) providing information of better quality on a more timely basis

 d) providing an increased ability to correlate data from different agencies of the enterprise

 e) providing more sophisticated business planning methodologies

9.15 Hardware now represents a diminishing percentage of the total costs of a system while labor costs are increasing at dramatic rates. How does this trend affect designers' goals for system performance?

9.16 Give several examples in which the cost of late information may be many times the cost of underutilization of the machine.

9.17 If two programs are run together in a multiprogramming mix, they may tend to delay one another. It is possible for them to get into each other's way so badly that each will take longer to complete than if each ran alone. Explain.

9.18 Explain how it is possible for the economic cost of an overloaded machine to be as high as or higher than the cost of an underloaded machine.

Section 9.6

9.19 The process of controlling the work flow is a burden on the flow itself. Explain.

9.20 Discuss the view of a computing facility as a continuous process mechanism.

9.21 Discuss the view of a computing facility as a production facility, capable of being planned.

9.22 The planned scheduling process can be applied to choices and combinations of jobs that are not reasonably available to a dynamic mechanism trying to make fast decisions. Explain.

9.23 There is an interesting danger in running stable work loads on a dynamic system. Explain.

Section 9.7

9.24 The fundamental assumption of resource management is that its consumption of resources will enable the net remaining resources to sustain greater loads. Explain.

10
Processor Management

10.1 FUNDAMENTAL NOTIONS OF MULTIPROGRAMMING AND TIME-SHARING

Although mechanisms designed to achieve *multiprogramming* and *time-sharing* are somewhat similar, and both multiprogramming and time-sharing are concerned with enabling shared use of a machine, there are some differences in underlying concepts worth stating before describing mechanisms that apply to both.

The essential goal of multiprogramming is to maximize the utilization and concurrent operation of all elements of a system. The technique may be constrained by response requirements stated in terms of priorities, but its essential goal is to minimize the cost of computing by distributing the cost of hardware use across a large set of concurrent users. *The success of multiprogramming depends on a large population of available jobs of heterogeneous resource needs.* The heterogeneity is important. In order to run hardware well, it is necessary that programs that are I/O-bound run with programs that are CPU-bound and/or memory-bound. When a perfect multiprogramming mix is formed, a particular program A is using the processor when program B is using channel 1 and program C is using channel 2, etc. A, B, and C never wish to use resources at the same time, no contention develops, and each program runs as if it were alone on the machine. The effect of multiprogramming is to fill in gaps in the utilization of equipment during times when a running single program is not using that equipment. In order to do this perfectly, it is necessary that there be an infinite number of spontaneously available heterogeneous units of work so that whenever a gap appears there is a unit of work to use it, and that unit of work will cause no contention for other resources. This ideal is not achieved, of course, but to the extent that it is not achieved the effectiveness of multiprogramming declines. Thus a very small population of equally CPU-bound jobs all using the same device for I/O and all occupying so much memory that others cannot coexist in memory (a homogeneous population) is a poor multiprogramming mix.

Time-sharing, on the other hand, very often profits by maximum homogeneity of use. A set of terminal users who are all doing the same thing may considerably improve the responsiveness of the system because sharing of code can be maximized and the resource management burden may be minimized. Movement of system functions in and out of memory may be minimized, the complexity of dispatching algorithms may be minimized, and very stable operating environments may be achieved.

10.2 HIGH-LEVEL SCHEDULING

A *high-level scheduler* is a mechanism that selects jobs from a set of jobs waiting for entry on a queue from which they can receive CPU service. (See Fig. 10.1.) It is commonly associated with a batch environment. The classical card deck submission procedures, however, need not be present in an environment substantially thought of as batch. Request for activation from a terminal of a job that will run *absentee* or *unattended* may be supported by a scheduling mechanism distinct from those used to support *conversational operation*.

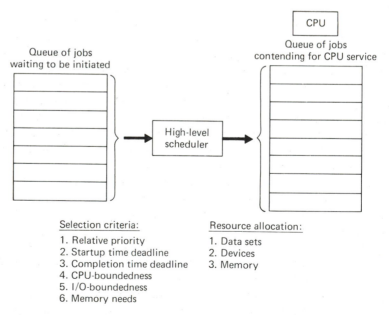

Queue of jobs
waiting to be initiated

Queue of jobs
contending for CPU service

CPU

High-level
scheduler

Selection criteria:

1. Relative priority
2. Startup time deadline
3. Completion time deadline
4. CPU-boundedness
5. I/O-boundedness
6. Memory needs

Resource allocation:

1. Data sets
2. Devices
3. Memory

Fig. 10.1 High-level scheduling.

10.2.1　Selection Criteria

A high-level scheduler may select a work unit from a queue of waiting jobs on the basis of a given relative priority or on the basis of a given startup or a given completion requirement time. All of these criteria are service-oriented. Other service-oriented criteria may be applied by defining a class of preferred jobs and indicating the membership of any job in some preference group. The basis of preference can be any installation-perceived characteristic. Shortest-Job-First is an example.

Sometimes *preference classes* are defined on the basis of resource utilization patterns, such as I/O-boundedness or memory needs. In general, it is not good practice to use relative priority as a means of indicating resource usage. Some early systems recommended that I/O-bound jobs be given high priority and CPU-bound jobs be given low priority. (We will discuss the reason for this later.) The difficulty with this approach is that there is then no mechanism for describing the relative importance of the work to the enterprise. An initial use of job classification schemes in operating systems was to relieve the relative priority parameter of the burden of describing resource usage.

The concept of *relative priority* is often criticized for not giving sufficient predictability to a user since the priority may be more or less effective depending on the priority of jobs in the mix. A concept of "absolute priority," "two-hour turnaround," or "finished by 3 P.M." may be enforced by the operating system or supported by an informal "express-normal-overnight" classification defined by an installation beyond the context of the operating system.

10.2.2　Allocation

After selecting a candidate, the scheduler may undertake to accumulate some resources for it. In multiprogramming systems, the high-level scheduler does not allocate CPU time or channel time, but it may allocate data sets, devices, and memory. It is possible to require a user to state resource requirements in control language, and to require the granting of resources as a precondition for starting the program. In such a design, the act of scheduling and the act of allocating are closely intermingled. The problem of such a design is that a requesting job may experience indefinite delays before it is started since all resources must be jointly acquired. The problem of such a design to the system is that it commits a resource that may not really be needed by a program, denying that resource to the other potential users. A goal of a dynamic system is to minimize the difference between nominal use of a resource and real use. *Nominal use represents those intervals during which a resource is allocated and held by a program but is not actively being used. The advantage to a user of having all resources allocated prior to execution is that after being started the job is guaranteed service until it is completed.*

A completely opposite approach is to select a candidate without giving it any resources whatsoever. Resources are acquired by run-time macros submitted after startup. Scheduling becomes the act of granting permission to contend for resources. The advantage to a user of this approach is quick startup, and the advantage to the system is dynamic retrieval of unneeded resources. The effectiveness of the approach, of course, depends on the programmer's care in releasing resources when they are not needed. The burden on run time increases because of multiple acts of allocation and de-allocation.

As allocation overhead decreases, more dynamic allocation becomes more feasible. Systems have tended over the years to allow more and more dynamic resource allocation. Memory is a particular example. In early systems it was allocated at scheduler time. Then some macro capability to acquire and release was provided. Currently, in paging systems, memory is allocated and de-allocated dynamically in a way transparent to a running program.

10.2.3 Deadlock

One of the problems of dynamic allocation is the possibility of intermittent delay because a requested resource cannot be made available. When this occurs, the requesting program must be suspended until the resource becomes available. During this time it may hold resources that it is not actively using.

A possible consequence of unavailable resources is *deadlock* or *deadly embrace*. In a system in which resources of any type can be requested in any order, and some resources are nonpreemptible (i.e., they cannot be taken away from a holder), a deadlock may occur. Consider a program A that requests and receives a resource R1. (See Fig. 10.2.) A program B requests and receives a

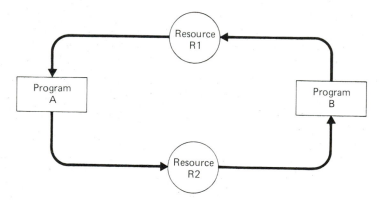

Fig. 10.2 Deadlock. Program A has been allocated Resource R1. Program B has been allocated Resource R2. Program A is requesting Resource R2 that it must have in order to proceed. Program B is requesting Resource R1 that it must have in order to proceed. The system is deadlocked. Neither of the two programs can proceed.

resource R2. Program A requests R2 while holding R1, and program B requests R1 while holding R2. These two programs are in a deadly embrace unless R1 or R2 is a preemptible resource.

10.2.4   Work Unit

An issue closely related to when resources are given is what the scheduled work unit is. The larger the work unit scheduled, the greater the exposure of the system to the overcommitment of resources; the smaller the work unit scheduled, the greater the exposure of the requestor to intervals of delay between work units. In IBM control language, a concept of STEPs within a JOB is defined. Allocation may be made at a JOB level or at STEP level, when a step is an individual program. The trend of recent years has been to allocate more discretely at the STEP level in order to confine overcommitment.

10.2.5   Staging and Aging

Techniques called *staging* and *aging* are sometimes used to reduce the exposure of users to indefinite delay when resources are allocated prior to execution. *Staging involves defining classes of resources and allocating each class from a separate queue.* The advantage of staging to a user is that it enables the program to ease onto the system. All resources need not be jointly available. As one class is acquired, the program holds the resource and advances to the next queue. The disadvantage to the system is that resources are held during periods of time that other resources are being waited for. Staging prevents deadlock.

   Aging is the process of increasing a program's priority over time or upon each denial of a resource request. A threshold priority may be defined that, when reached, will preclude the system from further allocation of resources until the aging requestor's requirement is fulfilled. This prevents smaller requestors from withdrawing returned resources, and allows the resources to accumulate. A further threshold may be defined through which the system will undertake to deprive other programs of their resources in order to fulfill the request of the substantially delayed requestor.

10.3   LOW-LEVEL SCHEDULING

Low-level scheduling is performed by the dispatching mechanism of the operating system. (See Fig. 10.3.) The dispatch control blocks form a queue of elements contending for CPU service. The dispatcher replaces a program with a new program

- when the running program indicates it wishes to voluntarily release control,

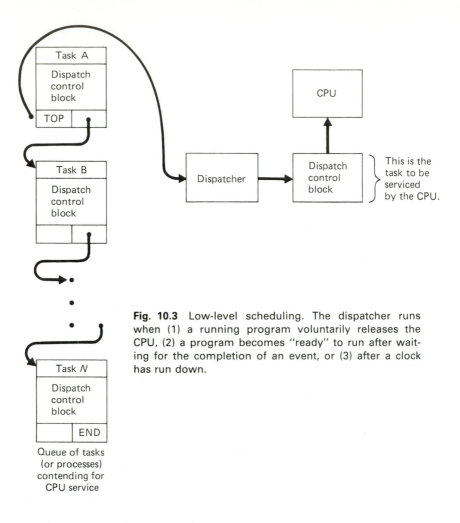

Fig. 10.3 Low-level scheduling. The dispatcher runs when (1) a running program voluntarily releases the CPU, (2) a program becomes "ready" to run after waiting for the completion of an event, or (3) after a clock has run down.

- when an event has occurred that makes a program ready to run that was previously unready because it was waiting for an event,
- when a clock has run down.

In both interactive programming systems and batch systems, a fundamental difference between scheduling and dispatching lies in the assumption that programs will requeue after intervals of service. That is, while scheduling is a one-time event for a program, dispatching is something that may occur frequently as the program receives discontinuous intervals of service. Real-time and inquiry systems may undertake to complete the service of a transaction in one dispatching event.

The dispatcher controls the rate of progress of programs in a mix by determining the frequency with which they will be given control and the length of time they will be allowed to maintain control. The ability of the dispatcher to completely predict the rate of progress of a program is limited by the program's ability to consume service. This ability is dependent on its need for I/O, its relationship to other processes and, in some systems, its page reference pattern.

10.3.1   Round Robin

In the simplest time-sharing environments in which each terminal works with a defined work space, where each work space is fixed in memory, and where no I/O can be done from the terminal, the dispatcher has absolute control over the distribution of computing power among users. If the population of work is homogeneous, each request from a terminal requiring approximately the same amount of service and each terminal using the same set of requests, then a perfect distribution of service can be achieved by use of a simple, time-driven, *round-robin* dispatcher.

Basic round-robin dispatching associates a time interval with the execution of a program. At the end of this interval (*time slice* or *quantum*), a successor program is started for an identical period of time. The dispatcher cycles around the queue, giving each program exactly the same share of processor time at a fixed interval.

It is possible to make the round-robin dispatcher more elaborate by changing the amount of time given to a program on the basis of some priority. A program with priority three might receive three time slices, a program with priority six might receive six time slices, etc.

In environments in which there is considerable heterogeneity among users, in which not all users can fit into memory at once, in which there is a possibility that a program will be unable to proceed, a considerable elaboration of the round-robin structure is necessary.

10.3.2   Feedback Cycle Queues

A *feedback cycle queue* is a queue structure partitioned into *n subqueue elements*. There is a rule for residence of any program on a subqueue element and a set of relationships for subqueue elements. Figure 10.4 shows the conceptual structure. The arrows indicate that a dispatch control block either may remain on a subqueue after an interval of service, or may be moved to another subqueue. The residence and relationship rules may be fixed in a system, or they may be opened to parameterization by using installations.

One use of this structure is in time-sharing systems in which a program is loaded into memory whenever it is to be executed and removed from memory when an interval of execution is complete. Such a system experiences a large

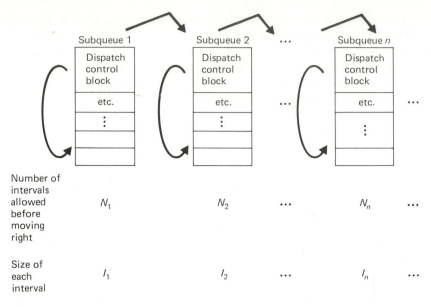

Note: Commonly, if $i > j$, then $N_i > N_j$ and $I_i > I_j$.

Fig. 10.4 Feedback cycle queues. A process starts running in subqueue 1. It percolates to the head of the queue and receives I_1 time units of service from the CPU. It then cycles to the bottom of subqueue 1, percolates to the top again, and receives another I_1 CPU units. This cycle is repeated N_1 times at which point the process moves to the bottom of subqueue 2. The process receives N_2 "shots" of length I_2 each before moving to subqueue 3. Once a process reaches the rightmost queue, it remains there until it completes execution. At any time subqueue x can cause a process to run only if no processes are waiting to run in subqueue y for any $y < x$.

number of memory loads during which the processor is idle. It is possible, using basic round robin, to partition memory into three areas, "last," "current," "next," and on an overlap machine, take advantage of the perfect predictability of basic round robin by reading in the memory load for the "next" while writing out the "last" and having the CPU processing the "current."

In order to actually reduce the number of memory loads, however, a form of feedback cyclic queue structure is used. Consider a program that requires 5,000 microseconds in order to make a response to the terminal. If it receives 50 microsecond "shots," it will require 100 such shots and consequently 100 memory loads. The number of memory loads is directly connected to the length of the individual intervals of service. If the program were to receive all of its time in one shot, then only one memory load would be required.

If there is a set of users each requiring different amounts of service before a terminal response, it is convenient to distinguish the long jobs from the short jobs and try to reduce the memory loads for long jobs. Feedback queues are used for this segregation of work. The top queue contains dispatch control blocks that have received fewer than n shots. Whenever a program receives a shot, a count is made to record the total number of shots received. When an nth shot is given, the program is moved from the top queue to the next queue. There it remains for some number of shots until, if it does not complete, it is moved right once more to another queue. At any time, therefore, from left to right across the subqueues there is a partitioning of jobs into short, longer, and longer still, in terms of the time they have already used.

Associated with each subqueue is an interval of service. If the first subqueue receives 50 microsecond intervals, the second might receive 150 microsecond intervals, the third 400 microsecond intervals, etc. If a system allowed six shots on the first queue, twelve shots on the second, and the remainder on a third, then a job requiring 5,000 microseconds would receive 26 individual shots before completing, and the memory loads are consequently reduced from 100 to 26. When a terminal response is made, a system may leave the dispatch control block for that terminal at a lower level on the assumption that this terminal is using long-service functions, or each terminal response may be treated individually and the next requested function may start fresh as a new job on the top queue between terminal responses.

The increase in the service interval associated with lower subqueues builds a considerable bias toward long jobs into the system if each queue is visited sequentially, if the round-robin cycle goes from the top of the top queue to the bottom of the last queue. The interval between instances of service for jobs on the top queue becomes enormous, and longer jobs are executing a high percentage of the time. For example, if there are six dispatch control blocks on each queue, using the numbers associated for shots in the previous paragraph, it would take 3,600 microseconds to service all three queues one time. The short jobs on the top queue would be given 300 microseconds, the jobs on the middle queue would be given 900 microseconds, and the long jobs on the bottom queue would be given 2,400 microseconds. Long jobs would be executing 66 percent of the time. The time between intervals of service for a short job would be 3,550 microseconds.

There are two ways to redress the strong bias to long jobs we have just built into the system. One way is simply to change the ratio of execution times from queue to queue. Note that giving a larger number of shots on each queue does not really redress the balance. It merely delays the time at which a long job is recognized.

The usual way to redress the balance is to define "visit" rules that control the servicing of the individual subqueues. These rules may be more or less severe. The severest rule is that the top queue always receives service whenever an element on it can use the service. In a system in which there is never a reason for the top queue not to have an element ready to go, then some fixed ration of service cycles may be established. Thus if it is desired to guarantee the set of small jobs 66 percent of the CPU's time, the top queue should be serviced completely 22 times (a total of 6,600 microseconds) before a visit to the second queue is made.

A similar vigorous short-job preference in environments in which it is possible to have occasional intervals in which no job on a queue is ready to run is to visit lower subqueues only when a leftmost queue can't take service and to preempt service from an element on a lower subqueue when an element on a higher subqueue becomes ready to receive service.

The severest top subqueue preference rules define a foreground–background environment in which it is possible to mix conversational and batch jobs, the batch jobs dropping to the bottom queues and receiving service only when no foreground job can proceed. Individual program priorities can be respected on each queue by modifying the time for each shot (within some limit) for each job on any queue. Note that real-time or inquiry environments may be supported by setting the time of service on a foreground queue to a level at which a terminal response can be made in one service interval.

More elaborate classifying rules may be applied to the structure. For example, jobs may be distributed among queues on the basis of use of main memory as well as length of execution time.

The dynamic recognition of short and long jobs is a first example of the application of the principle of *heuristic resource management. The basic principle underlying the movement from subqueue to subqueue is the assumption that a job that has consumed the most service has the most service yet to consume.* The concept is that the history of a unit of work is the basis for making a prediction about its future. This idea forms the basis of dynamic resource management in many environments.

10.3.3 Feedback and Batch

We will demonstrate the power of feedback cyclic enqueueing by showing how the same structure can be used in an entirely different way. In batch, there is a need to maximize the utilization of the I/O components of the system partially because they represent ever increasing percentages of total system cost and partially to achieve system balance. In order to achieve maximum I/O load, a variation of a thruput-oriented rule called *shortest job first* can be used as the dispatching policy. The fundamental rule is always to give the CPU to the program that will run the shortest time until it issues an I/O request. This effectively gives highest priority to I/O-bound jobs that generate I/O commands in the shortest intervals. This approach may tend to maximize the dispatching rate if a program that has issued an I/O is assumed unable to proceed and loses the CPU. There is a relationship between dispatching, channel, and device allocation that affects the dispatching tactic very directly.

Consider a system with many channels. It is desirable to run as many channels as possible concurrently. In order to do this, one might allocate all of the data sets of a particular program to a single channel. This would deprive the program of the ability to overlap its own I/O, but would eliminate shared use of channels and the queues that might consequently form on shared channels or devices. It would give each program maximum performance predictability because of isolation from contention with other programs.

Such an allocation tactic is consistent with the dispatching algorithm that finds the job that will run most quickly to an I/O event, runs it, and when it submits the I/O, gives control to another program. The ideal sequence is that program 1 runs and places a load on channel 1, program 2 runs and places a load on channel 2, program n runs and places a load on channel n. Concurrent use of channels is maximized (potentially), system balance is achieved, and CPU utilization is sustained except when the mix is excessively I/O-bound. The reader will note that buffering I/O in an attempt to balance a particular program undermines the intent of the system and represents an instance in which programming stylistics interferes with resource management.

A channel allocation algorithm that tends to spread the allocation of data sets across channels for a particular program will also distort the effect of the dispatching algorithm. When data sets for a particular program are distributed horizontally, there will be a strong tendency for programs to share channels. The effect of a maximum dispatching rate may be to increase channel imbalance. For example, if program A uses channel 1 and program B uses channel 1 and program B is run immediately after program A starts channel 1, then B may reference 1 and find it busy. In a system that must commonly share channels, the selection of a proper combined dispatching–allocation strategy is very complex and usually must involve not only a calculation of who will run the shortest time before submitting an I/O but also what the expected ratio of run time to I/O completion time may be.

An amusing paradox is related to these issues. Consider a system in which programs must share channels. Assume it is running at very low CPU utilization. It is desirable to increase the utilization by adding a CPU-bound job to the mix. Postulate that a job is found that is CPU-bound in the sense that it takes five times as long to process a record than the job takes to read it and write it. This program is added to the mix. The unexpected result is that CPU utilization goes down. What happens (when things in fact go wrong) is this: Instances of CPU idle time occur because the dispatcher cannot find a job on the queue that is ready to run. The probability of not finding a ready job is related to the length of time between the submission of an I/O request and its successful completion. This interval is a function of the queueing and arm movement patterns associated with shared use of disk devices. The CPU-bound addition to the mix applies a steady, if light, incremental load to the I/O system. Because of the presence of other users of I/O, the ratio of process time to I/O time for this program changes. It is no longer truly CPU-bound because the total time to do I/O is its own time plus the time of all elements enqueued before it. Each other element also experiences an incremental extension of its I/O completion time because of the new, nominally CPU-bound program. As a result of these extensions, the rate at which programs become ready to run slows, the instances in which the dispatcher cannot find a program ready to use the CPU increase, and CPU utilization goes down.

Let us see how feedback queues can be used to assure that the program that is most I/O-bound always gets the CPU. The top queue residence rule may be set so that it represents a maximum period of time that a program may run before submitting an I/O request. If a program submits an I/O before that time, it remains on the top queue. If a program uses its entire time slice, it is removed from the queue and moved rightward to a queue with a larger upper bound. At any time, the queues of the feedback structure represent subsets of programs of various degrees of I/O-boundedness with very I/O-bound jobs on the top queue and very CPU-bound jobs on the bottom.

The assumption made here is that a job submitting I/O requests at a fast rate will continue to submit I/Os at that rate. When a program slows its rate, it moves to a queue that receives longer intervals but less frequently.

The issue that immediately comes to mind is what to do when a program on a lower queue submits an I/O request very quickly. Should the program be immediately moved up to the top queue or should it be moved gradually back toward the top? This is a rather profound question that is essentially enquiring about how long the past should be.

One of the problems of using past performance to predict the future is how to treat the historical data. A programmer predicting how long a program will run has a collection of data about how long it has run in the past. The programmer may predict that its next running time will be most like its last. The programmer who does this is minimally smoothing his or her data and reacting in a maximum way to the last event. He or she may take an average, draw a trend line, take a weighted average, median, mode, or use any number of data manipulation techniques. To the extent that the programmer includes older data, he or she is smoothing the prediction and extending the concept of recent, relevant past further and further back.

A heuristic dispatcher faces exactly the same problem. Maximum smoothing for a dispatcher is to take some statement about I/O-boundedness given to it by a programmer to apply to the entire execution of the program. The difficulty in this is that if the program truly has a variation in its CPU–I/O-boundedness during its lifetime, it will, at times, be receiving either inappropriately good or bad treatment. The feedback partitioning attempts to change the treatment of a program on the basis of dynamically observed behavior.

The analog of maximum responsiveness to the most recent event, or to the last event, is to immediately move a program that seems to be entering an I/O-bound phase up to the top queue. A smoothing effect is applied when the program is either maintained on a lower queue until it has submitted a number of quick I/Os or gradually moved up queue by queue. There are dangers in maximum response in that the quick I/O request may not be a true signal of a change in pattern. The danger of smoothing is that by the time a program reaches a preferred position, it may be out of its I/O-bound phase once more. In both cases an error means inappropriate service for some time.

A variant form of feedback queue used to support high utilization involves the ordering of a single queue by a CPU/wait time ratio used as an index to CPU-boundedness. The list is ordered from the top with I/O-bound programs ahead of CPU-bound programs. Moving down the list always finds a more CPU-bound program. The list can be reordered after every dispatching interval, or over periods of time on the basis of collected statistics.

10.3.4 Feedback and Priority

The trade-off between service to a particular program and high utilization of components of a system is clearly seen when the concept of *relative priority* is mapped onto the structure we have just described. If programs are allowed to have service priorities, one way of using them is to influence the basic service interval. Consider a top queue that gives basic 50-microsecond slices. The actual amount of time given to a program may be extended by applying a priority factor to the basic interval. Thus a program of lowest priority will receive the 50-micro-second slice, but a program of higher priority will receive an expanded slice. This expanded slice is the amount of time the program can run without being penalized for not submitting an I/O request. Thus a very important CPU-bound program with a high priority might receive considerably longer service intervals without being penalized for not submitting an I/O request. The reader can see how this enlargement of service interval could dampen the I/O rate of the system by enlarging intervals of time during which I/O requests are not being generated.

There are several ways to balance utilization and priority service. One way is to provide the administration with a parameter describing the impact that priority is to have on the basic service interval. For example, on UNIVAC's EXEC VIII, a number may be provided that is used to divide into a program priority. When the number is high, the resulting quotient is low, and that low quotient is used to alter the service interval thus minimizing the effect of priority. When the number is low, the quotient of the division by the biasing factor of the priority is high and priority has a greater impact on the service interval. IBM's VM/370 has a set of similar biasing factors used to weight the ability of a program to receive CPU cycles.

Another approach used in IBM's OS/VS2 operating system is to define the priority to be subjected to I/O–CPU ratio balancing. Any job of a higher priority will take service cycles without a consideration of its boundedness, strictly on the basis of its priority. Those jobs at the priority level designated for APG service, "automatic priority grouping," are serviced on an ordered "mean-time-to-wait" basis, where mean-time-to-wait is an index of CPU-boundedness.

10.4   INTERMEDIATE-LEVEL SCHEDULING—THREE-LEVEL SYSTEMS

So far we have discussed two levels of scheduling, a "Dean of Admissions" that allows programs into a mix and a run-time environment dispatcher that decides which program is next to receive CPU service. Many large-scale multiprogramming and general-purpose (mixed batch and interactive) systems introduce a third level of scheduling that we characterize as an intermediate-scheduling level. (See Fig. 10.5.) Examples of components at this level in contemporary systems are the Systems Resources Manager of IBM's OS/VS2 and the Dynamic Allocator of UNIVAC's EXEC VIII. These mechanisms have been developed in order to increase the flexibility of the system without overburdening the dispatching function.

As systems become more heuristic and adaptive, more statistics are collected and more on-line analysis must be done. The structure of a two-level system becomes inadequate for a number of reasons.

■   The dispatching decisions become too complex. Because dispatching is a frequently executed function, the association of analysis functions is limited by a desire to have each instance of dispatch as fast as possible.

■   Some of the collected statistics of systems behavior are not really meaningful in the brief time frames of dispatching intervals. Some longer scheduling interval must be defined so that the concept of the recent past can be extended beyond "last dispatched" behavior.

■   The introduction of conversational services suggests that the number of individual requestors for CPU service might be much larger than a reasonable set of elements on a dispatching queue, and some standby queueing mechanism is needed between the entry queue and the dispatching queue to hold additional admitted but not serviced work.

■   The enlarged concepts of guaranteed rates of progress, deadline, and dynamic mix balancing require an intermittent systems analysis function for a fuller review of system status than is available or desirable at the dispatcher level.

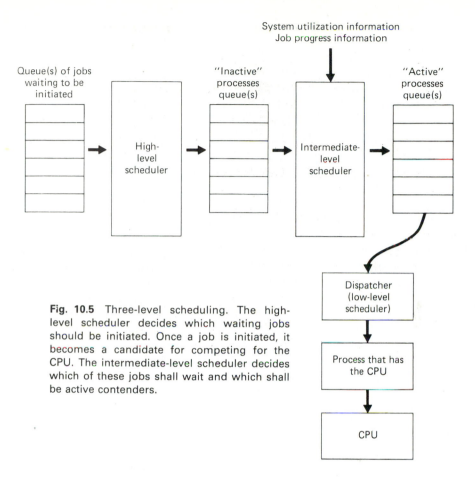

Fig. 10.5 Three-level scheduling. The high-level scheduler decides which waiting jobs should be initiated. Once a job is initiated, it becomes a candidate for competing for the CPU. The intermediate-level scheduler decides which of these jobs shall wait and which shall be active contenders.

The essential idea of the intermediate level is that there will exist a queue of work available to the system that has either come on conversationally or passed through the high-level scheduler, but that is not available to the dispatcher until the intermediate-level scheduler defines a dispatch list for the dispatcher. The intermediate-level scheduler may operate on a fixed time basis, commonly in seconds, or in response to a specific event such as the observation that a resource has become seriously overused. For example, on OS/VS2, the SRM may be started by the memory manager when the number of available page frames (usable free areas of memory) goes below a certain amount. This will cause the SRM to reduce the multiprogramming level (number of elements on the dispatch queue) and free the storage used by the suspended program. (The program is "swapped out.") The suspended program is placed on the OUT queue, the queue from which the SRM organizes a dispatch list. The availability of the OUT queue allows the changing of multiprogramming levels under the conditions of preempt resume rather than preempt abort. The program can be started at some later time whereas in the earliest versions of IBM's OS/MVT an overload of memory was handled by an operator aborting a program and losing productive work up to that point.

The intermediate-level scheduler can be used to balance systems utilization by transferring work between the *OUT queue* (also called *suspended queue,* or *eligible set*) and the *dispatching queue* on the basis of the balance of the mix. If, for example, all jobs are CPU-bound and are grouped at the bottom of the feedback cyclic dispatching structure, the intermediate-level scheduler can remove some of the CPU-bound jobs and replace them with I/O bound jobs on the suspended queue. The SRM, for example, will solicit from a Work-load Manager, a CPU Utilization Manager, and a Channel Manager recommendations for removal and replacement on the dispatching list. The Work-load Manager attempts to analyze whether programs in certain performance groups are progressing at the desired rates. The CPU Manager determines whether CPU utilization targets are being realized. On the basis of a weighting for the recommendations of Work-load Managers and Utilization Managers provided by the installation, the SRM will perform swaps from the dispatch queue to the OUT queue.

The idea of a guaranteed rate of progress for certain jobs is most extremely supported in a system that attempts to guarantee deadline. A simple concept of deadline involves the nomination of one deadline job in any particular mix. When this job is started, a computation is made of how many *service units* (see Chapter 15—Intermediate-Level Scheduling) it requires to run to completion. Let us say that a particular deadline program has a requirement for 1,200 service units and a three P.M. deadline. The system can provide 2,400 service units an hour. If the job is started at two P.M., let us say, in order to complete on time the job must receive 50 percent of the service units performable by the system in an hour. We will discuss the meaning of a service unit below. Let us postulate that there are going to be six intermediate scheduling intervals during the hour so that of the 2,400 available service units each interval provides 400. In each interval, in order to be "on-schedule" the deadline job must receive 200 units.

An initial priority is calculated by the system that will provide 50 percent of the service units of the system and the job is placed onto the dispatch list at that priority. Because of contention for resources, or because of the balancing of the program, the program may actually consume more or less than 50 percent. At the end of a dispatching interval, the intermediate scheduler determines how many units the job received and whether it is on, ahead of, or behind schedule. If it is behind schedule, the priority is raised to try to have the program catch up. If it cannot catch up in the next interval, more extreme measures, such as the preemption of memory space, might be undertaken until the entire machine resource may be given over to the deadline job.

The complexity of managing to deadline with more than one deadline job is very high in the batch environment unless very extensive policy is formulated to tell the system what to do if two deadline jobs fall behind schedule, etc. Some systems impose a deadline concept only on job initiation. They undertake to apportion time by trying to achieve rates of progress for performance groups in the run-time environment without going all the way to managing by deadline. "Guaranteed rate of progress" is a calculation that determines whether or not programs are receiving service at a requested rate.

Intermediate-level schedulers are particularly useful in interactive environments. Here the concept of deadline may be strong. In versions of IBM's TSS/370, there is a concept of *delta-to-run* that effectively time stamps a program with a number representing the clock time by which it must be run again. The intermediate scheduler puts those programs on the dispatching list whose delta-to-run time has been reached by the system "wall" clock.

A program on the dispatching list, after it has been transferred there by the intermediate-level scheduler, is subject to the rules of the dispatcher. It receives service during its time on the list in discontinuous intervals according to its I/O-boundedness, priority, terminal response pattern, etc. That is, there are periods of readiness and inactivity for programs on the dispatching list that may be subjected to round-robin or feedback dispatching.

The concept of a service unit, a basic measure of the rate at which programs are progressing, is present most clearly in OS/VS2. There a formula exists that undertakes to relate CPU cycles, I/O starts, and memory requirements into a single service-unit number. This enables programs of very different resource consumption patterns to express their level of load upon the system in a comparable way. The concept is by no means entirely sufficient, but it represents a means by which a richer concept than CPU cycles consumed can be used to measure a job's rate of progress.

TERMINOLOGY

aging

APG

automatic priority grouping

background

basic round robin

Channel Manager

CPU-bound

CPU Utilization Manager

deadline scheduling

deadlock

deadly embrace

dispatch list

dispatching

feedback cycle queue

foreground	quantum
heuristic resource management	queue of waiting jobs
high-level scheduler	real use of a resource
intermediate-level scheduler	round robin
I/O-bound	scheduling
JOB level	shortest job first
low-level scheduler	SRM
mean-time-to-wait	staging
memory-bound	STEP level
multiprogramming mix	swap out a program
nominal use of a resource	Systems Resources Manager
nonpreemptible resource	time slice
preemptible resource	Work-load Manager

EXERCISES

Section 10.1

10.1 What is the essential goal of multiprogramming?

10.2 The success of multiprogramming depends on a large population of available jobs of heterogeneous resource needs. Why?

10.3 What is a ''perfect'' multiprogramming mix?

10.4 Time sharing profits from homogeneity of use. Why?

Section 10.2

10.5 What is a high-level scheduler?

10.6 List several criteria used by a high-level scheduler for selecting jobs to run.

10.7 In what circumstances does it make sense to give higher priority to I/O-bound jobs than to CPU-bound jobs?

10.8 Criticize the concept of relative priority scheduling.

10.9 Why might it be undesirable to require that all resources a job may need be assigned to that job before the job may run? Why might it be desirable?

10.10 A goal of a dynamic system is to minimize the difference between nominal use of a resource and real use. Explain.

10.11 What is deadlock?

10.12 Distinguish between allocation at the JOB level and allocation at the STEP level.

10.13 Discuss staging and aging.

Section 10.3

10.14 What is low-level scheduling?

10.15 List several events that might cause a dispatcher to replace one program with a new program.

10.16 Distinguish between scheduling and dispatching.

10.17 Discuss the operation of basic round-robin dispatching.

10.18 What is a feedback cycle queue?

10.19 The severest top subqueue preference rules define a foreground–background environment in which it is possible to mix conversational and batch jobs, the batch jobs dropping to the bottom queues and receiving service only when no foreground job can proceed. Explain.

10.20 A basic principle of heuristic resource management is that a job that has consumed the most service has the most service yet to consume. Comment on the validity and usefulness of this principle.

10.21 Discuss shortest-job-first dispatching.

10.22 Give an instance in which programming stylistics interferes with resource management.

10.23 Explain how feedback queues can be used to assure that the most I/O-bound program always gets the CPU.

10.24 Discuss the validity of the resource management heuristic that says a job submitting I/O requests at a fast rate will continue to submit I/Os at that rate.

Section 10.4

10.25 Give several reasons for the need for intermediate scheduling.

10.26 Distinguish between the alteration of multiprogramming levels under the conditions of preempt/resume and preempt/abort.

10.27 Discuss how intermediate scheduling may be used to enforce job completion deadlines.

11
File and Object Management

11.1 FILE MANAGEMENT

An important function of an operating system is file management. *File management maintains a catalog of files known to the system in a file directory and provides information and access on request to other elements of the operating system.*

The availability of large amounts of on-line disk storage has provided the ability to leave data or program files organized into libraries more or less permanently on a system. The nature of the devices is such that it is necessary to maintain a directory that associates a file name with a particular allocation of space. It is also necessary to associate various restrictions on file accessibility and sharing with files known to the system. There are various advantages to providing these services as system functions. A standard set of services for entering, deleting, and altering entries in the catalog can be established, and data files can be made available to more than one program or system on a controlled basis.

The actual use of the file management function depends on what kinds of elements may be put in the catalog, when an element may be put in the catalog, and exactly what information is kept in a catalog entry. A generalized file system allows both programs and data files to be represented in a file directory, and some operating systems make constant use of the file system on behalf of a running program during run time. Some file management functions also undertake automatic *archiving,* the movement of files from drums to disks, or from disks to tapes as space becomes precious and certain files are discovered to be infrequently used.

11.2   THE MULTICS FILE SYSTEM

One of the most effective file management systems that has been implemented is that of Multics. In Multics, the file mechanism is intimately integrated with I/O, program linking, protection, and memory management.

There is an element of the Multics operating system called the Basic File System. The nature and structure of this element derive from a number of underlying concepts.

- The programs and data of a system are a collection of objects with unique names and attributes.

- All objects are represented in the system in a hierarchical tree structure containing an entry for each object and a set of attributes for each object.

- A running process has a set of objects that are known to it at any time. The set of objects known to it represents the name space of a process.

- On-line files can be referenced as objects without the need for a distinct I/O interface.

- A list of authorized users and their rights to an object can be associated with the definition of each object.

The heart of the file system is the directory structure. The Multics directory is a tree structure containing branches and links. A branch is an entry in a directory describing an object (a segment). A link is an entry that allows cross-referencing of elements in the system beyond that afforded by the basic tree structure. For each object in the system there exists a branch that provides its attributes. The directory structure contains directory and nondirectory elements. A directory element contains branches that point to and describe nondirectory elements, data objects, and procedures. A directory element may also point to other directory elements.

The root node of the Multics structure is a directory with branches pointing to a Systems Library Directory, a User Directory Directory, and a Process Directory Directory. The Systems Library Directory contains branches that describe a collection of available programs. The User Directory Directory points to a set of User Directories. Each User Directory represents a particular programming project that has its own internal structure. The project directory may have branches pointing to subprojects consisting of small development teams. Each small development team may have a directory pointing to a set of private programs and private data objects. Thus the User Directory Directory structure permits the description of a hierarchical structure of users each of which has an associated collection of objects of which it is the author and owner. The Process Directory Directory contains a directory for each active process and points to a

Process Directory that points to a table of objects known to a process and to other structures unique to Multics design.

A particular User Directory, for example, might contain a set of branch entries for all programmer managers associated with a project. Each branch might point to a directory with branches for all programmers associated with a particular manager. Each programmer directory might then contain branches for each program or data object associated with a programmer. The name of any particular object in the system is a concatenation of all directory entries describing a path from the root node to that object in the tree. Shortened names—names starting from some assumed starting directory—may be used where appropriate.

A directory entry contains attributes such as the author (or creator) of the element, the size of the element, the allocation of space on disk for the element, and the date the element was last used and/or modified. An entry also contains an *access control list* describing exactly who may use the object, and how they may use it. In addition, each entry contains *ring* information that associates the rings with the access rights described in the access control list.

The structure and the file system that surrounds it provide a command and run-time language capability for the explicit manipulation of elements in the directory structure. For example, segments may be created and deleted, authorization lists may be modified by authors, and *aliases* (alternate names) may be provided.

11.3 DYNAMIC LINKING IN MULTICS

In addition to the explicit use of the file system to catalog and protect objects in the system, the directory structure has another interesting use that is associated with *dynamic linking,* the ability of a program to refer to a program to which it has not been previously linked.

We have described the combination of separately compiled programs into a single program by the resolution of unresolved references. The linking of a procedure to another procedure is accomplished in run time at the time of an actual reference. A process that refers to a procedure while it is running may cause a file system search for the referenced procedure in the directory. When the referenced procedure is found, and if the caller has appropriate rights, the system makes the referenced procedure known to the referring process.

Making a segment known involves creating an entry in an element of the Process Directory called the Known Segment Table. The actual process of making a segment known is performed by a run-time system element called the *Linker,* a primary user of the file system. The full act of making a reference link involves forming an entry on the Known Segment Table and searching a symbol table of external references associated with a segment. The actual address provided the caller is an indirect address in a system structure called a Combined Linkage Segment that is used as a kind of directory. A reference is completed by placing an address in an indirect reference word in the Linkage Segment location associated with the reference. The level of indirection allows a referenced segment to be relocated even though its segment name, as it appears to a referencing program, remains unchanged. Thus programs can be dynamically linked to each other at instance of reference by a run-time Linker using the services of the file system. IBM's TSS/370 is another system that permits dynamic, run-time linking of this type.

11.4 PROTECTION AND INTEGRITY

The discussion of resource management in other parts of the text is preoccupied with the effective use of hardware resources. There are some ideas associated with resource management that concern themselves with ideas of protection, integrity, and operating systems structure.

Issues of protection and integrity affect the nature of allocation mechanisms. These mechanisms not only must determine what resources are available but also must enforce policies related to who may refer to them in order to assure legitimate reference and limit the scope of impact of erroneous reference.

The idea of a resource may be made rather abstract and general. Thus the collection of resources a system must manage is more than the set of hardware resources. It includes *objects* whose attributes and characteristics have been defined to the system, and whose use must be managed, not with an eye to performance, but with an eye to protection and integrity. The most general idea of a system is as a collection of objects. Objects have attributes such as name, type, capabilities, and data. An object may be a procedure object or a data object. A procedure object is one consisting of pure code and limited private local data. A data object consists of data that may be manipulated by some set of procedures.

The term *capability* represents a fundamental notion about resource management. A capability is the name of an object in the system, and a set of expressed rights to that object. Therefore a *capability list* associated with an object is a statement of other objects in the system to which the object has certain rights.

An authorization list for an object names the objects that may use it. The idea of a capability is somewhat the reverse of this idea as it represents the concept that an object states the objects it is allowed to reference. Using HYDRA terminology, the idea of an authority list is a mapping of objects onto Executors; the idea of a capability is a mapping of Executors onto objects. These two notions are associated with each other in different ways in various conceptual models of operating systems.

11.5   AUTHORITIES AND CAPABILITIES IN MULTICS

We have described the file system of Multics and its use in connection with dynamic linking. We have also discussed the ideas associated with rings of protection. These topics are relevant to the relationship between *authorities* and *capabilities* in Multics.

When a running process makes reference to an object named X and there is no current association between the process and the object, a *system fault* is generated. The *linking mechanism* calls upon the *directory system* to locate object X and provide enough information so that the process may reference X. The directory system uses the identification of the process to determine if the process has *rights* to the referenced object. This determination is made by searching the *access control list* of the referenced object, and finding the name of the referring process on the list. If the name is not found, access to the object is denied. More precisely, the identification used for the search is the name of the user of the process, for example, the password or codeword of the programmer on whose behalf the process is running.

If the user–process identification is found on the access control list of the referenced object, the object is made known to the referencing process. The objects known to a process represent the capabilities of that process. The *Known Segment Table* is a collection of the known objects representing a kind of local directory. In addition to the Known Segment Table there is, for each process, a *Segment Directory*—a collection of local names for objects that allow reference. When a process running in a particular procedure object makes either CALL or data reference to another object, it does so through the Segment Directory. It is only when no entry is found in the Segment Directory that an attempt is made to find the referenced object by name, first in the Known Segment Table and then in the system directories.

An entry in the Segment Descriptor contains the access rights, a real or virtual storage location, and the size of the object. The address in the entry is *real* if there is no paging mechanism beneath the object mechanism and *virtual* if there is. That is, *paging,* which we will shortly describe in some detail, *suggests yet another level of mechanism for relocation of objects in memory.*

The idea of a local name for an object is supported by the set of locations in the Segment Directory. Any address associated with an instruction contains a number that indexes a particular location on the Segment Descriptor Table at which is the Segment Descriptor Word for the object. The formation of these addresses involves linkage and the basic addressing mechanism of the machine. What is most interesting, in the context of this chapter, is that a particular process has a local name used for addressing objects in the run-time environment that is different from that object's systemwide name. The usefulness of this is in not having to undergo systemwide object name translation every time an object is referred to after being made known.

11.6 GENERALIZED NOTIONS OF OBJECT MANAGEMENT

Any procedure in the HYDRA system may have a capability list formed at its creation. In addition, any procedure may have a set of capabilities passed to it when it is invoked as a process. A mechanism called a *Template* is used to map capabilities passed from a caller onto the capabilities of a called procedure. When a procedure is invoked, a *Local Name Space* is created for the incarnation of the object. In HYDRA, a process is a stack of Local Name Spaces. A Local Name Space is a capabilities list defining the domain of objects the running procedure can reference.

There are several interesting notions in HYDRA. One is that a data object, as well as a procedure object, may have capabilities. This notion gives the ability to acquire addressability to various objects by acquiring addressability to an object that is another step in a path of capabilities. A second notion, closely related to the above, is the idea of forming the capabilities of a Local Name Space by merging the capabilities of the caller with the capabilities of the called object.

The idea of a nonprocedure object having capabilities is useful in the construction of complex resource types that can be defined in terms of known resource types. Thus sets of increasingly complex objects, and operations on objects, can be defined by specifying the capabilities these new objects have to existing objects.

The idea of formed capabilities for a Local Name Space has some important structural implications for HYDRA. It is upon this notion that the rejection of strict hierarchic structures is based. The call of a procedure involves the passing of capabilities to the called procedure. The called procedure itself has capabilities. It is possible that the called procedure has greater rights to an object than the caller has, and the caller must be prohibited from acquiring the rights of the called object. This prohibition is provided by a kernel function of the operating system that operates whenever a procedure is invoked. In order to invoke a procedure, a Local Name Space must have a capability to do it. Thus if a process wishes to write onto a file, it must have a capability to a procedure to do the writing, and a capability to the object that is to be written on. On the CALL, the operating system determines whether the arguments of the caller are consistent with the parameter templates of the callee. The rights passed down by the caller must be in accordance with the rights the callee is expecting. Thus if the caller wishes to write on a certain object, the callee must be expecting a write request for an object of that type, and a specification of the rights of the caller to that object. If the expected rights and the passed rights do not agree, the CALL is not allowed. If the rights do agree, a new Local Name Space for the called procedure is created. The rights of this Local Name Space may even be greater than the rights of the caller, but the caller may not gain access to greater rights because they are not available in the caller's own Local Name Space.

The merger of capabilities in HYDRA suggests that a hierarchic structure with increasing rights associated with descent down the hierarchy is not a necessary notion. Regardless of where in a structure a process is performing, it does not acquire increased rights as it approaches the heart of the system. Rather, rights are a function of a monitored relationship between callers and callees. The rights' relationships can be altered in different versions of the system, and more flexible operating systems structures can be devised. These ideas are important to the basic HYDRA notion that the kernel of an operating system should be seen as a building block for subsystems.

A complete operating system is seen as a set of procedure objects and a set of data objects in which the procedure objects represent the actions that can be performed upon the data objects. Except for CALL and RETURN, HYDRA functions are implemented as procedures. Generic functions are defined that perform operations on objects, and functions that are object-specific are also defined. In building a subsystem, a user defines higher-level functions and data objects in terms of the provided primitives.

These notions directly relate to allocation and resource management because the forming of capabilities lists is a result of an allocation process. The created Local Name Space is, in effect, being allocated resources. Allocation is the act of passing names and rights to an invoked procedure.

In general, capability-based systems present certain integrity and control problems. The acquisition of rights to refer to a resource is passable from a process to another process in the form of a capability. This passage is truly an instance of resource allocation that is not monitored by the operating system. If program A has a capability to file B, it may pass that capability to program C. Program C now has access to B. In effect, it has been allocated B, but the operating system has no knowledge of this.

An obvious problem arises when the operating system is called upon to "clean up" or retrieve resources at a point of termination. Another problem is that synchronization and locking may be required for an object, but the operating system is unaware that the object is being shared.

Passing of capabilities between processes represents an independent resource allocation mechanism beyond the control of the system. There is the allocation mechanism that is used to acquire rights from the system and a dual mechanism that allows these rights to be dispersed.

Several solutions have been suggested. One is to define a set of resources to which a user has rights and to define some of the resources as controlled and some as uncontrolled. The operating system manages controlled resources in the usual way and takes responsibility for cleanup and synchronization. Uncontrolled resources are managed by some function in the application. Capabilities may be freely dispersed within the application structure for uncontrolled resources at the application's own risk.

A related problem is that of whether procedures or processes have rights to resources. One danger in capability systems is that a running process receives a capability that it records in itself in such a way that the capability cannot be taken away.

Consider a running process with a capability that it passes to another running process. The receiving process writes the capability in some private section. When the process is terminated, the operating system deletes the capabilities list for that incarnation. The capability is now resident in the dormant procedure.

In order to control illegitimate passing of capabilities and illegitimate retention, some systems propose elaborating capability-handling rights. These rights apply to what can be done with the capability itself as opposed to what can be done with the object. For example, the right to copy a capability may be restricted. Also, the system may restrict the storing of capabilities to special sections that are automatically destroyed by the operating system when the process completes.

The idea of capabilities introduces an important potential change in the relationship between an operating system and application programs. In traditional operating systems the application program is seen to run within a context created by the operating system. The running application is represented by a process. Each program accesses resources that are allocated to a process control block. In order to switch the set of referencible resources, it is necessary to do a process switch or to escape from the process environment by invoking the operating system. The operating system has addressability to all resources in the system.

In a capabilities-based system it is possible to have a resource domain switch without a task switch. Since each called procedure has its own capabilities, the running process does not define the context of referencible resources. It is therefore possible to invoke operating systems services without escaping from the process context or executing a process switch. A call to an operating system program places it on the stack of activation records where it has the rights defined by its own capabilities statements. In this context no differentiation need be made between a call to an application program procedure and a call to an operating system function. In addition it is neither necessary nor desirable to think of the operating system as having universal access rights to all objects in the system. An operating system program running on the process stack has its capabilities constrained by the capabilities of its caller. This means that more secure systems may be built since there is no software component in the system that has universal rights.

11.7   MONITORS

There is an intersection here with the idea of monitors. *A monitor is a collection of procedures associated with a type of resource. It is responsible for allocating the resource and for controlling references to it. Each resource in the system has a specific monitor.* There may be, for example, a memory monitor, a set of I/O monitors, and a CPU monitor. *Each monitor has exclusive access to any tables or other structures containing information about the resource for which it is responsible.*

As the notion of a resource becomes generalized, one must generalize the idea of a monitor so that monitors for resources more abstract than CPUs and devices can be built. These abstract monitors can be built in terms of fundamental abstract objects such as lists, queues, locks, and fundamental manipulation mechanisms for these structures.

The distinctive feature of a monitor is that it contains a section of data that is designed for public use but that cannot be accessed except through the monitor. This concept permits the relaxation of some structural restrictions while achieving many of the benefits. Data structures can be freely changed without impacting modules other than the monitor, and synchronization and authority functions can be performed by the monitor.

The monitor has full responsibility for all functions associated with the resource class for which it is responsible. A monitor may have multiple entry points for various functions and be constructed as one module. Alternatively, a monitor may be a collection of modules gathered in a set.

Monitor construction has been used in experimental and small systems very successfully. It is not clear, however, how generalization to very rich and diverse resource environments will succeed.

TERMINOLOGY

access control list	Combined Linkage Segment
access rights	data object
alias	directory
authorization list	dynamic linking
automatic archiving	execute access
Basic File System in Multics	Executor
capability	file directory
capability list	file management
catalog of files	HYDRA

IBM's TSS/370

integrity

Known Segment Table

Linkage Segment

Linker

load time

loading

local name for an object

Local Name Space in HYDRA

monitor

Multics

password

private local data

procedure object

Process Directory

Process Directory Directory

protection

pure code

read access

rings of protection

scheduler

segment

Segment Descriptor

Segment Directory

system fault

Systems Library Directory

Template in HYDRA

User Directory Directory

write access

EXERCISES

Section 11.1

11.1 How has the availability of large amounts of disk storage affected operating systems design?

11.2 What is a file directory? What information does it contain?

11.3 Discuss the meaning of each of the following.

    a) read access

    b) write access

    c) execute access

11.4 Various combinations of read, write, and execute access may be given to a segment. Discuss the relative usefulness of each of the following hybrid access types. Give examples of how each access type might be used.

    a) read-only access

    b) write-only access

    c) execute-only access

    d) read-write access

    e) read-execute access

f) write-execute access

g) read-write-execute access

h) no access at all

11.5 What is automatic archiving?

Section 11.2

11.6 Discuss the underlying concepts of the Basic File System of Multics.

11.7 What is the name space of a process?

11.8 Discuss briefly each of the following items of the directory structure of the Multics file system.

a) branch

b) link

c) root node

d) Systems Library Directory

e) User Directory Directory

f) Process Directory Directory

g) User Directory

h) access control list

i) ring

Section 11.3

11.9 What is dynamic linking?

11.10 Explain how dynamic linking is handled in Multics.

Section 11.4

11.11 Briefly discuss the issues of protection and integrity.

11.12 The collection of resources a system must manage is more than the set of hardware resources. Explain.

11.13 What is a capability? What is a capability list?

11.14 What is an authorization list?

Section 11.5

11.15 Discuss the relationship between authorities and capabilities in Multics.

Section 11.6

11.16 Briefly discuss each of the following items and concepts in the HYDRA file system.

a) capability

b) Template

c) Local Name Space

d) merging the capabilities of the caller with the capabilities of the callee

e) rejection of strict hierarchic structures

Section 11.7

11.17 What is a monitor?

12
Asynchronous
Concurrent Processes

12.1 PROGRAM SYNCHRONIZATION

There are two basic situations relative to program synchronization in a multipro-gramming or time-sharing environment. The first is one in which *the programs know of each other's existence and explicitly coordinate the use of a shared resource*. The second situation is one in which *the programs do not know of each other and rely upon a monitor or kernel function to accomplish coordination*.

There are two fundamental relationships that cooperating programs may have: (1) They may *share a resource* that neither of them has produced or (2) they may be dependent on each other's operation as a *producer or consumer* of the resource around which they are synchronized.

The decisions that must be made about synchronizing programs are rather numerous and complex. One decision is related to the prerun-time–run-time environment trade-off, and is essentially a decision about the degree of sharing that may be undertaken in the run-time environment. If a program has been admitted to the mix as a holder or creator of a file, it is possible to prevent another program that references that file from entering the mix. The programs are *mutually exclusive* at the file level. For example, a program that wishes to create a file is mutually exclusive of a systems task that will print that file if the system task cannot be started until the creating program completes. Similarly, a program that wishes to write a file may be made mutually exclusive of any program that wishes any kind of reference to that file.

The refusal to admit two programs into a mix because they share a resource is a severe form of mutual exclusion imposed in the prerun-time environment. The ability to do it requires a full statement of all resources that are going to be used for each program attempting to enter the mix. The status of the resource, *free* or *used,* determines whether a program requesting the resource may proceed. It is possible to elaborate the concept somewhat by introducing the notion of a SHARED resource. Thus a file manager may allow several programs to enter the mix if the file they require has the SHARED attribute. A particular user (perhaps one who is known by the system to be the owner or creator of the file) determines the shareability of the file at the time it is created. The general population of users may be allowed to request EXCLUSIVE use of the file for particular runs. Thus the attribute of shareability depends on both an inherent attribute of the file and an attribute of the way a holder of the file may be granted exclusive use for the update period. Programs that wish only to inspect the file may be happy to have other programs inspecting the file at the same time. Some control should be applied to the exclusive use of shareable files. The authorization list can be used to indicate who has a right to deny access to others. The concept of capability rights may be similarly expanded so that whenever a capability list is formed, an exclusion right may be recognized and appropriate status recorded in an object.

A system might also contain some mechanism that determines mutual exclusion strictly on the type of use. Thus without concepts of user privilege, a basic mechanism that records that a file has been allocated for reading only, for updating, or for writing only suggests conditions under which the file can be shared. If no mechanisms exist for coordination in the run-time environment, only multiple reads may be allowed. If some coordinating mechanisms do exist in the run-time environment, then some combination of reads and update or write may be allowed.

12.2   LOCK TACTICS

Earlier we introduced certain concepts of P- and V-operators and semaphores in connection with mutual exclusion, and some notions of process synchronization using WAIT and CHECK in the run-time environment. This chapter explores these notions further and builds a more general environment for exclusion and synchronization.

The notion of sharing some external object, that is, an object to which a process has been given a right of access, involves contexts in which it is practical to permit a program to request specific synchronization. A mutual exclusion mechanism can be made available to a program for the protection of an object while it is using it. The simplest of these mechanisms is based upon Dijkstra's P- and V-primitives. In order to be meaningful, a program must know the name of the object to be protected and must execute a *locking instruction* (a P-operation) and an *unlocking instruction* (a V-operation). A usual form of these functions involves the declaration of a *lock name* and the execution of a lock/unlock pair using the lock name as an operand.

With this usage it is not actually the object that is being locked but an area of code in an executing process called a *critical section*. It is while it is in a critical section that a process makes actual references to the object that a lock protects. Locks are commonly supported with TESTANDSET instructions that determine if the lock is set by inspecting a character for zero. Within the execution time of a TESTANDSET, reference to the lock location is not permitted in the system.

When a lock is set and the holding process is executing in the critical section, it is possible that it may lose control of the processor because of mechanisms in the dispatcher. Therefore *it is possible that a nonrunning process can be holding a lock*. This may become inconvenient for the system if other programs are delayed because of the unavailability of the locked object.

There are various ways to design around the *lock contention problem*. A great deal depends on the anticipated duration of the locks relative to the interrupt, dispatching, and queue management mechanisms of the system. For critical sections of short duration, it is probably desirable to inhibit the causes of a *process preemption*. It is possible to design so that while a process is operating in a critical section, it cannot lose control of the CPU or, if it loses control, the operating system immediately returns to it. This might be done directly if an *inhibit interrupt instruction* is available to the process entering the critical section. This is the case for critical sections in the kernel. However, except for dedicated real-time systems, it is commonly not advisable to allow an application program to guarantee itself contiguous periods of time. Therefore, if it is desired to prevent a process from being preempted, it is necessary to enter the operating system in order to have preemption mechanisms disabled. Since the operating system is going to prevent preemption, it is reasonable to enter the operating system one time to obtain lock preemption protection and the lock.

An alternative, of course, would be to combine *preemption exclusion* and locking as a single instruction and make it an unprivileged instruction, *but this carries the danger of an application program locking out the system.*

A simple approach to preventing the suspension of lockholding processes is to allow the interruptions that might cause process preemption, but prohibit the dispatcher from actually taking control away from a process holding the lock. The interrupt-handling mechanisms would accept and record the interrupt, but the process holding the lock would be returned to immediately thereafter. This could be accomplished in two ways. One is to mark the activation record of a lockholding process as nonpreemptible. The other is to set a system flag that would inhibit operation of the dispatcher. These indicators can be set when the lock is granted.

There may be situations, however, in which it is not meaningful to prevent the suspension of a holder of a lock. The lockholder may, while in a critical section, request access to a resource, such as in an I/O activity, that will involve a long period in which the lockholder can do no meaningful work and should lose control of the system.

Another aspect of lock design involves a decision regarding how the system should respond to a request for a lock found to be set. There are a number of possible responses. The simplest is to allow a process to *spin on the lock*. This involves the repeated testing of the lock in a loop. A process finding a lock ''set'' may be able to find other things to do until the lock is open and do those things rather than spin on the lock.

A closely related alternative is the execution of a DELAY macro that stops the process from operating but does not release the processor or cause the process to be blocked. This idea is appropriate in situations in which there is physical support such that a clock is quickly accessible and in which the execution of instructions associated with spinning on a lock may set up undesirable memory interference as it would in noncache multiprocessor systems. The intent is to put a processor in a wait state for an interval of time so that it will not generate unproductive interference in the system.

What more should be done about encountering ''set'' locks relates directly to the expected time a lock will be held. Elaborate lock treatment is a subtle design area. The more one tries to do, the greater the exposure to taking longer to do it than merely spinning on the lock. There is also frequently an exposure to encountering other locks that will further delay clearing an initial lock condition. For this reason, blocking a process and dispatching a successor are not appropriate in short critical sections.

Many systems have notions of short locks and long locks that are conceptually similar to short and long critical sections. *In MVS a short lock is a spin lock and a long lock is a suspend lock. A suspend lock implies a long critical section and the profitability of suspending a denied process with a WAIT, and then dispatching another process.* If a process is suspended, it becomes a blocked process with an indication it is waiting on a named lock. Some enqueueing mechanism associating blocked processes with particular locks is necessary.

The operating system must always know when an object is unlocked so that it may unblock a waiting process. When an unlock is received, the system unblocks and may immediately run the dispatcher. The dispatcher will attempt to activate a process waiting on the lock. It is also possible to unblock but not dispatch until the next normal dispatch event.

A system may also involve scheduling policy and priority considerations in a lock-resolution policy. This is called *process promotion*. The system may inspect the priority of a process denied a lock to determine whether it is higher or lower than processes eligible to replace it on active status. If the priority of the denied process is high, then the system may elect to activate a waiting holder of the lock with the temporary priority of the denied process in order to *clear the lock* quickly. Similarly, the system may associate time periods with locks, and begin to raise the priorities of lockholders as the time during which they hold the locks increases.

12.3 PARALLEL PROCESSES

In the programming of parallel processes, the objects controlled by locks may be very small. In fact they may not be objects in the sense of an externally addressable structure, but variables whose values are to be shared by virtue of parameter passing, or by virtue of the processes executing on the same procedure. Thus a process may start another process by FORKing and the two processes may reference the same variables or have the same capabilities. It is the responsibility of programs written in this manner to place proper locks around shared variables in order to sequentialize operations upon them. Programming of this type is of theoretical interest but rare in practice because most popular programming languages do not support the concepts, and underlying system and machine architectures do not execute highly parallel structures efficiently. New languages such as Concurrent PASCAL and MODULA are generating real interest in concurrent programming, but it will be some time before their use is industrywide.

The notion of parallel processes involves the decomposition of functions into a set of concurrent processes that can run independently of each other for significant periods of time. On a multiprocessor, for example, the job of searching a long list can be separated into shorter searches, each executing on a separate processor and searching a portion of the list. There may be points at which the processes must be sequentialized because they refer to some data used in common. It is these points that represent the critical sections. The profitability of the notion depends on the degree to which elapsed time is actually reduced by the parallel structure. To the extent that the locking activities are rather long, the effort of synchronization begins to delay the progress of all processes, and the net elapsed time may be longer than it would be if the entire search were executed by a single process. The efficiency of the lock activity describes a lower bound on the size of programs that can profitably run as concurrent processes.

12.4 OPERATING SYSTEM STRUCTURE

The structure of operating systems that support multiprocessors must reflect the notion of possible concurrent operation of function by more than one processor. There are many design techniques that apply. One technique is to package operating system functions vertically so that multiple functions of the operating system may be run in parallel. Thus memory management, dispatching, and I/O are packaged so that a process wishing a service can enter at a number of defined points without encountering a lock. In the usual form of this, multiprocessors share common code, although the actual dedication of physical processing stations to these functions is beginning to interest designers. Lock contention is minimized because only those processors wishing to execute the same function get in each other's way.

Another technique is to organize the system so that critical regions are as small as possible. Thus as much parallel execution as possible is allowed before entering the critical section. For example, instead of locking the memory management function, lock only the code that is absolutely critical to sequentialize, and design so that that section is as small as possible.

One technique associated with design is the idea of local and global locks and a lock structure. A *local lock* is one that is private to a particular application and that need not be managed by the general lock mechanisms of the operating system. A *global lock* is one that relates to a systemwide object. In order to minimize the effects of global locks, a lock structure is developed that allows a lock to be held at the lowest possible point. The lock structure expresses a relationship between the locked objects so that deadly embraces may be avoided and critical sections may be minimized. The lock structure may be a tree structure. Whenever a lock is requested, an analysis of the tree is undertaken to determine whether the lock should be granted. Thus a lock may be obtained at the bottom of the tree structure to protect a primitive object. Another process requiring a lock on the entire collection would request a higher-level lock. When a higher-level lock is held, lower-level locks will not be granted. However, different locks at the same level may be held within the structure. Thus small objects may be locked with fine granularity. Larger structures may also be locked as coherent units when it is meaningful to do so.

So far, we have been discussing the temporary denial of access to a resource by using *mutual exclusion* techniques. The LOCK/UNLOCK and WAIT/SIGNAL pairs set a Boolean variable to true or false.

12.5   PRODUCERS AND CONSUMERS

Earlier we described the relationship between a process writing to a buffer and a process reading the buffer to an output device. This relationship is controlled by an event-posting mechanism, a checking mechanism, and a waiting mechanism. We will now discuss relationships of this type, between deliberately cooperating processes, in terms of a well-known formulation called the *producer–consumer relationship*. The set of ideas related to producers and consumers leads us from mutual exclusion into the area of *interprocess communication*, which will be discussed later.

When we reduce the exclusion level from a filewide level imposed by the prerun-time environment to a record level, it is possible to admit one writer and

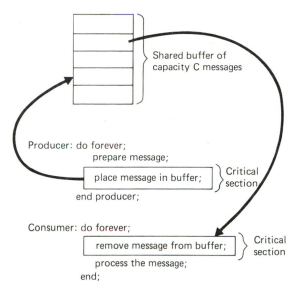

Fig. 12.1 Producer—consumer relationship with a shared buffer. When the shared buffer is full, the producer must not attempt to place another message in the buffer. Instead, the producer must WAIT. The consumer must SIGNAL the producer when a slot in the buffer is freed so that the producer may proceed. When the shared buffer is empty, the consumer must WAIT. The producer must SIGNAL the consumer when another message has been placed in the buffer.

one reader to the mix and to relate them in a manner reminiscent of UNIVAC's concept of the symbiont. The fundamental mechanisms are a buffer into which the writer places elements and from which the reader removes elements, and a mechanism to determine the status of the buffer. (See Fig. 12.1.)

The reader is said to be the *consumer* and the writer is the *producer* of these elements. The relationship between the processes has changed in an important way. They are no longer sharing some previously developed object but are reflexively dependent on each other for input and output. The support of this notion involves a generalization of semaphores so that they become counters rather than Boolean variables.

In the most direct implementation of the producer–consumer relationship, each process has accessibility to the shared buffer and each process executes operations directly upon the generalized semaphores. Whenever the producer places an item in the buffer, it increments the *buffer contents semaphore* and decrements the *buffer space semaphore*. Whenever the consumer removes an item from the buffer, it decrements the *buffer contents semaphore* and increments the *buffer space semaphore*.

If the producer and consumer processes are running on a multiprocessing system, the semaphores must be adjusted within a critical section so that semaphore modification is sequentialized. The producer may run whenever there is space in the buffer, and the consumer may run whenever there is an item in the buffer. Thus the two processes may coordinate their operation through the use of the shared semaphores.

These notions are commonly represented by the ideas of WAIT and SIGNAL. A WAIT(S) operation may invoke the operating system to block a process that has found the buffer empty or full. A SIGNAL(S) may invoke the operating system to unblock the process that was blocked because of the buffer condition. (See Fig. 12.2.) Thus the producer attempts to place a produced item with a WAIT (buffer space) that lowers the buffer space count. If the buffer space count is already zero, the producer will be blocked. If the buffer space count is not zero, it is reduced by one and the producer places the element in the buffer. After placing the element in the buffer, the producer performs a SIGNAL (buffer contents) that increases the buffer contents count. If the consumer is blocked, the SIGNAL (buffer contents) causes the system to unblock it. For example, if the buffer is initially empty and the consumer does a WAIT (buffer contents) and finds the item count zero, this causes the consumer to be blocked. The SIGNAL (buffer contents) from the producer allows the consumer to run. (See Fig. 12.3.)

It is not necessary to force blocking of a process because of a buffer-full or buffer-empty condition. It is possible to allow the process to loop or delay just as it was possible to do so in connection with locking.

Since the operating system is going to be invoked for WAIT and SIGNAL, it is possible to relieve both producer and consumer of the buffer management function by interposing a queue manager between them and the shared queue. The producer ENQUEUEs items using the queue manager and the consumer DEQUEUEs items. Actual queue manipulation and semaphore control become the responsibility of the queue manager. The control of activating the processes

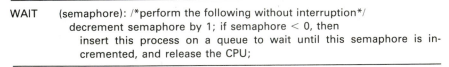

WAIT   (semaphore): /*perform the following without interruption*/
              decrement semaphore by 1; if semaphore < 0, then
                    insert this process on a queue to wait until this semaphore is incremented, and release the CPU;

SIGNAL (semaphore): /*perform the following without interruption*/
              increment the semaphore by 1; if semaphore ≤ 0, then
                    remove one of the processes waiting in the queue for this semaphore and place that process on the "ready" list for CPU allocation;

Fig. 12.2 The WAIT and SIGNAL synchronizing primitives.

```
share:  begin semaphore (buffer-contents, buffer-space, mutex);
           initialize (buffer-contents, 0); /*initially the buffers are empty*/
           initialize (buffer-space, C); /*capacity is C messages*/
           initialize (mutex, 1); /*semaphore to control critical section mutual exclu-
           sion*/

           cobegin; /*start producer and consumer as parallel processes*/

               producer:  do forever; /*create messages and deposit in shared buffer*/
                          prepare a message; /*create the message*/
                          WAIT (buffer-space); /*is buffer available for message?
                                               no—wait*/
                          WAIT (mutex); /*yes—may I enter critical section? no—
                                        wait*/
                          place message in buffer; /*critical section*/
                          SIGNAL (mutex); /*I am leaving critical section*/
                          SIGNAL (buffer-contents); /*add one to message count*/
                          end producer;

               consumer:  do forever; /*remove messages from shared buffer and pro-
                                      cess*/
                          WAIT (buffer-contents); /*is a message ready for me? no—
                                                  wait*/
                          WAIT (mutex); /*yes—may I enter critical section? no—
                                        wait*/
                          remove message from buffer; /*critical section*/
                          SIGNAL (mutex); /*I am leaving critical section*/
                          SIGNAL (buffer-space); /*add one to empty buffer count*/
                          process the message; /*use the message*/
                          end consumer;

           coend;

end share;
```

Fig. 12.3 Using WAIT and SIGNAL to control a shared buffer.

may be vested in the operating system that may take other systems factors into account in deciding the pattern of activations for the producer or consumer. This is a natural structure for a transaction system in which the producer receives messages from the outside world and asks the queue manager to place them in a buffer. When the queue manager operates, it can determine whether the consumer should operate immediately and so inform the dispatcher.

Since the ideas of WAITing and SIGNALing on a semaphore are so closely related to ideas of process blocking, we will review process synchronization. Systems may take different approaches to the status of the producer and the consumer when they cannot run. Both producer and consumer may have existing process control blocks that are maintained even when the processes cannot run. When a process cannot run, it is said to be *blocked*.

Blocking a process involves recording that the process cannot be run, and associating the inability to run with some specific event that must occur before the process can run again. *Unblocking a process* involves reporting the completion of that pending event. Because process activation records and event blocks are commonly accessible only to the operating system, the system must be invoked both to record the block and to remove the block. WAIT can be issued by a process or by an operating system function that decides that the process should wait. Its general form is WAIT (condition) in which condition describes the event that must occur. When WAIT relates to an I/O operation, the system is entirely responsible for running the process that performs the I/O, and then running the unblocking process. The unblocking process may be called POST or SIGNAL or WAKEUP. It is merely a mechanism for recording completion.

When the WAIT is issued as a result of a relationship between two application processes, the application process that is to perform the function must be activated by the WAITing process before it WAITs. It is then the responsibility of this process to SIGNAL or POST completion, probably invoking the operating system since it itself cannot access the activation records or event blocks that must be manipulated.

Any particular operating system may provide distinct macros for coordination of cooperating application processes, and for coordination of an application process with a function of the operating system. Any particular operating system may reveal the notion of a lock or may conceal it, providing coordination implicitly. All of the notions of P and V, LOCK, WAIT, POST, SIGNAL (and ultimately ENQUEUE and DEQUEUE) depend on a mechanism that provides for serialization of processes that may be running in a certain pattern because of a dispatcher that knows nothing about logical relationships. On uniprocessors, advantage can be taken of the knowledge that only one processor is really running at any time. On multiprocessors, additional hardware must be provided to allow exclusion and synchronization at an individual instruction level.

An alternative design is to delete or destroy a process control block whenever a process has completed a particular transaction or responded to a particular event. A producer placing an item of production on a queue is eliminated when it has done so. A consumer taking an item from a queue is eliminated when it is through processing that item. Instead of blocking processes to achieve synchronization, the processes are removed from the system. Instead of unblocking processes when there is work to be done, the process is recreated for each instance of work.

Such a design is appropriate when the population of work units is dynamic enough and process logic is so granular that a stable population of recurringly active processes cannot be defined. Process deletion occurs only when a work unit is completed, of course, and not for intrawork unit resource requests. Systems that use this design often guarantee all required resources to a process before creating the process.

Some systems use both process blocking and process deletion and creation. In the IBM MVS system, for example, the control blocks that represent application programs are blocked and unblocked as required. However, there is a set of specialized operating system functions specially scheduled as services are needed for authorized programs. A different control block is used for these functions. When they are requested, the control block is created and scheduled. When the function is complete, the control block is deleted from the system rather than put into a wait state for a new request.

12.6 INTERPROCESS COMMUNICATION

In the producer–consumer relationship two processes communicate with each other to synchronize their activities. We have seen that the relationship depends on an extension of notions of mutual exclusion to permit conditional exclusion based upon the status of an intervening shared buffer. Further extension of the ideas of interprocess communication leads to a rich set of possible designs. In particular, a running process may wish to send a message to another running process for any reason at any time, and a running process may request a message from another running process for any reason at any time. Further, the ability of a process to run may be dependent on receipt of a message or the receipt of an answer to a message so that message mechanisms are closely related to ideas of process blocking and unblocking. As an additional dimension, current interest in distributed processing suggests that the sender of the message may not know where the receiver of the message is physically located so that the system must intervene to determine whether memory sharing or channel-to-channel or tele-communications ''pipelines'' should be used for transport of the message.

The fundamental notion of interprocess communication involves functions generically called SEND and RECEIVE. In order to SEND a message, a process must have already established some connection to the process that is going to receive the message. In some systems, messages can be sent only to processes that are associated with the sending process by virtue of being a child process of some common ancestor. In other systems, any process can send a message to any other process whose name the sending process can determine. The SEND function, in its simplest form, names the process to which the message is to be sent and provides the address of the message. The message is copied onto a buffer that is added to a queue for the intended receiver. In more complex forms, the SEND may broadcast so that the message is placed in multiple queues or held on a single queue until some specified number of processes (or some designated set of processes) has received the message. The SEND may also indicate whether the sending process should be blocked until the message has been received.

The queue to which the message is written may be invisible to the sender. In a system with a queue manager of the type suggested previously, a sender may name a process as the recipient of the message. The queue manager will copy the message onto a queue that it has established for messages from the sender for the named receiver. The queue manager may then interrupt the intended receiver and force the message on it. Queues between senders and receivers are dynamically established and grow and shrink in size under the management of the queue manager. It is also possible that the message may not be handed to the receiver until the RECEIVE function is executed by the receiver, or unless there is an outstanding RECEIVE that names the process it wishes to receive a message from, in effect directing the queue manager to a particular buffer from which it provides a message. Thus a simple one-to-one relationship is established between sender and receiver by virtue of their knowing each other's names and sharing a ''pipe'' between themselves under control of an intervening enqueueing and dequeueing mechanism. A receiver, on finding no message, may elect to ask for blocking until a message is received on the indicated queue (from the named process).

The SEND/RECEIVE mechanism just described can be used to support the request for access to an I/O resource or allocation to any serially reusable resource. The ENQUEUE/DEQUEUE functions described previously are in fact a special case of SEND/RECEIVE. A process wishing access to a particular resource SENDs a message describing the resource, and the message is enqueued on a queue associated with the resource manager. The resource manager may be immediately invoked to process the resource request, or may process requests on the queue as it becomes active for other reasons. This simple mechanism restricts the communications path between processes, and provides support only of the producer–consumer relationship where message traffic is unidirectional.

In order to generalize interprocess communications, it is necessary to introduce ideas of acknowledgment, bidirectional communication, and multiple paths between processes for different kinds of messages. Acknowledgment communication relates to the idea that a process may wish notification of message receipt by the queue manager or receiver independently of a response to a particular message.

Sometimes, acknowledgment is all that is required. Acknowledgment of a receipt need not involve the message queue, but may be performed by POST or SIGNAL. The acknowledgment of receipt may be used to unblock a process that is waiting for such acknowledgment, or it may be passed to a running process that can continue past a SEND point but wishes to know whether its messages have been received. It is possible to provide a CHECK command to determine if a message has been received by querying the queue manager or testing some status field. If multiple messages may be sent before a CHECK is performed, it is necessary to identify each message uniquely so that the queue manager can look for a specific message in the appropriate queue.

A process can SEND particular identified messages to a named process or multiple processes, and then CHECK to see which messages have been received. The unique identification of a message must include sender identification when the queue is a "mailbox." *A mailbox is a queue associated with a receiver that can receive messages from more than one sending process.* A mailbox develops when sending processes know only the name of the receiving process (and not a queue name) and all messages are placed on the single implicitly named queue. Each message must be uniquely identified by sender and message identification. The receiving process may now send acknowledgments by SIGNALs identifying the process and message that it is acknowledging.

The idea of an answer associates the message identifier of the initially sent message with a message sent in response. Thus the receiver processes the message and sends a message to the sender that is identified as an answer to a particular message. This answer may be placed upon the same queue used for initializing messages. Thus the queue (which begins to lose some of the formal properties of a queue) may contain a mixture of messages and answers intended for different processes. There is, therefore, a need to distinguish between RECEIVEs and RECEIVE ANSWERs. A RECEIVE requests a message from a queue; a RECEIVE ANSWER requests the response to a previously sent message. Blocking may be associated with both functions. It is not necessary for an operating system to undertake message–answer mapping that may be left to the communicating processes.

We now have the ability for a process to receive messages from multiple sources on a single queue and to identify elements of the queue as either messages or answers to messages. An additional generalization of communication involves the ability to associate multiple queues with a process. These queues are frequently called *ports* and represent a species of internal file that processes *read from* and *write to*. Each process may open some number of ports and SEND or RECEIVE from these ports in a manner not unlike PUT and GET. Communicating processes share files, and producer–consumer relations can be supported. The close relationship between files and ports has caused interest in the application of a unifying SEND/RECEIVE notion to interprocess communication and I/O. Some flexibilities associated with this notion would allow SENDing to remote processes, spooling buffers, cooperating processes, or I/O channels depending on the nature of the device that was assigned as the medium for the buffer.

Ports may be input ports, output ports, or bidirectional, and may be one-to-one or many-to-many. When a process wishes to SEND, it may name the port as well as the process it wishes to address. When a process wishes to receive, it names the port it wishes to receive from. The idea of ports provides multiple paths between processes and enables a simplification of message and answer analysis that must be undertaken when multiple message types and answers are combined on the same port. Certain kinds of SEND/RECEIVE matching operations must still be performed in order to associate messages and answers from sending programs that must satisfy an outstanding RECEIVE.

There are many problems that must be addressed in the design of a SEND/RECEIVE mechanism. Most obvious among them is the management of message spaces and the responses a system should make when a queue is filled. There is also a problem associated with the possibilities that the target process of a SEND has been deleted from the system, or the receiver dies before sending an answer. Some mechanism must be provided for notification of the sender or for recreation of the target process. It is also possible to allow messages to accumulate on some repository device until the target process is created. It would be possible to design so that the rate of interaction is on a message-by-message basis if both processers are active, but on a file basis if they are not. If this is logically acceptable to the processes, then they may be run concurrently or not depending on the other goals of the system. One case in which this would apply is in the relationship between an application program and an output spooler. If a printer, for example, is available for the spooler, and the load and schedule are such that the spooler and program can coexist, then print lines can be sent to a named port and be printed concurrently. If, however, a printer is not available, then the process associated with the port would be a disk writer that would collect the entire file for later printing.

TERMINOLOGY

block a process

CHECK

consumer

critical section

ENQUEUE/DEQUEUE

FORK

global lock

hold a lock

interprocess communication

local lock

lock

lock tactics

LOCK/UNLOCK

locking instruction

long lock

mailbox

mutual exclusion

P- and V-operators

parallel processes

ports

POST completion

process "promotion"

producer   "spin" on a lock

producer–consumer relationship   suspend lock

program synchronization   symbiont

semaphores   TESTANDSET instruction

SEND/RECEIVE   unblock a process

shared resource   unlocking instruction

short lock   WAIT

"spin" lock   WAIT then SIGNAL

EXERCISES

Section 12.1

12.1 Two fundamental relationships that cooperating programs may have are
   a) they may share a resource that neither of them has produced, and
   b) they may be dependent on each other's operation as a producer or consumer of
      the resource around which they are synchronized.
Discuss each of these relationships briefly.

12.2 The refusal to admit two programs into a mix because they share a common resource
is a severe form of mutual exclusion imposed in the prerun-time environment. Explain.

12.3 If no mechanisms exist for coordination in the run-time environment, only multiple
reads of a shared file may be allowed. If some coordinating mechanisms do exist, then
some combination of reads and update or write may be allowed. Discuss.

Section 12.2

12.4 Discuss the use of Dijkstra's P- and V-primitives.

12.5 What is a critical section?

12.6 How is it possible for a nonrunning process to be holding a lock?

12.7 It is commonly not practical to allow an application program to guarantee itself
contiguous periods of time. Most systems require that the operating system be entered in
order to have preemption mechanisms disabled. Why?

12.8 Suppose preemption exclusion and locking were combined as a single unprivileged
instruction. What problems might occur?

12.9 Glen Myers's SWARD architecture introduces the idea that privileged operations
may be provided to a machine as a supplemental instruction set. Discuss the merits of this
scheme.

12.10 A simple approach to preventing the suspension of lockholding processes is to
allow the interruptions that might cause process preemption, but prohibit the dispatcher
from actually taking control away from a process holding the lock. Give several ways of
implementing such a scheme.

12.11 What does it mean to allow a process to "spin" on a lock?

12.12 How is the CHECK macro used?

12.13 Explain the operation of the DELAY macro.

12.14 Elaborate lock treatment is a subtle design area. The more one tries to do, the greater the exposure to taking longer to do it than merely spinning on the lock. Give some criteria for evaluating whether a given lock-handling mechanism is actually better than spinning on a lock.

12.15 Distinguish between a "short" lock and a "long" lock.

12.16 Discuss the concept of process "promotion."

Section 12.3

12.17 Give several examples of processes that can be profitably executed in parallel.

12.18 The efficiency of the lock activity describes a lower bound on the size of programs that can profitably run as concurrent processes. Explain.

Section 12.4

12.19 Distinguish between local locks and global locks.

Section 12.5

12.20 Why is it desirable to have one process creating records and placing them in a buffer, and a separate process reading the buffer to an output device?

12.21 Precisely explain the operation of the WAIT and SIGNAL primitives in a producer–consumer relationship involving shared buffers for spooling. Use semaphores to indicate buffer contents and buffer space counts.

12.22 Blocking a process involves recording a notation that the process can not be run, and associating the inability to run with some specific event that must occur before the process can run again. Unblocking a process involves reporting the completion of that pending event. Explain the use of process blocking and unblocking during the initiation, operation, and completion phases of an I/O operation.

Section 12.6

12.23 The fundamental notion of interprocess communication involves functions generically called SEND and RECEIVE. Discuss the operation of these primitives.

12.24 What is a "mailbox"?

12.25 Distinguish between RECEIVE and RECEIVE ANSWER.

12.26 What is a port?

12.27 Discuss several problems that must be addressed in the design of a SEND/RECEIVE mechanism.

13
Real Storage

13.1 INTRODUCTION

This section is restricted to some basic concepts in the management of "visible" (to the programmer) primary storage, and to relationships between memory management and scheduling/dispatching.

We have mentioned that there is a succession of binding times when a program can be associated with locations in memory, and a set of times when programs can be associated with one another. We have also mentioned that various multiprogramming operating systems may have different strategies about when memory sections are defined for the use of programs in the mix. There are some reasonably recognizable approaches to memory management in multiprogramming systems.

13.2 REAL MEMORY SYSTEMS WITH ABSOLUTE COMPILING

Absolute compile, fixed partition, real memory

In such a system, fixed partitions of memory are defined at systems definition time, and programs are compiled to operate out of specific partitions. (See Fig. 13.1.)

Absolute compile, flexible operator partition, real memory

In such a system, the partitions of memory may be changed by an operator. Compilation is to fixed partitions whose existence must be created by the operator at the time a program compiled for a partition of a certain extent and origin is to be run.

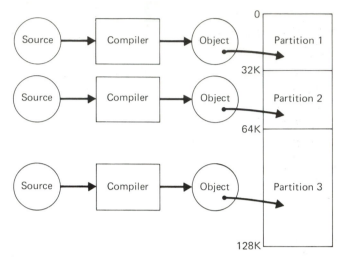

Fig. 13.1 Absolute compile, fixed partition, real memory. Object modules produced by the compilers contain absolute code and must be run in the particular partitions for which they were compiled. Programs are loaded by an absolute loader.

13.3   REAL MEMORY SYSTEMS WITH RELOCATABLE COMPILING

Relocatable compile, fixed partition, real memory

In such a system, the compiler produces relocatable code so that a program may be started in any free partition. (See Fig. 13.2.)

Relocatable compile, allocate partition, real memory

Here the amount of memory that a program is to have and the actual addresses are determined at allocation time just before the program enters the run-time environment. The program is constrained to operate within its partition and may not leave its partition. Some control over the use of space in the partition may be given through run-time macros. GETMAIN and FREEMAIN, however, do not actually acquire and release space. Instead they organize space within the allocated partition. IBM's OS/MVT is such a system. MVT's partitions are called *regions*. A real advantage of this type of system is that the partition exists only for as long as the program exists. The problem of distributing programs across fixed partitions disappears.

Relocatable compile, dynamic allocate, real memory

Such a system allows a program to grow and contract dynamically over time. GETMAIN and FREEMAIN take from, and return to, a common pool of

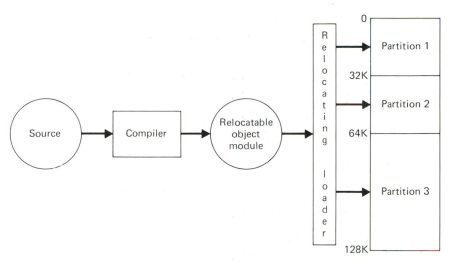

Fig. 13.2   Relocatable compile, fixed partition, real memory.

memory. Also, a program may be removed from memory and replaced at some other place in memory at the convenience of the system.

In all of the systems above, the term "real memory" means that the programmer is constrained by the number of physically available memory locations. The partitions are defined onto actual addresses of available storage.

13.4   FIXED-SIZE BLOCK ALLOCATION

Whether allocation of real storage is done in the run-time environment or at allocate time, the fundamental mechanisms are roughly similar. One decision to be made is whether space will be allocated in fixed-size blocks or in arbitrary sizes as required. If space is allocated in fixed-size blocks, then a memory map may be maintained by a *memory contents manager* that has an "on" or "off" bit for each block. As space is requested, the allocator searches for a number of contiguous blocks until it satisfies the request or determines that it cannot.

13.5   VARIABLE-SIZE BLOCK ALLOCATION

If space is to be allocated in variable-size blocks (usually with some minimum defined by the characteristics of the hardware), then a list of free space must be maintained. Each free area is represented by an entry that gives its location and its size. This may be a sequential list or a linked list in which each element actually resides in the first word of a free storage area.

13.6   FIRST-FIT VERSUS BEST-FIT

The process of *allocating storage* is to follow the *free space list* until an area of adequate size is located, and to bind that area to the requesting program by means of a *base register* or *offset register*. The list may be ordered by address or by size of available area. If ordered by address, then a *first-fit algorithm* takes space out of the first available free area large enough to be used. If ordered by size, then a *best-fit algorithm* is used that takes the smallest space large enough to fill the request. (See Fig. 13.3.) There is quite a controversy about whether first fit or

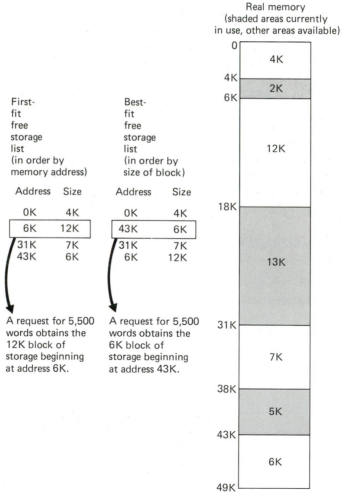

Fig. 13.3 First-fit versus best-fit placement algorithms.

best fit is the better algorithm. The preferability of one over the other depends on average request size, rates of requests and returns, and other factors having to do with the maintenance and ordering of the lists themselves.

13.7 CONTIGUOUS STORAGE ALLOCATION

A constraint in most real storage management systems is the necessity for allocating contiguous space so that protection can be applied over an entire addressable area. Certain architectures allow for some discontiguity in the allocated space, but it is more usual to find contiguous memory allocation in the implementation of real storage systems.

Consider a mix of five programs, each 64K long bordering each other in memory, 0 to 64K—1, 64K to 128K—1, etc. Assume that there is a block of 16K unused memory locations at the upper edge of storage. Program A in locations 64K to 128K—1 desires to grow by 4K and it issues a GETMAIN. The storage is available but cannot be given to the program because it is not contiguous with the program's current addressable area. In order to make the space available, it is necessary to rearrange memory so that the additional 4K borders program A. One technique is a form of *garbage collection* involving the movement of program A and its neighbor. Another technique is to preempt program A's neighbor and free its storage for A's use. Garbage collection is a disruptive and expensive project and even the most heuristic of real storage systems will undertake it only in special circumstances, for example, on behalf of a very high-priority job, or a deadline job behind schedule.

13.8 MEMORY COMPACTION

Similarly, consider a mix in which there is a fragment of unused space of 4K between each neighbor and a program desires 16K. A total of 16K is available but not contiguously. In order to grant the request, it is necessary to relocate programs to bring together a continuous 16K area. This technique is called *memory compaction*.

13.9 FRAGMENTATION

The problem of unusable fragments of space requiring garbage collection or preemption to achieve more effective usage of memory is called the *fragmentation* problem. It occurs as the result of the dynamics of mix management wherein programs terminate at different times and are replaced by programs of different sizes. The fragmentation problem not only affects the growth of programs in the mix but also the ability of the system to start new programs.

13.10   CPU AND I/O LOAD IN THE MULTIPROGRAMMING MIX

The tendency of a mix to be memory-bound is high in real storage management systems; i.e., the CPU and I/O devices may be underutilized because not enough programs can be placed in storage to generate sufficient load on the other hardware components. Therefore, it is not desirable, from a utilization viewpoint, to restrict the size of the mix by memory limitations alone. It is desirable to find ways of generating additional load on the CPU and I/O devices from a given memory size by utilizing the memory more effectively. This has led to the paging and relocation systems described in the next chapter.

TERMINOLOGY

absolute compile, fixed partition, real memory

absolute compile, flexible operator partition, real memory

best-fit algorithm

binding times

contiguous memory allocation

first-fit algorithm

fragmentation

free space list

FREEMAIN

garbage collection

GETMAIN

IBM's OS/MVT

memory-bound job mix

memory compaction

memory contents manager

partition of memory

real storage

regions

relocatable code

relocatable compile, allocate partition, real memory

relocatable compile, dynamic allocate, real memory

relocatable compile, fixed partition, real memory

run-time macros

"visible" primary storage

EXERCISES

Section 13.1

13.1 Review the sequence of "times" presented in Chapter 4. Explain how the binding of programs to memory locations can be effected at different times.

Section 13.2

13.2 Discuss the operation of each of the following real memory schemes.
  a) absolute compile, fixed partition, real memory

  b) absolute compile, flexible operator partition, real memory

Section 13.3

13.3 Discuss the operation of each of the following real memory schemes.
   a) relocatable compile, fixed partition, real memory

   b) relocatable compile, allocate partition, real memory

   c) relocatable compile, dynamic allocate, real memory

Section 13.4

13.4 Discuss the operation of a memory contents manager oriented to fixed-size block allocation.

Section 13.5

13.5 Discuss the operation of a memory contents manager oriented to variable-size block allocation.

Section 13.6

13.6 Discuss the relative advantages and disadvantages of the first-fit and best-fit memory allocation algorithms.

Section 13.7

13.7 Why is it more difficult to allocate memory in discontiguous storage blocks than in contiguous ones?

13.8 What is garbage collection?

Section 13.8

13.9 What is memory compaction? Give an example in which performing memory compaction is extremely worthwhile despite its overhead.

Section 13.9

13.10 What is fragmentation?

13.11 How does fragmentation manifest itself in fixed-partition real memory multiprogramming schemes?

13.12 How does fragmentation manifest itself in variable-partition real memory multiprogramming schemes?

Section 13.10

13.13 The tendency of a mix to be memory-bound is high in real storage systems. Why? What options are available to the administrators of a real storage system to alleviate this problem?

14
Virtual Storage

14.1 PAGING AND SEGMENTATION SYSTEMS

Paging is a relocation and address-to-physical-location binding mechanism. Segmentation is essentially a program-to-program linking, sharing concept. The addition of paging or segmentation mechanisms to the architecture of a system provides two advantages.

■ *Programmers may behave as if they have considerably larger memory spaces than are really available,* thus avoiding efforts involved in planning overlays or opening small working files. This is the concept of *virtual memory.* In IBM's virtual memory system OS/VS1, the concept is supported as an enlarged linear name space of 16 million bytes shared by many users or programs in a mix. A single virtual memory larger than the real memory of the machine is defined. In OS/VS2, each user or program has a virtual memory of 16 million bytes (multiple virtual memories). The concept of virtual memory may also be supported by entirely abandoning the idea of a *linear address space* of any size. In Multics, a user owns a set of segments that are logical objects such as files or named procedures, and the idea of a linear memory space with a maximum address entirely disappears.

■ The existence of the paging and segmentation mechanisms provides a solution to the fragmentation problem by allowing programs to map portions of their virtual memory into real memory locations that are not necessarily contiguous.

14.2 PAGING

Paging depends on the organization of memory into a number of fixed blocks called *page frames*. The size of a page frame varies on different systems. IBM's page frames are 2K or 4K bytes long. Any particular IBM system will use either a 2K or 4K block. There are differences of opinion about the proper size of a page frame. Those arguing for smaller page frames point out that the page frame is effectively the smallest unit of allocation, and if it is large relative to request sizes, then a good deal of empty space will be hidden on pages. This is called *internal fragmentation* and occurs when 4K-page frames hold data or programs of smaller size. (See Fig. 14.1.)

Advocates of larger page frames point out that the number of individual pages referenced in an interval is large, potentially increasing the burden of managing the movement of program elements into and out of page frames. Various compromise proposals have been offered. These generally are similar to an idea of *page clusters. A page cluster is a collection of page frames that become associated by virtue of the page frames' joint usage and may be managed as a unit.*

Associated with the definition of page frames is a mechanism of some sort used to address a page frame, and a mechanism that translates the addresses of a program into page frame addresses. These mechanisms are some form of formalization of base registers and indirect addressing.

Consider Fig. 14.2 that shows a 36,000-word memory organized into 36 page frames of 1,000 words each. Next to the memory, the figure shows a page table that represents the assignment of program pages to page frames. We will later discuss the physical or logical implementation of this table and how assignments are made. The table shows that a program has been allocated

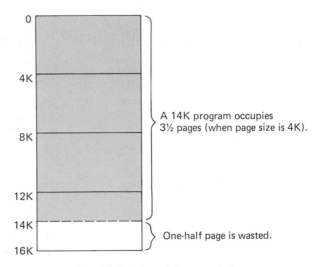

Fig. **14.1** Internal fragmentation.

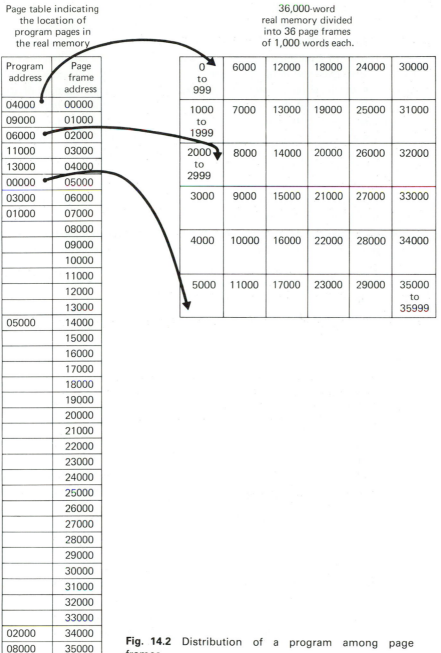

Page table indicating the location of program pages in the real memory

36,000-word real memory divided into 36 page frames of 1,000 words each.

Program address	Page frame address
04000	00000
09000	01000
06000	02000
11000	03000
13000	04000
00000	05000
03000	06000
01000	07000
	08000
	09000
	10000
	11000
	12000
	13000
05000	14000
	15000
	16000
	17000
	18000
	19000
	20000
	21000
	22000
	23000
	24000
	25000
	26000
	27000
	28000
	29000
	30000
	31000
	32000
	33000
02000	34000
08000	35000

0 to 999	6000	12000	18000	24000	30000
1000 to 1999	7000	13000	19000	25000	31000
2000 to 2999	8000	14000	20000	26000	32000
3000	9000	15000	21000	27000	33000
4000	10000	16000	22000	28000	34000
5000	11000	17000	23000	29000	35000 to 35999

Fig. 14.2 Distribution of a program among page frames.

memory such that its addresses 0–999 are in memory at 5000–5999, its addresses 1000–1999 are in memory at 7000–7999, addresses 2000–2999 are in memory at 34000–34999, etc. The program has been, in effect, *scatter loaded* into page frames in some apparently arbitrary way. Let us conjecture that the first instruction to be executed in this program is at address 00025. This address will be placed in the location counter. The *address translation mechanism* of the machine will decompose this address into a *page address* and a *relative page displacement*. The first two digits, 00, will be used to search the table. This search will find 00 with an associated page frame address of 05. The system will form the full address 05025 and bring the instruction from that address to memory. Similarly, each address brought into the instruction counter or used as an operand address will be decomposed with the upper two digits used as an entry to reach the table and the lower three digits used as an offset to find the specific location on the page frame.

Various implementations of the page frame map have been undertaken. It is possible to build a fast *associative array* that allows the translation of virtual addresses to real addresses very quickly. Memories of millions of bytes, however, cannot be fully represented by associative arrays because of the high cost of such devices.

An alternative way of mapping page frames is to use a software structure. When a program begins to operate, a control register in the machine is set to point to the origin of an area in regular memory called the *page table*. Each address is decomposed, as above, and the upper digits are added to the origin register to form an index to the table. The indexed location contains the page frame address of the assigned location.

Consider Fig. 14.3. An operand address of 04673 has been submitted to the translation mechanism. A software page table exists in memory at location 1000. The origin register is set to 1000, and 04 is added to it to form 1004. At 1004 there is an entry 8000. This entry is added to 673 to form the real location address 8673. Note that on this table the real and virtual addresses are not both explicitly shown; only the real address is recorded and the virtual address is used as an index to the real address.

The difficulty with a page table in regular memory is that an additional memory reference is required for every address and this seriously slows the machine. Many virtual memory machines attempt to resolve the speed problem of software paging tables and the cost problems of associative arrays by building arrays that map some of the memory. The management of the contents of these partial maps of memory depends on an application of the concept of locality of reference. This concept forms the basis for most dynamic memory management schemes in paging systems. We will first see it applied to managing the references of one program.

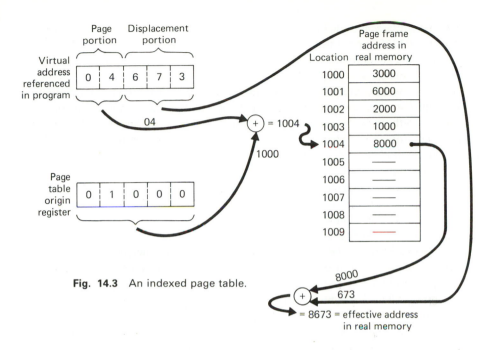

Fig. 14.3   An indexed page table.

14.3   LOCALITY AND THE TABLE LOOKASIDE BUFFER

Since it is too expensive to map all of memory in an associative array, at any time only a portion of memory is mapped on a device called, by IBM, a *table lookaside buffer*. The actual organization of this array varies from machine to machine. A simple implementation is an eight-entry table with a virtual address and a page frame address in each entry. It is necessary to represent both addresses because no ordering of the array is possible since entries will be made according to the dynamics of program address references. The eight entries in the array will represent the eight most recently referenced page frames. Thus the eight page frames that constitute a map for most recently referenced addresses will be available without a need for the additional memory references of the software table. On any address reference, a machine first inspects the array and if it finds an appropriate entry, it generates a location address. This process does not add time to the execution cycle of the machine. Only when an entry is not found in the array is it necessary to index into the software page table in memory.

At the start of the execution of a program, the array is empty. The first reference by a program finds no entry and uses the software table for the mapping. The failure to find an entry on the array causes the creation of an array entry consisting of the page frame origin and the origin address of a program page that contains the address used by the program. For example, if the program address is 01776 and the page frame address is 33776, the entry would be 01,33. Any subsequent address in the program range 1000–1999 would find an entry in the array.

The array will fill in accordance with the addressing pattern of the program. The actual entries and the rate at which new entries are made are entirely functions of how the program is addressing memory. If the program, during a particular dispatching interval, constrains its addressing to three pages, then only three entries will be made on the array. If the program constrains its addressing to eight pages, then all eight entries on the array will be used.

When a program references a ninth page, it is necessary to replace one of the eight entries on the array. Some algorithm must be developed to select an entry for replacement. The entry that one desires to replace is the one that has the least probability of being needed. The system makes use of heuristics and attempts to predict what the immediate referencing pattern of the program will be. The page frame with the least probability of being used in the immediate future must be selected. Heuristic reasoning suggests that this page frame is the one that has not been referenced for the longest time.

The array itself has a natural time ordering in that the entries at the bottom of the array are older than the entries at the top. It is possible to apply a FIFO (*first-in–first-out*) algorithm and always select the top entry for replacement by a new entry. FIFO actually reflects time of first usage. In some programs the reference pattern may well be such that the time of first usage is the time of last usage and FIFO accords with the idea of a *least recently used* (LRU) page frame selection algorithm.

The reference patterns of many programs, however, may be such that a page referenced very early, and consequently represented in an array entry at the top, has since been referenced. Thus the first reference does not reflect the actual reference pattern. In order to handle this, and in order to more closely reflect what really are the most recently referenced page frames, some mechanism for recording the order of page frame references must be devised. The general approach is that of *dynamic least recently used,* and it is supported by many possible implementation approximations. It is possible to actually time stamp each reference so that when a replacement page is sought, a time-ordered list can be formed. Most hardware mechanisms that are used in connection with memory management actually use a concept of *least frequently used* (LFU) in order to approximate least recently used. A very simple form of this is used in connection with the associative array.

Associated with each entry on the array is a reference bit that will be set ''on'' whenever a new entry is placed on the array. Before the array is filled, there is a set of empty entries with the reference bit ''off'' and a set of used entries with the reference bit "on." The array is filled whenever all reference bits are "on."

When all entries are filled, all reference bits are set to "off." After this, a pattern of addresses will set some reference bits back to "on" and will leave some reference bits "off." A reference finding no entry on the array will choose one of the entries that has not turned the reference bit back on. The selection involves a search from the top to the first "off" reference bit. This position is used for the new entry.

The mechanism depends on the idea that at some starting point all entries are equally recent and the reference bits are reset. In the ensuing interval, those entries that are referenced constitute a set of more active entries. The most frequently referenced entries will have a higher probability of resetting the reference bit first, and consequently have the highest probability of being "on" when room for a ninth entry is sought. When all entries are again "on," then the entire array is again reset.

The effectiveness of gathering a subset of program page to page frame associations is directly related to the addressing pattern of the program. There is a notion of *locality of reference*, or the *neighborhood of a program*, that says that over an interval of time a program will concentrate its references in a particular area. It is the same notion that supports cache design and the page management schemes we will shortly discuss. If a program is addressing within an eight-page area, and that area changes slowly over time and does not grow beyond eight pages, the array will minimize the number of times a reference to the software page table in memory must be made. To the extent that a program's neighborhood changes rapidly or grows beyond eight pages (the program is intensively referencing across nine or more pages), fewer "hits" will be found in the array. If the program's neighborhood is rapidly changing, then entries that are overwritten will not be later reformed. If the program is addressing over too large a neighborhood, there will be a pattern of reforming entries already deleted. At the array level there is only a small difference in the effect of a changing neighborhood or an excessively large neighborhood. At the next level up there are considerable differences in penalty to the system's performance.

14.4   VIRTUAL MEMORY, MEMORY MANAGEMENT, AND PAGING

The idea of locality and neighborhood can be extended to apply to the addresses of any program in memory at any time. Beyond the level of what pages are being referenced intensively enough to be in the associative array, there is a level of what pages are being referenced intensively enough to be in memory at all.

In order to provide service to larger populations of users, or to generate additional load on the CPU and I/O devices, it is convenient to minimize the amount of memory space occupied by any particular program. We desire to constrain a program's occupancy to some set of locations that are heavily used during some sequence of dispatching intervals when the program is on the dispatching list.

Virtual memory operating systems separate the notion of program size from the notion of size of memory, and rely upon the paging and segmentation mechanisms to dynamically associate virtual addresses with real locations. The virtual memory is an address space that is maintained in the form of blocks on peripheral storage devices such as disks and drums. An operating system mechanism called an *auxiliary storage manager* maintains a map of the association of program addresses with backing-store locations. On single virtual memory systems, the concepts of partitions and regions, and all real memory management functions may be defined on and performed on the virtual memory. Thus allocating, loading, GETMAIN, FREEMAIN, and all logical operations that are performed on real memory in real memory management systems may be performed on virtual memory by manipulating the image of the virtual memory on backing stores. Generation-to-generation compatibility provides much of the motive for the preservation of these functions. The essential effect of the virtual memory concept is to enlarge the apparent size of the memory on which the usual operations of definition and allocation are performed. All of these operations have no effect upon what portions of the virtual memory are mapped onto real memory at any particular time. That mapping is the sole responsibility of a *paging manager* that brings pages of virtual memory into real page frames by some set of algorithms keyed to actual program reference patterns. Thus any of the types of real memory systems described earlier may be simulated on a single virtual memory system.

IBM's Multiple Virtual Memory System (MVS) presents each user with a complete virtual memory private to himself or herself. This memory space is not that of a "clean" machine since many addresses of the virtual memory contain operating system functions and operating system tables. The image of each memory comes very close to the image of a unique and separate machine, a *virtual machine*, except that the user does not have the ability to determine what operating system will run in his or her virtual machine. Some details of the functions of real memory management that are mapped onto virtual memory are not entirely consistent with the concept but represent concessions to compatibility with earlier systems. IBM's TSS/370 and Honeywell's Multics represent two multiple virtual memory systems that are not constrained by compatibility. IBM's OS/VS2 (MVS) contains some concepts that have been maintained to ease the transfer of programs from earlier operating systems to MVS. Among them, for example, is the lingering concept of a region.

Regardless of whether a system is a single or a multiple virtual memory system, the management of real storage depends on a page table structure, a mechanism for recognizing a referenced page not present in main storage, a mechanism for assigning pages to page frames, and a mechanism for managing page replacement. Those mechanisms that are associated with the management of space in the translation lookaside buffer array must be replicated, in somewhat more elaborate form, to manage space in memory.

The fundamental operation of a paging system involves a system event whenever a memory reference not only fails to find an appropriate entry on the array but also fails to find an entry on the software page table or segment table. Consider Fig. 14.3 once more. An address 05896 has been developed and the index to the table 05 is being used to find the associated page frame. The 05 location, however, is found to be empty, indicating that the program page containing addresses 05000 to 05999 is not in memory. The response to this event is a *paging exception interrupt* that causes the paging manager to (eventually) receive control. The paging manager must find an available page frame to assign to 05000–05999 of the program. The paging manager has a table of available page frames and chooses one from the table. The origin location of this frame is placed in the page table of the program giving the program the ability to reference that frame. Now the paging manager (itself or through the auxiliary storage manager) finds the address on disk of the blocks representing program addresses 05000–05999. An I/O request for this page is issued and the page eventually comes into the system to occupy the assigned page frame.

This sequence is an instance of paging. During the interval after the enqueueing of the page I/O and its arrival, the program that experienced the paging exception is placed in a nondispatchable state and other programs are dispatched. *Page wait status in most systems does not remove a dispatch control block from the dispatching queue.*

The constraint on the amount of memory given to a program can lead to an excessive number of page exceptions. This constraint, justified by the notion of locality, creates a potential additional load on both the CPU to analyze and respond to the paging exceptions, and on the I/O subsystem to bring in pages. In systems already CPU-bound or I/O-bound, this incremental load may disrupt the performance of the mix. This problem, called *thrashing,* will be examined later in this chapter.

14.5 MANAGEMENT STRATEGIES AND PAGING

The use of paging in multiprogramming systems avoids the *fragmentation problem* and the *contiguity problem* by allowing discontiguous association of page frames with program addresses. The effectiveness of the technique, however, is limited by the amount of paging that must be done and the time required to do it. Policy decisions about when addresses and page frames should be associated, how the system should distribute memory among contending programs, and how the system should react when there are no page frames available must be made in order to keep paging within acceptable limits.

One essential constraint on management is to remove a certain portion of the memory from the pool of page frames that will be dynamically allocated. The kernel of the operating system, and important subsystems, for example, may be "locked into memory," i.e., made nonpageable by design or by parameter from the installation. The designation VIRTUAL = REAL on IBM systems not only locks pages into memory but locks pages into specific locations. Another level of lock, of course, is to specify that the program can be allocated anywhere but is not subject to paging after it is brought into memory. VIRTUAL = REAL means the same addresses that are used in virtual memory to represent a program are used in real memory. Locking a program into real memory, or making it nonpageable, must be closely guarded, naturally, since it reduces the area of memory that the system may dynamically manage.

Another aspect of a system that constrains, from time to time, the set of completely manageable page frames is I/O. The details of this vary from system to system depending on whether the addresses used by the channels are real or virtual addresses and on whether the machine is *channel relocatable*. In general, it may be necessary to *pin pages to real storage* when they have been named as addresses to which input will be directed using the usual I/O access methods. While I/O may be flowing to or from addresses, it is necessary that the page frames on which they are mapped are not considered available.

Certain data associated with all programs may be considered nonpageable by the system. For example, the segment and page tables themselves, although logically suitable for paging, are characteristically locked into memory while a program runs.

14.6   SIMPLE DEMAND PAGING

Within the constraints of I/O "pinning" and nonpageable areas, a system has broad discretionary power over the management of real memory. The memory management strategies are closely intertwined with the scheduling and dispatching mechanisms of the system. We will describe the simplest memory management strategy first in the context of a system with a dispatch queue in which all pageable memory is to be distributed among the members of this dispatch queue.

Initially, memory is empty and the first program on the queue operates for an interval and generates page references. Each early reference causes a paging incident and results in the next program on the queue being given the CPU. After a few cycles around the dispatching list, the programs accumulate enough pages to operate for intervals of time without causing a page exception. The page rate, initially very high, falls off and responds to changes or growth in established neighborhoods. If the total number of page frames in the system is large enough to hold the combined neighborhoods and to accommodate growth, then there will never be instances of contention or unavailable space. The amount of space held at the end of a program represents all of the pages it has referenced. The input of a page and allocation of a page frame upon reference is known as *demand paging*.

It is possible that an instance of demand will find no available page frames or so few available page frames that the system may decide to free some space. The mechanism used here is called a *page replacement algorithm*. This page replacement activity is an elaborate software version of the hardware mechanism used to make space on the associative array. One basic algorithm used to make space available is global least recently used.

Global LRU is based upon a mechanism that records the page references of all programs in the mix and orders "recency" of use by reference across all programs. Recency of use is partially related to the algorithms of dispatching because the pages used by programs most recently run will tend to be most recently used systemwide. Similarly, smaller programs that tend to reference a higher percentage of their pages during a dispatching interval will have a higher percentage of recently used pages than will larger programs that reference more sparsely over an interval. The dispatching interval, of course, determines how many page references may be made by a program while it is active. The length of the dispatching queue will also determine "recency" of reference for any page frame. A long dispatching list will increase the number of page frames referenced between dispatching intervals of a particular program, emphasizing the bias of global LRU to protect the pages of most recently run, smaller programs.

When a page frame must be freed to meet the demand for an additional page, the simple global LRU manager will find the systemwide least recently used page and make it available. A potential paradox is that this page may be least recently used in the system because the program that referenced it ran longest ago. It may have lost control because it desired another page. When that page comes in and that program is made ready and eventually started again, it may well do nothing more than recall the page it lost while waiting for a requested page. *This recall of pages because of errors in determining neighborhoods is called thrashing.* One of the reasons for constraining the size of dispatching lists and using intermediate schedulers is to minimize this.

It is usual for a paging manager to add one other factor in selecting a page frame to free. Over an interval, any page frame may be in one of four states.

- referenced and changed
- referenced and unchanged
- unreferenced and unchanged
- unreferenced and changed

The last possibility comes out of the fact that a page was changed on a reference at some previous time but has not been referenced since the "reference bits" were reset.

It is pragmatically preferable to free an unchanged page frame because this eliminates the necessity for executing both a page push and page pull. A *page push* is an instance of having to write out the contents of a page frame onto the image of virtual memory maintained on the backing store. This is necessary whenever a changed page frame is to be freed. By preferring to release least recently referenced unchanged page frames, the system may reduce its real I/O load for paging.

Not all operating system designers are content with the necessity for suppressing page pushes because it may tend in some cases to protect obsolete data pages and release currently used procedure pages. There are various suggestions for giving some page release control to a program so that it can indicate its current neighborhood and distinguish among changed pages that are really outdated and should be taken from the system.

In simple demand paging with global LRU, programs steal pages from each other and rather indiscriminately grow and contract at each other's expense. It is possible to constrain this by associating with each program a minimum set of page frames beyond which it cannot be deprived of pages. It is also possible to define a maximum set of pages that a program will be allowed to acquire. This minimum or maximum set may be predefined for each program or may be determined dynamically by the system.

The concept of a program's *working set of pages* is widely discussed in the literature. This is a concept of the number of pages a program has referenced over an interval of time. There are many diverse methods in hardware and software for approximating something like a working set. What is attempted is a means of tracking the number of different pages referenced during the last dispatching interval or during the last few dispatching intervals. This number of page references is the size of the working set, and it represents *the minimum number of page frames that a program should hold to run efficiently without generating excessive paging activity.* (See Fig. 14.4.)

One fundamental difference between the algorithm associated with the array and unconstrained global LRU is an assumption about whether, when a reference to a new page is made, the neighborhood is enlarging. Since the array cannot be increased in size, it must fundamentally assume the neighborhood is shifting but staying the same size. If this assumption is wrong, there will be intense replacement in the array. Global LRU makes the fundamental assumption that the program is enlarging its neighborhood when it refers to a new page. Working set attempts to correct this to some extent by trimming the neighborhood back to size.

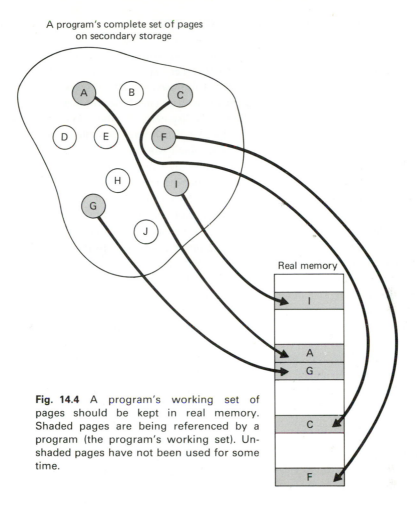

A program's complete set of pages
on secondary storage

Real memory

Fig. 14.4 A program's working set of pages should be kept in real memory. Shaded pages are being referenced by a program (the program's working set). Unshaded pages have not been used for some time.

Once a page frame has been released and is scheduled for a push or a pull, there is an interval of time during which the decision is reversible; i.e., the frame is recapturable if a reference is made by a program before the push or pull is actually submitted. This recoverability is called a *page retrieval capability*. It is nice to have but if it scores a high degree of recapture, it is a sign that there is something wrong with the page replacement mechanism. Every recapture represents the fact that the system guessed wrong about the likelihood that the released page frame would not be referenced in the near future.

14.7 INTERMEDIATE-LEVEL SCHEDULING

On a system that reorders the dispatching list from time to time, the issue of memory management becomes reasonably central.

It is usual to associate some number representing a working set size with a program that has come off the dispatching list. One criterion that the intermediate-level scheduler will use for forming a dispatch list is the sum of the working sets of all programs that will go on the list. Experience has shown that serious problems in overpaging occur if the combined working set sizes are allowed to exceed the amount of available real storage. Commonly, some constraint is applied so that only around 80 percent occupancy is planned for an interval. Programs may grow into available space during the interval, but a dispatching list will not be formed that reflects an initial occupancy for all of storage.

In many systems, the intermediate-level scheduler will not place a program on the dispatching list unless it can guarantee its working set size initially. An intermediate-level scheduler that not only guarantees working set size but actually recalls to memory the working set of pages as they were at the time the program left the dispatching queue is moving as far as possible from demand paging. Such a technique is called *swapping*. A program's working set is swapped in when it is placed on the dispatching queue and swapped out when it leaves the queue. During its time on the queue, it may grow or contract; its working set size may be dynamically redefined depending on the system.

Swapping is an idea based upon the observation that a chained read of pages is much faster than separate reads of the same number of pages. Since the first action of any program newly on the dispatch list is to accumulate its pages, it seems reasonable to provide these pages immediately and allow the dispatch list to begin having long periods of program execution without a preliminary collection process. Some of the elements on the new dispatch list are carry-overs from the old interval, of course, so there is no really massive initial swap-in sequence for the entire new list.

One problem with swapping is that there may be a neighborhood shift coming right at the point at which the program lost its place in the dispatch queue. This means that some of the pages brought in by the swap may not really be in the neighborhood the program will be using when it gets control. Additional paging will have to be done to get the appropriate pages, and this will hurt the system by artificially enlarging the space occupied by the program until some working set redefinition is done. A defense of swapping would point out that neighborhood shifts can be expected to be gradual and represent a small percentage of the initial working set. Given the tremendous efficiency of swapping as an I/O activity (i.e., the time to swap in 20 pages as a linked I/O command is much smaller than 20 individual page reads), neighborhood definition errors are

tolerable. Some systems have experimented with allowing a program to explicitly define what pages it wants prepaged, but the results have not been conclusive.

One of the times an intermediate scheduler may run is when the paging
manager has determined that the page availability is too low. Instead of attempting to trim the size of programs in memory, the system may request the
intermediate-level scheduler to decrease the level of multiprogramming by removing a program from the mix and releasing its pages as a group.

14.8 PROGRAM PROGRESS, PAGING RATES, AND THRASHING

The concept of program progress was mentioned earlier. The ability of a program
to progress, that is, to use the CPU cycles that the scheduler allocates to it, may
be constrained by the memory it has available to it. The idea of letting a program
grow is related to the idea that it can effectively consume more processor cycles
and therefore progress more rapidly if its memory is larger.

A related idea is that the paging rate generated by the program will decrease
as its memory is larger. This idea is connected to the notion that a high paging
rate implies that a program has too little storage, and also implies that a system is
overcommitted.

Some programs will not run faster with additional memory, and there are
programs with paging rates that show some degree of insensitivity to memory
space.

Whenever a program makes a request for a new page frame, that request
may be because its neighborhood is enlarging or its neighborhood is changing. It
is profitable to grant the request for a new frame only if the neighborhood is
enlarging. If the neighborhood is just changing, it is more profitable to have the
program replace one of its own pages. This suggests that LRU might profitably
be applied locally to pages within each program. If one does this, it is necessary
to provide a mechanism that does not constrain a program from ever growing.

*If the neighborhood of a program is merely shifting, then the paging rate of
the program will not go down as a function of how much space it is able to
acquire.* It will continue to refer to different areas of address space and continually request new page frames. The system will observe a program with a
chronically high paging rate. Programs with chronically high paging rates are
prime candidates for being suspended.

This program may be making really splendid progress. That is, its paging
rate may represent legitimate I/O operations that have been collapsed into the
structure of the virtual memory. The programmer has been able to put a set of
files or a large matrix into his or her virtual memory, replacing traditional I/O
with paging I/O on references to the data, just as he or she was encouraged to do.
His or her program's paging rate is a high I/O rate and the program is deserving

of highest priority because it is truly I/O-bound. Sadly, in place of this, it is treated as a sick, badly formed chronic pager.

So far, we have seen that program progress may not be related to memory size in that one can't achieve a desired CPU consumption rate by expanding memory allocation, and in that programs with high paging rates may not be undesirable. This implies that a systemwide, very high paging rate may also not be, in and of itself, undesirable. Thus to the extent that the paging rate represents legitimate I/O or legitimate retirement of function, the paging rate is not an index of malfunction.

Thrashing is not merely a high paging rate. It is properly a measure of the repaging rate, and is an index of the tendency of the page replacement manager to make wrong guesses about the future. The indicator of trouble for a system is the degree to which pages released from page frames must be brought back into the system. This suggests that a better indicator of trouble is not a high paging rate but a high page reclaim rate.

Associated with this observation is the possible use of a page recall rate to determine for each program whether or not a new page frame request should be filled with a new page frame or by releasing a page frame already held by this program. *A program with a high paging rate but low repaging rate will not profit from more space, while a program with a high repaging rate will profit from more space.*

14.9 SEGMENTATION

The concept of a *segment* varies somewhat from system to system. In its purest form, *a segment is a logical object* with a name and an extent and perhaps other attributes such as being owned or owning resources. A segment is a structure of variable size, taking on the size of the object that it represents.

It is possible to implement a segment machine without paging. The Burroughs B5500, for example, manages segments without an underlying paging scheme. Both Honeywell's Multics and IBM's systems have a segmentation level above an underlying fixed-size page scheme.

In IBM's systems, the segment level is supported by a segment table pointed to by a segment origin register. Each entry on a segment table is a pointer to a page table. The variable size of a segment is reflected in the length of the segment table. The segment level is used to

- allow segments to share code by pointing to the same tables,
- reduce the size of page tables and allow dynamic growth, and
- allow a concept of nonlinearity in the organization of user space.

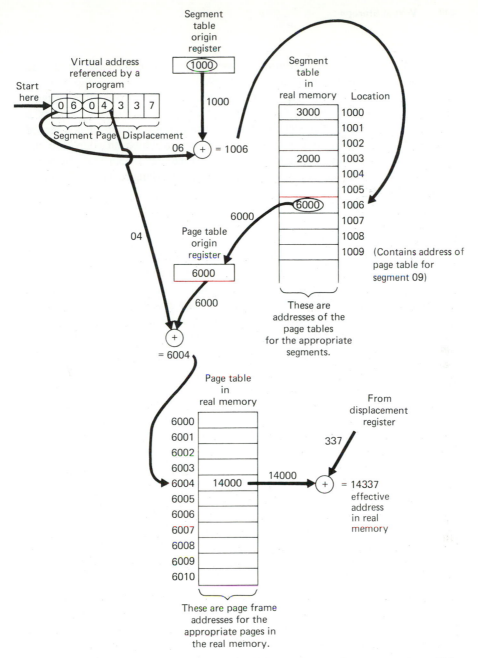

Fig. 14.5 Two-dimensional addressing with paging and segmentation. This scheme requires enormous overhead if a process is just beginning to run. Once a process is started, however, the segment and page table registers for a process have values and this "dynamic address translation" proceeds efficiently.

Previously, in our discussion of resource management, we have introduced the ideas of objects and capabilities. There is a conceptual relationship between segments, file systems, and capabilities that is used in many operating systems including HYDRA, Multics, and UNIX. In Multics, memory is seen as a collection of segments. The concept of the linear single-address space is replaced by the notion of a *two-dimensional address space* in which an address is the name of an object and a place within the object. (See Fig. 14.5.) Thus the name space of a process at any time is its collection of known objects. The same is true of HYDRA.

In a system that, like Multics, implements the idea of a single-level store, I/O operations are hidden from a process that gains accessibility to files as objects in the same way it gains accessibility to program segments. Thus the single-level store concept includes the ideas not only of a dynamic mapping from an apparent address to a physical address but also of the elimination of explicit I/O by mapping file references into the single-level address space.

Segmentation naturally leads to the idea of each process having a collection of small address spaces. This idea is useful in debugging since the *reach* of any process is limited to its private collection of objects to which access is specifically controlled. The name space of any process may consist of a set of locations to which it has private addressability because they are part of its compiled module, and a set of capabilities that it acquires. The idea of encapsulating a procedure in a small address space encourages modularization and well-defined formal relationships between procedures.

A procedure runs in a well-defined virtual address space that overlaps with the defined address space of a caller only to the extent that the caller desires. This logical isolation does not affect the degree to which procedures or data in real memory locations may be shared. Thus the management of name spaces becomes quite distinct from the management of physical space, and segmentation and paging schemes become conceptually quite separate. Name space management involves capability granting, object naming, and rights definition. It goes on independently of the mapping of objects to real storage locations.

TERMINOLOGY

address space	FIFO
associative array	first-in–first-out
cache	global least recently used
chained read of pages	internal fragmentation
contiguity	least frequently used
demand paging	least recently used

LFU

linear memory space

locality of reference

LRU

memory management

multiple virtual memory system

page frame

page pull

page push

page reclaim rate

page replacement algorithm

page table

page wait status

paging

paging rate

"pin" a page to real storage

real address

referenced and changed page frame

referenced and unchanged page frame

scatter load

segment

segment table

segmentation

single virtual memory system

software page table

swapping

table lookaside buffer

thrashing

unreferenced and changed page frame

unreferenced and unchanged page
   frame

virtual address

VIRTUAL = REAL

virtual memory

working set of pages

EXERCISES

Section 14.1

14.1 In virtual memory systems, programmers may behave as if they have considerably larger memory spaces than are really available. Give several advantages of working with the "larger" memories. Give some disadvantages.

14.2 Briefly distinguish between the virtual memory structures of IBM's OS/VS1 and OS/VS2 operating systems.

14.3 Explain how, in Honeywell's Multics system, the idea of a linear memory space with a maximum address entirely disappears.

Section 14.2

14.4 Most paging systems use a single page-frame size so that any page may fit in any page frame. Give a rationale for using several page-frame sizes on the same system. List several advantages and disadvantages of this scheme over the single-page-frame-size scheme.

14.5 What is internal fragmentation? How is it related to page-frame size?

14.6 Give several arguments pointing to the need for larger page frames.

14.7 What is a page cluster? Briefly describe how a memory manager might detect and organize page clusters. Is the additional overhead of a page-clustering memory manager justified?

14.8 Describe how an address translation mechanism in a paging environment translates addresses referred to in the program into real memory addresses.

14.9 Explain how the use of software page tables (without the availability of hardware associative arrays) can severely degrade program performance.

Section 14.3

14.10 Describe the organization of the table lookaside buffer.

14.11 Consider an eight-entry table lookaside buffer. When a program begins executing the table is empty. Explain how entries are made for the table.

14.12 When a table lookaside buffer becomes full and it is desired to add a new entry, how does the system decide which entry to replace?

14.13 In what circumstances does FIFO become identical with LRU?

14.14 Explain the operation of the dynamic least recently used scheme for recording the order of page-frame references.

14.15 Explain the operation of the LFU approximation to LRU.

14.16 Explain the notion of locality of reference.

Section 14.4

14.17 Beyond the level of what pages are being referenced enough to be in the associative array, there is a level of what pages are being referenced intensively enough to be in memory at all. Explain.

14.18 Regardless of whether a system is a single or multiple virtual memory system, the management of real storage depends on

     a) page table structure

     b) a mechanism for recognizing a referenced page not present in main storage

     c) a mechanism for assigning pages to page frames

     d) a mechanism for managing page replacement

Comment briefly on each of these items.

14.19 What is a paging exception interrupt?

14.20 Page wait status in most systems does not remove a dispatch control block from the dispatching queue. Why?

14.21 The constraint on the amount of memory given to a program can lead to an excessive number of page exceptions. How?

Section 14.5

14.22 The use of paging in multiprogramming avoids the fragmentation problem and the contiguity problem by allowing discontiguous association of page frames with program addresses. Why is this statement not completely true?

14.23 Why is the kernel of the operating system normally "locked into memory"?

14.24 The right to lock a program into real memory must be closely guarded. Why?

14.25 How does the normal functioning of the I/O system affect the set of page frames that may be paged?

14.26 Why are segment tables and page tables characteristically locked into memory while a program runs?

Section 14.6

14.27 Explain the operation of simple demand paging.

14.28 Explain the global least recently used page replacement algorithm.

14.29 Explain how global LRU could actually result in the replacement of a page that will be referenced almost immediately.

14.30 What is thrashing?

14.31 Why is it preferable to replace an unchanged page?

14.32 What circumstances can cause a page frame to be in each of the following states?

    a) referenced and changed

    b) referenced and unchanged

    c) unreferenced and unchanged

    d) unreferenced and changed

14.33 A page replacement algorithm has access to a table classifying every page frame according to the four states mentioned in Exercise 14.32. Arrange these four states in order from "most desirable page frames to replace" to "least desirable page frames to replace."

14.34 Describe how you might implement a system in which some capability for page release control is given to a program.

14.35 Explain the concept of a program's working set of pages.

14.36 Global LRU makes the fundamental assumption that the program is enlarging its neighborhood when it refers to a new page. Working set attempts to correct this to some extent by trimming the neighborhood back to size. Explain.

14.37 What is a page retrieval capability?

14.38 Why is it undesirable for a page retrieval mechanism to score a high degree of recapture?

Section 14.7

14.39 Experience has shown that serious problems in overpaging (thrashing) occur if the combined working set sizes are allowed to exceed the amount of available real storage. Why?

14.40 In many systems, the intermediate scheduler will not place a program on the dispatching list unless it can guarantee its working set size initially. Explain how this strategy can still lead to overcommitment of real storage.

14.41 What is swapping?

14.42 Some systems have experimented with allowing a program to define explicitly what pages it wants prepaged, but the results have not been conclusive. List several advantages and disadvantages of such a scheme compared with conventional demand paging.

Section 14.8

14.43 Does a high paging rate necessarily imply that a program has too little storage or that a system is overcommitted?

14.44 Some programs will not run faster with additional memory, and there are programs with paging rates that show some degree of insensitivity to memory space. Explain.

14.45 Explain the difference between a program attempting to enlarge its neighborhood versus attempting to shift its neighborhood. How might a memory manager detect the difference?

14.46 Thrashing is not merely a high paging rate. Explain.

Section 14.9

14.47 What is a segment?

14.48 Discuss briefly each of the following functions of segmentation.

    a) allow segments to share code by pointing to the same tables

    b) reduce the size of page tables and allow dynamic growth

    c) allow a concept of nonlinearity in the organization of user space

14.49 Explain the Multics concept of the single-level store.

14.50 The idea of encapsulating a procedure in a small address space encourages modularization and well-defined formal relationships between procedures. Explain.

14.51 Name space management involves capability granting, object naming, rights definition, and goes on independently of the mapping of objects to real storage locations. Explain.

15
Intermediate-Level Scheduling

15.1 OVERVIEW OF THE SYSTEMS RESOURCES MANAGER

Throughout the text we have made passing references to the Systems Resources Manager (SRM) of IBM's OS/MVS operating system. Since it was first announced, the SRM has undergone continuous evolution. In general, the maturation of the component has been in the direction of better balancing of the intensity and complexity of system heuristics with more predictable responsiveness to user-supplied parameters. There is reason to believe that a high-water mark in heuristic resource management has been achieved. The current version of the system has a greater tolerance for periods of overcommitment and undercommitment than did previous versions, and actually undertakes less extensive corrective action than did earlier versions in some cases.

The SRM is actually an intermediate scheduler that is an outgrowth of the TSO driver. Higher-level scheduling is performed by the JES (Job Entry Subsystems) associated with the IBM OS family of operating systems. (See Fig. 15.1.) The idea of the SRM is to give more global systemwide control over a system that characteristically runs batch jobs with significant numbers of on-line terminals. Associated with the goal of providing more global system control is a considerably expanded set of functions for expressing user policy, and for expressing the balance between meeting response and completion requirements and achieving good processor, memory, and I/O utilization levels. Finally, an expanded concept of the dynamic intensity of systems management is intended to make the systems maximally self-tunable in response to observations of systems load and the rates of progress of processes in the multiprogramming mix. Self-adjustment is based on a coordination of the algorithms associated with component utilization and schedule enforcement.

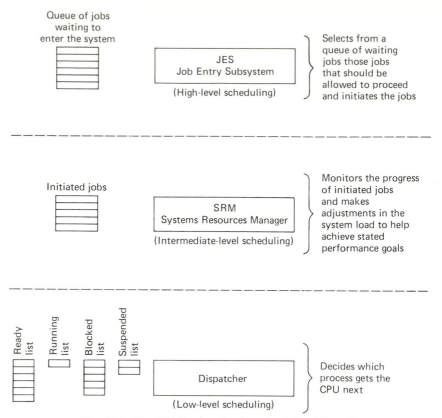

Fig. 15.1   The SRM's place in the scheduling hierarchy.

At the heart of the *policy-driven* concept is a user-provided policy statement called an IPS (Installation Performance Specification) that describes how an installation wishes service to be given to various transactions. A batch transaction is a job or step. A TSO transaction is a command.

15.2   THE SERVICE UNIT

The concept of service involves a somewhat abstract notion of a *service unit* that is used to describe a rate of service to be accorded to a transaction of a certain type. The service unit consists of four major components.

■   A CPU utilization component describing the rate at which CPU service should be accorded to the process (i.e., active time in terms of model-dependent IBM/370 CPU units)

- An I/O units component involving a count of I/O blocks transferred

- A memory utilization component describing the number of page frames to be accorded over various intervals of collected CPU service (a time–space concept)

- A system service component describing the time the operating system spends on behalf of servicing a running process

The complexity of the service unit concept derives from a desire to achieve a uniform statement of a rate of service for processing that varies widely in the balance of resource usage. The *service rate* of a transaction is expressed in terms of service units per second to be received during its lifetime.

15.3 WORK-LOAD LEVELS, OBJECTIVES, AND PERFORMANCE GROUPS

There is a concept of a *work-load level* that describes the burden of work on the system. Thus an installation may define a number of discrete work-load levels (total demands for service) in which the relationship between total demand and total capacity varies from characteristic oversupply to characteristic undersupply of systems resources. The concepts of service rate and work-load level are combined to form the idea of an objective. An *objective* is a statement of the rates of service a group of programs should receive under varying conditions of load. The set of programs associated with an objective are members of a *performance group*. Thus an installation can associate a program with a performance group, and a performance group with an objective. (See Fig. 15.2.) An objective may indicate, for example, that at work-load level 1, performance group 1 is to receive 500 service units per second; at work-load level 2 (the load on the system is heavier), it is still to receive 500 service units per second; at work-load level 3, it should receive 300 service units per second. This objective would be appropriate for describing very critical batch or on-line jobs of maximum importance to the installation. It is desired that excellent service be given to programs in the group at all times, but under conditions of extreme load the service rate may be allowed to decline.

Similarly, an objective may indicate that at work-load level 1 (light use), the group may receive 500 service units per second; but at work-load level 2, only 100 service units are to be accorded; at work-load level 3, no service units need be given. This describes a group of programs of marginal importance that should receive service when it is available, seriously degraded service when any serious load is placed on the system, and no sustained service when there is significant load on the system.

In making out these objectives, it is necessary for an installation to be sure that the set of objectives is feasible and reasonable. Otherwise, the system will

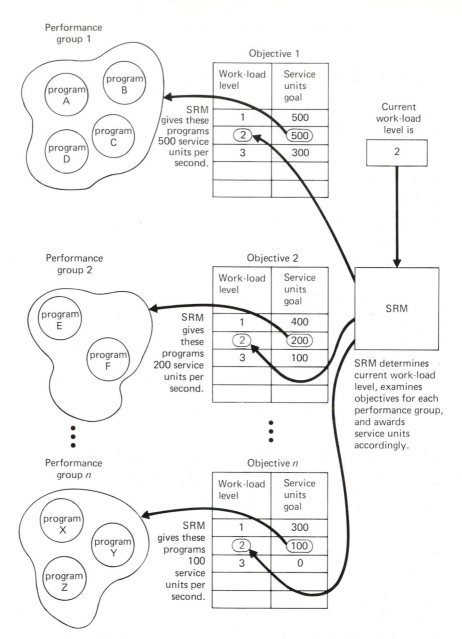

Fig. 15.2 Work-load levels, performance groups, and objectives.

invest increasing amounts of self-tuning effort in order to attempt to achieve unachievable work-load management goals. Note that *the service goals are rates of service rather than stated response requirements so that the SRM is not a deadline scheduling mechanism. An attempt is made to warranty rates of service, not to manage toward achieving a stated completion time.*

The SRM also receives parameters describing utilization goals, and the relative weight to be accorded to utilization versus service goals can be manipulated. We shall later see that the SRM balances response and utilization goals in determining the multiprogramming level, and the exact composition of the multiprogramming mix. Work-load level numbers are used as recommended values in analyzing the desirability of removing a particular process as a candidate for CPU service for some interval of time.

15.4　PERFORMANCE PERIODS

There is an additional dimension associated with rate of service specification. It is possible to define performance periods across the life of a transaction, and associate a transaction with different objectives at different periods in its existence. This mechanism can be used to effect a change in service to transactions as they age in the system. For example, if very good service is to be given to short terminal commands, then a time period can be defined that is associated with high-service-unit levels. The objective will be applied, for example, to all commands that have not yet achieved 200 service units. When 200 service units have been given, those commands that have not completed processing can be defined as entering a new performance period. A new service objective can be associated that calls for a lower rate of service for a defined duration. Commands still not complete enter a third service period in which they are associated with yet another diminished service objective.

15.5　INTERVAL SERVICE VALUE

The performance period concept can be used with a concept called *interval service value* (ISV) to achieve an effect similar to the feedback queueing described earlier. The interval service value is the number of service units a transaction must receive before it can be removed from memory. A process in its interval service value that has not yet received the service it is to get cannot be removed from memory. Remember our earlier notion of a short job living on a top queue receiving frequent but short intervals of service, then moving to a lower queue to receive less frequent but longer periods of service. Although we are not speaking now of dispatching intervals, but of intervals on the dispatching queue, the reader will note the similarity of the notions in the next paragraph.

Consider a population of terminal commands associated with a performance period of duration 200 in turn associated with an objective that calls for a high rate of service and an ISV of 200. No command that has received fewer than 200 service units will be removed from the set of processes in memory or from the dispatching queue. Those completing in that period will not be swapped. Throughout the 200 service units of its life, the transaction will be in the dispatchable set. When the period ends, those transactions not completed may be assigned to a new objective that provides for a higher ISV, but a lower service rate that will tend to keep them in memory but give them fewer system cycles. The degradation of performance may be emphasized by associating the period with a lower dispatching priority.

A central intent of ISV is to reduce swapping by modifying the competition for memory that naturally occurs as the system makes decisions based upon service objectives. A beneficial reform of the system since it was first announced is the elimination of automatic aging that caused the system to increase the ISV of a process as it stayed longer in the system. This nonreversible aging is closely associated with the concept of the feedback queue as we described it for a small interactive environment. However, the effect on a large system running interactive and batch in an environment in which memory is a critical resource is to enable old batch programs to begin to take over the system by remaining in memory with artificially elongated ISVs.

15.6 RESPONSE VERSUS UTILIZATION

The objectives provided by an installation give considerable policy-expressing power when combined with a set of statements about resource-utilization goals describing the balance of importance between response and utilization. The system may be directed to run with no consideration of I/O or CPU load whatsoever or it may be provided with a value associated with interest in resource utilization. The mechanism works as follows.

The work-load level definitions given to the system are integers of arbitrary size. These values are used as a component of a dynamically computed recommendation value. This recommendation value, we shall soon see, is used to determine whether a process should be considered for removal from the mix of dispatchable programs. If the system has been parameterized to consider loading factors, it will modify recommendation values by numbers (CPU-load adjustment recommendation and I/O-load adjustment recommendation) provided in the parameters. There is a maximum adjustment factor associated with the work-load objectives of the system. The objective specifying no service at the highest work-load level provides a limit on utilization adjustments such that a load adjustment may not be greater than 20 percent of the work-load level. Consider a set of three performance objectives that specifies a no service level at work-load levels 20, 50, and 100, respectively. The highest load-adjustment factor may be 20. Thus the impact of load adjustment on objective three (100) will be considerably less than on objective one (20). Programs associated with better performance goals will tend to be serviced with less sensitivity to system resource usage.

The entire process of determining a recommendation value will be discussed shortly. The essential notion is that the system collects dynamic statistics about how close processes are to their service objectives and how the resources are being used. It then reforms the dispatch list as a result of the recommended swap values determined by this analysis.

15.7   SRM GOALS AND TECHNIQUES

The essential goals of the SRM, as an intermediate scheduler, are to distribute service as the installation directs, to maximize utilization within service constraints, and to prevent serious resource imbalance resulting in chronic contention. The techniques the SRM uses to accomplish these goals are control of the level of multiprogramming and periodic definition of the specific components of the mix. The earlier comments about a high-water mark and moderate retreat relate to the intensity with which the SRM attempts the management of the mix, and its tolerance for periods of overcommitment and undercommitment.

15.8   THE EARLIEST VERSION OF THE SRM

In the earliest version of the system, the SRM runs as a result of a set of particular events, or on a timed basis. The events that result in SRM operation and a swapping occurrence are, for example, a terminal entering a wait state, or a recognition that memory is overcommitted and insufficient space exists. Similarly, an ENQUEUE on a resource held by a swapped-out process causes the SRM to mark the swapped-out holder as a candidate for swap in.

When the SRM runs as a result of the passage of a defined interval, it does an analysis of the schedule and resource usage. The analysis involves the CPU-load adjustment algorithm, the I/O-balancing algorithm, and the work-load management algorithm. Each of these runs and provides recommendations for swapping that the SRM considers jointly.

The CPU algorithm determines if the statistics kept on CPU utilization indicate an overutilization or an underutilization of the CPU.

The I/O-balancing algorithm monitors the use of system logical channels, and if it finds underutilization or overutilization, it nominates candidates for swap in or swap out in order to bring channel usage into balance within desired limits.

The work-load management algorithm monitors the actual amount of service a process is getting, and compares it with service objectives for the load at which the system is operating.

The SRM swap analysis forms a swap list based upon the recommendations of the three algorithms, and the predicted effects on service distribution of suggested swap-out candidates.

The system is managed as a single global entity and there is a single global multiprogramming mix whose level represents the goal of the system unless constraints in service or utilization do not allow that goal to be met.

Several undesirable properties were observed in this early version of the SRM. The system was highly sensitive to undercommitment or overcommitment and tended to overreact causing intensive swapping operations that, in turn, caused performance to degrade rapidly at high-utilization or high-multiprogramming levels. This was caused by the swapping of entire programs to alleviate memory constraints and also by the extensiveness of the analysis and the amount of swapping being undertaken. In a sense, the system was too ''high-strung'' making it difficult to predict how a mix would behave.

15.9 DOMAINS

In order to provide more stability and user control, several internal calculations have been changed and certain new control concepts have been added, including the concept of a *domain*.

A domain is a special compartment of work intended to distinguish types of users from each other, and to be individually controlled. In place of a single multiprogramming level, each defined domain is associated with a unique multiprogramming level representing the minimum and maximum degrees of multiprogramming desired for each domain. These multiprogramming levels indicate the number of programs in each domain to be swapped in at any time. The SRM manages each domain to a preferred multiprogramming level in response to the load and responsiveness of the system. Complete control over the multiprogramming level of a domain can be exercised by the installation that sets the minimum and maximum equal to each other. In this case the SRM makes no decision about the optimal multiprogramming level.

Thus an installation may partition its work into batch, short interactive, long interactive or short batch, long batch, interactive, or any other grouping of work that seems meaningful. Any program that is a member of a particular domain is also a member of a performance group by virtue of its association with a performance objective.

When the SRM is allowed to compute optimal multiprogramming levels for a domain, it must be provided with some notion of the relative importance of the domains. This is expressed by a weight used to compute a contention index between domains. The contention index is formed by considering the weight (relative importance of the domain), the optimum multiprogramming level, and the average number of ready processes associated with this domain. In making swapping decisions to increase total multiprogramming load, the SRM gives precedence for swap in to the domain with highest contention index that is below its maximum level of multiprogramming and that has a higher number of ready users than its current multiprogramming level. When the SRM wishes to decrease the number of programs in the mix, it lowers the multiprogramming level for a domain that has the lowest contention index and is not at its minimal level.

The swapping analysis attempts to maintain each domain at its optimum levels and to periodically adjust optimum levels. When a level is reduced, the process with the lowest recommended value is swapped out. This is a unilateral swap that can affect only one process in the system. For a domain with a current level less than its optimal level, the SRM swaps in the process with the highest recommendation value. When the domain is running at its optimal level, an exchange swap involving the highest and lowest recommended values will occur.

The SRM will also swap in the process that has been out of storage for the longest time and that holds a resource. This may be a unilateral swap or an exchange swap depending on whether the domain of the process is, or is not, at its optimal level.

Thus the SRM computes optimal multiprogramming levels for each domain and assures that the number of processes representing that domain on the dispatch list is at that level. However, only one swap in decision is made about each domain reducing the total number of swap decisions, introducing a notion of tolerance for periods of undercommitment and overcommitment, and increasing the stability of the system. The system is a logically partitioned system in which work of the same kind tends to compete rather than in which there is a general competition for all users of the system.

Later versions of the system involve some modifications to page management. Initially, the notion of swapping was very strong in the system, and its primary response to a memory shortage was to swap out a process. There was a process called periodic trimming that redefined working sets in terms of most recently referenced pages. This mechanism has been replaced by a global LRU replacement algorithm that involves stealing pages on demand.

15.10   OTHER ASPECTS OF BALANCING AND TUNING SYSTEMS

There are many aspects of balancing and tuning a system we have not yet discussed. Among these are parameters beyond the ken of the SRM, and algorithms such as device allocation and job start selection that are closely related. Within the context of the SRM, there are various parameters beyond the workload and resource-load objectives we have discussed. For example, an installation may specify the range of permissible CPU utilization levels, the range of permissible paging rates, the SRM invocation interval, the levels of available memory and storage considered critical, and various other parameters. In addition, there are mechanisms that report the usage statistics the SRM uses to determine system load and status. Data must be reported on CPU activity for each process, channel activity, paging rates, available page frames, etc. in order to support system analysis. Closely connected to these mechanisms are components that collect, summarize, and format data for the inspection and analysis of the members of the professional staff who are responsible for mapping the workload onto the system.

15.11 DISPATCHING MECHANISMS AND TACTICS

We conclude our discussion of the SRM by considering the nature of the dispatching mechanisms and tactics available to control the rate of CPU service. The dispatch control mechanisms of the OS/MVS system are part of the SRM. These mechanisms apportion CPU service to those processes on the dispatch list, while the mechanisms we have just discussed decide who is to be on the dispatch list. More specifically, a particular range of the dispatching priorities available in the system is put under the control of the SRM. These priorities are called the APG priorities (the Automatic Priority Group). The phrase, which once meant those priorities that may be adjusted as a result of CPU–I/O-bound ratios, has been expanded to mean those priority levels under control of the SRM. The full internal range of dispatching priorities the MVS system uses is 0–225. The SRM controls the set 70 to 7F (hexidecimal). Thus there may be programs running at higher priorities that are not subject to SRM control.

Within the set of priorities managed by the SRM, particular dispatching tactics are associated with particular priorities. Thus priority levels 70 and 71 are subject to round robin, 72 to 76 by CPU-I/O "mean-time-to-wait," 7B by rotation, and the remaining levels by a fixed priority scheme.

By assigning priorities to various processes, the installation determines that none of the dispatching machinery is under control of SRM, that all of it is, or some balance is made. Programs may also be assigned priorities for different periods. A particular process from period to period may be dropped from fixed to mean-time-to-wait priority levels.

Mean-time-to-wait is a number periodically calculated for each process in a MTW group. Those processes that are CPU-bound are assigned lower priorities within the group than are I/O-bound processes. The method achieves something like the feedback queue method described earlier, but it affords a finer calibration of CPU–I/O balance. The mean-time-to-wait calculations are periodically performed on programs that have achieved a certain amount of accumulated CPU service since the last calculation. The calculation itself divides the number of waits experienced while the CPU time is being accumulated. Thus CPU time divided by waits gives a mean-time-to-wait. Actually the MTW is not a true index of CPU–I/O ratios since the calculation is truly a mean time of continuous CPU service. In a system in which CPU and I/O processing can be overlapped for the same process, the I/O load the process is applying to the system would be understated by the concept of mean-time-to-wait.

Rotate priority is a scheme for balancing service between processes of equal priority. The SRM periodically rotates processes of the same priority by placing the process at the top of the group at the bottom of the group, and moving all other processes up. The frequency is a system-defined rate of the order of 100 ms, giving rise to rotations on the order of ten per second.

Finally, there is a mechanism for time slicing that permits the user to specify a program as a member of a time-slice group for designated time periods (not the same as performance periods). A particular priority within a time-slice group can be assigned to each program. When a process is not in a time-slice time period, it dispatches at its normal dispatch priority. When it is in a time-slice time period, it is dispatched at its time-slice dispatching priority. Members of a particular time-slice group may come from multiple performance groups across domains. The effect of time slicing is to permit a process to be moved ahead on the queue for some interval of time in order to get carefully controlled preferred service for limited periods of time.

The importance of time slicing lies in the fact that the major means of control the SRM has over the mix is through swapping. Before the addition of time slicing, two major subsystems, for example, both made ineligible for swapping, could not be directly controlled by the SRM since it had no mechanism at the dispatch level to control how much CPU time the subsystem would obtain. By virtue of the ordering of the dispatch list, one would always be more important than the other, even if they had equal priorities. The time-slice capability allows the system to limit the amount of service a subsystem can be given over an interval of time.

15.12 CONCLUSION

This has been a compressed description of a rich mechanism that has been constantly evolving and will certainly continue to evolve.

The future of such ambitious mechanisms is not clear. There are those who are anxious for their extension and perfection. There are those who say that the diminishing cost of hardware makes such mechanisms unprofitable because less hardware will be shared. There are those who feel that such mechanisms should be taken "off-line" onto auxiliary processors that manipulate schedules without disturbing the performance of the load of applications. There are those who believe that trying to provide good batch and interactive service in the same system is difficult at best and leads to excessive system overhead.

TERMINOLOGY

APG	Job Entry Subsystem
Automatic Priority Group	mean-time-to-wait
contention index between domains	MTW group
CPU-load adjustment algorithm	multiprogramming level
deadline scheduling	objective
domain	performance group
heuristic resource management	policy-driven
high-level scheduling	recommendation value
Installation Performance Specification	service rate of a transaction
intermediate-level scheduler	service unit
interval service value	SRM
I/O balancing algorithm	swapping
IPS	Systems Resources Manager
ISV	work-load level
JES	work-load management algorithm

EXERCISES

Section 15.1

15.1 The current version of the SRM has greater tolerance for periods of overcommitment and undercommitment than previous versions, and actually undertakes less extensive corrective action than did earlier versions in some cases. In what circumstances, do you suppose, might less corrective action on the part of the SRM yield better results?

Section 15.2

15.2 Discuss the purpose of each of the following components of a service unit.

    a) CPU utilization component

    b) I/O utilization component

    c) memory utilization component

    d) system service component

Section 15.3

15.3 Discuss the concept of work-load level.

15.4 What is an objective?

15.5 What is a performance group?

15.6 The SRM attempts to warranty rates of service, not to manage toward achieving a stated completion time. Explain.

Section 15.4

15.7 What is a performance period?

Section 15.5

15.8 What is an interval service value?

15.9 A beneficial reform of the SRM since it was first announced is the elimination of automatic aging that caused the system to increase the ISV of a process as it stayed longer in the system. Why did the elimination of this feature improve performance?

Section 15.6

15.10 Discuss the response versus utilization trade-off.

Section 15.7

15.11 What are the essential goals of the SRM?

Section 15.8

15.12 Discuss the functions of each of the following SRM components.

    a) CPU-load adjustment algorithm

    b) I/O-balancing algorithm

    c) work-load management algorithm

    d) swap analysis

15.13 What were some of the undesirable properties of early versions of the SRM?

Section 15.9

15.14 What is a domain?

Section 15.11

15.15 How is mean-time-to-wait calculated?

15.16 Discuss the rotate priority scheme for balancing service between processes of equal priority.

15.17 What are the major means of control the SRM has over a multiprogramming mix?

16

Virtual
Machines

16.1 SEVERAL OPERATING SYSTEMS SHARING A SINGLE MACHINE

The idea of a *virtual machine* involves providing a base on which different operating systems can share a machine and logically behave as if each is the only operating system running on the machine.

Situations often arise in which it is desirable to run programs on different machine systems. One machine may be down or overloaded or unable to respond to additional load while another machine system has the physical capacity to run the program. Unfortunately, even if the second system is hardware compatible, it may be running an operating system whose interfaces are not the same as the operating system for which the program was written. Thus the program may be written for a DOS environment but the available machine is running OS. In order to run the program, it is necessary to seriously disrupt the operations of the OS machine, bring up DOS on that machine, and dedicate it under DOS to the DOS program.

Similarly, it is possible that variations in the versions of the same operating system running on machine 1 and machine 2 are such that it is very difficult to run a program on machine 1 under its operating system if that program was intended for machine 2. Differences in cataloged control language procedures, for example, may necessitate some modifications to the request if it is to be run on another system.

Problems of system development arise from the pattern of system extension and enhancement of software products, and the notion of versions. When a new version of an operating system is delivered, it is necessary to "bring it up" and then to do some preliminary testing before committing production work to the

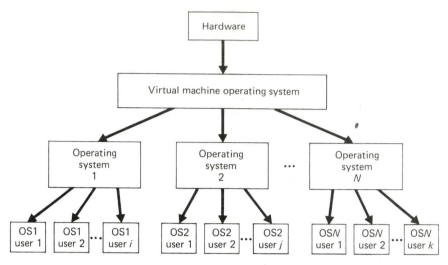

Fig. 16.1 Virtual machine operating system environment.

new version. Since it is impossible to run two versions of an operating system simultaneously on the same machine in the absence of the virtual machine concept, such activity must also be specially scheduled on a dedicated machine.

The early motivating concepts of virtual machine systems included system portability and development. The essential notion of the virtual machine was applied so that a DOS program could run under DOS while the system was running OS on its usual work load, or that the production version of OS could be running while the new version was under test. In order to accomplish this, these operating systems had to be run essentially as subsystems. (See Fig. 16.1.) A hardware–software base involving an underlying kernel that isolated the operating systems from one another was provided as the virtual machine operating system.

The earliest work in virtual systems was the IBM 7044X–7044M project. It was this project that first defined the notion of a multiprogramming mix running as distinct virtual machines rather than as processes under a single multiprogramming system.

16.2 INFLUENCE OF VIRTUAL MEMORY

The development of virtual memory concepts was an important element in the development of virtual machine concepts. With the relocation mechanisms of virtual memories, it became feasible to implement virtual machines whose concept of memory space could be completely isolated from the concept of real memory locations. This served not only to provide apparent user spaces but also to protect critical memory locations from access by a running operating system that would normally have access to these locations.

16.3   CONTROL STATE AND PROBLEM STATE

The function of the virtual operating system is to provide the illusion that the operating system, running as a subsystem, can enter control state without actually allowing it to do so. Thus the operating systems are always kept in problem state, and the virtual system records whether or not the operating system thinks it is in control state. If the operating system thinks it is in control state, the virtual system acts upon its control state functions. If a control state function is requested while the virtual system records a particular operating system as being in problem state, the same result is induced as would occur if the operating system was running on the bare machine.

16.4   INPUT–OUTPUT

In addition to mapping addresses and intercepting control functions, the virtual system must execute all I/O on behalf of the operating systems, maintaining maps relating the virtual assignments the operating systems have made for their running programs to the real device addresses known only to the virtual system.

16.5   MINIMIZING PERFORMANCE BURDENS

The additional levels of mapping impose a performance burden upon programs running on virtual systems. This burden is strongly felt when the operating systems are themselves virtual memory operating systems doing their own memory mapping. In order to alleviate this burden, two approaches have been taken. One is to eliminate the double mapping by combining the mapping function of the operating system with the virtual system wherever practicable. Thus manipulating page and segment tables in such a way that double mapping can be minimized has been attempted in IBM's VM/370. Another approach to minimizing the performance burden is to place as much of the second level of mapping as possible in microcode. This has also been done with versions of IBM VM/370 that run on machines with a microcode capability.

16.6   RUN-TIME ENVIRONMENT

Because the virtual operating system is itself an operating system, it must perform some of the usual functions of an operating system beyond supplying a virtual system interface. The run-time environment of a virtual system does not contain service interfaces of interest to the operating systems it is running. By definition, such interfaces are excluded. However, the implicit and global systems functions of multiplexing CPU time and scheduling I/O operations must still be performed. A dispatching mechanism to allocate processor power between the operating systems must exist, and a scheduling mechanism to enforce some notion of policy must exist. The scheduler for VM/370 is functionally rich including notions of priority, working set size, suspend queues, and dispatch queues associated with intermediate-level scheduling.

In addition, a set of installation interfaces allowing the installation to deal with the virtual operating system as an operating system must be provided. An operator's language, performance tuning tools, etc. must exist for the virtual system. Some set of user commands may also exist to support intervals of time during which a terminal user is dealing directly with the virtual operating system before establishing his or her own operating system context. Thus a user LOGs on to the virtual operating system, using its conventions, before a user IPLs his or her virtual machine.

16.7   CONVERSATIONAL MONITOR SYSTEM

Because the virtual operating system wishes to impose minimum burden and maximum isolation on the operating systems it runs, the functional capacity of the kernel is restricted to what is absolutely necessary to support the concept. In order to support a population of users not yet committed to a particular operating system, it is common to provide an associated subsystem containing command language and file management capability. An example of such a subsystem is the CMS (Conversational Monitor System) associated with IBM's VM/370. CMS includes a set of utilities, debugging aids, programming languages, and a command language. It was written explicitly for running on VM/370, and runs efficiently in the virtual machine environment. A user can use CMS as a time-sharing conversational operating system without regard to the essential ideas of a virtual machine system.

Any particular operating system running under a virtual machine system may itself be a batch single-stream, batch multiprogramming, or time-sharing multiaccess system. Thus while VM is running DOS and MVS, these systems in turn may be running mixes of applications programs and/or subsystems. VM has no notion of what they are doing, and they have no notion of the existence of VM.

16.8   DISTRIBUTED PROCESSING AND NETWORKING

The notion of a virtual machine has been receiving attention within the context of distributed processing and networks. Many of the advantages of distributed processing come from functional specialization of a machine. Thus there is the idea, for example, in DATAPOINT's ARC system that one processor might be dedicated to an application, another processor dedicated to communication, and a third processor dedicated to file management. The advantages of this depend on economy of scale, performance predictability and stability, and increased programmer productivity as applications are written as small separate processes to reside in small processors. Many of the advantages of distributed processing come from the illusion that a terminal user has of owning his or her own machine, and from the effects of good subsystem definition, and enhanced user interfaces.

The virtual machine concept may be applied to distribution and networking in instances in which the interaction between applications requires faster hardware support than channel interconnections or teleprocessing lines permit. Thus a family of specialized virtual machines can simulate the existence of a network of real machines by providing a file management virtual machine, a telecommunications virtual machine, and a virtual machine for each application. Resources can be partitioned in such a way that the performance stability of separate processors can be approached, and interfaces of similar quality can be provided by subsystems running under a virtual machine system.

An interesting notion involves the idea that a process talking to another process or to data uses the same interface regardless of whether the process is talking to a process in another virtual machine, in the same real machine, or in another real machine. Thus processes may be "exported" or "imported" from real machine nets to virtual machine nets.

As an example of this, consider programs that share no data and rarely talk to each other. These might well be implemented on separate minicomputers. Now over time the enterprise changes its view of how it wishes to be organized and managed so that the programs must talk to each other quite frequently. The programs really become functions of the same application rather than separate applications. A bank that previously managed checking, savings, and credit quite independently, so that movement of money from savings to checking involved two separate transactions, might decide to provide a single "move from savings to checking" transaction. The savings account processor and checking account processor that never talked to each other in the past may now be asked to talk to each other quite frequently. One solution to this reorganization of functional relations is to reorganize the database to integrate checking and savings accounts, probably a difficult task. An alternate solution is to leave the databases as they were originally organized, but bring them to a larger disk file, and then to take the applications programs from the small dedicated processors into virtual machines. These virtual machines would then talk to each other via a memory-based intercommunication protocol that allows them fast interaction.

16.9 CONCLUSION

Originally quite distinct from other notions of operating system structure, the notion of virtual machine is beginning to coalesce with current work on defining the minimum kernel and moving functions upward in the structure in order to limit the scope of errors and provide architectural support for increasingly distinct systems functions.

TERMINOLOGY

address mapping

address space

"bring up" an operating system

cataloged control language

CMS

control state

Conversational Monitor System

DATAPOINT's ARC System

dedicated machine

DOS machine

double mapping

IBM 7044X-7044M Project

IBM's VM/370

interception of control functions

IPL a virtual machine

kernel of a virtual operating system

memory space

microcode

multiprogramming mix

OS machine

problem state

program portability

real device addresses

real memory

relocation

subsystem

version of an operating system

virtual device assignments

virtual machine

virtual machine operating system

virtual memory

virtual system interface

EXERCISES

Section 16.1

16.1 What is a virtual machine?

16.2 Explain how system development and portability motivated the virtual machine concept.

Section 16.2

16.3 Why was the development of virtual memory concepts important to the development of virtual machine concepts?

Section 16.3

16.4 Explain how a virtual operating system provides the illusion that an operating system, running as a subsystem, can enter control state (even though the subsystem is always kept in problem state).

Section 16.4

16.5 Discuss how a virtual operating system executes I/O on behalf of an operating system running as a subsystem.

Section 16.5

16.6 Discuss the relative merits of each of the following means of minimizing performance burdens in virtual operating systems that run virtual memory systems as subsystems.

    a) Eliminate double memory mapping.

    b) Place second level of mapping in microcode.

Section 16.6

16.7 The run-time environment of a virtual system does not contain service interfaces of interest to the operating systems it is running. Explain.

Section 16.7

16.8 Discuss the motivation for CMS.

Section 16.8

16.9 Explain the usefulness of virtual machines in the context of distributed processing and networking.

17
An Assessment

17.1 THE VALUE

The particular systems we use and understand today are based upon a set of economic facts and assumptions relating the cost of implementing functions in hardware, the cost of implementing functions by programming, and the cost of the particular split of programming responsibility between vendors and users. The function of software is to maximize the net economic value of computing machinery to users by

- reducing the cost to use the machinery

- assuring timely delivery of information

- increasing the effective use of machinery when the cost of hardware is nontrivial

Software fills the gap between affordable hardware function and affordable user interfaces. This idea is pictured in Fig. 17.1. The layers of rectangles represent levels in the hierarchic structure of a system. The idea is that the couple looking at the outside box is seeing an interface that will impose upon them a set of activities and learning experiences that constitute a cost of using the system. This interface, however, will provide certain functions that will reduce the work load on users of the system by providing a work-oriented or a system-oriented capability that would otherwise need to be done by hand. The interface is economically sound if its total cost, including its price, the hardware resource it consumes, and the cost of using it, is less than the cost of not having the interface available.

In different situations, different interfaces may or may not be economically

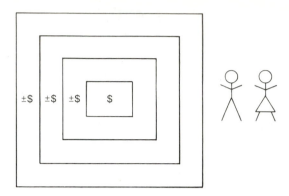

Fig. 17.1 Layers of value.

sound. For example, in an environment with a common, stable application, the purchase of an applications package might be economically sound because purchased instructions generally cost less than developed instructions. However, in an environment in which problem solving is the requirement and the development of new algorithms is the essence of the work, then a good programmer's interface becomes economically valuable. In general, the constraint on any software product is that the cost of using it is, in fact, less than the cost of not using it.

Currently, there is a certain amount of uncertainty about the economics of software. Figure 17.2 shows the nature of this concern. The x-axis represents some notion of richness of function and potentially associated complexity of use. The costs of very rich systems are a function of the nature of the parameters that must be supplied, the information that must be gathered to tune the system and install and maintain components. These costs are represented as complexity on the x-axis.

The y-axis represents a notion of the total cost of installing and supporting a system throughout its lifetime. No one really knows what the curve should look like, but Fig. 17.2 represents a concern that there may be a "software knee." This software knee occurs at the point at which the costs associated with delivered software exceed the costs of not having the function at all, or the costs of implementing the function in user applications. The knee can be thought of as the profitable point of "roll your own," the point at which it is more economical for an installation to forgo function or to program it itself than to accept function from a software package.

The curve of Fig. 17.2 poses a very basic question about the economics of software by suggesting that there is a point at which users may perceive a

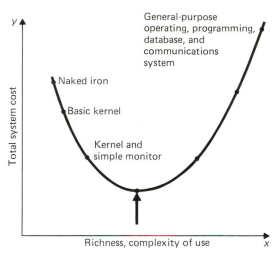

Fig. 17.2   Is there a software knee?

software package to be uneconomical; namely, the cost to use it is more than the value it delivers.

17.2   THE COSTS

Some of the costs associated with using an operating system are

- system overhead
- learning
- organizational impact
- reliability
- stability
- parameterization

System overhead refers to the level of withdrawal of machine resource in order to perform systemwide management services. It also refers to the increments in time and space caused by the generalization of programs inherent in the provision of shared function.

Learning involves the effort required to master the interfaces provided by the system in terms of formal schooling, on the job training, and associated misuse of the system at various intervals in the learning curve.

Organizational impact refers to the organizational costs associated with using the system. A computing device can impact an organization in a number of ways. The actual impact is partially a function of the size of the system and the scope of its work load. The authors like to think of four organizational impact levels.

■   The *tool level* at which job descriptions change. At this level the computer replaces a slide rule or a desk calculator, and performance at a particular job involves some competence in the use of the device as a personal tool.

■   The *specialist level* at which new jobs must be described within a department. The nature of the computing device is such that job descriptions must be created that have computer skills and responsibilities as a primary requirement and objective.

■   The *organizational level* at which departmental missions change. At this level, the computer is a significant enough device so that the mission of a department is modified to reflect the use of a computer.

■   The *enterprise level* at which new departments are formed in order to support computer operations and are solely responsible for providing computer services.

If one considers the full spectrum of computing devices, then different classes of machines in this spectrum will have characteristic organizational impacts. A handheld calculator has a tool-level impact. A microcomputer used to perform an administrative function associated with a department has a specialist-level impact. A minicomputer installed to perform the primary function of a department has an organizational-level impact. A large centralized database management information system has an enterprise-level impact.

Since the size of hardware suggests the nature of the software and operating system associated with it, and the software presents the user his or her view of the nature of the system, software characteristics relate a computing device to a particular organizational impact.

Reliability relates to the probability that the software will function properly and defines a cost in terms of the lost value of the computing system if it becomes inoperative because of software malfunction, as well as a cost of problem determination, analysis, and repair.

Stability refers to the costs associated with the recurring extension, modification, and enhancement of the system due to the pattern of the announcement of new functions or new versions by a vendor, and the rate at which a vendor withdraws support of earlier versions.

Parameterization involves the costs of initially defining the system, providing performance policies, tuning and adjustment, and establishing required directories and profiles.

17.3 PROBLEMS

This section describes what can go wrong in operating systems design. The intent of design is to avoid these problems.

■   *System undermanages or overmanages the machine resource.* In an intensely competitive market, a misconceived resource management level can destroy a machine by reducing its delivered application service rate to a level at which it may become more economical to purchase smaller machines, minimize sharing, and tolerate underutilization. A well-conceived resource management level can make sharing economically attractive. The requirements associated with a proper resource management level are almost overwhelming. The first requirement is a proper perception of the machine and how sophisticated the resource management algorithms should be. The second requirement is that the actual code faithfully represent the algorithms under all work-load conditions. The third requirement is that the code be of sufficient quality that the algorithms for resource management do not become too heavy for the machine because of the burden of code.

■   *The system cannot be learned.* This might be because the user interface is atrocious, because the level of knowledge required is just too high, or because the documentation is poor. The explosion in the number of modules or lines of code delivered with a system has been matched by an explosion in the number of manuals that must be read. Literally thousands of pages must be read to master a large system, and although not everyone must read everything, the mass of material is still overwhelming. Small systems reduce the amount of reading but do not necessarily improve the accuracy, completeness, or coherence of the material.

Associated with the cost of learning the system is the cost of learning to use it well. A system may encourage marginal use because the level of effort associated with really mastering the system to use it effectively is just too high. The effect of this may be to make the capacity of the system, or its responsiveness, a disappointment to the installation.

■   *The system generates too many jobs, and the jobs cannot be coherently defined because the interfaces of the system are not coherent.* The installation requires too many systems specialists to use the system. The particular functional split of interfaces maximizes the learning costs; specialists' jobs must embrace too many syntactically and semantically unique systems services and subsystems interfaces. Associated with this notion is the idea of the cost versus the value of a parameter. There is no methodology for cost-justifying a parameter so that over the life of a system the cost to a user of making a parameter decision can be shown to be less than the value of making that decision. Thus systems have too many parameters and sometimes don't provide parameters that would be important control points for an installation.

▪ *The performance of the system cannot be predicted at reasonable cost* because of the complexity of the interaction of various resource algorithms, various hardware balances, and various work-load characteristics.

▪ *The cost to extend the system is prohibitive.*

▪ *The structure of the system has become pathological* because of a change in the way work is conceived (a switch from batch to on-line, for example) and the structure itself imposes unacceptable burdens on work passing through the system. Another aspect of this is that the cost of a particular system change is too widespread in scope, involving too many modules.

17.4   THE UNIVERSALIST–PERFECTIONIST VIEW

In the opening chapters, we expressed the view that it is not clear exactly what an operating system is. There are two extreme views of this issue, one that, borrowing a phrase from C. A. R. Hoare, we will call the *Universalist– Perfectionist View,* and the other we will call the *Toolmaker's View.*

The Universalist–Perfectionist View holds that all of the software provided for a machine is part of a generalized, well-integrated, coherent structure. A proper design and implementation involve careful definition of the relationships between all of the languages of the system, and provide universal access to all resources in syntactically consistent ways regardless of how a user is accessing the system. An extreme of this view suggests a complete top-down design with the user manuals written first and the software design accomplished before the hardware is designed. The goal of hardware design is to provide a reasonable price to run the required software.

The underlying concept is to design from an image of how the system will be used, to recognize that software interfaces define the marketplace for a piece of hardware, and that it is the software that defines the system. To illustrate this view, consider an installation with an IBM 370/168 running MVS and IMS. Consider the impact of the announcement that as of a certain day the system will be changed to TSS/370 or ACP. Consider an alternate whimsical possibility that UNIVAC has produced a system with identical logical capability and identical interfaces that runs on an 1100/80. It is obvious that the hardware base change has much less impact on the user community than the software base change, and consequently hardware design should always follow and support software design.

The problem with this viewpoint is that the task cannot be accomplished.

This is true partially because of the state of the art in the software design and implementation process when large systems are involved. It also cannot be done because a sufficiently precise universal image of use is almost impossible to define in a way sufficiently complete to really constrain design. It cannot be done because of a phenomenon that we call *software lag*. Software lag refers to the common phenomenon that software design and implementation always seem to require more time than hardware design. This may be because large software products are inherently more complex. There are orders of magnitude of difference between the number of instructions in a large operating system and the number of circuits in a large processor. Consequently, hardware design tends to drive software design. What results from the extended view is a kind of fragmented universalism that, when well done, provides coherent subsystems and, when badly done, leads to the problems mentioned in the previous section.

Another problem with the Universalist–Perfectionist View is that it is insensitive to rates of change. The problem lies in the fact that what constitutes a view of a general-purpose system at the time of a design may not be sufficient during the lifetime of the system. A prime example is the introduction of on-line transaction processing into a general-purpose system. A very rich and elaborate system that appears to be general-purpose may find itself badly structured at the midpoint of its life because of trends in the way systems are used.

17.5   THE TOOLMAKER'S VIEW

The *Toolmaker's View* is that an operating system supplies a set of mechanisms that provide control over a set of abstract resources. The operating system is a minimum basic subset of building blocks and a minimum extension of the machine. An operating system is a set of mechanisms that do not impose policy and that do not impose structure. The essential idea is that the building of user-level functions can be more effective by using building blocks than by trying to specialize and parameterize general-purpose systems. Rather than have systems programmers parameterize and specialize database management function into some generalized system, use the building blocks to build as many different kinds of systems as are desired in the installation. The entire package may be more reliable because each building block is a well-defined mechanism.

The essential problem with this approach is that the building blocks may not be well chosen, and the burden of structuring a system can be heavy for both builder and system because of inefficient layering techniques.

The presence of such divergent viewpoints reflects observations regarding the nature of use and rates of change in usage and hardware economics. The hope of current workers is that some reasonable balance between providing high function and flexible underlying structures can be achieved.

17.6 STRUCTURAL CONCEPTS

There is another dimension to how one views operating systems that is essentially structural. The opening section of this chapter alluded to a set of layers of incremental functions providing interfaces intended to reduce user cost by transferring functions from person to machine. This view is a horizontal view of structure. There is also a vertical view suggesting that, for any machine system, a set of operating systems should be provided so that a user may select structures optimum for time-sharing, database, real-time, etc.

In a market in which software components are purchased, it seems clear that each of the vertical operating systems would have an individual price. It is less clear what kind of pricing would be done for the horizontal structure. It is possible to price very granularly so that each level is individually priced. Alternatively, it is possible to include software systems through a monitor level with the basic price of the system and charge for software above that level. If this is done, it is still possible to provide mechanisms for the user to suppress the levels he or she does not find economical to use.

A very provocative set of thoughts must immediately occur to a systems programmer thinking about horizontal and vertical structures. A notion of intersection begins to form. How does one combine ideas of vertical and horizontal offerings in a meaningful way? It is an issue at the edge of the art. What is implied by the issue is that there is both an OEM (Original Equipment Manufacturer) and a packaged function market in the operating systems marketplace. It is desirable to approach these markets in the way hardware producers approach the markets for OEM and integrated systems, that is, by offering basic units to OEMs and by using the same basic units to build more integrated offerings for systems markets. Such notions relate to ideas of a family of operating systems built out of sets of fundamental structures.

There is a dimension to the problem of doing this for software that does not exist in hardware. This addresses a structural issue and a module relationship issue. Take, for example, the idea (once more and for the final time) of there being a database-level GET, a record-level GET, and READ and DEVICE levels associated with I/O support. It is undesirable in the time-sharing version of the system to include the database-level GET as a resident function of the kernel. If it is to be used at all, it will be used in a subsystem context. However, in the database version of the system, this function should not only be in the basic resident kernel but should be in a form that provides the most efficient operation, integrated with all lower levels. Therefore the design issue is presented. Is it possible to define and implement a set of functions in various functional modules that can be structurally reorganized and recombined to support the idea that both OEM and various packaged systems can be built with the same set of modules? Associated with this question is an issue of how operating systems built in this way might be brought to the market. The answer lies in the fact that documentation encapsulates software in the same way that software encapsulates hardware. Therefore, regardless of the fact that different offerings are built from a common set of modules, each version must be supported by a unique set of publications containing what is necessary for the user of that, and only that, version.

The user running a time-sharing version on machine A and a database version on machine B will be amazed to discover that should he or she want A and B to interconnect in the context of a distributed system, the interconnection can be accomplished by adding an identical module to essentially identical systems.

All of this is somewhat whimsical because it is not in the current state of the art, nor is it clear that it ever will be. However, it is clear that some refined notions of building blocks, systems integration, and systems presentation are beginning to emerge and are certainly in order. Many people feel that issues of proper structure are philosophical abstractions until they wish to market a system and discover that the marketplace application of function and the designers' appreciation of structure are mismatched.

17.7 THE COMPATIBILITY-INNOVATION ISSUE

There are those who feel that it is time for all major vendors to develop major new operating systems because the old ones are structurally obsolete and the interfaces are archaic. There is a desire for maximum innovation partially supported by the view that the building of a new system is essentially less complex and burdensome a process than is a process of trying to restructure older ones. There are those who feel that it is impossible to undertake new operating systems (especially large ones) because there has been no real advancement in design and implementation methodology sufficient to guarantee such an effort would meet its goals. However, the major thrust against new systems is that regardless of whether or not current structures are optimal or economical, they are known and they support a population of programs whose net economic worth is sometimes estimated to be exceeded only by the Gross National Product.

The difficulty arises from the fact that both viewpoints are partially right (and, in consequence, partially wrong). There is a dollar value for compatibility that a user may assess and balance against innovation. While it is true that there are many programs that must have old interfaces preserved for them, it is also true that there are more programs not yet written, and that users show a willingness to learn and use new systems (if they are attractive) for the support of new work.

Certain design questions arise from this balance between a need to preserve old interfaces and a desire to find improved interfaces and improved structures.

■   What degrees of freedom are allowed behind a set of preserved interfaces if restructuring looks desirable?

■   Can compatibility be precisely calibrated and priced so that various compatibility packages can be offered with a new system to link it to the old? Compatibility package approaches are to provide macro interfaces that look like the old package, run the old package as a subsystem in the context of a new system, and provide degrees of compatibility for a price.

■   Is it sufficient merely to provide protocols for new systems to talk to old systems? Enhanced application functions can be designed for the new system but still be able to communicate with functions and data running on the old system.

It is inconceivable to abandon large populations of users who are running on current systems. It is also inconceivable that a hundred years from now there will be populations of DOS users. Between now and then something is going to happen. The balance between the economics of continuance and compatibility versus the economics of innovation and change is going to tilt decisively.

17.8   DISTRIBUTED SYSTEMS

The idea of distributed systems is rather vague and ill defined at this moment. There is some notion that a system running at one place should be able to talk to a system running someplace else more efficiently than it is possible to do now. There is an abundance of literature emerging in this area. There is concern about how incompatible operating systems may talk to one another.

We have taken the view that a distributed system is not a special class of system but rather a new set of configuration options. However, there is a possibility that sufficient changes in the context of machine design and use will occur so that a truly new class of system will emerge. There are some fascinating operating system design issues that emerge in the presence of a system that can be built with the processor-to-processor interaction rate of a tightly coupled multiprocessor but in which each processor is capable of having its own private operating system in a private local memory.

This section introduces the nature of these design issues. Consider the system shown in Fig. 17.3. Each station potentially consists of a computational processor, a memory, an interconnect device, and a local control processor. Any station may consist of only a memory, and the entire address space of the system is available to any processor. It is possible to add processors of heterogeneous architecture to the system.

The following operating systems questions need to be explored in such a system.

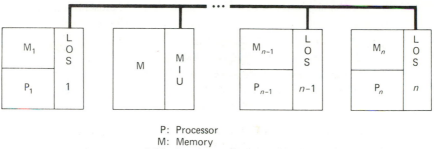

P: Processor
M: Memory
LOS: Local operating system
MIU: Memory interface unit

Fig. 17.3 Hypothetical distributed system.

- What are the global functions of the operating system?
- What are the local functions?
- Is it possible to decompose global functions into local form?
- Is it desirable to provide global and local forms for the same function?
- Does one decompose the system vertically or horizontally?

One notion of design, which we call the *multiprocessor-biased design,* is to nominate a set of specialized functional processors to perform various vertical cuts of the operating system; for example, a system scheduler, a file manager, a START processor, a SEND/RECEIVE processor, or a memory manager processor. Thus each computational station requests the services of these processors as needed. Instead of all processors executing protected shared code as in classical multiprocessor design, services would come from a set of specialized stations. This ties the system together very tightly. For example, a process wishing to start a cooperating process on another processor would locate an eligible processor and assign the process to it or enqueue the request until a processor notifies the system of its availability. In this design, the role of the local control processor would be rather small, constraining itself to such things as local task switching for the processes already assigned to a processor.

The idea of a distributed system, however, suggests a possibly different operating system view. A counterdesign, which we call a *distributed-biased design,* would maximize the role of the local operating system and either eliminate the functionally specialized processors or combine them into very high-level functions. Thus a system scheduler would be admissible but only as an application running at a normal computational station.

Consider the design of a START in such a system. The local processor executes a START causing parameters to be passed to its local control processor.

The local processor may then proceed with its work or be task-switched by the local control processor (which has a private list of processes running at this station). The local control processor broadcasts a request for all processors of a certain type and status. This broadcast provides the ability to collect a preferred processing environment. For example, the requesting processor may indicate that it wishes to start a process on a processor with no multiprogramming. The processors receive the broadcast and do an analysis of their status and either reject the request or send back a code indicating their willingness to undertake the new work. The requesting processor then makes a selection, notifies all but one processor that they are not going to get the work, and requests one processor to start a process in accordance with parameters it receives. While the entire selection process is going on, the local processors are not disturbed in any way. Only the local control processors are involved.

The interesting operating system problem is to determine whether harmoniously synchronized cooperative algorithms can be devised so that all the functions of an operating system can be decomposed into replicated cooperative kernels. The goal of this is to provide support for distributed systems that are bus-interconnected at very high speeds, but allow considerable choice and flexibility in how processors and, consequently, processes are going to relate to each other. Specific issues relate to whether memory management is really a global or local function, and what kinds of partitions should be built around subsets of processors that will cooperate more closely than with other subsets.

Of course, there is always the issue of what the operating system really is. For example, it is possible to provide a complete system of all packaged functions at each station, in effect building a hardware-supported virtual machine. On the other hand, the idea that we find most useful is to provide the kernel functions in each local operating system, such as send/receive, start/stop, lock/unlock, and dispatch, but to allow higher levels to reside in specialized processors. Thus each processor uses primitives like SEND to communicate with the file manager or the global systems scheduler.

Problems of design at this level involve entirely new notions of machine organization that are emerging and that make the study of the structure and functions of operating systems vital for the future.

17.9 CONCLUSION

It is hard to conclude when we feel that we are so much at the beginning. There is an atmosphere today recalling that of the mid-1950s. Then there was a huge collection of ideas waiting to happen, and these ideas fueled the activities of the 1960s and 1970s.

Enormous progress has been made. By and large, when it is important to achieve good utilization on a piece of expensive equipment, we know how to do it (whether or not we like the details of doing it). When it is important to provide responsiveness, we know how to do it (whether or not we can do it with equal success in all systems). We have learned to construct massive systems, with millions of lines of code, and make them serviceable—and valuable. Regardless of what purists and grouchy people may say, the systems constructed and delivered in the 1960s and 1970s added enormously to the net value of computing, and to the growth of computing in the world.

Now the industry is told it must rethink some assumptions, improve interfaces, contend with new hardware organizations, and formalize some notions about what it has been doing. We are in a period of reassessment preliminary to a great leap forward. As far as we have come, most of the work is yet to be done.

TERMINOLOGY

compatibility–innovation issue

completion of a machine by
   programming

distributed systems

distributed-biased design

local control processor

local processor

machine consumption

microcode

multiprocessor-biased design

OEM

overmanage a machine

software knee

software lag

Toolmaker's View

top-down design

undermanage a machine

Universalist–Perfectionist View

EXERCISES

Section 17.1

17.1 The function of software is to maximize the net economic value of computing machinery to users. Comment on this.

17.2 Why do you suppose purchased instructions generally cost less than developed instructions?

Section 17.2

17.3 Comment on each of the following costs associated with using an operating system.

   a) machine consumption
   b) learning
   c) organizational impact
   d) reliability

e) stability

f) parameterization

17.4 Discuss each of the following organizational impact levels associated with using an operating system.

a) the tool level

b) the specialist level

c) the organizational level

d) the enterprise level

Section 17.3

17.5 What problems are associated with undermanaging the machine resource? What problems are caused by overmanaging the machine resource?

17.6 A system may encourage marginal use because the level of effort associated with really mastering the system to use it effectively is just too high. Give several reasons why this is true.

Section 17.4

17.7 What is the Universalist–Perfectionist View?

17.8 Software lag refers to the common phenomenon that software design and implementation always seem to require more time than hardware design. Why, do you suppose, is this true?

Section 17.5

17.9 In the Toolmaker's View, the operating system is a minimum basic subset of building blocks and a minimum extension of the machine. The essential idea is that the building of user-level functions can be more effective by using building blocks than by trying to specialize and parameterize general-purpose systems. What is the main problem with this approach?

Section 17.6

17.10 There are both an OEM and a packaged function market in the operating systems marketplace. How should this affect a vendor's strategy for operating systems design?

17.11 Documentation encapsulates software in the same way that software encapsulates hardware. Explain.

Section 17.7

17.12 Some designers feel that the building of a new system is essentially less complex and burdensome a process than is the process of trying to restructure older ones. Comment on this.

Section 17.8

17.13 List several operating systems design issues that need to be explored in distributed systems.

Bibliography

Bibliography

Abernathy, D.H., et al., "Survey of Design Goals for Operating Systems," *OpSys Review,* Association for Computing Machinery, Vol. 7, No. 2, April 1973; Vol. 7, No. 3, July 1973; Vol. 8, No. 1, January 1974.

Agoston, M.K., "An Operating System for the Intel MDS System," *SIGMini Newsletter,* Vol. 3, No. 2, April 1977.

Aho, A.V.; P.J. Denning; and J.D. Ullman, "Principles of Optimal Page Replacement," *JACM,* Vol. 18, No. 1, 1971, pp. 80–93.

Anderson, H.A.; M. Reiser; and G.L. Galati, "Tuning a Virtual Storage System," *IBM Systems Journal,* Vol. 14, No. 3, 1975, pp. 246–263.

Andrews, G.R., and J.R. McGraw, "Language Features for Process Interaction," *OpSys Review,* Vol. 11, No. 2, April 1977, pp. 114–127.

Aron, J.D., "Real-time Systems in Perspective," *IBM Systems Journal,* Vol. 6, No. 1, 1967, p. 49.

Attanasio, C.R.; P.W. Markstein; and R.J. Phillips, "Penetrating an Operating System: A Study of VM/370 Integrity," *IBM Systems Journal,* Vol. 15, No. 1, 1976, pp. 102–116.

Auerbach Corporation, *Rethinking Computer Operations:* Part I: Where Is Operations Going? Part II: Automated Scheduling; Part III: On-Line Scheduling by Computer, *Auerbach Data Processing Manual,* 1974.

Auslander, M.A., and J.F. Jaffe, "Influences of Dynamic Address Translation on Operating System Technology," *IBM Systems Journal,* Vol. 12, No. 4, 1973, pp. 368–381.

Baily, J.H., et al., "The Job Entry Subsystem of OS/VS1," *IBM Systems Journal,* Vol. 13, No. 3, 1974, pp. 253–269.

Belady, L.A., "A Study of Replacement Algorithms for a Virtual Storage Computer," *IBM Systems Journal,* Vol. 5, No. 2, 1966, pp. 78–101.

Bender, G., et al., "DOS/360 and TOS/360," *IBM Systems Journal,* Vol. 6, No. 1, 1967, pp. 2–21.

Benoussan, A.; C.T. Clinger; and R.C. Daley, "Multics Virtual Memory," Proceedings of Second Symposium on Operating Systems Principles, *ACM,* October 1969, pp. 30–42.

Bernstein, A.J., and T. Sharpe, "Policy Driven Scheduler for a Time-sharing System," *CACM,* Vol. 14, No. 1, February 1971, pp. 74–78.

Birch, J.P., "Architecture and Design of DOS/VD," *IBM Systems Journal,* Vol. 12, No. 4, 1973, pp. 401–411.

Bobrow, D.G., et al., "TENEX, A Paged Time-sharing System for PDP-10," *CACM,* Vol. 15, No. 3, March 1972, pp. 135–143.

Brawn, B., and F. Gustavson, "Program Behavior in a Paging Environment," AFIPS Conference Proceedings, *FJCC,* Vol. 33, 1968, pp. 1019–1032.

Brinch Hansen, P., "Concurrent Programming Concepts," *Computing Surveys,* Vol. 5, No. 4, December 1973, pp. 223–244.

Brinch Hansen, P., "Structured Multiprogramming," *CACM,* Vol. 15, No. 7, July 1972, pp. 574–578.

Brinch Hansen, P., "The Nucleus of a Multiprogramming System," *CACM,* Vol. 13, No. 4, April 1970, pp. 238–241.

Brinch Hansen, P., *Operating Systems Principles,* Englewood Cliffs, N.J.: Prentice-Hall, 1973.

Brinch Hansen, P., "Short-term Scheduling in Multiprogramming Systems," Proceedings of Third Symposium on Operating Systems Principles, *OpSys Review,* Vol. 6, Nos. 1 and 2, June 1972.

Brown, J.C., et al., "Interaction of Multiprogramming Job Scheduling and CPU Scheduling," AFIPS Proceedings, *FJCC,* 1972, pp. 13–21.

Buzen, J., and U. Gagliard, "Introduction to Virtual Machines," *Honeywell Computer Journal,* Vol. 7, No. 4, 1973.

Casey, L., and N. Shelnes, "A Domain Structure for Distributed Computer Systems," Proceedings of Sixth Symposium on Operating Systems Principles, *OpSys Review,* Vol. 11, No. 5, November 1977.

Coffman, E.G., Jr., and L. Kleinrock, "Computer Scheduling Methods and Their Countermeasures," Proceedings AFIPS, *SJCC,* Vol. 32, 1968, pp. 11–22.

Coffman, E.G., Jr., M.J. Elphick, and A. Shoshani, "System Deadlocks," *Computing Surveys,* Vol. 3, No. 2, June 1971, pp. 67–78.

Coffman, E.G., Jr., "Analysis of Drum Input/Output Queue under Scheduled Operation in a Paged Computer System," *JACM,* Vol. 16, No. 1, January 1969, pp. 73–90.

Cohen, E., et al., "Protection in the Hydra Operating System," Proceedings of Fifth Symposium on Operating Systems Principles, *CACM,* November 1975.

Cohen, E., et al., *Hydra—Basic Kernel Reference Manual,* Department of Computer Science, Carnegie–Mellon University, November 1976.

Comeau, L., "Study of Effect of User Program Optimization in a Paging System," Proceedings of First Symposium on Operating Systems Principles, *CACM*, October 1967.

Courtois, P.J., "Decomposability, Instability, and Saturation in a Multiprogramming System," *CACM*, Vol. 18, No. 7, July 1975.

Cutler, D.N., et al., "The Nucleus of a Real-time Operating System," *ACM Conference Proceedings*, 1976, pp. 241–246.

Daley, R.C., and J.B. Dennis, "Virtual Memory Processes and Sharing in Multics," *CACM*, Vol. 11, No. 5, May 1968, pp. 306–312.

Denning, P.J., "Working Set Model for Program Behavior," *CACM*, Vol. 11, No. 5, 1968.

Denning, P.J., "Fault Tolerant Operating Systems," *Computing Surveys*, Vol. 8, No. 4, December 1976. pp. 359–390.

Denning, P.J., "Virtual Memory," *Computing Surveys*, Vol. 2, No. 3, September 1970, pp. 153–189.

Denning, P.J., "Thrashing: Its Causes and Prevention," Proceedings AFIPS, *FJCC*, Vol. 33, 1968, pp. 915–922.

Denning, P.J., "Third-generation Computer Systems," *Computing Surveys*, Vol. 3, No. 4, December 1971, pp. 175–216.

Denning, P.J., "A Note on Paging Drum Efficiency," *Computing Surveys*, Vol. 4, No. 1, March 1972, pp. 1–5.

Denning, P.J., "Effects of Scheduling on File Memory Operations," Proceedings AFIPS, 1967, *SJCC*, Vol. 30, pp. 9–21.

Dennis, J.B., and E.C. VanHorn, "Programming Semantics for Multiprogrammed Computations," *CACM*, Vol. 9, No. 3, March 1966, pp. 143–155.

Dijkstra, E.W., "The Structure of T.H.E. Multiprogramming System," *CACM*, Vol. 11, No. 5, May 1968, pp. 341–346.

Dodd, G.G., "Elements of Data Management Systems," *Computing Surveys*, Vol. 1, No. 2, June 1969, pp. 117–132.

Doherty, W.J., "Scheduling TSS/360 for Responsiveness," Proceedings AFIPS, *FJCC*, 1970, pp. 97–111.

Ekanadham, K., and A.J. Bernstein, "Some New Transitions in Hierarchical-level Structures," *OpSys Review*, Vol. 12, No. 4, October 1978.

Fabry, R.S., "Capability-based Addressing," *CACM*, Vol. 17, No. 7, July 1974, pp. 403–412.

Feiretag, R.J., and E.I. Organick, "Multics Input/Output System," Proceedings of Third Symposium on Operating Systems Principles, *OpSys Review*, Vol. 6, Nos. 1 and 2, June 1972.

Fernandez, M., and H. Hartson, "Comparative Study of Environments for Database System Implementation," Proceedings Symposium on Small Systems, *SIGMini Newsletter*, Vol. 4, No. 4, August 1978.

Flink, C.W., II, "EASY—An Operating System for QM-1," *SIGMicro Newsletter*, Vol. 8, No. 3, September 1977.

Fogel, M.H., "The VMOS Paging Algorithm," *OpSys Review*, Vol. 8, No. 1, January 1974.

Foster, C.C., "An Unclever Time-sharing System," *Computing Surveys*, Vol. 3, No. 1, March 1971, pp. 21–48.

Fry, J.P., and E.H. Sibly, "Evaluation of Database Management Systems," *Computing Surveys*, Vol. 8, No. 1, March 1976, pp. 7–42.

Gaines, R.S., "Control of Processes in Operating Systems: The Boss-slave Relation," Proceedings of Fifth Symposium on Operating Systems Principles, 1975.

Gaines, R.S., and N.Z. Shapiro, "Some Security Principles and Their Application to Computer Security," *OpSys Review*, Vol. 12, No. 3, July 1978.

Gonzalez, M.J., Jr., "Deterministic Processor Scheduling," *Computing Surveys*, Vol. 9, No. 3, September 1977, pp. 173–204.

Gray, J., "Control Structure of an Operating System," *IBM Research*, RC–3949, July 1972.

Gray, T.E., "Job Control in a Network Computing Environment," *Compcon*, Vol. 76, Spring, p. 146.

Greif, I., *Semantics of Communication Parallel Processes*, M.I.T., Project MAC, MAC TR–154, September 1975.

Habermann, A.N., "Synchronization of Communicating Processes," *CACM*, Vol. 15, No. 3, March 1972, pp. 171–176.

Habermann, A.N., et al., "Modularization and Hierarchy in a Family of Operating Systems," *CACM*, Vol. 19, No. 5, May 1976, pp. 266–272.

Habermann, A.N., "Prevention of System Deadlock," *CACM*, Vol. 12, No. 7, July 1969, pp. 373–377.

Handzel, G.; D.L. Parnas; and H. Wurges, *Design and Specification of the Minimal Subset of an Operating System*, Software Systems Engineering, 1976, pp. 23–38.

Harrison, M.A., et al., "Protection in Operating Systems," *CACM*, Vol. 19, No. 8, p. 461.

Hatfield, D.J., and J. Gerald, "Program Restructuring for Virtual Memory," *IBM Systems Journal*, Vol. 10, No. 3, 1971, pp. 168–192.

Havender, J.W., "Avoiding Deadlock in Multitasking Systems," *IBM Systems Journal*, Vol. 7, No. 7, 1969, pp. 74–84.

Heistand, R.E., *ACP System Concepts and Facilities*, IBM Corporation, GH20–1473.

Heistand, R.E., "Executive System Implemented as a Finite State Automation," *CACM*, Vol. 7, No. 11, November 1966, p. 669.

Hellerman, H., "Some Principles of Time-sharing Scheduler Strategies," *IBM Systems Journal*, Vol. 8, No. 2, 1969, pp. 94–117.

Hoare, C.A.R., "Montiors: An Operating System Structuring Concept," *CACM*, Vol. 17, No. 10, 1974, pp. 549–557.

Holt, R.C., "Some Deadlock Properties of Computer Systems," *Computing Surveys*, Vol. 4, No. 3, September 1972, pp. 179–196.

Huxtable, D.H.R., and M.T. Warnick, *Dynamic Supervisors—Their Design and Construction*, Proceedings of First Symposium on Operating Systems Principles, *ACM*, 1968.

IBM Corporation, *IBM Virtual Machine Facility/370: Introduction*, IBM Corporation, GC20–1800.

IBM Corporation, *IBM/System/360 OS: Job Control Language*, IBM Corporation, C28–6539.

Ivie, E.J., "The Programmers Workbench: A Machine for Software Development," *CACM*, October 1977, Vol. 20, No. 10, p. 746.

Jensen, E.D., and E. Boebert, "Partitioning and Assignment of Distributed Processing Software," Compcon, 1976, p. 348.

Kleinrock, L. "A Continuum of Time-sharing Scheduling Algorithms," Proceedings AFIPS, *SJCC*, 1970, Vol. 36.

Lamport, L., "Concurrent Reading and Writing," *CACM*, Vol. 20, No. 11, November 1977, p. 806.

Lampson, B.W., and H.E. Sturgis, "Reflections on an Operating Systems Design," *CACM*, Vol. 19, No. 5, May 1976, p. 251.

Lans, M.G., "The Subsystem Approach to Enhancing Small Processor Operating Systems," Proceedings of First Symposium on Small Systems, *SIGMini Newsletter*, Vol. 4, No. 4, August 1978.

Lausen, S., "A Large Semaphore-based Operating System," *CACM*, Vol. 18, No. 7, July 1975, pp. 377–389.

Liposvski, G.J., "On Virtual Memories and Micronetworks," Proceedings of Fourth Annual Symposium on Computer Architecture, *ACM*, 1977.

Liskov, B.H., "The Design of the Venus Operating System," *CACM*, Vol. 15, No. 3, March 1972, pp. 144–156.

Lister, A.M., and P.J. Sayer, "Hierarchical Monitors," *Software Practice and Experience*, Vol. 7, No. 5, September 1977, pp. 613–623.

Lister, A.M., and K.J. Maynard, "An Implementation of Monitors," *Software Practice and Experience*, Vol. 6, No. 3, 1976, pp. 377–385.

Lomet, D.B., *Process Structuring, Synchronization and Recovery Using Atomic Actions*, IBM Research, RC6287, November 1976.

Liu, C.L. and J.W. Layland, "Scheduling Algorithms for Multiprogramming in a Hard, Real-time Environment," *JACM*, Vol. 20, No. 1, January 1973, pp. 46–61.

Lynch, H.W., and J.B. Page, "OS/VS2 Release Two Systems Resources Manager," *IBM Systems Journal*, Vol. 13, No. 4, 1974, pp. 274–291.

MacEwen, G.H., *Hierarchic Structure in Operating Systems Software Systems Engineering*, Chameleon Press, 1976, pp. 125–150.

McGee, W.C., "The Information Management System IMS/VS," *IBM Systems Journal*, Vol. 16, No. 2, 1977, pp. 84–168.

Margolin, B.H.; R.P. Parmalee; and M. Schatzoff, "Analysis of Free-storage Algorithms," *IBM Systems Journal*, Vol. 10, No. 4, pp. 283–304.

Mealy, G.H., *System Design Cycle,* Proceedings of Second Symposium on Operating Systems Principles, *CACM,* 1969.

Mealy, G.H., and Clark Witt, "Functional Structure of OS/360," *IBM Systems Journal,* Vol. 5, No. 1, 1966, pp. 3–61.

Melendez, K., et al., *Evaluation of UNIX Time-sharing System,* Los Alamos Scientific Laboratory, University of California, LA–6755–MS, April 1977.

Milles, D.L., *Basic Operating System for the Distributed Computer Network,* Department of Computer Science, University of Maryland, TR–416, AD AO21989, October 1975.

Mohan, G., "Survey of Recent Operating System Research," *OpSys Review,* Vol. 12, No. 1, January 1978.

Morrison, J.E., "User Program Performance in Virtual Storage Systems," *IBM Systems Journal,* Vol. 12, No. 3, 1973, pp. 216–237.

Meuller, J.H., "Aspects of Gemini Real-time Operating System," *IBM Systems Journal,* Vol. 6, No. 3, 1967, pp. 150–162.

Needham, R.M., and D.F. Hartley, "Theory and Practice in Operating System Design," Proceedings of Second Symposium on Operating Systems Principles, *CACM,* 1969.

Nielsen, N.R., "Allocation of Computer Resources—Is Pricing the Answer?" *CACM,* Vol. 13, No. 8, August 1970, pp. 467–474.

Noble, S., "Integrated Programming and Operating System—Part I: Systems Considerations and the Monitor," *IBM Systems Journal,* Vol. 2, 1963, p. 153.

Parmelee, R.P., and T.I. Peterson, "Virtual Storage and Virtual Machine Concepts," *IBM Systems Journal,* Vol. 11, No. 2, 1972, pp. 99–130.

Parnas, D.L., "On a Buzzword: Hierarchical Structure," Proceedings IFIP Congress 1974, Stockholm, August 1974, pp. 336–339.

Parnas, D.L., and D.P. Siewiorek, "Use of Concept of Transparency in the Design of Hierarchically Structured Systems," *CACM,* Vol. 18, No. 5, May 1975, pp. 401–408.

Parnas, D.L. "On the Criteria to Be Used in Decomposing Systems into Modules," *CACM,* Vol. 15, No. 12, December 1972, pp. 1053–1058.

Pettersen, O., *Synchronization of Concurrent Processes,* Computer Science Department, Stanford University, STAN–CS–75–502, AD A016808, July 1975.

Presser, L., and J.R. White, "Linkers and Loaders," *ACM Computing Surveys,* Vol. 4, No. 3, September 1972, pp. 149–169.

Prieve, B.P., and R.S. Fabry, "VMIN—An Optimal Variable-space Page Replacement Algorithm," *CACM,* Vol. 19, No. 5, 1976, p. 295.

Randell, B., and C.J. Kuehner, *Dynamic Storage Allocation Systems,* First ACM Symposium on Operating Systems Principles, October 1967.

Randell, B., and C.J. Kuehner, "Dynamic Storage Allocation Systems," *CACM,* Vol. 11, No. 5, May 1968, pp. 297–306.

Ritchie, D.M., and K. Thompson, "The UNIX Time-sharing System," *CACM,* Vol. 17, No. 7, 1974, pp. 365–375.

Rosin, R.F., "Supervisory and Monitor Systems," *Computing Surveys,* Vol. 1, No. 1, March 1969.

Ruschitzka, M. and R.S. Fabry, "A Unifying Approach to Scheduling," *CACM,* Vol. 20, No. 7, 1977, p. 469.

Ryder, K.D., "Optimizing Program Placement in Virtual Systems," *IBM Systems Journal,* Vol. 13, No. 4, 1974, pp. 292–306.

Saltzer, J.H., "Research Problems of Decentralized Systems with Largely Autonomous Nodes," *Operating Systems Review,* Vol. 12, No. 1, January 1978.

Schroeder, M.D.; D. Clark; and J. Saltzer, "Multics Kernel Design Project," Proceedings of Sixth Annual Symposium on Operating Systems Principles, *Operating Systems Review,* Vol. 11, No. 5, November 1977.

Schroeder, M.D., and J.H. Saltzer, "A Hardware Architecture for Implementing Protection Rings," *CACM,* Vol. 15, No. 3, March 1972, pp. 157–170.

Scherr, A.L., "OS/VS2–2 Concepts and Philosophies," *IBM Systems Journal,* Vol. 12, No. 4, 1973, pp. 382–400.

Scherr, A., and D. Larkin, "Time-sharing for OS," *FJCC* Conference 1970, pp. 113–117.

Senko, M. E., "Data Structures and Data Accessing in Database Systems," *IBM Systems Journal,* Vol. 16, No. 3, 1977, pp. 208–257.

Shaw, A., et al., "Multiprogramming Nucleus with Dynamic Resource Facilities," *Software Practice and Experience,* Vol. 5, 1975, pp. 245–267.

Shaw, A., *Logical Design of Operating Systems,* Englewood Cliffs, N.J.: Prentice-Hall, 1974.

Smith, A.J., "Bibliography on Paging and Related Topics," *OpSys Review,* Vol. 12, No. 4, October 1978.

Sorenson, P.G., "Interprocess Communications in Real-time Systems," Fourth Symposium on Operating Systems Principles, *OpSys Review,* Vol. 7, No. 4, October 1973.

Spier, M.J., and E.I. Organick, "The Multics Interprocess Communication Facility," Proceedings of Second Symposium on Operating Systems Principles, *ACM,* 1969, p. 83.

Spier, M.J., "A Critical Look at the State of Our Science," *OpSys Review,* Vol. 8, No. 2, April 1974.

Spier, M.J.; T.N. Hastings; and D.N. Cutler, "A Storage Mapping Technique for the Implementation of Protective Domains," *Software Practice and Experience,* Vol. 4, 1974, pp. 215–230.

Wettstein, H., "Implementation of Synchronizing Operations in Various Environments," *Software Practice and Experience,* Vol. 7, 1977, pp. 115–126.

Wood, D., "An Example in Synchronization of Cooperating Processes: Theory and Practice," *OpSys Review,* Vol. 7, No. 3, July 1973.

Wulf, W.A., et al., "Hydra: The Kernel of a Multiprocessor Operating System," *CACM,* Vol. 17, No. 6, 1974, pp. 337–345.

Index

Index

Abort a job, 88
Absentee job, 238
Abstract notion of system, 107
Access control list in Multics, 259, 261
Access method, 144
Access right, 48
Accessibility, 64
ACP, 91–94, 342
Activation record, 124, 135, 165, 169, 271
Activation time, 108, 109
Adaptive system, 250
Address error, 9
Address field of an instruction, 7
Address mapping, 13
Address offset, 191
Address space, 190
Address translation mechanism, 296
Addressing mechanism, 73
Addressing pattern of a program, 298
Addressing scheme, 1, 21
Addressing structure, 6
Advanced batch multiprogramming, 81, 87
Advanced memory manager, 164
Advanced multiprogramming system, 229
Aging, 241
Airlines Control Program, 65, 91
ALGOL, 49

Alias, 259
ALLOCATE, 48, 150, 205, 216
Allocating storage, 109, 179
Allocation of data sets, 34, 109
Allocation of devices, 54, 109
Allocation in HYDRA, 263
Allocation mechanism, 260
Allocation time, 174
Allocators, 115
Analog/digital converters, 65
APG, 250, 324
APL, 21, 22, 42, 47, 49
Apparent instruction set, 16
Applications package, 25, 338
Applications programmer, 2
Archiving, 257
Assembler, 40, 113
Assembler library, 113
Assembly language, 2, 51
ASSIGN, 85
ASSOCIATE, 48
Associative array, 296–298
Asynchronism, 82
Asynchronous channels, 62
ATTACH, 44, 153, 154
Attended operation, 48
Authorities in Multics, 261

Authorization list, 260
Autocoder, 74
Automatic Priority Grouping, 250, 324
Auxiliary storage manager, 300

Backend processor, 66
Background, 71, 246
Backing store, 126
BACKSPACE, 141
"Bare" machine, 331
Base register, 7, 288, 294
BASIC, 22, 43, 53, 215
Basic batch multiprogramming, 81
Basic file system, 164
Basic file system in Multics, 258
Basic multiprogramming systems, 229
BASIC subsystem in Multics, 43, 45
Batch, 48, 238, 316
Batch access, 43
Batch job, 34, 215, 317
Batch multiprogramming, 89
Batch multiprogramming mix, 52
Batch operating systems, 74
Batch systems, 63, 73, 194, 197
BDAM, 144
Best-fit, 194, 288
Bind a program to another program, 115
Bind a program to devices, 115
Bind a program to machine locations, 115,
    189
Binding, 112, 293
Binding loader, 74
Binding time, 121
Binding times, 285
Black box, 6
Block handling, 140
Block a process, 169, 272, 277, 278
Blocking, 87, 174
Block-level management, 130, 141
Block size 74, 173
BMEWS (Ballistic Missile Early Warning
    System), 66
Bottlenecking, 84
Branch, 258
Brinch Hansen, 203, 204
BSAM, 144

BTAM, 144
Buffer, 6, 41, 119, 225, 274
Buffer contents semaphore, 275, 276
Buffer control, 140
Buffer control routines, 87
Buffer pooling, 145
Buffer space semaphore, 275
Buffering, 144, 145, 174, 247
Buffering levels, 49
Burroughs B1700, 20
Burroughs B5500, 308
Burroughs' Master Control Program
    (MCP), 180

Cache hit probability, 19
Cache memory, 17, 299
CALL, 34, 153, 205, 215, 261–263
Capabilities, 260, 264, 310
Capability list, 260
Capability list in HYDRA, 262
Capability-based systems, 263
Card reader, 44
Catalog, 173, 221, 257
Cataloged procedures, 46
Cataloged segments, 162
Cataloging of on-line data sets, 88
CDC 6600, 6, 18
Central Processing Unit, 6
CHAIN, 75
Chained read of pages, 306
Changed priority of a job, 88
Channel, 1, 140, 172, 221
Channel allocation algorithm, 247
Channel availability, 173
Channel command word, 176
Channel interrupt, 9, 10
Channel manager, 252
Channel programs, 176
Channel queues, 177
Channel relocatable, 302
Channel status, 179
CHECK, 138, 148, 270, 280, 281
CICS, 92
Clock, 71, 170
Clock-driven software dispatcher, 148
Clock interrupt, 46

Clock manipulation instructions, 147
CLOSE, 74
Closed execution, 86
CMS, 48, 332
COBOL, 2, 21, 49, 74, 202
Code generation, 2
Code optimization, 2
COGO, 89
Collecting loader, 74, 191
Combination time, 108
Combine, 48
Combine time, 114
COMBINE, 188
Combined linkage segment in Multics, 260
Combiner control language, 109
Command language, 3, 33, 47, 153, 188
Command language interpreter, 174
Communication protocol, 52
Communications controller, 97
Communications devices, 142
Compare and swap instruction, 125
Compatibility-innovation issue, 345
Compilation target, 40
Compilation time, 108
Compile, 188
Compile/load/go, 44, 75
Compile-time, 109
Compiler, 1, 39, 108
Computational public utility, 48
Computational slave device, 66
Computing nodes, 94
COMTRAN, 202
Concurrent PASCAL, 273
Concurrent programming, 41, 273
Condition code, 165
Configurability, 98
Console typewriter, 44
Consolidated work-load environment, 62, 98
Consumer, 275, 277, 278
Contention index in SRM, 323
Contiguity of a function, 120
Contiguity problem, 301
Contiguous storage allocation, 289
Continuous process mechanism, 229
Control application, 65

Control block, 72
Control language, 42, 50, 87, 188
Control language syntax, 42
Control memory, 16
Control point, 110
Control processors, 23
Control state, 13, 40, 41, 71, 132, 135, 146, 162, 165, 178, 331
Control store, 23
Control stream, 44, 73, 74, 188
Control stream processor, 108
Control stream reader, 25, 188, 189
Control unit, 1
Conversational entry, 86
Conversational monitor system (CMS), 332
Conversational operations, 238
Conversational systems, 63
Cooperating processes, 80, 274, 281
Cooperative, 81
COPY, 43, 47
Core image, 75
Cost of computing, 226
Cost/performance, 98
CPU, 6
CPU allocation, 88
CPU-bound, 80, 194, 237, 252, 301
CPU-I/O concurrency, 6
CPU loop program, 92
CPU monitor, 265
CPU utilization manager, 252
CREATE, 36
Create process, 130, 133
Critical section, 271, 274–276
CRJE, 52
Cross-assembler, 71
Cross-compiler, 71
CTSS at M.I.T., 89
Cylinder, 143, 221
Cylinder address, 177
Cylinder group indices, 142

Dartmouth BASIC, 89
DASD device, 188
Data chaining, 176
Data Control Block (DCB), 173

Data definition statement, 45
Data description language, 211
Data dictionary, 196
Data Extent Block (DEB), 175
Data General NOVA, 66
Data management, 34
Data object, 260
Data set allocation, 115
Data set characteristics, 174
Data set name, 174
Data set objects, 34
Database, 91, 333
Database-level GET, 344
Database machine, 213
Database management, 202
Database management subsystems, 211
Database management system, 25, 340
Database manager, 37
Database systems, 162
DATAPOINT's ARC system, 332
DATE card, 44
Date, C.J., 213
DB/DC, 142
DBM, 203
DCB, 173, 175, 176
DD statement, 45, 173, 174, 176
Deadline scheduling, 55, 252, 253, 289, 319
Deadlock, 240
Deadly embrace, 240, 274
Deallocating storage, 179
DEB, 175–178
Deblocking, 87, 130, 144
Debugging process, 3
DEC PDP-11, 66, 90
DECNET, 95
Default, 46
Deferred queue, 92
DELAY, 272
Delta-to-run, 253
Demand paging, 302
Demand processing, 93
DEQ, 153
DEQUEUE, 276, 278
DESTROY, 36

DETACH, 153
Device, 140, 172, 221, 344
Device allocation, 115
Device availability, 173
Device characteristics, 175
Device handler, 174
Device handling, 130
Device independence, 44, 62, 74, 172
DEVICE keyword, 45
Device mounting, 25
Device objects, 34
Device population, 45
Device sharing, 172
Device start, 147, 203
Dijkstra, 123, 164, 270
Direct access, 142, 144
Directory system in Multics, 261
Disk, 46, 81, 86, 143, 257, 300
Disk arm, 143
Disk handler, 141
Disk seek, 177
Disk space requirements, 174
Disk writer, 282
Dismounting directives, 54
DISP, 173
DISP keyword, 45
Dispatch control block, 169, 241, 301
Dispatch list, 251
Dispatch queue, 166, 332
Dispatcher, 123, 128, 166, 170, 241, 251, 253
"Dispatcherless" system, 168
Dispatching, 164, 166, 242, 273
Dispatching queue, 81, 252, 301, 320
Distributed-biased design, 347
Distributed computing, 94
Distributed processing, 53, 213, 332
Distributed systems, 346
Distribution, 98, 333
Diverse interfaces, 62
DL/1, 93
Domain in SRM, 322
Donovan, 128
DOS, 85, 329, 332
DOS POWER, 86

DOS/VS, 86
Double indexing, 7
DPPX, 130, 142
DPRTY keyword, 45
Drum, 81, 143, 257, 300
DSNAME keyword, 45
Dynamic allocator, 193
Dynamic Allocator in EXEC VIII, 250
Dynamic heuristic resource management,
     225
Dynamic least recently used, 298
Dynamic linking, 161
Dynamic linking in Multics, 259
Dynamic memory allocation, 240
Dynamic memory management, 87, 296
Dynamic resource management, 93
Dynamic scheduling, 62

ECB, 138
Economic cost of an overloaded machine,
     228
EDIT, 43, 215
Editor, 3
Electronically programmable read-only
     memory, 20
Eligible set, 252
Encapsulation of hardware by software,
     345
Encapsulation of software by documenta-
     tion, 345
End user, 42
ENQUEUE, 152–154, 276, 278, 321
Enqueueing of outputs, 54
Enterprise level or organizational impact,
     340
EPROM, 20
ESS interface, 130
Equipment utilization, 65
Event control block (ECB), 138
Event-driven design, 69
Event-posting mechanism, 274
EXCLUSIVE attribute, 270
EXCP, 154, 176, 179
EXEC statement, 45
$EXECUTE, 76

Execute Channel Program, 130, 154
EXECUTE privilege, 15
Execution cycle, 279
Executors in HYDRA, 260
Extended architecture, 39, 40
External events, 65
External symbol dictionary, 192, 193
External/timer interrupt, 164

Failsoft environments, 69
Feedback cycle queues, 243, 245
Feedback dispatching, 253
FIFO, 177
FIFO replacement of entries in associative
     array, 298
File closing, 34
File creation, 34
File directory, 257
File level I/O, 142
File management, 257
File manager, 347
File manipulation language, 52
File opening, 34
File reading, 34
File system, 90, 165, 173, 257, 310
File writing, 34
Firmware, 15, 97
First-fit, 288
First-level interrupt handler, 129, 164
Fixed length records, 173
Fixed partition real memory systems, 285
Fixed size records, 142
FLIH, 130, 164, 171, 179
"Flush" a completed program, 110
FMS, 44, 74, 75, 202
Foreground, 71, 246
FORK, 273
FORTRAN, 44, 74, 75, 89, 189, 202
FORTRAN Monitor System (FMS), 44,
     74, 75
Fragmentation, 289, 293, 301
Frame, 7
FREEMAIN, 87, 153, 286, 301
Free space list, 288
Front-end processor, 66

Front-end scheduling, 230
Function mapping to objects, 37
Functional compartmentalization, 38

Garbage collection, 289
Gather read, 176
GECOS, 87
General-purpose operating system, 145, 161, 343
Generalized call facility, 164
GET, 40, 41, 74, 96, 111, 119, 130, 140, 150, 152–155, 175, 202, 281
GETMAIN, 87, 132, 153, 195, 286, 300
Global functions, 122
Global lock, 274
Global LRU replacement algorithm, 303, 323

Handheld calculator, 340
Handle interrupts from I/O devices, 25
Hard copy, 52
Hardcore supervisor, 163
Hardware, 1
Hardware costs versus labor costs, 226
Hardware–software interface, 20
Hardwired instruction set, 15, 16
Heuristic resource management, 88, 246, 315
Heterogeneous resource needs, 237
Hewlett-Packard, 95
Hidden buffer, 18
Hierarchic structure, 126, 263
Hierarchical tree structure, 258
Hierarchically structured subsystem, 204
Hierarchy, 123, 146
High paging rate, 308
"High strung" system, 322
Higher-level programming language, 3
High-level scheduling, 164, 188, 193, 231, 238, 315
Hoare, C. A. R., 342
Hold a job on the queue, 88
Hold state, 169
Honeywell, 7
Honeywell 800, 148

Honeywell 6800, 13
Horizontal microcode, 17
"Hot job", 194
HYDRA, 162, 203, 205, 222, 260, 262, 263, 310
Hypervising, 92

IBM 370, 13, 22, 147, 151, 164, 177, 316
IBM 370/168, 94, 342
IBM 370/OS, 63
IBM 650, 44
IBM 704, 44
IBM 3704, 3705, 94
IBM 3790, 94
IBM 5100, 22, 42
IBM 7040, 44
IBM 7044X-7044M project, 330
IBM 7070, 79
IBM 7094, 63
IBM 8100, 130
IBM DOS (Disk Operating System), 47
IBM early DOS, 195
IBM OS/360, 45, 142
IBM OS/MVS, 7, 55, 80, 300, 315
IBM OS/MVT, 34, 52, 174, 180, 252, 286
IBM OS/VS1, 189
IBM OS/VS2 (MVS), 300
IBM series 1, 66
IBM TSS/360, 93
IBM TSS/370, 89, 300
IBM VM/370 operating system, 22, 250, 331
IBM VSPC, 90
IBSYS, 44
IBSYS/IBJOB, 74, 76, 190, 202, 204
IDB, 7
Illiac IV, 95
IMS, 92, 93, 212, 342
Incarnation record, 169
Incremental compilation, 47
Index register, 7
Indexed access, 142, 143
Indirect addressing, 7, 260, 294
Information hiding, 127, 146
Inhibit interrupt instruction, 271

Initial program load, 54, 195
Initiation of a function, 120
Initiator, 88
Input completion interrupt, 9
Input/Output Block (IOB), 176
Input queue, 92
Inquiry systems, 63
Installation Performance Specification
    (IPS), 55, 223, 316
Instruction set, 12, 16, 97
Integrity, 260
Intensive utilization of equipment, 4
Interactive batch submission, 52
Interactive programming access, 53
Interactive programming subsystem, 214
Interactive terminal command interpreters,
    25
Interactive Terminal Facility, 215
Interface, 1, 145
Interface for operations, 39
Interleaving processor service, 148
Intermediate-level schedulers, 164, 231,
    253
Intermediate-level scheduling, 250, 306,
    315, 321, 332
Internal fragmentation, 393
Internalized job queue, 83
Interprocess communication, 274, 279–
    281
Interprogram communication, 34
Interrupt, 7, 40, 41
Interrupt definitions block, 8
Interrupt handler, 10, 11, 41, 92
Interrupt handling, 66, 96, 129, 147, 164
Interrupt mechanism, 97
Interrupt sequence, 10
Interrupt status word, 179
Interrupt structure, 6, 7, 21
Interrupts disabled, 11, 147, 165
Interrupts enabled, 9, 147
Intertask communication, 72
Interval service value, 319, 320
Interval timer, 92
Intralevel service calls, 129
I/O, 41

IOAS, 130
IOB, 176, 177, 179
I/O-bound, 170, 194, 237, 239, 246, 248,
    252, 301, 308
I/O completion, 10, 92, 178, 179
I/O control program, 172, 175, 176
I/O control system, 25, 74
I/O-CPU overlap, 98
IOCS, 74, 78
I/O device allocation, 76
I/O device buffering, 90
I/O device handling, 147
I/O FLIH, 178
I/O handler, 164
I/O hardware architecture 176
I/O interrupt, 80, 146, 164, 178
I/O management 87
I/O monitors, 265
I/O program, 6
I/O request element, 173, 176
I/O subsystem 301
I/O supervisor, 144, 152, 172
I/O support, 164, 172
I/O transfer, 10
IPL, a virtual machine, 195, 196, 332
IPO, 196
IPS, 55, 316
ISAM, 144, 145
ISV, 320
ITF, 215

JCL, 45, 74, 87, 173, 188, 215, 217, 218
JES, 95, 194, 201, 315
JFCB, 174–176
JOB card, 44, 45, 241
Job completion, 54
Job control language (JCL), 45, 74, 87,
    173, 188, 215, 217, 218
Job Entry Subsystem (JES), 95, 194, 201,
    315
Job File Control Block (JFCB), 174–176
Job management, 34
Job name, 174
Job queue, 86
Job scheduler, 193

Job setup, 43
Job steps, 45
Job submission mechanism, 201
Johniac Open Shop System (JOSS), 53
JOSS, 53

KEEP, 173
Keeping programs on schedule, 4
Kernel, 120, 161, 166, 203, 211, 262,
    263, 269
Kernel state in PDP-11, 182, 209
Key length, 173
Key position, 173
Keyword parameter list, 45
Known segment table in Multics, 259, 261

LABEL, 173
Label conventions, 46
Label definitions, 74
Labor costs versus hardware costs, 226
Language processor specialist, 2
Language specialist, 2
Least frequently used(LFU), 298
Least recently used(LRU), 298
Level of multiprogramming, 307
Level-of-view concept, 5
Levels of service, 154
Lexical analysis, 2
LFU, 298
Library systems, 88
Linear address space, 93, 192, 293
Linear name space, 293
Link, 258
Link a program to data, 34
Link pack area, 151
Linkage directives, 191
Linkage editors, 25, 39, 108, 191, 193
Linkage-edit time, 114, 191
Linked list, 287
Linker in Multics, 259
Linking, 293
Linking loader, 74
Linking mechanism in Multics, 261
List, 265
Lister, 130
LOAD, 47, 153

Load-balancing, 95
Loader, 39, 165, 190
Loader directive language, 190
Load directives, 114
LOADGO, 216
Load time, 114, 190
Loading, 190
Local batch submission, 52
Local control processor, 348
Local lock, 274
Local name space in HYDRA, 262, 263
Local versus global optimization, 225
Locality of reference, 296, 297, 299, 301
Location space, 190
Lock, 124, 265, 278
Lock contention problem, 271
Lock name, 270
Lock pages into memory, 302
Lock setting functions, 147
Lock tactics, 270
LOCK/UNLOCK, 274
Locking instruction, 270
Locking mechanism, 123
Logical channel, 177
Logical channel queue, 178
Logical device address, 76
Logical record, 37
Logical record length, 173
Logical resources, 39, 203
LOGON, 217
Long lock, 272
Low-level scheduling, 241
LRU, 298, 307
LSI, 11, 65

Machine language, 2
Machine sharing, 44
Machine utilization, 89
Macroassembler, 40, 74
Macro instructions, 121, 146
Macro languages, 153
Macrolevel I/O support, 74
Macro-supported linkages with the operat-
    ing system, 150
Madnick, 128
Mailbox, 281

Main chain, 80
Manage queues of I/O requests, 25
Master index, 142
Master mode, 13
Master/slave, 149
MCP, 87, 180
Mean-time-to-wait, 250, 324
Mechanisms versus policies, 33
Media conversion utilities, 25
Media services (MS), 130
Megamachine, 1, 146
Memory, 1, 221
Memory addressing, 96
Memory addressing hardware, 7
Memory addressing pattern of a program,
    225
Memory allocation, 6, 92, 115
Memory allocator, 124
Memory availability table, 126
Memory-bound, 237, 290
Memory bounds register, 13, 147
Memory compaction, 289
Memory contents manager, 179, 287
Memory contents table, 180
Memory cycle, 10
Memory hierarchy, 15
Memory image, 191
Memory-limited, 84
Memory load, 244
Memory management, 87, 190, 258, 273,
    285
Memory management policy, 181
Memory management strategies, 7
Memory manager, 251, 347
Memory monitor, 265
Memory partitions, 83
Memory protection, 119
Memory size, 45
Merge, 25
Message buffer, 80
Message control program, 216
Message processing programs, 70
Meta-assembler, 71
Microcode, 15, 120, 146, 182, 331
Microcomputer, 71, 340
Microprocessor, 16, 65, 95, 128

Microprogram, 95
Microprogramming, 15, 17
Military command/control systems, 67
Minicomputer, 66, 340
Mininets, 205
MODULA, 273
Modularity, 128, 310
Module, 145
Monitor, 75, 265, 269
Monitor state in PDP-11, 182, 209
Mounting directives, 54
MTW group, 324
Multics, 7, 43, 48, 89, 90, 93, 147, 161,
    162, 197, 203, 293, 300, 308, 310
Multics directory structure, 258
Multics file system, 258
Multiple virtual memories, 293
Multiplexing, 89, 148
Multiplicity of views, 3
Multiprocessing, 152, 276
Multiprocessor, 12, 125, 148, 272, 273
Multiprocessor-biased design, 347
Multiprogramming, 7, 41, 63, 80, 96, 152,
    205, 237, 269, 285
Multiprogramming level, 54, 88, 319
Multiprogramming mix, 45, 119, 224,
    227, 238, 290, 322, 330
Multiprogramming systems, 110
Multipurpose operating systems, 63, 93
Multitasking, 63
Mutual exclusion, 270, 274, 279
MVS, 137, 149, 182, 250, 272, 279, 300,
    332, 342
MVS/NCP, 94
MVT, 93

Name space of a process, 258
Negotiated scheduled access, 51
Network access, 53
Network control, 94
Network Control Program (NCP), 94
Network controller, 94
Networking, 53, 94, 333
Networks, 332
Nominal versus real resource utilization,
    225

Nondispatchable state, 301
Nonpreemptible resources, 240
Nonprivileged instructions, 97
Nonrelocatable instructions, 191
NOVA, 66
Nucleus, 76

Object manager, 38, 181
Objective in SRM, 317
Objects, 258, 260, 310
OEM, 195, 344
Off-line printer, 79
Off-line satellite computer, 79
Offset register, 288
On-line access, 43
On-line devices, 65
On-line interactive systems, 197
On-line jobs, 317
On-line transaction processing, 343
OPEN, 40, 74, 96, 111, 130, 154, 174, 175
Operate upon a program as data, 39
Operating system, 1, 24
Operating system process, 203
Operating systems taxonomy, 61
Operational interface, 53
Operator, 3, 53
Operator-driven partition redefinition, 85
Operator's language, 42
Ordering key, 142
Organick, 203
Organizational impact, 340
Original equipment manufacturer, 195
OS/360, 34
OS 1100, 7
OS JES, 116
OS/MFT, 87
OS/MVS, 7, 88, 90, 93, 94, 196, 324
OS/MVT, 7, 87, 92, 115, 144
OS/VS, 92, 153
OS/VS1, 293
OS/VS2, 251, 253, 293
OUT queue, 251
"OUT" state, 169
Output completion interrupt, 9
Output spooler, 282

Overlay, 75
Overmanage the machine resource, 341
Override, 46

P, 278
P and V, 124, 270
Packaged programs, 33
Page address, 296
Page cluster, 294
Page fault, 12, 164
Page frame, 251, 293, 294, 296, 301
Page frame map, 296
Page push, 304
Page reclaim rate, 308
Page replacement, 301, 303, 305
Page retrieval capability, 305
Page stealing, 304, 323
Page table, 296, 300, 302, 308
Page wait status, 301
Paging, 13, 86, 112, 129, 240, 261, 293
Paging exceptions, 301
Paging manager, 300
Paging rate, 307
Parallel processes, 273
Parameterization, 340
Partial system generations, 196
Partition, 72, 85, 195, 244
Partition redefinition, 195
PASCAL, 273
PASS, 173
Password, 46, 261
PDP-11, 95, 147, 182, 209
Peak loads, 65
Performance groups, 253, 317
Performance periods in SRM, 319
Performance prediction, 342
Performance timing and tuning, 55
Periodic trimming in SRM, 323
Peripheral devices, 66
Peripheral storage devices, 300
Personal computing, 63, 90
PGM keyword, 45
Physical channel, 177
Physical record, 37
Physical resources, 203
Physical unit address of a device, 174

Pin a page to memory, 129, 302
"Pipe," 280
PL/I, 3, 21, 49, 205, 215
Policy-formulating mechanisms, 222, 223
"Politeness reentry," 170
P-operation, 124, 270
Port, 281
Portability, 330
POST, 138, 148, 153, 172, 176, 178, 179, 278, 280
Postrun time, 108, 110
Preemptible resources, 226
Preemption, 171
Preemption exclusion, 271
Preference classes, 239
Prepaging, 307
Prepartitioning of memory, 83, 84
Prerun-time functions, 187
Presentation services, 130
Primary memory, 17
Primitive, 34, 119, 131, 162, 165
Printer handler, 140
Privilege, 96
Privileged instructions, 13, 40, 71, 97, 119, 146
Problem state, 147, 163, 331
Procedure, 222
Procedure library, 189
Procedure objects, 34, 260
Process, 119, 126, 131, 132, 222, 258, 262, 274, 330
Process activation record, 110
Process control block, 110, 169, 181, 278
Process coordination, 152
Process directory in Multics, 258, 259
Process-driven design, 69
Process hierarchy, 203
Process manager, 129
Processor, 1, 221
Processor error interrupt, 9
Processor management, 87
Process preemption, 271
Process promotion, 272
Process states, 169
Process Synchronization, 128, 161, 277
Producer, 275, 277, 278

Producer–consumer relationship, 80, 269, 274, 279, 281
Production line monitoring, 65
Program addressable memory, 16
Program check interrupt, 164
Program combination, 109, 190
Program development compilers, 72
Program fetch, 165, 190
Program initiation, 34
Program linking, 258
Program priorities, 45
Program reference table (PRT), 180
Program relocation, 74
Program structure, 2
Program synchronization, 269
Program visible register, 1
Programmer, 1
Programmer/operator, 53
Programmer productivity, 73
Programmer's workbench, 43, 64, 73, 89
Programmer-visible register, 16
Programming development system, 73
Programming language processors, 26
Programming stylistics, 224, 225, 247
Programming systems, 63
PROM, 19, 66
PROTECT, 36
Protection, 13, 39, 40, 96, 161, 258, 260
Protection key, 13
Protection mechanism, 6, 13, 21
PRT, 180
Pseudo-ops, 41
Public utility computer power, 42
Purchased versus developed instructions, 338
Push/pull, 304
PUT, 40, 41, 74, 138, 150, 175, 281

QISAM, 144
QSAM, 144
QTAM, 144
Quantum, 243
Queue, 152, 265
Queue-driven design, 69
Queue manager, 276, 277, 280
Queue-ordering discipline, 152

Queue visit rules, 245
Queueing disciplines, 224
QUICKTRAN, 89

Random access storage devices, 144
Random access to disk, 74
Rates of service, 224
RC4000, 204
RCT, 217
READ, 10, 36, 40, 122, 129, 130, 140,
    150, 152–155, 175, 344
READ privilege, 15
Read-only memory, 19
READ/WRITE heads, 143
Reader, 38, 88, 109, 275
Reader handler, 141
Reader/scheduler relationship, 189
Ready state, 169
Ready queue, 92
Real address, 296
Real memory, 287, 330
Real storage, 261, 285, 300
Real-time applications, 128
Real-time environment, 65
Real-time operating systems, 63, 149
Real-time software, 69
Real-time systems, 63, 226, 271
Recall of pages, 303
RECEIVE, 130, 154, 279, 280, 281
RECEIVE answer, 281
Receiver process, 280
Record advance, 40, 140, 203
Record-level GET, 344
Record prototype, 211
Record format, 74
Reentrant code, 152
Reference bit, 298
Region, 300
Region control program, 216
Region keyword, 45
Regions in MVT, 286
Register conventions, 112
Relational database system, 211
Relative page displacement, 296
Relative priority, 239

Reliability, 66, 340
Relocatable assembly, 85
Relocatable code, 286
Relocatable compilation, 85
Relocatable loader, 190
Relocatable program module, 190
Relocation, 13, 114, 165, 189, 261, 293,
    330
Relocation bits, 190
Relocation registers, 191
Remote job entry, 52
Repartitioning of memory, 195
Report writer programs, 212
Request element (I/O), 178
Request time, 108, 109
Resident, 87, 126, 162
Resource, 221
Resource allocation, 73, 161
Resource allocation tactics, 62
Resource allocator, 39
Resource availability tables, 114
Resource domain switch, 264
Resource management, 221
Resource manager, 39, 127
Resource recapture, 226
Response-utilization dichotomy, 222, 320
Responsiveness to the environment, 65
Resume a process, 166
RET, 173
RETURN, 132, 263
REWIND, 141
Rights in Multics, 261
Rings in Multics, 162, 259
ROM, 19, 66
Root node in Multics, 259
ROS, 19
Rotate priority in SRM, 325
Round robin, 168, 243
Round-robin dispatching, 253, 324
RPG, 50
RTE A, 95
RTE B, 95
RTE II, 95
RUN, 43, 53, 215
Running state, 169

Run-time, 50, 110, 108
Run-time environment, 40, 41, 110, 119,
    146, 149, 152, 161, 172, 175, 197,
    201, 225, 270, 286, 331
Run-time functions, 187
Run-time interface, 90, 116
Run-time macros, 108, 121
Run-time services, 108
RWE, 15

SACCS (Strategic Air Command Control
    System), 66
SAGE Air Defense Command Control Sys-
    tem, 66
SAVE, 43
Save area, 165
Sayer, 130
SCAN, 74
Scatter load, 296
Scatter write, 176
Scheduler, 4, 25, 52, 88, 109, 193
Scheduler objective functions, 223
Scheduling, 73, 242
SCOPE, 87
SDC Q-32 Time-Sharing System, 89
Search engine, 213
Secondary memory, 17
Seek, 74, 177
Seek queues, 177
Segment, 7, 93, 162, 258, 259, 293, 308,
    310
Segment descriptor in Multics, 261
Segment Directory in Multics, 261
Segment fault, 12
Segment origin register, 308
Segment table, 301, 302, 308
Segmentation, 13, 86, 308
Segmented two-dimensional addressing, 7
Select a job to run, 193
Select time, 108, 109
Selectable units, 197
"Self-loading," 113
Service routine, 165
Service unit, 253
Semantics, 97

Semaphores, 270, 275, 277
SEND, 130, 153, 154, 279–281
SEND/RECEIVE, 282, 347
Sender process, 280
Sequential access, 74, 142, 144
Sequentialization, 39, 86, 125
Serially reusable code, 152
Service rate of a transaction, 317
Service unit, 316
SHARED attribute, 270
Shared buffer, 80, 275, 279
Shared code, 87
Shared resources, 33, 39, 222, 269
Shared variables, 273
Sharing, 221, 293, 308
Short lock, 272
Shortest job first, 239, 246
Side effects, 2
SIGNAL, 275–278, 280
Single-level store, 310
Single-stream batch systems, 110
Single-time systems, 111
SIO, 154, 177
SIOT, 174
Slave/master, 149
Sleep, 120
Small-machine operating system, 62
SNA, 144
SNAP, 153
Software, 1
Software "knee," 338
Software lag, 96, 343
Software package, 25
Software page table, 296, 297
Software stacking of I/O interrupts, 11
Sort, 25, 49
Specialist level of organizational impact,
    340
Specialize by authority, 54
Specialize by function, 54
Spin lock, 124, 272
Spooling, 78, 115, 188, 281
SRB, 137
SRM, 251, 252, 315, 319, 321
Stability, 340

Stack, 264
Stack printer, 8
Staging, 241
"Stand-alone" seek, 177
START, 47
START processor, 347
Start a program, 25, 109
Starting an initiator, 111
Starting a reader, 111
STATIC, 205
Static relocation, 190
State of the art, 99
State vector, 7, 8
STEP, 241
Step Input/Output Table (SIOT), 174
Step name, 174
STIMER, 153
Stop a program, 25
Storage devices, 142
Storage management, 98
Structured programming, 122
SUBMIT, 86, 215
Submit I/O requests to devices, 25
Subqueue, 245
Subroutine call, 131
Subroutine linkages, 113
Subsystem, 107, 115, 201
Subsystem interfaces, 203
Supervisor, 76
Supervisor call (SVC), 13, 41
Supervisor state, 13, 75, 163, 203
Suspend lock, 272
Suspend a process, 166, 272
Suspend a program, 7, 33
Suspended queues, 252, 332
Suspended state, 169
SVC, 13, 40, 41, 132, 146, 148, 149, 175,
     176
SVC interrupt, 164
Swapping, 251, 306, 320
Symbiont, 80, 275
Symbolic device assignment, 85, 114
Symbolic file names, 114
Synchronization, 265
Syntactic analysis, 2
Syntax, 97

SYSGEN, 46, 195, 196, 218
SYSIN, 76, 85
SYSLIB, 44
SYSOUT, 44, 76, 85
System, 107
System driver, 217
System fault in Multics, 261
System generation (SYSGEN), 46, 195,
     196
System overhead, 339
System reconfiguration, 25
System reliability, 66
System scheduler, 347
System status modification, 25
Systems dynamics, 107
Systems Library Directory in Multics, 258
Systems Network Architecture (SNA), 144
Systems operator, 25
Systems programmers, 21, 48
Systems programs, 122
Systems Resource Manager, 55, 193, 250,
     315
Systems services, 108, 187, 201

Table lookaside buffer, 297
Table-driven scheduler, 170
Tape, 257
Tape handler, 141
Target for compilation, 1
Target process, 282
Task, 72, 134
Task control block, 110, 169
Task Input/Output Table, 174
Task management, 34
Task-switching, 66, 264
TCB, 110, 175, 177
Telecommunications, 26, 88, 91, 202
Telecommunications access method, 218
Teleprocessing, 85, 197
Template in HYDRA, 262
Terminal commands, 48
Terminal monitor program, 217
Test and set instruction, 125, 271
Text editors, 72, 90
T.H.E. multiprogramming operating sys-
     tem, 123

Thrashing, 301, 303, 308
Thruput, 81
TI 990, 65
Tightly coupled multiprocessor, 346
Time division multiplexing, 148
Time-division approach to operating sys-
    tems structure, 108
Time keyword, 45
Time-sharing, 53, 88, 93, 237, 238, 269
Time-sharing control task, 216
Time-sharing operating systems, 63, 110
Time-slice, 243
TIOT, 174–176
TMP, 217
Tool level of organizational impact, 340
Toolmaker's view, 342, 343
Top-down programming, 146
Track, 142, 221
Track index, 143
Traffic control, 69
Transaction processing, 64, 72, 91, 93
Transients, 120, 175
Transient area, 80, 165
Translation lookaside buffer, 301
Transparent hierarchy, 130
TSO, 43, 48, 88, 90, 92, 93, 182, 210,
    215, 217, 218, 315, 316
TSS/360, 170
TSS/370, 170, 253, 342
Turnaround time, 73, 81
Two-dimensional address space, 310
Two-state uniprocessor, 147

UCB, 76, 174, 176–178
Unattended job, 238
Unattended operation, 48
Unattended subsystems, 66
Unblock a process, 172
UNCOL, 113
Undermanage the machine resources, 341
Uninterruptible functions, 120
UNIT, 173
Unit Availability Table, 76
Unit Control Block (UCB), 76
Unit Function Table, 76
Unit symbolic name of a device, 174

UNIVAC, 7, 275, 342
UNIVAC 1100s, 18
UNIVAC 1107, 80
UNIVAC EXEC II, 80
UNIVAC III, 80
UNIVAC EXEC VIII, 93, 249
Universal computer-oriented language,
    112
Universalist–Perfectionist View, 342
UNIX, 48, 90, 310
Unlocking instruction, 270
Unresolved external reference, 193
User, 4
User Directory in Multics, 258
User interface, 5
User process, 203
User state in PDP-11, 182, 209
User-directed batch submission, 52
Utilities, 72
Utility routine, 3

V, 278
V-operation, 124, 270
Value of computing, 226
Variable length records, 173
Variable-size block allocation, 287
Variable-size records, 142
Versions of operating systems, 329
Vertical microcode, 17
Virtual address, 296
Virtual address space, 310
Virtual machine interface, 207
Virtual machines, 205, 300, 329
Virtual memory, 86, 93, 293, 330
Virtual memory management, 161
Virtual memory space, 190
Virtual memory systems, 190
Virtual operating systems, 52
VIRTUAL = REAL, 302
Virtual storage, 261
Virtual Telecommunications Access
    Method, 94
"Visible" primary storage, 285
VM/370, 332
Volume mounting, 73
Voluntary release, 170

V-operation, 124, 270
VSAM, 144, 145
VTAM, 94, 144

WAIT, 119, 138, 148, 153, 170, 179, 270, 272, 275–278
WAIT state, 148, 272
Waiting job queue, 188
WAIT/SIGNAL, 274
WAKEUP, 278
"Wall" clock, 110, 253

"Wired-down" functions, 120, 162, 180
Worker program state, 13
Worker programs, 108
Working set of pages, 304, 323
Working set size, 306, 332
Work-load level, 317
Work-load Manager, 252
Work unit, 241
WRITE, 36, 40, 129, 137, 148, 150, 175
Write privilege, 15
Writer, 38, 80, 274, 275
WTO, 153